Satiric Advice on Women and Marriage

Satiric Advice

ON

Women AND Marriage

FROM PLAUTUS TO CHAUCER

Warren S. Smith, Editor

THE UNIVERSITY OF MICHIGAN PRESS   ANN ARBOR

Copyright © by the University of Michigan 2005
All rights reserved
Published in the United States of America by
The University of Michigan Press
Manufactured in the United States of America
⊛ Printed on acid-free paper

2008   2007   2006   2005   4   3   2   1

A CIP catalog record for this book is available from the British Library

Library of Congress Cataloging-in-Publication Data

Satiric advice on women and marriage: from Plautus to
   Chaucer / Warren S. Smith, editor.
        p.   cm.
      Includes bibliographical references and index.
      ISBN 0-472-11426-3 (acid-free paper)
        1. Satire, Latin—History and criticism. 2. Satire, Greek—
   History and criticism. 3. Chaucer, Geoffrey, d. 1400—Political and
   social views. 4. Chaucer, Geoffrey, d. 1400—Characters—Women.
   5. Women and literature—To 1500. 6. Satire, Medieval—History
   and criticism. 7. Marriage in literature. 8. Women in literature.
   I. Smith, Warren S., 1941–
   PA3033.S28   2004   2004014328
   877.009'3543—dc22

For Anne Marie, Josh, Caleb, and Rachel

Preface

✍

The essays in this book examine satiric attitudes toward women and marriage in later classical literature, starting with Plautus (ca. 200 B.C.) and continuing into the Christian era as far as Walter Map (twelfth century A.D.). With the exception of two closing chapters on Chaucer (d. A.D. 1400), the emphasis will be on authors writing in Latin; this choice is based on the belief that there is a continuity of thought, ideas, and vocabulary throughout Latin satiric literature, from Plautus and Lucretius to Walter Map and beyond. Moreover, greater focus is gained by concentrating on Latin authors, making it possible to trace both a consistency of terms and a literary continuity between the classical and medieval periods, particularly in the case of the important transitional writers Tertullian and Jerome, who are a central feature of two of the essays. This book is not so much about women as about male attitudes toward women and marriage, particularly as that attitude is conveyed in the eccentric and distinctive context of satiric writing. It should also be added that the list of authors under consideration was chosen to reflect various points of view and was in no sense intended as exhaustive or definitive.

Chapter 1, "Satiric Advice: Serious or Not?" by Warren S. Smith (University of New Mexico), looks at the authors who discuss women and marriage from the point of view of what we can deduce about their attitudes and intentions: what makes such advice "satiric" and how the genres of satire and comedy influence our attitude toward the narrative voice, how seriously its message may be intended, and the reader for whom the message is intended.

The second chapter, " 'In a Different Guise': Roman Education and Greek Rhetorical Thought on Marriage," by Richard Hawley (Royal Holloway, University of London), shows how the education of the Roman male elite had an important focus on Greek moral values: teachers posing the question "Should one take a wife?" encouraged schoolboys to search through Greek literature, starting with Homer and the dramatists, for negative examples of married relationships.

Susanna Morton Braund (Standford University), in "Marriage, Adultery, and Divorce in Roman Comic Drama" (chap. 3), shows how often Plautus and Terence focus on tension in the married relationship. *Uxores dotatae* (dowried wives) are dangerous in Plautus, who seems to warn against a legal shift in which a wife becomes sui juris after the death of her father. In Plautus's *Amphitryo* and *Menaechmi*, where threats of divorce are a central theme, Plautus challenges the convention of the *palliata* (which avoided the theme of divorce), and Terence outdoes Plautus with his highly experimental play *Hecyra*, which shows a marriage held together by the manipulations of unsuspecting men by generous and intelligent female characters.

Warren S. Smith, in chapter 4, " 'The Cold Cares of Venus': Lucretius and Anti-Marriage Literature," discusses Lucretius as a satiric writer and describes his urging of the (male) reader against any sexual relationship that is accompanied by love, for fear it will distract his thinking and affect his objectivity in the search for philosophical truth. The force of love is finally seen as comparable to that of a plague or an invading army.

Karla Pollmann (University of St. Andrews, Scotland), in "Marriage and Gender in Ovid's Erotodidactic Poetry" (chap. 5), shows how Ovid, in his *Ars amatoria*, teaches young men and women how to refine, cultivate, and control the sex drive as a natural force. The status of the women courted in Ovid's poems is not always clear, and there is a blurring of boundaries between the married and unmarried. The addition of sex advice to women is unusual, even unique, and the female psyche and personality are seen as both complex and subtle.

Warren S. Smith, in "Advice on Sex by the Self-Defeating Satirists: Horace *Sermones* 1.2, Juvenal *Satire* 6, and Roman Satiric Writing" (chap. 6), shows how Horace and Juvenal warn against sexual relationships with a pessimism that ends up as self-defeating, not only since the sex drive itself is powerful, but because the resourcefulness and resilience of women gives them an unbeatable advantage in their encounters with men.

In chapter 7, "Chaste Artemis and Lusty Aphrodite: The Portrait of Women and Marriage in the Greek and Latin Novels," Regine May (Oxford University) points out that women are prominent in the idealized Greek novel and may have been intended readers. In the Roman novels of Petronius and

Apuleius, women are presented much more negatively (through the vehicle of the Milesian tale), as unscrupulous seducers. The vicious stepmother of Apuleius's book 10 outdoes anyone in Petronius as part of an indictment against the female sex.

Elizabeth A. Clark (Duke University), moving forward to the early Christian era in "Dissuading from Marriage: Jerome and the Asceticization of Satire" (chap. 8), analyzes the anti-marriage tracts of the Latin Christian authors Tertullian and Jerome. Jerome borrows and exaggerates much of Tertullian's material and is imbued with a far stronger anti-sexual animus than his predecessor. Jerome's purpose is not to reform marriage but to warn Christians away from it entirely.

Barbara Feichtinger (University of Konstanz), in "Change and Continuity in Pagan and Christian (Invective) Thought on Women and Marriage from Antiquity to the Middle Ages" (chap. 9), an overview of antigamous and antigynous literature, stresses the importance of historical and geographical context for judging each of these works. Feichtinger shows a change between pagan and Christian misogamy, a change stemming from a new attitude toward chastity. Sexuality to Christians is seen, in the post-Eden world, as the situation of fallen men. Tertullian, in his treatises on marriage, tries to instill in women good behavior, chastity, and subservience, but to Jerome (Tertullian's successor and imitator), marriage only has value in producing virgins. Both men and women must now be persuaded of the value of abstinence. Misogynistic misogamy is part of the takeover of married life by the medieval church, which attempts to control female authority by placing norms on women.

In chapter 10, "Walter as Valerius: Classical and Christian in the *Dissuasio*," Ralph Hanna III (University of Oxford) and Warren S. Smith see Walter Map's *Dissuasio matrimonii*, a popular twelfth-century antimatrimonial treatise, as "a riotous fabric of sources with an eye for the colorful and humorous," intermingling classical and Christian sources and achieving a rhetorical tour de force even while disdaining rhetoric.

P. G. Walsh (University of Glasgow), in his survey "Antifeminism in the High Middle Ages" (chap. 11), points out that an anonymous treatise like *De coniuge non ducenda* (On not taking a wife) had the specific interest of maintaining sufficient numbers of ordained clergy, by discouraging potential clerics from entering the married state. In such treatises as the third book of Andreas Capellanus's *De amore*, we find an astonishingly virulent onslaught on the female sex. The influence of Juvenal and Ovid is strongly felt here, as in other writers of the High Middle Ages, such as Walter of Chatillon and Bernard of Cluny, who update classical satire by applying it to the vices of contemporary women.

Chapter 12, "The Wife of Bath and Dorigen Debate Jerome," by Warren S. Smith, is another reminder of the great influence of Jerome's *Against Jovinian* in the Middle Ages and shows how Chaucer's work provides a kind of peaceful resolution to Jerome's anti-marriage theme. *Against Jovinian* is a central preoccupation in Chaucer's *Canterbury Tales*, where the Wife of Bath, in her prologue, debates with Jerome about the biblical position on marriage, while Dorigen, in the "Franklin's Tale," humanizes and provides a softer moral for many stories from Jerome about women who escaped or reacted to rape by suicide.

Acknowledgments

C♥

*T*he idea for this book began to take shape at a conference on Apuleius at Corpus Christi College, Oxford, in 1995. The conference was organized by Stephen Harrison, whose work on the Roman novel has always been a model for me. At that same conference, I met Peter Walsh, another of my longtime role models, who later agreed to write a chapter for this book, in which he surveys medieval Latin satire on marriage. Heinz Hoffman, at the University of Tübingen, had some helpful ideas on getting the book organized and made the happy suggestions of Karla Pollmann and Barbara Feichtinger as possible contributors. Susanna Morton Braund—then at Royal Holloway, University of London, and now at Standford University—suggested Regine May, who at that time was Steve Harrison's doctoral student at Oxford, to write on the Greek and Roman novel; she also introduced me to Richard Hawley, who eventually wrote the chapter on Greek rhetorical influence on the Romans. Susanna herself read an early version of my chapter on the Wife of Bath and encouraged me in that effort, and to top it off, she also contributed the chapter on attitudes toward women in Roman comedy. In a very real sense, she is a spiritual parent of this book. The other contributors, Ralph Hanna III and Elizabeth A. Clark, are well known in their fields and fortuitously joined the project when they were needed.

Many years ago, I heard Wendell Clausen lecture on Juvenal one summer at Harvard University, and this started my lifelong fascination with satire, which is still my first love in the classics, though my research gets sidetracked in other directions. My interest was renewed after a summer National

Endowment for the Humanities session at the University of California, Berkeley, with W. S. Anderson in the late 1970s. Other more recent fruitful contacts have come from Maaike Zimmerman at the University of Groningen; from Martin Winkler, a Juvenal and film scholar; from Barbara Gold, who was to have written a chapter on Juvenal's sixth satire but finally had to decline because of other commitments; and from the late Don Fowler, a generous and kind man, whose illness finally prevented him from completing a chapter on Lucretius.

I first read Jerome's *Against Jovinian,* a work that finds prominent mention in this book, in Migne's *Patrologia Latina* more than a decade ago, when I taught for a year at St. Andrews Theological Seminary in Manila in the Philippines. That I had extra time to spend and that the library was the only air-conditioned room in the complex drove me to these books at first out of boredom, which turned to fascination.

In conclusion, I thank Lori Czosnyka, who, as an editorial assistant, helped me prepare the bibliography; Joseph McAlhany, who read part of the manuscript and offered helpful suggestions; and John Owen, who continually supplemented my rudimentary computer skills.

Contents

ℒ❥

Contents

One

Satiric Advice

SERIOUS OR NOT?

Warren S. Smith

✐

This book includes a series of chapters on satiric advice on women (in particular, sexual involvement with women) and marriage. If the distinctions made between satire against women and satire against marriage (or perhaps against married women) often seem blurred, that is because they are so often blurred in satire. Susanna Morton Braund, in her essay in this book (chap. 3), shows how marriage, particularly to dowered wives (who retain a power of control over their husbands), is often the butt of jokes in Roman comedy. Married women in comedy are spendthrifts and full of complaints. This charge is spotlighted in Juvenal's sixth satire, which adds a host of other complaints against wives, while husbands are implicitly criticized for their passivity. Juvenal's satire implies a criticism of the institution of marriage itself for its negative effect on both partners. The Christian anti-marriage satire of St. Jerome adds a new twist, extolling celibacy itself as an ideal state, in imitation of the celibacy of Jesus and the Virgin Mary, and arguing that celibacy has always been the preferred state of right-thinking people, whether Jew, pagan, or Christian.

SATIRIC TWIST

Roman satirists, including Petronius and Apuleius in prose as well as Horace and Juvenal, go to an opposite extreme from the impersonality of Homer. They make the force of their personalities immediately felt. Indeed, their ostensible personal eccentricities quickly become part of the critical debate. The satirists, or their narrative personae, seem anxious to introduce themselves, to drag us into their world, with an earnestness that can have both absurd and disturbing overtones even as it succeeds in involving us emotionally. The satirists are immediately caught up in their subject; they take a stance, and, as defined by Horace in his program satire *Sermones* (1.4, 1.10, 2.1), they follow the tradition—going back to Old Comedy—of censuring vice with a smile (*multa cum libertate notabant, Serm.* 1.4.5). Supposedly, this Aristophanic tradition was taken up by Lucilius and refined and followed by Horace, though Horace and the other Roman satirists never went so far as to emulate Aristophanes' lampoons of prominent public figures. The personality of the satirist complicates the issue. Satirists have a perspective that, despite their show of objectivity and effort to appear as blunt, plainspoken speakers, is often flawed or exaggerated.

As far as actual autobiography is concerned, the trend in classical satire seems to have been away from the personal. In Old Comedy, one of satire's spiritual ancestors (see Horace *Serm.* 1.4.1–6), real historical personae (e.g., Cleon, Pericles, and Socrates) were impersonated and ridiculed by name, and the poet him/herself or his/her representative addressed the audience in the *parados* (song with which the chorus entered the theater). Some early Roman writers, such as Naevius, experimented with this kind of direct attack on contemporary political figures and were punished for it; already Plautus and Terence camouflage their Roman satiric targets under foreign and exotic names and give the plays foreign settings, although both Roman playwrights often use a *prologus* (speaker of a prologue) to address the audience and often refer to the playwright himself in the third person—while calling for silence, providing a plot summary, or expressing the relationship between the play at hand and its Greek model or models. The personal stamp took longer to die in the case of satire itself, where the individual personality of the narrator always leaves its mark even though the individual victims are not often singled out by name. We have Horace's word for it (*Serm.* 2.1.30–33) that Lucilius, one of the early masters of the genre, used his writings as a kind of confessional and, indeed, unfolds his whole life (*vita senis* [the old man's life], 2.1.34) in his satires. Horace himself takes or appears to take anecdotes from his personal experiences and uses his own misadventures—such as his uncomfortable trip to Brundisium (*Serm.* 1.5), his assault by an office seeker on the Via Sacra (1.9), or the verbal attack on him by his slave Davus (2.7)—to raise a laugh.

The two later verse satirists Persius and Juvenal are much more circumspect about introducing personal details (though Persius, uniquely in his third satire, seems to introduce himself as a character in his own skit, playing the role of a derelict schoolboy; cf. *findor* in line 9 and Smith 1969). Juvenal in particular teases the reader with what seems to be a promise to talk primarily about himself in his program satire (*ego*, the second word of the opening line of his first satire, teases us with false expectations, in a way that is matched by the enigmatic *ego* in the identical position in the opening paragraph of Apuleius's satiric novel *The Golden Ass*). In the long run, however, Juvenal gives us almost no information about his life except by implication, but he indirectly reveals much about his prejudices and feelings, as he turns our attention away from his pain to the issue at hand that is causing him such outrage. Where the situation seems to require more personal information, as in *Satires* 3 or 9, he retreats to the background or becomes the "straight man" as he introduces other characters as victims and chief complainers. Even in *Satire* 6, where the poet's personal fear and loathing of women seem so much in evidence, Juvenal still stays away from any personal experiences and avoids describing himself in any detail as a victim; instead, that poem either pushes forward as examples other actual or potential long-suffering husbands (Postumus at line 28, Claudius at line 115) or, by use of the second person singular, brings the male reader himself into the picture as potential victim, forcing him to imagine himself as exploited in various ways by his hypothetical wife (76, 201, 231, and passim).

DIATRIBE SATIRE, RHETORIC, AND MISOGYNY

Susanna Morton Braund (among others) has argued for the pervasive influence of the schools of declamation on both the "choice of subject and the framing of ideas"[1] in Latin satire. A favorite topic of the *Controversiae* of the elder Seneca is the suspected adultery of women.[2] Senecan *Controversiae* are often preceded by abstract headings that list the general law or principle around which the case is being judged (e.g., *Contr.* 1.1: "Children must support their parents, or be imprisoned"; 2.2: "A priestess must be chaste and of chaste parents, pure and of pure parents"). That principle is then debated by a variety of speakers using clever and pointed arguments and is tested against some peculiar or bizarre circumstance where its application is questionable. Like their rhetorical models, Latin satires often imply an arrangement around abstract topics like "Ought a man to marry?" or "Is the life of a parasite profitable?" with the satiric exempla drawn heavily from examples of bad conduct. The satirist is not merely taking a snapshot of contemporary life but has a point to make, often one of *dissuasio*, and he piles up all his powers of persuasion, paints lurid scenes, and presents evidence selectively to ensure that he wins the debate. The implied presence of a second voice, a rival or hostile interlocutor, adds to the picture of a rhetorical contest (cf. the explicit admission of Persius at *Sat.* 1.44 that he "has created someone to argue on the other side"). The resulting debate is passionate and involved, and the satiric persona takes a firmly defined stand that is almost bound to involve hyperbole and inconsistency, to the extent that the reader (at least the modern reader who imagines that he or she is attuned to nuances of narrative point of view) may well have doubts as to whether the author "really means" some of the more outrageous positions voiced by the narrator.[3]

Even given that they share some common sources of inspiration, such as the declamation schools, classical and medieval diatribes against women and marriage are of various kinds and with varied purpose. First of all, they are, almost all of them, written by men, and the misogynistic slant is almost a given, a topos. To make a sharp distinction between misogamy and misogyny in most cases is difficult and may be unhelpful;[4] arguments against marriage almost inevitably place a strong emphasis on the inferiority of women as partners due to supposed defects in the female sex. Though Braund, for example, persuasively argues that Juvenal 6 is a rhetorically based argument against marriage rather than a "catalogue of abominable women," she also argues that the narrator of that satire is an extreme—even obsessed—misogynist,[5] thereby seeming tacitly to concede the blending of the two themes. Elaborate explanations were devised by medical writers to account for the inferiority of the female physiology and temperament. Galen is part of a tradition of writers who relegated women to the status of "failed males"[6] whose sex was determined by the inadequacy of body heat their fetuses had received in the womb and who were consequently clammy, cold, and formless. Medieval writers sometimes connected women's supposed excess in body fluid with a greater tendency to lust: Guillaume de Conches, for example, argued that since a woman is cold and wet, the fire (of lust) is harder to start but burns longer.[7]

Women were also considered less able to exercise restraints over their greed and sexuality. Uncontrolled sexuality on the part of women is treated by Roman authors as if it were symptomatic of a general breakdown of order[8] and as if it had precipitated the downfall of the Republic. Women are seen as easily going out of control, as subject to sexual, emotional, and religious excesses, not to mention alcoholism. It is the wives who take the first plunge into frenzy, dragging their husbands along with them: the husbands in Juvenal's sixth satire are regularly seen as victims, a caricature of restraint to the point of seeming catatonic as their wives cavort in front of them.

SELF-REFERENTIAL ATTACKS

Many of the attacks against women, particularly those by Latin writers, must be understood as influenced by the peculiar slant of the self-referential genre of satire. The satiric spirit or intention is usually disclosed by a peculiar level of emotional intensity, such as is associated with rhetorical diatribe. Few issues are more highly emotionally charged than sex and marriage, and while the satirist ostensibly (even desperately) may try to turn the reader's attention away from the satirist's self-pity by inviting the reader to share in the indignation at the outrage at hand, the self-pity seems to keep gaining the upper hand and causes the satirist's suffering to seem exaggerated and absurd; the satirist almost inevitably becomes, at least in part, the butt of his/her own joke. The tendency is irresistible, in some scholarship, to regard chauvinistic attacks on women as suspect, as though they encouraged a judgment on the misogynistic speaker as well as one on his target; thus, for example, on Juvenal's sixth satire, the conclusion of Wilson and Makowski is representative: "how can the reader trust the observations of a person who repeatedly exposes himself as absurd, sensational, petty, and fanatical . . . ?"[9] This negative criticism, which finds the narrative point of view inconsistent or otherwise suspect, reverses the older view that the satirist (who is identified as the author himself) plays a serious role of moralist, flailing vice with the zeal and efficiency of a Sunday school teacher. The reliability of the satiric voice has been called into question by recent writers on satire, such as W. S. Anderson and Braund, who insist on distinguishing the view of the unreliable "satirist" from the author's own point of view.[10]

Roman writers have a tendency to preach, to take a moral stance or appear to do so, and moralistic passages have a tendency to insert themselves into surprising contexts; there is also a Roman tendency to link together various vices (e.g., licentiousness, drunkenness, and gluttony) in a kind of guilt by association, making the implication that where one is found, many others will be close behind.[11] In some instances, satirical passages that attack women or marriage have the impression of being inserted into their context as an afterthought, a compulsion that the author could not resist despite its lack of logic. For example, the digression on sex in *De rerum natura* 4.1037–287 seems to throw the detached tone of the main argument off track; the passage interjects into the argument the humor of a rhetorical diatribe and gives the appearance that Lucretius has been tempted for the moment to lose sight of his priorities as a philosopher and try his hand as a satirist. There is a related phenomenon in Juvenal's *Satire* 6, the diatribe against women, where there is a sense that the original basic theme of the poem has become inflated and has pulled the poet in too many directions; the diatribes take on a life and energy of their own, as the comic exaggerations pile up. Complicating the narrator's stance in satire even further is the "pattern of apology" that E. J. Kenney has detected in the program pieces of the Roman verse satirists (Horace *Serm.* 2.1; Persius *Sat.* 1; Juvenal *Sat.* 1).

> First, a pronouncement, lofty to the point of bombast, of the satirist's high purpose and mission. Second, a warning by the friend or the poet's *alter ego* of the voice of prudence—call it what you will. Third, an appeal by the satirist to the great voice of Lucilius. Fourth, a renewed warning. Fifth and last, evasion, retraction, equivocation.[12]

The reason for such equivocation by satirists is variously given; thus Kenney argues that no Roman writer ever thought he/she had the right to completely free speech, while Courtney argues that satirists wanted to associate themselves with Lucilius while simultaneously distancing themselves from his aggressiveness. But the pattern that Kenney detected can, I have argued elsewhere, be detected at many points in various genres of Latin literature, including the key elements with the exception of the reference to Lucilius: bold assertion, rebuttal by an interlocutor, and defensive reaction followed by equivocation or backing down by the narrator.[13] Particularly relevant are the aggressive stances against women and marriage adopted in such Latin writers as Lucretius and Jerome, where the narrator in many instances ends his diatribe by eventually compromising or retreating from the extreme position with which he had begun. It is perhaps all part of a satiric ploy, but the net thrown by satire is wide indeed.

Marriage at least had the potential of enhancing a man's economic status. In actual fact, or in "real life," to find a potential wife with a large dowry was considered by the Romans a socially acceptable motive for marriage, more acceptable, for example, than seeking a wife for her voluptuous charms.[14] But in popular essays and in comedy, this motive is often stood on its head, and a large dowry is seen as having a negative influence on the bride, giving her unrealistic expectations and encouraging her to overspend;[15] thus there is the common saying—probably with hypocritical overtones, yet eagerly picked up later by Christian writers—that wives ought to be adorned by virtue and modesty rather than by precious jewelry and clothing (Plutarch *Moralia* 141D–E).

6

In New Comedy, a fear of dowried—and hence independent-minded—wives is a common topos expressed by middle-aged bachelors, men of the world who have already made some money and are afraid of losing it; they are shown avoiding wealthy brides who will expect to be maintained in high style. Susanna Morton Braund points out in chapter 3 in this volume that in Roman comedy especially, marriage is a universal telos for young people, but once they have experienced it firsthand, all complain about it and wish to escape it. Middle-aged bachelors, who have a wider perspective on the issue, fear in particular a bride who will make financial demands, a variation on a fear of the wife taking the sexual initiative away from the husband. Similar is the diatribe of the bachelor Periplectomenus in the *Miles gloriosus* (680–714), who sees dowried wives as potential "yappers" barking after his money; brides should be selected by their virtue and modesty rather than by precious jewelry and clothing (cf. also Plutarch *Moralia* 141D–E). This view is not restricted to comedy; in Plutarch's *Dialogue on Love* (*Moralia* 752F), Pisias argues that excessive wealth makes women "frivolous, haughty, inconstant, and vain" and "often . . . elates them so much that they fly away."

SHOULD A PHILOSOPHER MARRY?

Marriage and philosophy are often seen as incompatible, as in the following anecdote sometimes quoted in the medieval period.

> Cicero post repudium Terentie uxorari noluit, dicens se pariter et uxori et philosophoie operam dare non posse.
>
> [*Cicero refused to marry again after divorcing Terentia, saying that he could not spare time at once for a wife and for philosophy.*][16]

"Philosophical misogamy," as discussed by Wilson and Makowski, uses arguments against marriage that are based not on the moral inferiority of the wife but on the inconveniences of marriage, which "impedes the philosopher's freedom to think and study."[17] The antipathy between philosophers and marriage is not necessarily a natural or inevitable one in all periods or literary genres. Aristotle writes in *Nicomachean Ethics* 8.12.7 that the friendship between husband and wife appears to be a natural instinct and is based on a combination of utility and pleasure. Philosophers, however, often are seen as falling under a special category, because due to their devotion to abstract reasoning, they may be remote from the problems of the real world and find a special difficulty in seeing what is good for them; thus Aristotle can say of Anaxagoras

and Thales that people applaud their wisdom but find it to be useless in application, "because it is not human good that they seek" (*Nic. Ethics* 6.7=1141b,
Ross). Such impracticality might easily lead philosophers to choose undesirable partners. In later antiquity, as Foucault points out,[18] there was in fact
considerable disagreement among the philosophers on the desirability of marriage, with Cynics and Epicureans tending to oppose marriage, while Stoics
tended to see marriage as a universal duty. However, when Epictetus describes
marriage as creating a distraction for the ideal Cynic philosopher (*Discourses*
3.22.67–82), the warning is made not on the basis of any defect in women but
on the idealistic ground that the responsibilities of a household would prevent the philosopher from fulfilling his/her obligations to the rest of humanity. Seneca, in his lost work *On Marriage*, apparently argued that "philosophers
should marry and that there were sound reasons for marriage,"[19] though Jerome,
in *Against Jovinian* 1.49, groups Seneca with Aristotle and Plutarch among
those who cautioned against the effects of excessive love.

The power of sexual attraction and the unpredictability inherent in inti-
macy easily give rise to incongruity and humor in stories about the private lives
of thinkers and ascetics. Since the start of philosophy, there have been widespread anecdotes about men lost in contemplation who, despite all their wisdom and ability to reason and argue, were exposed as physically inept or
inadequate or were otherwise bested by their own wives or mistresses or by
other women; the recurring irony highlighted by such stories is that these men
could advise others well with abstract theory but could not keep their own
houses in order when it came to real-life situations. An attractive servant girl
mocked Thales for falling into a well while he was observing the stars (Plato
Theatetus 174A). Lucretius himself, in a well-known anecdote reported by
Jerome,[20] was driven insane by an aphrodisiac that, according to later tradition, was administered by his wife (she is perhaps intended as the "Lucilia"
in Walter Map's *De nugis curialium* 4.3). The nagging and abuse of Socrates by
his shrewish wife Xanthippe are often reported—one of those making good use
of it is Jerome (*Against Jovinian* 1.48), who adds the nagging of a second wife,
Myron. A story about Aristotle, widely repeated in the Middle Ages and often
depicted in painting and sculpture, has the great philosopher equally humbled
by a woman. Supposedly he was tricked by "Phyllis," either the wife or mistress
of Alexander the Great, Aristotle's pupil, into allowing himself to be mounted
by her and ridden about like a horse, much to the amusement of Alexander.
According to Jacques de Vitry (d. 1240), who used this story in a sermon,

> If indeed the malice and cunning of the woman so prevailed that
> she deceived and held an old man captive, the most prudent of all

8

mortals, . . . how much more power she might have over you, (whom she could much more easily) deceive, allure, and defraud. . . . [21]

Another popular story in the Middle Ages, when Virgil was often regarded as a sage, had the ascetic author of the *Aeneid* falling in love with the daughter of the emperor of Rome—in real life, according to the ancient *Vita* of Suetonius, Virgil had little interest in women and was called *Parthenias* for his fastidiousness (*et ore et animo tam probum, Vita* 11). In the medieval tale, the lady tricks Virgil into entering a basket, which she then raises halfway to her window, suspending him there so that he may be mocked by the people of Rome the next day (according to one version of the story, he gets revenge on her the next day by requiring the townspeople to rekindle their fires by touching brands to her genitals). These humiliations of two famous sages were sometimes juxtaposed in art, wonderfully emblematic of the synthesis in satire of grave moralism and slapstick farce.[22]

According to the reasoning of Lucretius in *De rerum natura*, once a woman sets her designs on a man, he is trapped; the man may initially find a way to eventually resist the attraction of the woman, but she can find some way to break him down, to wrest his power away from him, like the ocean slowly succeeding in wearing down rocks by beating against them. Time is on the side of a persistent woman (cf. *consuetudo concinnat amorem* [custom paves the way for love], *DRN* 4.1283). For all his elaborate efforts to remain detached, the eligible man will eventually succumb to the woman, to the extent that she is able to emerge as an independently thinking and acting person able to assert her own needs and seize control of the courtship.

ANTI-SEX, ANTI-WOMEN, ANTI-MARRIAGE: SELF-DEFEATING VEHEMENCE?

The attacks of such major and influential satires as Juvenal's *Satire* 6 or Jerome's *Against Jovinian* rise to great heights in their rhetorical indignation but seem to collapse, at the end, under the weight of the powerful feelings they have aroused. The readiness of the satirists to acquiesce in defeat (cf. the backing down of Juvenal's narrator at the end of *Sat.* 1.171–72) reflects the notion of the lyric poets (going back to Sappho) who record and lament the incredible and invincible power of love. The satirist eventually is forced to admit defeat against the power of women and sexual attraction—or at least ultimately to admit that in the conflict between men and women, the odds are heavily stacked against men.

The sometimes astonishing vehemence of the anti-marriage literature—the single-minded, concentrated, and obsessive tone of many of the attacks—requires some explanation going beyond literary intention and touching on the psychology of the male satirist. One kind of answer comes from anthropology. As Susan Treggiari says, " 'Wife jokes,' like mother-in-law jokes, are only funny if there is some degree of male insecurity."[23]

Part of the explanation for such insecurity in the case of the Roman satirists may be sought in the fear that women, in moving upward socially, may usurp the sexual and economic rights of men, a fear that stands out clearly in the second century and is certainly a factor in the nearly pathological obsession of the sixth satire of Juvenal and in the epigrams of his contemporary Martial.[24] A variation on such fear—namely, the fear of sex with old women (cf. Horace *Epodes* 3, 8)—is explained by Amy Richlin as a possible "apotropaic satire that attempts to belittle and control the power of old women, pitting the phallus against the threat of sterility, death, and the chthonic forces."[25] In such ridicule, we have not moral indignation but loathing of the ugly and aged. But the old woman, as Richlin admits, is also seen as a sexual predator, particularly in her incarnation as a nymphomaniac witch, as in the case of Apuleius's Meroe in *Golden Ass* 1.13. In general the boundary violation that the satirists believe is perpetuated by sexually aroused women is well explained by an anthropologist. Mary Douglas, in her innovative study *Purity and Danger*, writes about the fear of sexual intercourse among primitive tribes, using language that can shed light on many of the authors considered in the present study. At issue is the idea of sexual attraction and intercourse as involving a boundary violation.

> Female pollution in a society of this type is largely related to the attempt to treat women simultaneously as persons and as the currency of male transactions. Males and females are set off as belonging to distinct, mutually hostile species. Sexual antagonism inevitably results and this is reflected in the idea that each sex constitutes a danger to the other. . . . Indeed the story of the Garden of Eden touched a deep chord of sympathy in Lele male breasts. Once told by the missionaries, it was told and retold round pagan hearths with smug relish.[26]

This male fear of boundary violation by women comes out clearly in the myth of Pandora. As Froma Zeitlin notes, in this story "woman remains a separate and alien being, whose presence in the household he [the husband] both requires and resents."[27] In the economically conservative worldview of Hesiod, the presence of a woman in the household is that of a drone who reaps the toil of others into her own belly (*Theog.* 599). In the famous comparison by Semonides of Amorgus to various animals, the luxurious mare is the wife who drains away household expenses (70).

Closely related to the fear of boundary violation is the idea that for men, sexual intercourse can in certain cases (according to Galen) hasten the onset of disease[28] or can bring about a diminution of virility. Peter Brown writes:

> A powerful "fantasy of the loss of vital spirit" lay at the root of many late classical attitudes toward the male body. It is one of the many notions that gave male continence a firm foothold in the folk wisdom of the world in which Christian celibacy would soon be preached. The most virile man was the one who kept most of his vital spirit—the one, that is, who lost little or no seed.[29]

OVID: PUTTING A HARNESS ON THE ILLOGICAL

Ovid presents his *Ars amatoria* as a guidebook to courtship, attempting or pretending, in a series of precepts, to show the reader how lovemaking can be regulated. A central presupposition of his work is that *amor* is capable of being taught and learned, just as chariot driving or lyre playing can be taught: he maintains that *arte regendus amor* [love must be controlled by skill] (*AA* 1.4). That such a precept seems almost an oxymoron does not deter the poet but simply adds to his zeal. By demonstrating how it is possible for the suitor to influence the behavior of women by manipulating them, Ovid picks up on a theme from Lucretius *De rerum natura* 4. Yet where Lucretius teaches how to drive seductive women away, Ovid aims at seduction performed with the proper flair: as Karla Pollmann says (in chap. 5 of the present volume), the *Ars* "intends to teach how to refine, cultivate, and control a natural force." At the start of the *Ars* (1.31–32), Ovid seeks to discourage noble women motivated by *pudor* from reading his book, maintaining that his target is only women of lower station. Yet despite this attempt by Ovid to excuse himself, it is clear that the satirical thrust of the *Ars* centers in part on its vision of the replacement or enhancement of marriage with illicit relationships. Thus this work was guaranteed to win the displeasure of the emperor Augustus, who wanted to strengthen family ties.

Ovid, who is seemingly the most happily heterosexual of Roman writers, tends to speak disparagingly of homosexuality (cf. *AA* 1.524, which jibes at the man of "doubtful sex" [*male vir*], who wants to have a man); he celebrates the love of man and woman in much of his poetry and has a genuine interest in the psychology of women. As Pollmann discusses in her contribution to this volume (chap. 5), the third book of the *Ars* is aimed at women in order to redress the imbalance of men getting all the good advice. This is an even-handed and even innovative strategy, which takes for granted the equal sexual desire and needs of women. Furthermore, "Ovid demands that women should not be stereotyped according to prejudices,"[30] and he maintains that courtship requires the mastery of an *ars* precisely because the female psyche is a complex and subtle mechanism.

However, in a concession with wide implications for the antimatrimonial literature, Ovid also acknowledges the negative and dangerous side of love. In his *Remedia amoris*, he goes back to the imagery of Greek lyric poetry and tragedy when he speaks of love with the wrong partner as driving many to suicide (17–22). As the title of the poem suggests, the *Remedia* sees love as a "disease" (at least for the unhappy lover) whose wicked seeds must be crushed (81). For such imagery, Ovid could find a precedent not only in such Greek poets as Sappho (frags. 31, 47) and Euripides (the illness of Phaedra in *Hippolytus*) but also in such Latin love poets as Catullus, who bewails his own love as a sickness (*taetrum hunc deponere morbum*, 76), and especially Propertius (who describes the illness in his program piece, 1.1). Ovid the love doctor turns such lessons to his own prescription for a systematic remedy. However, he warns that trying to turn aside love after it has already begun is like calling in a doctor when it is too late to save the patient or trying to pull up a tree after it has already sunk its roots. Ovid's acknowledgment of a negative side of love, structurally balanced in a separate book against the positive advice of the *Ars*, was to have an important influence on such medieval writers as Marbod of Rennes and Andreas Capellanus, who balanced "good against bad" women in successive poems (Marbod) or books of essays (Andreas).

JUVENAL: LOSING CONTROL

Juvenal's sixth satire has been called "probably the most horrifying of all catalogues of female vices."[31] It has been convincingly argued by Braund that this satire "is best understood not as a general diatribe against women but as a dissuasion from marriage."[32] But while Braund's general point remains, the sixth satire is a good example of how difficult it is to separate misogamy from misogyny as a literary theme. The highly rhetorical components of the argument have long been noted: these include a debate with a fictitious reader, rhetorical questions, hyperbole, and reasoning by gradation.[33] In an attempt to dissuade his friend Postumus from marrying, the narrator presents a slide show of horrors perpetuated by various hypothetical wives. Meanwhile, in a grim litany of over six hundred lines, Postumus seems to be imagined as actually entering into a marriage and undergoing various indignities, until he is finally enfeebled by a love philter (612) and murdered (659–60).

Juvenal includes many of the themes prominent in earlier antifeminist literature, especially female drunkenness, sexual promiscuity, and, above all, woman's exercise of power as a *domina* who wants to enslave, belittle, and enfeeble her male partner.[34] All such vices are shown as subverting her marriage. Indeed, abuse of power is an important underlying theme of Juvenal's sixth satire, the result of a husband's being compelled to submit to the yoke of a wife who will dominate his life (*ferre potes dominam,* 30). A Roman wife is supposed to enter the *manus,* or control, of her husband; and part of the injunction made by the *pronuba* (matron who escorted one bride to her chamber) to the bride in the Roman wedding ceremony was apparently that she should remain *morigera* (compliant) to her husband—her property was given to him as a dowry.[35] But the husbands envisioned by Juvenal have lost that control over their wives—and indeed over their own lives. Their wives have learned how to exercise imperium over them (*imperat ergo viro,* 224)—the same paradox deplored by Plautus in his *Casina* (409). Suicide is presented as a preferable alternative to submitting to a *domina.* Juvenal's husbands are passive to the point of cowardice, and their bold wives win out by their persistence (as Lucretius finally admits at the end of *DRN* 4) and by their increasingly bold behavior, which can lead to their murder of their husbands—Clytemnestra-style (i.e., by ax) if the men learn to fortify themselves against poison (*Sat.* 6.659–61).

Above all, Juvenal's approach is monolithic, meant to impress by its sheer size and repetition, in contrast with the complexity of Ovid. One point of view is hammered home, in the manner of rhetorical diatribe.

ENTER CHRISTIAN LITERATURE: NEW OPPORTUNITIES, NEW ATTACKS

The advent of Christianity appeared at first to open up new social opportunities for women. Several factors contributed to this change. Not only did Christians venerate the Virgin Mary as one of their primary patron saints; they pursued a cult of equality that broke down social, racial, and economic distinctions to the extent of seeming at times to put women on an equal footing with men before Christ.[36] Indeed, already in the Gospels, women have a place of relative honor. Jesus, ignoring the surprise of his own disciples at his forwardness (John 4:27), spoke with women naturally and casually, seemingly without self-consciousness about their difference in sex; he had female followers, notably Mary Magdalene; in John 4, his first revelation of himself as the Messiah is made to the Samaritan woman at the well; and women are the first witnesses of the resurrection (Mark 16:1–8; John 20:1–18).

St. Paul, in his letters, adopts a serious tone on the subject of male-female relationships and becomes a kind of intermediary between Hellenism and Judaism. As Barbara Feichtinger argues in this volume (chap. 9), Paul displays "an eschatological indifference toward marriage as the institution of a transitory world." Paul at times seems to imply that for those who had undergone baptism, the rite of entry into the church—the significance of social and sexual distinctions—has been wiped out by the Gospel of Christ and by the coming end of the world. Thus he makes the startling proclamation, "There is no longer Jew and Greek, there is no longer slave or free, there is no longer male or female; for all of you are one in Jesus Christ."[37] Now it was possible to become a child of Abraham merely by baptism, without being born a Jew or undergoing circumcision. Membership in the church—not belonging to a particular ethnic group and not membership in a particular city or nation—became the fundamental relationship between human beings.

Paul sees the "freedom" claimed by the Greek polis as an error, a mere self-indulgence, a wandering from the truth, which carries with it an enslavement to sin and brings its own punishment.[38] In this he carries over some of the assumptions of Juvenal (especially in the third and sixth satires), who sees the Greeks as introducing outlandish Eastern customs (3.60–66), effeminacy ("you would think it's a woman speaking, not a mask," 3.95–96), and immorality (6.191). The Christian freedom under the New Covenant is the alternative to the Hellenic licentiousness; it is in a new category, freedom from sin and the Law (Gal. 4:26; Romans 7:3) and enslavement to the will of God (Romans 6:22). In the diatribe against idolatry and sexual immorality that begins in Romans 1:18, Paul gives special prominence to the actions of homosexuals and lesbians, whom he finds revolting because they reverse the usual role of their sex. Both groups, especially the men, were frequent targets of the Roman satirists.[39] Paul's diatribe in Romans 1–2 has the style of a rhetorician-satirist turned up at loudest volume, making use of proverbial sayings (1:18), paradoxical *sententiae* ("claiming to be wise, they became fools," 1:22; " . . . served the creature rather than the Creator," 1:25), antitheses ("Invisible things . . . are seen," 1:20; "They exchanged the truth of God for a lie," 1:25), alliteration, asyndeton (1:29–31), and repetition of the same phrase leading to rhetorical climax ("God gave them up," 1:24, 26, 28).[40] Telling also are the rhetorician-satirist's direct engagement with the reader ("Therefore you have no excuse, whoever you are . . ." 2:1; this recalls the satirist's repeated debate with Postumus in Juvenal's sixth satire) and posing of a series of insistent and indignant questions (2:1–4). The style of this biblical passage is common to declamatory satire (cf., e.g., Juvenal *Sat.* 6.37, 42, 44, 59, 75, 104, 105). Such a passage, by its effective use of exaggeration and by sweeping the reader away with its display of clever effects, sets the rhetorical stage for the diatribes of Tertullian and Jerome. The view of the Greek world as bankrupt and obsolete, as degenerate with a tendency toward self-indulgence, is an attitude that Paul shares with Juvenal. The Greeks, in this view, are not the giants of the classical world but degenerate tricksters and libertines whose libertine attitude is corrupting the traveler to their land.

If the rite of baptism breaks down national distinctions and makes us all children of Abraham through Jesus Christ, so the breaking down of distinctions must extend to the body and further blur distinctions between male and female. This is made explicit by Paul in the triumphant declaration that unites Jew and Greek, slave and free, male and female in Jesus Christ (Gal. 3:28).

In some respects, early Christianity gave a push to women, starting them on the road to equality with men; marriage was even exalted as symbolically representing the love of Christ and the church. For the first time, women were offered a personal choice between marriage and celibacy. Moreover, the pro-celibacy Christian literature often sought to influence this choice by discouraging them from the bearing of children, the function that probably most dramatically distinguishes them from men. Those women who removed themselves from marriage and childbearing, according to reasoning in the early church, went even further toward social equality, and "a celibate woman thus became, in moral terms, a man."[41]

In New Testament Scripture, we find a condemnation of adultery, divorce, fornication, and homosexuality that reflects and, in the case of divorce, even goes beyond the conservatism of Jewish Scripture.[42] St. Paul does allow fornication within marriage, and he sees it as a normal part of that relationship (1 Cor. 7:3–5); elsewhere, he goes further, exalting the love of husband for wife by comparing it with that of Christ and the church (Eph. 5:25). The influential early Christian writing *The Shepherd of Hermas* (early second century A.D.) follows Paul in seeing Christian marriage as a way to avoid temptations to immorality (*Shepherd*, chap. 29). Though marriage may bring this negative benefit of preventing sexual immorality, Paul does not consistently ascribe any inherent positive value to marriage, and he would prefer that all stay unmarried, as he is (1 Cor. 7:7–8). An important subtext for Paul's judgment on social issues is that he sees the world as rapidly coming to an end, so new commitments or changes in relationships are discouraged.[43] In the Gospels, too, the commitment to the married state, along with other family relationships, is subordinated to the commitment to the kingdom of God (Luke 12:51–53; cf. Matt. 19:27–30), and those who marry and are given in marriage are typed as "children of this world" (Luke 20:23–26). Thus Paul's position on the issue of celibacy is moderate and conciliatory, if occasionally ambivalent, as is the message of the Gospels. However, regardless of how biblical discussions of marriage were interpreted, the virginity of Mary and the presumed virginity of Jesus himself were there to be held up as examples; a growing asceticism is seen already in the later first century in the exaltation of virgins in the passage (unusual for the Bible) at Revelation 14:4, where the 144,000 who have been redeemed from the earth are "virgins who have not defiled themselves with women."

In postbiblical Christian writing, such as *The Acts of Paul and Thecla* (perhaps as early as the second century A.D.), the slanting of Scripture toward chastity has begun full force. Paul has become a fervid advocate of chastity; his version of the Beatitudes begins, "Blessed are the poor in heart, for they shall see God; blessed are those who keep the flesh chaste, for they shall become a temple of God; blessed are the continent, for God shall speak with them. . . ." (*Acts of Paul and Thecla* 5), and he urges that those who have wives be as those not having them. Thecla, who hears Paul's message, abandons her fiancé and travels with Paul, much as Paula and Eustochium were to do with St. Jerome centuries later: "The Fathers begin to vie with one another in exalting the state of virginity."[44]

The story of the Fall is often interpreted as casting a more negative light on women than on men, and the implications of this lesson were worked out by the earliest commentators. Philo of Alexandria had already argued at length in his *Allegorical Interpretation of Genesis II* that Adam represents the mind (*nous*) while Eve represents sense perception (*aisthesis*), the latter of which is bound to the corporeal.[45] The serpent, according to Philo, stands for pleasure, with which Eve is closely allied (Philo 2.71–74). Philo's lead is often picked up in Christian discussions of the Fall. The deutero-Pauline 1 Timothy 14 has already shifted the blame for the Fall away from the man: "and Adam was not deceived, but the woman was deceived and became a transgressor" (cf. Romans 5:18–19). St. Ambrose found "an allegory in the Fall, whereby the serpent is 'a type of the pleasures of the body,' woman 'stands for our senses,' and the man 'for our minds.' "[46]

PAGAN AND CHRISTIAN SYNTHESIS

For a scholar such as Augustine, the Bible became the basis for a new Christian culture, a treasure house of stories and knowledge rivaling the old pagan classics, and a book that one could easily study alone from boyhood to old age without exhausting its riches.[47] What was not so clear was whether the Bible really preached a homogenous message on, for example, the subject of marriage and virginity. While it remained difficult to turn to Scripture for a clear precedent in the exaltation of virginity as an ideal state for humankind, early biblical commentators sought ways to find allegories and warnings about women in the stories, as part of an ongoing effort to harmonize or explain away differences between the Judeo-Christian and Greco-Roman traditions. In his treatises *On the Good of Marriage* and *On Holy Virginity*, Augustine took the decisive step of arguing that virginity could be praised without denigrating marriage, extolling the goodness of conception and birth against the extreme asceticism put forth by Jerome and others. He extolled the goodness of the sexual act, if only when used for reproduction.[48]

Misogynistic overtones in the Bible were sought out, exaggerated, and distorted by medieval Christian commentators, who tended also to see such Old Testament characters as Samson, David, and Solomon as providing negative lessons against marriage by exemplifying the dangers of coming under the power of a woman.[49] From the second century onward, there were groups of Christians who preached that Christ had come to earth to deliver mankind from sexuality and marriage.[50] It was claimed that Jesus had taught Salome that death would hold sway "as long as you women bear children" (cf. Matt. 20:20–22, *Gospel of Thomas* 61:2–5). St. Jerome (at least in his satiric writing) did not hesitate to interpret out of context Matthew 24:19, "woe to them that are with child and to them that give suck in those days," as "a condemnation . . . of the swelling womb and wailing infancy, the fruit as well as the work of marriage" (*Against Jovinian* 1.12; cf. *On the Perpetual Virginity of Blessed Mary* 23). Augustine, Jerome, and their successors found it easy not only to include pagan and classical exempla in the same treatise but to put them side by side and seamlessly move from one to the other. A single example from the French literature of the High Middle Ages will demonstrate this vividly. If we open the thirteenth-century *Romance of the Rose* to Jean de Meung's remonstration on women as spoken by the jealous husband (9079–360), we find, in the space of a few lines, the deceitfulness of women as proved by citations from Juvenal's sixth satire, followed closely by Hercules and Samson cited together as examples of husbands dominated by their wives.

TERTULLIAN: THE LOATHING OF SEX

Tertullian, among the earliest of the Latin fathers and "the first of the great Christian misogynists,"[51] is an important transitional figure between the pagan and Christian tradition. Christopher Dawson describes him as thoroughly "Roman in his thought and his ideals" and as "the last representative of the great Roman moralists, like Lucretius and Juvenal and Tacitus." According to Dawson, Tertullian's "moral indignation" made him "the champion of the Christian faith against the corruption of the pagan world."[52]

Women are an important focus of Tertullian's moral indignation. He is capable of addressing women as "the devil's gate, surrender of that tree, first to violate divine law" (*De cultu feminarum* 1). His treatises on women, sexuality, and marriage (including *De cultu feminarum*, *Ad uxorem*, *De exhortatione castitatis*, *De virginibus velandis*, *De monogamia*, and *De pudicitia*) display the results of his legal and rhetorical training. Consider a passage like *De monogamia* 3.2:

> Yes, you say, but the right to marry still remains. True, it does remain, ... it is already partially abrogated, however, in so far as continence is said to be preferable, *It is good*, he says, *for a man not to touch a woman*. Therefore, it is bad to touch one. For nothing is opposed to the "good" except the "bad."

Here we see the characteristic devices of the diatribe satirists in miniature, including engagement with the reader, pointed antithesis, and inexorable logic that quotes phrases out of context and admits to no compromise; the only allowable answers involve extremes.

Tertullian strengthens and exaggerates to the point of caricature Paul's preference for celibacy, since even marriage, he says, "in the shameful act which constitutes its essence, is the same as fornication" (*De exh. castitatis* 9.4). Tertullian's pro-celibacy views were of great influence in the early church, not least because his writings concerning marriage and chastity were extensively used as a source (usually without acknowledgment) by St. Jerome. Jerome, in his controversial but highly influential pamphlet *Against Jovinian*, copied many of the ideas and rhetorical flourishes from Tertullian for his refutation of the "heresies" of the monk Jovinian. It is as a satirist that Jerome, as Peter Brown cuttingly remarks, "placed the sayings of Jesus Christ on the same footing as the authors of Roman Comedy."[53]

JEROME: THE OPPOSITE OF SEX

Using all his rhetorical skills, Jerome, in *Against Jovinian*, turns to the views on marriage by St. Paul. Jerome espouses these views with enthusiasm but sometimes turns with impatience against Paul, when, in Jerome's view, Paul has failed to follow his arguments through to their logical conclusion.

Thus, on the whole, we get in Jerome's treatise a perspective that is remarkably rich and varied in its sources but whose point of view is also varied to the point of incoherence. Women are at times denounced as inferior partners, but faithful women are held up as examples to prove the superiority of virginity (or fidelity or chastity). Part of the reason for the confusion, certainly, is Jerome's inability to decide whether his primary target is marriage itself (from which both men and women must be dissuaded; thus he would be assuming a mixed audience) or the female sex (in which case he would be assuming only a male audience and attempting to polarize the men against women). By choosing such a wide target—by attempting to reconcile pagans and Christians, Old and New Testament, passages in favor of marriage with those against it or neutral—he achieves a narrative tone that is now reasoned, now hysterical, and finally rather sad and isolated, as the old churchman laments the enormous task of wiping out sin and watches the events of history sweep past him. Despite Jerome's extreme—even sometimes hysterical—views of female lechery and the perils of marriage, he himself, it can be argued, actually elevates the debate about male-female relations by his allowance of women into the audience and by offering them some of the benefits of celibacy that in the pagan world had only been available to men—namely, the ability to pursue spiritual goals through detachment from the cares of a sexual relationship, by remaining in one's room alone and reading Scripture (Jerome *Ep.* 22, *Letter to Eustochium* 24–25).

The voices of Jerome and Tertullian were ultimately not the definitive and final word in the church's position on marriage; their authority was overridden by the treatises of St. Augustine, which, while continuing to exalt the state of celibacy, attempt to elevate marriage to the special position it often occupies in Scripture, starting with God's admonition in Genesis 1:28 to "be fruitful and multiply." While marriage was acceptable, virginity was preferable: "'Honorable is marriage in all, and the bed undefiled.' And this we do not so call a good, as that it is a good in comparison of fornication. . . . Therefore marriage and fornication are not two evils, whereof the second is worse; but marriage and continence are two goods, whereof the second is better" (*De bono conjugali* 8). Marriage was good not merely for the sake of the begetting of children but because it provides natural society between the sexes (*De bono conjugali* 3). Yet chastity is a higher good; indeed, if it were somehow possible that all marriages would entirely cease, "much more speedily would the City of God be filled, and the end of the world hastened" (*De bono conjugali* 10). Augustine's concession to the good of marriage provided an important corrective to Jerome's extreme position that not only seemed to imply a moral equation between marriage and fornication but even condemned the begetting of children, which Augustine listed at the forefront of the benefits of marriage.[54]

FOR AND AGAINST

Among the priesthood or those intending a career in the priesthood (which theoretically required celibacy), there was a constant circulation and reworking of misogynistic material, partly as a show of learning and partly as part of a campaign by the church "to establish a fully celibate priesthood."[55] In his *Liber decem capitulorum*, Marbod of Rennes (ca. 1035–1123) displays some of the ambiguity of Jerome (and repeats many of Jerome's examples from *Against Jovinian*) by writing successive chapters on bad and good woman (*De meretrice* and *De matrona*). In the earlier work, woman's evil is almost cosmic, the greatest of "the traps that the scheming enemy has set through the world's paths and plains," and the examples given are balanced between the Bible (Eve, Lot's daughters, Delilah, Salome) and classical literature, especially Ovid (Eriphyle, Clytemnestra, Procne, Helen of Troy). Jerome's sailing metaphor is picked up in section 84, but now the ship is a bizarre blending of the church and of the ship of Odysseus; the passenger must stay fastened to the timber (the cross) and block up his ears with "sound doctrine" in order to avoid being shipwrecked by the alluring songs of the Sirens.

The second treatise by Marbod, *De matrona*, praises the constancy, modesty, and chastity of women; this positive picture, contradicting the view of the earlier treatise, is formally parallel to the antithesis of Ovid's tour de force (*Ars amatoria* balanced by *Remedia amoris*) but is also matched by Jerome, even if unconsciously so, in that part of Jerome's *Against Jovinian* (1.41–44) in which examples of female constancy, bravery, and chastity seem oddly juxtaposed with negative examples of women.

In the twelfth century, Hugh Primas of Orleans, in his three Oxford poems against harlots (poems 6–8), presents himself or his satiric persona as one who has been wronged by a harlot, Flora (Witke 1970, 200–232). In poem 6, Flora has abandoned him for another man and mocks him in his grief (*Set tu mendosa rides me flente dolosa* [while I weep you laugh, full of lies and tricks], 28). This theme widens in poem 7, where the greed and fickleness of women is decried. In a kind of mock consolation, the reader is advised to be *sapiens* (wise), to face adversity with *pectore forti* (a brave heart, 7), and to endure the vicissitudes of fate with patience; he is warned that women will stick by him only so long as his money holds out. Poem 8 contrasts the sordid home life of a *meretrix* with the elegance she affects when she is with a young client. The poems alternate between self-pity and mock consolation for a narrator who has trusted a whore. Their realism, their worldly cynicism, and the frank admission by the narrator of his personal experience in the lifestyle against which he is warning make these poems memorable for their "subjectivism and self-pity"[56] and their combination of lyricism with satiric bite at the heart-lessness of women.

CAPELLANUS'S COMPLEX POINT OF VIEW

Andreas Capellanus was certainly influenced by Ovid (whom he frequently quotes) in the structure of his *De amore*.[57] His three-book plan seems to have as its model the three books of Ovid's *Ars amatoria* (except that Andreas's third book corresponds more naturally to Ovid's *Remedia amoris*). Andreas's work is a remarkable example of the complexity that can result from the influence of Ovid (as opposed to the more monolithic approach, say, of Jerome): he attempts to see courtship from a woman's perspective and offers a balancing of views and a series of dialogues between men and women of varying social stations. The third book of *De amore* is a diatribe against love (like Ovid's *Remedia amoris*), teaching the reader reasons for falling out of the love into which he has been enticed by the earlier books. Using scriptural as well as classical authority, Andreas's third book argues, in the old tradition that opposes philosophy and love, that the *sapiens* should renounce all acts of love (3.3) and that the lover cannot concentrate because of constant fear and jealousy (3.14–16). As so often occurs in the anti-sex literature, Andreas makes an easy transition from the arguments against passion itself (3.1–64)—arguments that might be applicable to either sex—to passages denouncing the supposed evil of women in particular (3.65–112). Then, after listing in detail stock feminine vices (inconstancy, drunkenness, lechery, and jealousy are only a few), he finally concludes, with a broad stroke that manages to combine echoes both of Juvenal's sixth satire (*nullane . . . tibi digna videtur?* 6.161) and of the Bible (Ecclesiastes 7.28), *femina nulla bona* (3.109).

MAP: PAGAN AND CHRISTIAN WITTILY COMBINED

After Jerome, the writer having the most widespread influence among all the medieval satirists against marriage was Walter Map, a diplomat of the twelfth century and at one time archdeacon of Oxford.[58] He wrote (perhaps in the 1170s) *A Dissuasion of Valerius to Rufinus the Philosopher, that He Should Not Take a Wife*. This treatise originally circulated separately and had a life of its own but was eventually incorporated by Map into his *De nugis curialium* (Courtiers' trifles), becoming the most finished and crafted part of that work. The *Dissuasio* is alluded to, for example, under the name of "Valerie," in Chaucer's Wife of Bath's prologue (672). Two important sources of this work are Ovid's *Metamor-*

phoses and Jerome's *Against Jovinian* (it was sometimes considered a part of the latter and copied along with texts of Jerome), but as the treatise's recent editors have argued, Map juggles a variety of other sources as well; for example, the dramatic form of the work (an address to a marrying friend) recalls the situation of Juvenal's *Satire* 6. In the final section of Map's essay, he "bounces back and forth between Christian and classical argumentation," and "mythological references alternate with passages redolent with biblical diction."[59] As was the case with Jerome, Map seeks to arrive not so much at a specifically Christian truth as at a set of principles universal for all humankind, pagan as well as Christian. With wonderfully mixed metaphors, Map argues that marriage is the honeyed poison served by the cupbearers of Babel, which goes down sweetly but "at last will bite like an adder and inflict a wound that no antidote can cure."[60]

Walter Map's *Dissuasion*, though unconventional as a piece of Christian moralizing, exerted a wide influence on clerics; it ends on a note that is already familiar to us from Jerome—that the reader should learn to imitate the lifestyle of virtuous pagans, especially philosophers who trained themselves to abstain from marriage. But again like Jerome, Map seems very doubtful of the efficacy of his own advice. He points out sadly that few things are impossible to a woman, and he concludes with a prayer that Rufinus may not be deceived by the deceits of the "Almighty Female."[61]

CHAUCER AND THE "MARRIAGE DEBATE"

In the character of the Wife of Bath, Chaucer grapples with the anti-marriage views of St. Jerome and Map and perhaps also responds to other antifeminist tirades closer to Chaucer's time, such as the *Corbaccio* of his older contemporary Boccaccio.[62] Much of the prologue to the "Wife of Bath's Tale" engages in a close debate with Jerome, particularly on the issue of biblical interpretation of marriage and the role of women. The debate continues and seems to reach a resolution in the "Franklin's Tale," where *Against Jovinian* is again an important source, in this case for Dorigen's lament.

Nearly a century ago, in his famous essay "Chaucer's Discussion of Marriage," George Kittredge described how the "Franklin's Tale" provides a resolution for Chaucer's marriage debate. In particular, Kittredge believed that the Franklin finds a solution for the demand to dominate made so often by the wives of the satirical anti-marriage literature.

> It was the regular theory of the Middle Ages that the highest type of chivalric love was incompatible with marriage, since marriage brings in mastery, and mastery and love cannot abide together. This view the

Franklin boldly challenges. Love *can* be consistent with marriage, he declares. Indeed, without love (and perfect gentle love) marriage is sure to be a failure. The difficulty about mastery vanishes when mutual love and forbearance are made the guiding principles of the relation between husband and wife.[63]

Chaucer's use of Jerome's anti-marriage treatise (particularly in the Wife of Bath's prologue—as I argue in chapter 12 in this volume—and in the "Franklin's Tale") comes to grips with his arguments in a devastating way, correcting and moving beyond them to a higher concept of the equality between partners and the validity of marriage.

REFORMATION: FAITH AND WORKS

Chaucer begins to see in marriage a possible alternative to the specter of domination by wives that is so effectively raised by Jerome. However, in the Reformation, with its vast new perspective on the nature and limitations of a Christian life, theorists developed ideas on the subject of chastity and marriage that were intended to blunt the polarizing effect of Jerome's theories. Erasmus minimized Jerome's attacks on marriage by pointing out that they were written before marriage had become one of the seven sacraments of the church. Erasmus believed that the Christian church had to be renewed by a return to its sources, which included the early patristic writers as well as the Bible. He stressed the example for Christians of Jerome's scholarship and learning and ranked Jerome's moral teachings of secondary importance.

The Protestants, in contrast, found less to praise in Jerome. Luther, in his lectures on 1 Corinthians 7, which Jerome notoriously had read as a warning against marriage, naturally defends the advice of "better to marry than to burn" and types Jerome as one who stresses works rather than faith.

St. Jerome, who glorifies chastity and praises it most solemnly, confesses that he was unable to subdue his flesh with fasts or wakes, so that his chastity became for him an unimaginable plague. Oh how much precious time he must have wasted with carnal thoughts! . . . You see, the man lay in heat and should have taken a wife. There you see what "aflame with passion" means. For he was of the number that belong in marriage, and he wronged himself and caused himself much trouble by not marrying.[64]

Elsewhere, Luther goes even further, arguing that Jerome should not be numbered among the doctors of the church and saying: "I know no writer whom I hate as much as I do Jerome. All he writes about is fasting and virginity."[65] As the debate on marriage and virginity begins to enter the modern world, the emotional and intellectual level of the discussion begins to sound more reasoned, less desperate; the stridency of the old satirists begins to soften and take on a lighter humor.

ℒ♥

Notes

1. Braund 1996, 44. See also Richlin 1983, 81, 143.

2. De Decker (1913, 23) refers to his "critique general des moeurs feminines."

3. E.g., Mason (1968, 127) writes on Juvenal, "The total effect . . . is to diminish our concern for the reality of what he is saying." On role-playing in satire, see Braund 1996, esp. 1–9, "The Masks of Satire."

4. This is argued in Hanna and Lawler 1997, 6 n. 14.

5. Braund 1992, 72, 82.

6. P. Brown 1988, 10.

7. See Ferrante [1975] 1985, 7.

8. See Edwards 1993, 43.

9. Wilson and Makowski 1990, 34.

10. Braund 1992, 72, 82, and Anderson 1982, esp. 293–361, "*Lascivia* vs. *Ira*: Martial and Juvenal."

11. See Edwards 1993, 5.

12. Kenney 1962, 36.

13. See Smith-Werner 1996; the examples given there include Catullus 10 and the trickster scene from Plautus's *Trinummus* (843ff.).

14. See Treggiari 1991, 96.

15. Cf. G. Williams 1958, 18.

16. Walter Map *De nugis curialium* 4.3 (Hanna and Lawler 1997, 135); cf. Jerome *Ad. Iov.* 1.48.

17. Wilson and Makowski 1990, 5.

18. Foucault 1986, 150–64.

19. Treggiari 1991, 218.

20. Jerome *Eusebii Pamphili Chronici Canones*; see Kenney [1971] 1994, 6–9.

21. Quoted in S. Smith 1995, 76.

22. See S. Smith 1995, 156.

23. Treggiari 1991, 210 n. 25.

24. See Sullivan 1991, 206; Rudd 1986, 204.

25. Richlin 1983, 113.

26. Douglas 1966, 152–53.

27. Zeitlin 1995, 59.

28. See Foucault 1986, 119.

29. P. Brown 1988, 19.

30. Pollmann, chap. 5 in this volume.

31. Rogers 1966, 38.

32. Braund 1992, 85.

33. See De Decker 1913, 112.

34. See W. S. Smith 1980 for my analysis of the sixth satire as a kind of dramatic skit, passing through the stages of courtship, disillusionment, enfeeblement, and murder.

35. See Treggiari 1991, 29.

36. See, e.g., McLeod 1991, 36.

37. Galatians 3:28. Cf. P. Brown 1988, 49–50.

38. Romans 1:27. See also Van Leeuwen 1964, 140.

39. On the rare attacks on lesbians in the ancient literature, see Richlin 1983, 134.

40. For a list of such devices, see De Decker 1913, 154–72.

41. McLeod 1991, 38.

42. See Grant 1970, 270.

43. See, e.g., 1 Cor. 15:24; Wilson and Makowski 1990, 36.

44. Giordani 1944, 219.

45. See Bloch 1991, 29–30.

46. Blamires, Pratt, and Marx 1992, 3.

47. See P. Brown 1967, 263.

48. See Clark 1991.

49. See Rogers 1966, 5.

50. See P. Brown 1988, 85.

51. F. F. Church in Scholer 1993, 200.

52. Dawson 1967, 112. Translations of Tertullian in this chapter are from Le Saint 1951.

53. P. Brown 1988, 376. Cf. Jerome *Ep.* 54.9; *Adv. Iov.* 1.1.

54. This position is argued at length in W. S. Smith 1997. Translations from Augustine's *De bono conjugali* are by C. L. Cornish (1994).

55. Blamires, Pratt, and Marx 1992, 4.

56. Witke 1970, 225.

57. See Parry [1941] 1969, 18.

58. See Hanna and Lawler 1997, 44.

59. Hanna and Lawler 1997, 51.

60. Hanna and Lawler 1997, 123.

61. Hanna and Lawler 1997, 147.

62. See the translation and essay on Boccaccio's *Corbaccio* by A. Cassell (1975).

63. Kittredge 1911–12, 467.

64. Quoted in Oswald 1955, 28:28.

65. Quoted in Rice 1985, 62.

Two

"In a Different Guise"

ROMAN EDUCATION AND
GREEK RHETORICAL THOUGHT
ON MARRIAGE

Richard Hawley

*I*n her excellent book *Roman Marriage* (1991), Susan Treggiari offers a careful survey of Greco-Roman theories concerning marriage. Her focus, however, is mainly philosophical thought as recorded in the works and fragments of writers such as Xenophon, Aristotle, and Hellenistic thinkers from the Stoic, Epicurean, and Peripatetic schools. Treggiari rather neglects rhetorical discussion of marriage. Donald Russell (1979) has helpfully filled this gap by showing how Greek rhetoricians indeed discuss marriage at some length and in a variety of contexts. Treggiari (1991, 184) holds that most Romans inherited Greek moral conventions "through the theatre and through street culture, if not through written literature." However, another angle from which one may approach Roman absorption of Greek ideas about marriage is to consider how Greek literature was embedded in the Roman educational system from an early stage and what messages and images this in turn may have implanted in the developing minds of Roman schoolchildren. These children, the boys from the ruling elite, would later grow up into writers and thinkers in their own right and might draw upon childhood-learned texts and images to illustrate and enhance their writing.[1]

In this brief chapter, I aim to suggest how a consideration of the education of the Roman male elite enhances our appreciation of their reception of Greek moral attitudes. When we realize how commonplace remarks about and examples of good and bad marriages were in the texts read and discussed in schools, we begin to appreciate more sensitively why certain examples, opinions, and authors are cited so frequently. We are lucky that we have access to a fair amount of ancient source material on ancient rhetorical education.[2] Although the theoretical texts surviving to us today may range across several centuries and derive from Greek and Latin writers, it is remarkable how consistent and relatively constant certain educational practices remained throughout antiquity, especially in the hands of Greek teachers.[3] The Romans essentially followed a Greek system of education inspired and driven by Greek educationalists.[4]

I do not intend to repeat here Russell's general examination of rhetorical thought on marriage, nor shall I rehearse at length Treggiari's survey of Greco-Roman theories both for and against marriage, although some summary is required to show how philosophical and other literary texts offered complementary views of marriage. Instead, I shall limit my focus to a few ancient authors who, I feel, can contribute to an understanding of the development of the anti-marriage tradition in particular in Roman literature. Hence negative images and stereotypes will abound. I base my discussion upon Quintilian's suggested reading program for prospective orators (1.8, 10.1). He includes Homer, Euripides, and Menander. If we look first at the presentation of marriage in these three authors, we soon see epic and dramatic parallels for the later explicit theorizing of marriage by authors such as Xenophon, Aristotle, Theophrastus, and Seneca. Finally I turn to the quotations on marriage collated by John of Stobi (henceforth referred to—for shorthand—by his Latin name, *Stobaeus*). An analysis of his selections offers insight into the types of texts that may have been circulating in handbooks of "potted philosophy" often used in schools and that provided elite readers beyond their schooldays with a wealth of material for deployment in cultivated conversation or more serious literary activity.

The teachers Quintilian (first century A.D.), Theon (probably Quintilian's younger contemporary), and Aphthonius (fourth century A.D.) all report the important rhetorical preparatory exercise of the *thesis*. This was one of the progressive exercises in rhetoric (Greek *progumnasmata*) taught as preparation for the more complicated *suasoriae* and *controversiae* that in turn prepared pupils for a career in law or politics. The category of *suasoriae* comprised two types of exercise: those that were widely speculative on broad philosophical issues and those that were more immediately applicable to everyday life—on topics such as marriage or political ambition.[5] Suetonius indeed notes that *theseis* were often of practical use (*De rhet.* 1). These preparatory *progumnasmata* exercises probably developed during the Hellenistic age—as rhetoric rapidly became more self-conscious and sophisticated[6]—and went on to flourish under the empire. Theon's handbook is unusual in that he illustrates his theory at some length, adding confirmation and refutation exercises at each progressive stage. His examples give us a real flavor of what such exercises may have been like in practice. In the *thesis* exercise, pupils who are by now fairly advanced in their educational program of rhetoric with the *grammaticus* would be given a topic for debate, for and against. Among those exercises listed by the rhetorical theorists as common is the *thesis ei gameteon* (question whether one should marry), or as Quintilian puts it, the *ducendane uxor* (should one take a wife? 2.4.25). Quintilian also notes that this thesis can easily be turned into a *suasoria* "if only characters are added" [*personis modo adiectis*] (2.4.25). Aphthonius's teacher Libanius indeed includes first among his examples of worked-out *theseis* a detailed and lengthy *thesis ei gameteon*.[7] Pupils would be praised for the way they selected and presented examples to support their case. But from where might they draw such examples if not from their background preparatory school reading? This reading would not necessarily present a positive image of marriage, as we shall see.[8]

The theorists and others tell us how young pupils started their education by tackling Homeric epic.[9] While, of course, the most famous positive examples of marriage are found in the *Iliad* and the *Odyssey*, and while Hector and Andromache and Odysseus and Penelope are commonly cited in many ancient theoretical texts as explicit ideal examples (Greek *paradeigmata*, Latin *exempla*),[10] we ought not to forget the negative images of marriage that Homeric epic offers. We can think of the contrast of good versus bad marriage on the mortal plane by means of the figures of the two daughters of Tyndareus who epitomize bad wives, Helen and Clytemnestra, who counter the ideally positive Penelope and Andromache. However, perhaps the best—or technically worst—examples of marriage are those shown between gods on the immortal plane: Zeus and Hera or Hephaestus and Aphrodite. These immortal relationships illustrate many anti-marriage characteristics that later become conventional in the literature of the Greeks and, in turn, the Romans: weak husbands manipulated by domineering wives, male suspicions of female infidelity, female abuse of sexual charms, nagging wives, cuckolded husbands who are the butt of jokes. Indeed, in many ways, the negative images of marriage in epic are perhaps more memorable than the positive. Even the fervent wish of Odysseus for the young Nausicaa to find a like-minded husband with whom to share a happy marriage is couched as a hope for the future (*Od.* 6.182–84). This wish is frequently recalled by ancient theorists, such as Clement of Alexandria (*Stromata* 2.23.143), who closely echoes the Latin translation of pseudo-Aristotle's *Oeconomica* 3.4.[11] However, the wish is recorded more often with a tone of pessimistic hope than with one of positive certainty.

The negative images and examples with which epic armed school pupils were merely the beginning. Greco-Roman education also devoted much time to the learning and discussion of classical Greek drama.[12] Quintilian firmly believes in the importance of studying and imitating the effects used by Euripides and Menander (10.1.69–72).[13] Euripides, of course, was a model for Ennius, Ovid, and Seneca for their respective Medeas. These authors and the genres they represent contain excellent rhetorical speeches and examples of characterization. However, the plays also offer a wide range of anti-marriage commonplaces. One of the most common is that of the domineering wife, given superior power through status and/or wealth. Euripides' *Phaethon* (158–59), for example, speaks of a husband as "slave of the marriage bed, body sold for dowry." Menander's *Plokion* features the infamous domineering, dowered Crobyle. Spartan wives had a reputation in Athens for controlling their husbands, who allegedly called their wives *despoinai* (mistresses).[14] Euripides draws on this stereotype when presenting, for example, the overweening Hermione in his *Andromache*. Such domination by wives was neatly termed in Greek *gunaikokratia* (woman/wife power)[15] and offered a neat model for structuring even historical narratives such as that of Antony and Cleopatra.[16] The dowered wife, which is a motif exploited by many writers of Greek New Comedy,[17] becomes in Latin comedy the stereotypical character of the *dotata uxor* (wife with a dowry).[18]

Greek drama also illustrates the commonplace of conjugal conflict. Philosophical texts discouraged such marital arguments. Socrates' shrewish wife Xanthippe is explicitly described as "the most difficult woman there ever has been or ever will be" (Xen. *Symp.* 2.10), and numerous stories circulated that confirmed her image as the tormentor of her much enduring sage-husband. Cleoboulus advised husbands "not to fight with your wife . . . when others are present" (10.3 Diels-Kranz). Martial terminology (*machesthai, nike, kratos,* etc.) is given an extra, highly memorable twist by Clytemnestra as she uses it to persuade her general-husband, Agamemnon, to submit to her wishes (Aesch. *Ag.* 940–43). In the play bearing her name, Euripides' Andromache refers to quarrels with a husband as a *hamilla* [contest] (214). In Menander's comedy *Epitrepontes*, Habrotonon asks Chairestratus "not to fight" (952). In Menander's *Dyskolos*, the verb *zugomachein* (to fight under the same yoke) is used to describe Cnemon's behavior with his wife (17).[19]

Attic tragedy and comedy (both old and new) worked together as genres to present consistent and consonant positive and negative images of marriage for Athenian and later audiences. The perspective was still predominantly male, although glimpses of a more sympathetic feminine outlook did occur, most notably in Euripides' *Alcestis*, Artistophanes' *Lysistrata*, or Menander's *Samia*. When pupils were learning how Euripides and Menander used rhetorical persuasive devices and developed characterization, they may well also have absorbed the content and plot context of the dramatic speeches as resources for later use.

Attic drama would thus be able to supply plenty of material for any school pupil or school-trained writer arguing against marriage and could be suitably adapted to complement more explicit philosophical theory. A good example of this technique can be found in Jerome's infamous tirade against women in *Against Jovinian* (1.47.317a–b); here we see a list of Euripidean women (Pasiphae, Clytemnestra, and Eriphyle) cited as examples of the dangers of seductive, adulterous wives.[20]

Philosophical theorizing about the respective roles of husband and wife developed in Athens during the period of the city's own self-examination as a polis, with Plato (especially *Republic* and *Laws*), Xenophon (*Oeconomicus*), and Aristotle (especially *Politics*) being the most famous extant examples. They all in turn show the influence of or at least echo images of marriage found in drama. Through the combined reading of Greek drama in school and later of these more developed philosophical works, Greek conventions and stereotypes leaked into Roman consciousness and thus Roman writings on marriage. For example, Cicero translated in his youth Xenophon's *Oeconomicus*, which was also explicitly critiqued by Philodemus in part of his surviving *On Vices and Corresponding Virtues*, where he discusses the virtues of a wife.

The major Greek philosophical tracts that discussed the benefits or pitfalls of marriage and that have clearly influenced later Roman writers were works by Xenophon, Aristotle, and Theophrastus. It is worthwhile looking at them briefly here to complete the overall picture of the influences at work in the developing Roman literary psyche.

Although not what we might consider philosophy today, Hesiod's didactic poems offered influential comments on the nature of women and marriage that are reproduced and quoted often by later authors. His discussions of Pandora in both his *Theogony* (570–612) and his *Works and Days* (60–105) present a negative—or perhaps, more accurately, pessimistic—view of marriage. More extreme—and thus more memorable—was the even less "philosophical" satire *On Women* by Semonides (frag. 7). Hesiod and Semonides have been seen by several scholars as the originators of the "misogynist" tradition of Greek literature,[21] although it is also important to remember that there are also significant examples of archaic Greek writers who offer positive images of women (e.g., Homer, Alcman, Sappho).

The first full-scale account of women's roles within marriage and of the value of marriage per se is Xenophon's treatise on household management, the *Oeconomicus* (ca. 361 B.C.).[22] For our purposes here, as we trace the anti-marriage tradition, Xenophon is not very helpful, for his depiction of marriage is generally positive, with husband and wife having complementary duties that are clearly identified. Both parties are needed to produce a happy and prosperous household, although the wife is expected to follow her husband's lead (71e). This virtue of submission *(huperesia)* is echoed often by Greek drama and is developed more theoretically by Aristotle.[23]

Aristotle's *Politics* offers a discussion of marriage as part of a broader discussion of civic organization.[24] The management of a household is frequently compared to that of a state. The husband's virtue is to order and the wife's to obey *(Pol.* 1.13.1260a21–24); she is to be silent before her husband and do everything through him *(Pol.* 1.13.1260a28–31). These sentiments neatly echo the words spoken by an ideally positive woman from Greek tragedy, Aithra in Euripides' *Suppliant Women* (40–41). Euripides presents the husband in some plays as the "lord" *(kurios, Androm.* 54; *themisteuon, Ino* 383). This necessity for men to lead is, in Aristotle's view, a natural consequence of woman's inferior deliberative faculty, yet marriage is both crucial to the city for reproduction *(Pol.* 1.13.1252a) and natural (1253a).

Aristotle is similarly in favor of marriage in his *Nicomachean Ethics,* where marriage is discussed as a type of friendship *(philia).* Nevertheless, Aristotle still sees the husband as the leader or ruler and the wife as subject, even though their friendship is considered natural for both utility and pleasure (1160b32–1162a33). Aristotle therefore, although presenting a poor picture of woman, is strongly pro-marriage. The same is not true, however, of one of Aristotle's most influential pupils, Theophrastus.

Jerome, in his *Against Jovinian* (1.47.313c), refers enigmatically to a "golden book on marriage" by Theophrastus.[25] Here Theophrastus apparently urged that the philosopher ought not to marry. This may be a surprising departure from the general Peripatetic inclination to support marriage. The difference, however, is that here Theophrastus was apparently talking about marriage in a particular special case, that of the philosopher. For the philosopher, marriage offers numerous dangerous distractions that recur later as motifs in satirical treatments of marriage (e.g., Juvenal *Sat.* 6):[26] women require expensive clothes, attendants, and furniture; they chatter all night; they are jealous and suspicious. In short, says Theophrastus, it is hard to support a poor wife and torture to endure a rich one. The traditional argument that a man needed a wife as a companion, which is common in other works on marriage (especially in Plutarch's *Coniugalia praecepta*), did not apply to a philosopher; nor did the need for children, for the philosopher was better to choose friends as his support for old age.

Further detailed discussion of marriage came in a series of miscellaneous treatises and letters from the Hellenistic revival of the Pythagorean school.[27] As these support marriage, they need not be considered here, except to say that they develop further the characteristics of ideal wifely behavior that were found in epic's Andromache or Penelope (who often indeed figure as named examples) and in drama's ideal wives (e.g., Alcestis, Andromache).

The positive drive toward marriage continues generally in Roman literature. Seneca's lost work *On Marriage* urged that a philosopher ought to marry because it is natural.[28] He adhered to the general Stoic view that women were relatively moral equals of men, with virtues similar to those of men. Both husband and wife were to be loyal, with Seneca stressing women's chastity, or *pudicitia*—the same *pudicitia* that departs the earth at the start of Juvenal's sixth satire. This Stoic view is best illustrated in the extensive discussion of women, marriage, and education by Seneca's older contemporary the Stoic Musonius Rufus, whose works take the form of the diatribe treatise on a specific proposition, like a rhetorical *thesis*.[29] For Musonius, marriage was certainly no obstacle to philosophy; indeed, a philosopher ought to marry for love of his country (14). Moreover, a wife could herself be a philosopher, although Musonius's description of her application of philosophy reverts to typically domestic duties (3).

If we are looking for anti-marriage texts in early Latin literature, we must turn to satire. Lucilius wrote two satires on wives (*De mulierum ingenio et moribus* and *De nuptiarum et matrimonii molestiis*), which openly exposed the disadvantages of marriage and the vices of wives. He appears to have drawn on Greek anti-marriage sources for inspiration (especially satirists such as Hipponax or Aristophanes),[30] for his wives also abandon their housework and disappear on alleged visits to shopkeepers and relatives.

Juvenal's *Satire* 6 is, however, perhaps the most extensive and virulent example of anti-marriage tradition literature in early imperial Rome. This text will be discussed in a later chapter in this book, so I shall restrain my comments here to Juvenal's relationship to earlier Greek comic motifs and to rhetorical commonplaces. Juvenal's tirade against women has received much scholarly attention because he includes so many vivid vignettes of contemporary elite women's behavior, whether exaggerated or not. The satire combines elements familiar from Greek satire and comedy with specifically Roman features, such as stress on female status, the rites of Isis, and mockery of intellectuals and of athletes, including female gladiators. Traditional motifs include women's lust, greed, untrustworthiness, deception, domination, and jealousy. These traditional motifs are also picked up and exploited by Martial, although obviously in a less systematic way, through isolated and specific satirical epigrams. While he offers many examples of comic attacks on vices and women in particular, it is hard to formulate a consistent picture of Martial's attitudes toward marriage as an institution.

Both Juvenal and Martial draw heavily upon rhetorical commonplaces (topoi). Barwick (1959) has shown how Martial's epigrams naturally recall the contemporary fascination with rhetorical *sententiae* in both their form and content. His attitudes toward women are often very negative and based upon traditional misogynistic commonplaces.[31] However, the sheer number of remarks against women and about scandalous adulterers do not offer any sustained or deliberately thought-out anti-marriage strategy; they are most often expressed first and foremost to shock and amuse.

A more carefully structured anti-marriage tirade is Juvenal's sixth satire, which comprises Juvenal's entire second book of satires and is more than twice the length of his attacks on male sexuality found in *Satires* 2 and 9. Scholars such as Courtney (1980), Winkler (1983), and Braund (1992) have analyzed this poem in detail. I shall here simply summarize their findings. The poem adopts initially the form of a speech arguing against marriage (*logos apotreptikos gamou*) but rapidly develops into a broader denunciation of women (*psogos gunaikon*), albeit confined chiefly to women of rank.[32] The structure is deliberately loose, suiting the persona of an outraged man and echoing the hodge-podge that satire is by nature (*farrago, Sat.* 1.85–86).[33] The poem comprises a series of variations on the theme that women are bad and that marriage is therefore to be avoided. Unity is lent by the overarching moral theme rather than by any careful stylistic devices.[34]

The structure therefore recalls a rhetorical exercise against the proposition that marriage is a good thing (cf. the discussion of Stobaeus later in this chapter). Catalogues and lists of women were common in Greek literature from Hesiod's *Catalogue of Women* on—through tragedy and comedy to imperial prose. Juvenal adopts this structure to expand on certain negative traits of women and to prepare for successive waves of climax within his text. The commonplace that a good woman is hard to find (*Sat.* 6.47–51) leads into examples of lustful women, in the same way that the Greek Semonides' satire *On Women* (frag. 7) catalogues nine types of flawed women to isolate the one rare good woman who is hard to find. The individual examples chosen by Juvenal are suitably Roman (Eppia, Messalina), but the vices are familiar from Semonides' satire and Greek comedy.

The traditional Greek dramatic character of the henpecked husband is also translated into a Roman context by Juvenal. Firstly, Caesennia's stupid husband loves her only for her money, which makes her the boss in their household (*Sat.* 6.140–41). Secondly, Sertorius is presented as fickle in loving Bibula only for her beauty, which Bibula uses to rule her husband (6.143, 149). These examples then lead Juvenal to characterize the ideal woman, but in the form of a neat rhetorical paradox. Her virtues are listed in a series of striking adjectives (6.162ff.), which, as Courtney notes (1980, ad loc.), parody similar lists of positive adjectives in women's epitaphs. She is also dehumanized by her description in animal terms, again very much like the use of animal and nature images to characterize Semonides' ten types of women. The paradox is that this ideal woman is hard to find but, if she were found, would drive her husband to distraction by her sheer virtue and the pride this would inevitably inspire in her. Here Juvenal, by his reference to the mythological Niobe, signposts that he is debunking the traditional idealization of mythological women such as Andromache or Alcestis: they may have been virtuous, but they must have been hell to live with! His conclusion is therefore that it is better to remain unmarried (*Sat.* 6.210–11).

There then follow other commonplaces that derive from the Greek satirical tradition: the corrupting mother-in-law, marital strife, gossip, excessive use of makeup. Such commonplaces remained firmly in the Greek tradition well into the empire: for example, the *Loves* attributed to Lucian includes many of the same motifs,[35] as do the passages collated by Stobaeus (discussed shortly).

Juvenal finally closes with startling Roman examples of feminine excessive immorality: they induce abortions out of vanity (*Sat.* 6.595ff.)—thus going against their biological nature—and even go so far as to send their husbands mad or kill them (6.610ff.). The crescendo is the result of a carefully crafted piece of rhetorical diatribe that mixes traditional Greek motifs with contemporary Roman concerns. I therefore think it quite short-sighted of Courtney to comment (1980, 252) that it is "unprofitable" to consider the poem from the point of view of the rhetorical tradition. My own focus here has been on Greek literary echoes, but De Decker (1913, 23–29) has also shown how many passages in Juvenal's anti-women tirade recall the world and rhetorical culture of Roman declamation.

We have seen thus far how the study of certain genres of Greek literature in school and the reading of more sophisticated philosophical treatises on marriage may have fed images and commonplaces into the Roman anti-marriage tradition. A clear indication of how pervasive these commonplaces were can be found in a later text that valuably illustrates my argument that the Roman anti-marriage tradition owed much to the rhetorical deployment of preexistent and preselected passages of Greek literature. Here we may now turn to consider the collections of Stobaeus.

The anthologist John of Stobi (Stobaeus), who lived in the fifth century A.D., offers an extremely valuable collection of quotations on a wide range of subjects in his *Anthologies* and *Florilegium*. Many quotations are extensive and are the sole source for an ancient fragment or author. His categories comprise moral and political topics, under such titles as *On the State*, *On Laws and Customs*, *On Rule and the Qualities of a Ruler*, and *On Youth* (*Anth.* 1, 2, 5, and 11, respectively). Several categories are discussed in balanced sections that provide evidence for and against a proposition in the manner of a *progumnasma* exercise, such as *Praise of Bravery* and *Denunciation of Military Bravery and Strength* (*Anth.* 10 and 12) and a pair of passages that first praise and then denounce "Aphrodite" (i.e., sexual love) as base and dangerous (*Anth.* 20.1 and 20.2). It is not surprising that soon after discussion of "Aphrodite," we find sections on beauty (*Anth.* 21.1 and 21.2) and then a series of sections on marriage (*Anth.* 22–23).

Stobaeus's section 22, on marriage, is subdivided into seven smaller categories. These include discussions on marriage as a very good thing (2:494–512 Wachsmith and Hense), on marriage as not a good thing (2:513–23), on union as beneficial for some and not for others (2:524–31), on courtship (2:532–41), on the need to marry someone of the right age (2:542–44), and on considering not birth or wealth but disposition in marriage (2:545–49); finally, Stobaeus offers a general denunciation of women (2:550–68). This section is followed in turn by one titled *Marriage Advice* (2:569–99), which is followed by further sections on whether or not to have children, whether to respect parents, and so forth. It is telling to note that while there is a (lengthy) section specifically devoted to the denunciation of women (*psogos gunaikon*), there is no balancing praise of women (*epainos*).

The positioning of the sections on marriage so early in the *Anthologies* and so soon after those on civic issues again shows how often the social relationship of marriage was considered central to any debate on civilization and culture. The headings of Stobaeus's sections conveniently illustrate the perpetuation of handbook compilations upon which he must have drawn to compile his great work. For our purposes, the sections on marriage neatly show what subjects attracted such compilers and which authors were popular enough to be excerpted and anthologized.

In most sections, Stobaeus positions his excerpts from poetry before those from prose: for example, in *Anthologies* 22.2 we are given sixty-five verse quotations before he closes with one prose excerpt from Antiphon the Sophist.[36] Within the verse quotations, there appears to be little attempt to order the texts, whether by author, alphabetically, or by date. *Anthologies* 22.1, for example, starts with four quotations from Euripides and Apollonides before adding one from Theognis and then returning to drama with Sophocles. Often the name of the author is all that is given in the genitive at the start, while sometimes the work is also added. Excerpts from the same (usually prose) work may be split up with the simple tag "from the same work" between them. There is no attempt to offer a compilator's comment; no introduction is given to the sections other than the title; the texts are given barely and without discussion for the reader's use.

A survey of the authors cited confirms how popular Euripides and Menander still were by Stobaeus's time.[37] Euripides is by far the most popular author quoted (forty-two times). It is interesting to note that we are given the play title more often with Euripides than with other dramatists: perhaps this might hint at a special Euripides compilation upon which Stobaeus (or even an earlier anthologist) drew. The plays drawn upon in each section appear to reflect what we know of their content elsewhere as regards marriage. For example, in *Anthologies* 22.2 (where it is argued that marriage is not a good thing), we have Euripides' *Ino*, *Alcestis* (twice), and (not surprisingly) *Stheneboea*; in 22.3 (where it is argued that marriage is a mixture of good and bad), *Alcmaeon*, *Protesilaus*, *Melanippe* (twice), *Alcestis*, *Orestes*, *Hecuba*, *Oedipus*, and *Alexander*; in 22.4 (on courtship), *Melanippe* (twice), *Phoenician Women*, *Antiope* (twice), and *Meleager*; in 22.5 (on age and marriage), *Phoenix* (twice), *Aeolus*, and *Danae*; in 22.6 (on disposition and marriage), *Andromache* (three times), *Cretan Women*, *Electra*, *Bellerophon* (or *Stheneboea*), *Antiope*, *Meleager*, and *Melanippe*. By contrast, most other authors seldom exceed one quotation per subsection.[38]

Menander gets the next highest number of quotations (fifteen), yet the plays are not specified. This clearly points to a different compilation as source. The comic poets in general provide many quotations, while few are from lyric (there is one from Sappho in *Anth.* 22.5). Moralistic hexameters/elegiacs are quoted, especially from Hesiod and Theognis. Although neither of these poets is quoted in *Anthologies* 22.2 or 22.6, they are otherwise quoted at least once per subsection. It is perhaps not surprising that *Anthologies* 22.2, where it is argued that marriage is not a good thing, draws more heavily on comedy. This subsection has the smallest number of quotations from Euripides (four) and the highest from Menander (six).

The passages collated by Stobaeus can be found quoted in many other texts that discuss women and marriage, especially in the works of Plutarch, who also seems to have used books of commonplaces extensively to add literary sparkle and authority to his moral and historical works. It is here that we find Semonides' satire *On Women* (*Anth.* 22.7 [2:561–66]), extensive quotations from the Stoics Hierocles and Antipater of Tarsus (e.g., *Anth.* 22.1 [2:502–12]), and Musonius Rufus (e.g., *Anth.* 22.1, 22.3 [2:497–501, 530–31]). Stobaeus's collation of pro- and anti-marriage texts offers us a helpful behind-the-scenes snapshot of literary figures, a clue to the cheats they used to display classical Greek reading. Such books of commonplaces must lie behind the works of other great figures whose classical learning appears at first sight impressive, figures such as Clement of Alexandria or Eusebius.[39]

Stobaeus's collations show that in the world of the fifth century A.D., anyone who wanted to enter the literary arena to discuss marriage would have a wealth of earlier Greek literary texts to use as inspiration or as direct sources. Hellenized Romans could thus draw upon their own memories of childhood schoolroom exercises, *sententiae*, and textual exposition and confirm this by referring to the increasing range of resources of "potted philosophy" or "canned culture" offered by the service industry for rhetoricians that produced books of commonplaces. Imaginative writers like Juvenal could take such material, adapt it, and add a Roman coloring, thus creating their own Roman anti-marriage tradition that grew in parallel and subsequently took over from the Greek as the dominant anti-marriage tradition in Western literature.

Notes

1. On drawing upon childhood memories for *sententiae*, see Seneca *Ep.* 33.7; Phaedrus 3, epilogue 33.

2. On Roman declamation, see Bonner 1949; on Greek declamation, Russell 1983. Translations of Theon and Aphthonius may be found in Matsen, Rollinson, and Sousa 1990, 253–88.

3. See, further, Bonner 1977, 251.

4. See Bonner 1977, 165.

5. See Theon 121.6ff.; Hermog. 17.26ff.; Aphth. 49.15.

6. See Bonner 1977, 250.

7. It comprises eleven pages of Foerster's Teubner text (1903–27, 8:550–61).

8. On women in Greek declamation, see Hawley 1995.

9. See, e.g., Quint. 1.8.5; Horace *Ep.* 2.2.41–44; Petr. *Sat.* 5; Pliny *Ep.* 2.14.2.

10. E.g., Penelope is cited in Seneca *Ep.* 88.7–8.

11. Note that the desired quality of *homophrosune* is translated into Latin as *unanimitas*.

12. On tragedy and epic read and expounded, see, e.g., Martial 8.3.13–16.

13. Cf. Quintilian's admiration for Menander elsewhere (1.8.7–8).

14. Plut. *Lyc.* 14. Cf. Aristotle *Pol.* 2.1269b31; Plut. *Agis.* There were stories that Spartan men were humiliated for not marrying (Plut. *Lyc.* 51; Pollux *Onomast.* 3.48), humiliations given by women (Athenaeus *Deipn.* 13.555c). In Thessaly, *despoina* = *gune* (Hesychius *Lex.* G707).

15. Cf. Plut. *Marc. Cato* 8; Aristotle *Pol.* 5.9.6.1313b34–39. On *imperium* usually used of household control in Roman drama, see, e.g., Plaut. *Asin. argumentum* 2, 87, 506, 509. For *servitus* to a dowered wife, see Plaut. *Aul.* 169. *Kratos* could be both acceptable or unacceptable power within a household. On *kratos* as acceptable, see *Od.* 1.359; Eur. frags. 463, 503.3 (Nauck and Snell 1964); Plut. *Con. praec.* 6, 139a. On *kratos* as ambiguous, see Aesch. *Ag.* 10, 258, 1673; *Choe.* 71. On *kratos* as unacceptable, see Aesch. *Septem* 189; Eur. *Hec.* 863.

16. On Antony, see J. Griffin 1977; Pelling 1988 (introduction).

17. It recurs in, e.g., Menander, Diphilus, Philemon, and Demophilus: see Fraenkel 1960, 416.

18. Cf. Fantham 1975, 73.

19. Cf. Menander's *Kubernetai* frag. 251.6 (Korte and Thierfelder 1953), where a *gune* is said "to be in control of everything, to give orders, to be always fighting." Later, Plutarch (*Con. praec.* 38, 143d) observes the pain of domestic discord and urges its resolution, often with "Aphrodite" (i.e., sex). (On Plutarch's *Coniugalia praecepta*, see Pomeroy 1999; Hawley 1999.)

20. Hermione's remark in *Adv. Iov.* 317a is also found in Plut. *Con. praec.* 40.

21. The first major proponent was Arthur (1984).

22. See Pomeroy 1994; Allen 1985, 53–57.

23. Cf. Treggiari 1991, 202–3.

24. For a useful introductory survey on Aristotle's view of women, see Allen 1985, 83–126.

25. See Bickel 1915 (for a discussion of the possible content of this work and its relationship to Seneca *On Marriage*); Wiesen 1964, 153–58.

26. Cf. Courtney 1980, 261.

27. For texts, see Thesleff 1965 and Centrone 1990; for translations, Guthrie 1987. Cf. Stadele 1980. On Pythagorean women, see Hawley 1994.

28. See Bickel 1915; Treggiari 1991, 215–20.

29. On Musonius, see Van Geytenbeek 1962; Allen 1985, 173–80; Lutz 1947; Manning 1973.

30. See, e.g., Treggiari 1991, 206.

31. On Martial's attitudes toward sex, see Sullivan 1979.

32. See Courtney 1980, 252; M. Winkler 1983, 147.

33. See M. Winkler 1983, 149.

34. See M. Winkler 1983, 151.

35. These motifs include cosmetics (*Loves* 38–39), hair (40), clothes and jewelry (41), and superstition (42).

36. Yet in *Anthologies* 22.4, the sayings of Chilon, Cleobulus, Pericles, and Democritus follow excerpts from Callicratidas, Nicostratus, Antipater of Tarsus, and Musonius Rufus. Perhaps this was due to Stobaeus taking up another preexistent compilation after having added the prose passages.

37. We may here appropriately note the greater number of Euripidean and Menandrian fragments preserved on papyrus.

38. The four from Hierocles in *Anthologies* 22.1 are all from the same work.

39. One thinks especially of the *Stromateis* of Clement and Eusebius's *Praeparatio evangelica*, both of which themselves read at times like patchworks drawn from books of commonplace.

Three

Marriage, Adultery, and Divorce in Roman Comic Drama

Susanna Morton Braund

Two's company, but three's a couple.
—Adam Phillips, *Monogamy*

*I*n this chapter, I shall examine three plays of surviving Roman comedy that deviate from the usual paradigm of making marriage or sexual union the goal: Plautus's *Amphitryo* and *Menaechmi* and Terence's *Hecyra*. In each case, the dramatist focuses on a marriage already in existence and puts that marriage under pressure by bringing close the specter of divorce, which in effect shifts the goal from achieving marriage to retrieving it. In examining the mechanisms and implications of this shift from the usual paradigm, it becomes clear that all three plays break the rules of *fabula palliata* (New Comedy in its Latin manifestation with Greek names and settings), which suggests to me that the genre had difficulties accommodating the theme of divorce. All three plays, I conclude, are experiments that press at and perhaps even rupture the boundaries of the genre.

A CENTRAL ISSUE

Roman comic drama takes marriage as a central theme.[1] The evidence of the *fabula palliata* is abundant. The same is also suggested by the surviving titles and fragments of the *fabula togata* (comedy in Roman dress set in Roman country towns). Titles such as Afranius's *Divortium* (The divorce), *Mariti* (The husbands), and *Repudiatus* (The rejected husband) and Atta's *Socrus* (The mother-in-law) suggest plots involving marriage; the surviving fragments substantiate this.[2] In the genre of the mime, which seems to have grown in popularity during the late Republic, one of the most (in)famous exemplars is "the adultery mime."[3] In this chapter, I shall occasionally introduce details from these two popular genres, but since the evidence of the *fabula palliata* is so much more substantial, I shall largely confine my attention to the treatment of marriage and divorce there.

Marriage: A Comic Paradox

I want to confront the essential paradox of Roman comedy: that while marriage is the objective of the essential comic plot, already-established marriage is portrayed as a negative experience about which husbands and wives complain and from which husbands fantasize their escape. These antithetical perspectives are usually divided between the two different generations involved, so that the young couples want to marry and the older couples are at loggerheads. That goes some way to reconciling the paradox. But there is more to it than that.

Northrop Frye, in his *Anatomy of Criticism*, presents a scheme of interpretation of comedy yet to be superseded (illustrated in fig. 1): boy wants girl; boy cannot get girl because of obstacle; obstacle is removed; boy gets girl.[4] This pattern is basic to virtually all the extant plays of New Comedy, whether the union takes the form of legitimate marriage between citizens or of the joining of a young lover with his adored *meretrix* (lady friend).[5] This applies even when the part played by the two lovers in the play is minimal (the young woman does not appear at all if she is of respectable status, in accordance with the social constraints applied to respectable young Greek women; in addition, the young man may play only a minor part, as in Plautus's *Mostellaria* and *Pseudolus*) and even when the lovers never actually appear on stage (as in Plautus's *Casina*). Frye points out that our sense of "the comic norm" is so strong that when Shakespeare tries, in *All's Well That Ends Well*, to reverse the standard pattern of the young having to overcome resistance of their elders in order to marry (by having the older generation force two younger people to marry), this creates a sense of unease.

Initial situation:
Desire of adulescens to be united with beloved

▽

Obstacles:
E.g., blocking characteristics include father, pimp, rival

▽

Resolution:
Blocking character outwitted or changes opinion

▽

Result:
Marriage or sexual union

Fig. 1: Marriage/sexual union as objective of *fabula palliata*

This view of comedy as aiming at marriage (or another form of sexual union) is part of Frye's larger picture of the integrative tendency of comedy, whereby most—if not all—characters, including "blocking characters" and even misanthropes, can be integrated into the new society established at the end of the play.[6] Classic examples of the integrative thrust of New Comedy include Menander's *Dyskolos* and Plautus's *Aulularia* (and, on the same pattern, Shakespeare's *The Tempest* and *The Merchant of Venice*), which hinge upon changes of heart by grumpy misanthropes and misers,[7] as illuminated by David Konstan in his discussion of *Aulularia*.[8] The end of Terence's *Adelphoe* sees the integration of Demea and the marrying off of his brother Micio, a dedicated bachelor. The resolution of a comedy presents the ideal of an integrated society.

Frye's formalistic interpretation, necessarily schematic, is reinforced by the study of New Comedy in its social context, as exemplified by the work of David Konstan on Greek and Roman comedy and Maurizio Bettini on Plautus. Konstan's view of marriage as a social transaction between two families in which the women along with their dowries are commodities illuminates the way in which New Comedy explores some of the difficulties inherent in interacting with another family.[9] Virtually all the extant plays focus upon the period before marriage, but just occasionally the period following marriage is scrutinized, especially when insurmountable difficulties arise.[10] Bettini's anthropological view of the plot structures of Plautine comedy complements Konstan's approach, once it is expanded by seeing prostitution as an analogic financial transaction between two parties. According to Bettini's narratological model, the transferral of a commodity—usually a woman but sometimes a sum of money, transferred from one party to another and between the spheres of the permitted and the forbidden—is the central plot event in the Plautine corpus.[11]

Though marriage or another form of sexual union is the fundamental aspiration of the plots of New Comedy, three plays of extant Roman comedy—each of which focuses upon a marriage that is already in existence—make separation and divorce central.[12] One of these, Terence's *Hecyra*, is widely acknowledged as an experiment (whether successful or not). But Terence's experiment was anticipated by Plautus in two of his most experimental plays, *Amphitryo* and *Menaechmi*, and I find it significant that these are the two plays that offer most resistance to Bettini's narratological schema. I suggest that in these plays, the dramatists are trying to extend the genre by treating material normally eschewed as too uncomfortable. Accordingly, in part 1 of this chapter, I will establish some of the parameters of the normative treatment of marriage and divorce in Roman comedy, which will entail glancing at the abuse of wives, praise of the bachelor life, dowries, and the double standard involved in adultery and divorce. Then, in part 2, I will indicate the ways in which these three plays extend or break the rules of New Comedy. A brief postscript will consider the way in which the same themes are tackled in a more obviously normative play, *Miles gloriosus*.[13] Anyone already familiar with the Roman social context of marriage, adultery, and divorce might wish to proceed directly to part 2.

PART 1

The Double Standard

Many of the plays of Roman comedy present marriage as the goal yet give marriage "bad press."[14] The plays reflect a tension in society. There were of course reasons to marry, most obviously for the procreation of legitimate children,[15] but also as a means of controlling women and property and thereby offering a certain stability to social and family structures—thus Afranius, in one of his comedies, can describe marriage as *firmamentum familiae* [the mainstay of the family] (*Com.* 241).[16] Nevertheless, exhortations to marriage suggest a reluctance to marry, as epitomized in the speech delivered by the censor Q. Caecilius Metellus Macedonicus in 131 B.C. encouraging marriage and procreation (Gell. *N.A.* 1.6.1).

> si sine uxore esse possemus, Quirites, omnes ea molestia careremus, set quoniam ita natura tradidit ut nec cum illis satis commode nec sine

illis ullo modo vivi possit, saluti perpetuae potius quam brevi voluptati consulendum est.

[*If we could exist without a wife, citizens, we would all be free of that nuisance, but since nature has so ordained that it is possible neither to live with them comfortably enough nor to live without them at all, we should give priority to our lasting well-being rather than to transient pleasure.*][17]

Matching the censor's dilemma—that men find it difficult to live with wives but impossible to live without them—is the double standard applied by Roman men to responsibility for unhappiness in marital relationships, which blames women for things going wrong. Hence, there is a differentiation between men and women in the law on adultery and in the justifications for divorce: in both cases, women's conduct is much more tightly regulated. This emerges clearly from another text from the second century B.C., the speech *De dote* (On the dowry) by the hard-line moralist Cato, recorded by Gellius (*N.A.* 10.23.4–5).

vir cum divortium fecit, mulieri iudex pro censore est, imperium quod videtur habet, si quid perverse taetreque factum est a muliere; multatur si vinum bibit; si cum alieno viro probri quid fecit, condemnatur. . . . in adulterio uxorem tuam si prehendisses, sine iudicio inpune necares; illa te si adulterares sive tu adulterarere digito non auderet contingere neque ius est.

[*When a man initiates divorce, the arbitrator is like a censor to the woman. He has the authority to impose what seems good to him, if the woman has acted in any wrong or disgusting fashion. She is fined if she drinks wine; if she has had a dishonourable relationship with another man, she is condemned. . . . If you were to take your wife in the act of adultery, you could freely kill her without a trial; whereas if you were to commit adultery or to be defiled, she would not dare to lift a finger against you, nor is it right.*][18]

Jo-Ann Shelton provides a lucid summary of the situation with regard to adultery and divorce.

A woman was considered to behave improperly if she had a sexual relationship with any man other than her husband. . . . A man, on the other hand, whether single or married, was reproached only if his sexual relationship was with the wife of another man. The intent of these moral standards was to ensure that a married woman would become pregnant only by her husband. Thus male sexual infidelity was a moral issue only if it compromised the integrity of another man's family. Wives were expected to tolerate their husbands' "affairs" with slaves, prostitutes, and other "disreputable" women . . . , but husbands could divorce wives involved in similar behaviour and kill the "other" man. The definition of adultery was limited to any sexual infidelity by a married woman or with a married woman.[19]

Plautus on the Double Standard

Plautus includes a complaint or lament about the double standard at *Mercator* 817–29.

ecastor lege dura vivont mulieres
multoque iniquiore miserae quam viri.
nam si vir scortum duxit clam uxorem suam,
id si rescivit uxor, impunest viro;
uxor virum si clam domo egressa est foras,
viro fit causa, exigitur matrimonio.
utinam lex esset eadem quae uxori est viro;
nam uxor contenta est, quae bona est, uno viro:
qui minus vir una uxore contentus siet?
ecastor faxim, si itidem plectantur viri,
si quis clam uxorem duxerit scortum suam,
ut illae exiguntur quae in se culpam commerent,
plures viri sint vidui quam nunc mulieres.

[*Good God! Women live under hard conditions, poor things, so much more unfair than the men. It's a fact that if a husband brought home some tart without his wife knowing and she finds out, the husband gets off scot-free. If a wife simply leaves the house without her husband knowing, he has the grounds he needs and she's divorced. I just wish the same law applied to wives and husbands. Now a wife, a good wife, is content with just her husband— so why should a husband be less content with just his wife? Good God! If husbands were taken to task for bringing in their tarts without their wives knowing, the same way as wives who are guilty of an offense are divorced, I guarantee there would be more solitary men than there are now solitary women!* [trans. Braund]]

44

This speech indicates the ideal that was established for women, that she be *contenta . . . uno viro* (824).[20] We have ample other evidence for this—especially from inscriptions—and for the closely related ideal expressed in the single word *morigera* (compliant).[21] For example, at *Amphitryo* 839–42, the noble wife Alcmena describes her contribution to the marriage in elevated terms,[22] as proper behavior, compliance, and generosity.

> non ego illam mihi dotem duco esse, quae dos dicitur,
> sed pudicitiam et pudorem et sedatum cupidinem,
> deum metum, parentum amorem et cognatum concordiam,
> tibi morigera atque ut munifica sim bonis, prosim probis.

> [I don't regard as my dowry what is called a dowry, but instead purity, propriety, self-control, respect for the gods, devotion to my parents and affection for my family, and being compliant with you and generous with kindnesses and helpful through my behaving well.]

What it is to be *morigera* emerges more clearly from a significant conversation at the start of *Casina* between two neighboring but contrasting wives. Cleustrata is miserable because she feels her rights to her property have been infringed by the designs of her husband (the lovesick *senex* Lysidamus) on her slave girl, whom she has raised at her own expense. Myrrhina not only scolds Cleustrata for owning personal property (199–202) but argues for turning a blind eye to her husband's love affairs—provided her home life is comfortable—because of the risk of divorce (204–11). Still more revealing is the later scene in which the "bride," the slave Chalinus, dressed as the slave girl Casina, is given advice on how to handle her new husband by deceiving him and getting the upper hand (815–24). This is a wonderful inversion of what it is to be *morigera*.[23] Then, when the *senex's* slave Olympio emerges embarrassed and reeling from his encounter with the new "bride," he is asked: *satin morigera est?* [Is she nice enough to you?] (896), which indicates that this concept included sexual compliance.

Further corroboration of this picture of what it is to be *morigera* comes from the conversation in *Menaechmi* between the wife of Menaechmus and her father, whom she has summoned because Menaechmus is treating her so outrageously, as she thinks, by stealing her property. First comes the remarkable soliloquy by the *senex* in which he reflects, rather evenhandedly, on the difficulties of marriage, seeing that there could be fault on either side or on both sides (764–71).

verum propemodum iam scio quid siet rei:
credo cum viro litigium natum esse aliquod.
ita istaec solent, quae viros subservire
sibi postulant, dote fretae feroces.
et illi quoque haud abstinent saepe culpa:
verum est modus tamen quoad pati uxorem oportet,
nec pol filia umquam patrem accersit ad se
nisi aut quid commissi aut † *iurgi est iusta causa*.[24]

[*Actually I have a pretty good idea what's up—I think a quarrel with her husband has arisen. That's the way they behave—they expect their husbands to slave for them, those wives with dowries, so fierce. And the husbands are often at fault too. But there is a limit to how much a wife should put up with. And good lord! My daughter never summons her father unless something's wrong or there is a just cause for complaint. [trans. Braund]*]

In the conversation that follows, the father reminds her that she should *morem geras* [be compliant] (788) and is not moved by her revelations that her husband spends time next door drinking and making love to the prostitute who lives there; provided the husband keeps the wife in comfortable circumstances, he says, she has no complaint. In short, in these texts, *concordia* between husband and wife is established as the ideal for marriage, but the prime responsibility for the achievement of such *concordia* is almost invariably placed upon the wife, especially through the wife being *morigera*, that is, compliant with her husband in domestic and sexual matters.[25]

Abuse of Wives in Comedy

The verbal abuse of wives is pretty routine in Roman comedy, typically in conversations between two *senes* or a *senex* and his slave.[26] It usually happens in the absence of the woman concerned, but sometimes in the fictive absence of the wife, when she is eavesdropping. For example, the opening scene of *Asinaria* contains much casual abuse of Artemona by her husband, Demaenetus, abetted by his slave Libanus: she is described as *importunam atque incommodam* [high-handed and hard to get along with] (62). But in a later scene, the wife hears her husband's abuse, though he is unaware that she is listening as he talks to the *meretrix*: *nauteam / bibere malim si necessum sit, quam illam oscularier* [I'd rather drink bilgewater, if it came to that, than kiss her] (894–95); *perisse cupio* [I want her dead] (901); *te Philaenium mihi atque uxoris mortem* [My dearest wish is to have you, Philaenium, and to have my wife dead] (905).

At *Mercator* 760–61, the tension is higher still when a cook reminds the husband that he hates his wife "like she was a snake," something he tries to deny because his wife is standing right there.

The exception to this pattern is provided by *Menaechmi*, where abuse is delivered direct to the wife. In fact, the play's action starts with lively abuse of his wife by Menaechmus, who comes on stage singing a *canticum* directed back inside (110–22, quoted later in this chapter), which begins with direct insults and proceeds to threats of divorce. Plautus makes it absolutely clear that the wife can hear all this, when he has Menaechmus say, *euax, iurgio hercle tandem uxorem abegi ab ianua* [That's excellent, with my abuse I've finally driven my wife away from the door, by god] (127). This strikes me as unusual. But worse is to come. Later in the play, there is an extended episode of verbal abuse of the wife and her father, along with threats of physical violence. At lines 714–18, Menaechmus's twin tells Menaechmus's wife that she is like Hecuba, and at line 837, in his pretend fit of insanity, he calls her *illa . . . rabiosa femina . . . canis* [that rabid woman-bitch]. I shall discuss this episode more fully later; for now, I simply want to establish that *Menaechmi* appears to break the convention that abuse of wives usually takes place in their absence.

In Praise of the Bachelor Life

Another locus in comedy for criticism of marriage and wives is the praise of bachelor life. An excellent example occurs in *Miles gloriosus*, where the *senex* Periplectomenus, a self-styled *adulescens* as far as his *mores* go (661), congratulates himself on his philosophy of life (673–707). He boasts, for example (678–81):

> liberae sunt aedis, liber sum autem ego: mei volo vivere.
> nam mihi, deum virtute dicam, divitias meas
> licuit uxorem dotatam genere summo ducere;
> sed nolo mi oblatratricem in aedis intro mittere.

> *[My house is a free house and I'm a free man. I like to live my own life. I'm rich enough, thank the gods, to get myself a rich and aristocratic wife—but no thank you—I'm not letting any barking bitch into my house.]*

There follows the typical Plautine catalogue of the expenses created by wives (686–98). The *senex* is emphatic that he prefers indulging himself to winning the approval of society by raising children, displaying a clearly antisocial attitude without blushing.[27]

Aulularia provides a similar catalogue of the things on which wives spend money, in the mouth of another character who proposes opting out of marriage.[28] Rich Megadorus has been a bachelor all his life. When his sister insists that he marry, he rejects her proposal of a wealthy middle-aged woman as his wife (158–59) and instead makes the novel proposition that he marry a girl from a family too poor to provide a dowry, saying that he regards a large dowry as a form of slavery for husbands (167–69). Later, he explains his position in a soliloquy. He believes the policy of rich men marrying daughters of poor without dowries would create more unity in society (481), make wives more obedient to their husbands (483), and reduce the costs of married life (484). He quotes the "offensive" words of rich wives who claim rights over the money they have brought to the marriage (498–502), then he provides a hilarious catalogue of all the tradesmen who call (505–22). He concludes that these are the inconveniences and expenses of a big dowry (532–33). He explains: *quae indotata est, ea in potestate est uiri. / dotatae mactant et malo et damno uiros* [A wife without a dowry is under her husband's control. It's the ones with dowries that afflict their husbands with misery and bankruptcy] (534–35). So here we have it: it's all about money and power. The *uxor dotata* is resented because her money gives her more freedom and independence than is acceptable to the male ego.

The Dowry System: Necessary but Resented

So, we might ask, what is wrong with Megadorus's proposal? In his discussion of the play, Konstan clearly demonstrates the role of the dowry in securing the cohesion of the community as a whole.[29] According to the social code, for women to be married without dowries could instigate a breakdown in social relations. The risks are spelled out in *Trinummus*, where the young man Lesbonicus is afraid that people will think he is betrothing his sister into concubinage if there is no dowry (688–93).

> nolo ego mihi te tam prospicere, qui meam egestatem leves,
> sed ut inops infamis ne sim, ne mi hanc famam differant,
> me germanam meam sororem in concubinatum tibi,
> si sine dote <dem>, dedisse magis quam in matrimonium.
> quis me improbior perhibeatur esse? haec famigeratio
> te honestet, me conlutulentet, si sine dote duxeris:
> tibi sit emolumentum honoris, mihi quod obiectent siet.
>
> *[I wish you wouldn't take such measures to relieve my poverty without realizing that I'll be broke and a laughingstock, with people spreading the word*

48

that I have given my own sister to you in concubinage rather than in marriage, if I give her without a dowry. Who would have a more rotten reputation than me? And if you did take her without a dowry, all this spread-the-word would glorify you and muddify me. You'd get the honor and the glory and I'd get whatever they'd throw at me. [trans. Braund]]

As Konstan says: "The dowry is the sign of the communal sanction. Without it, marriage is not a bond but an appropriation."[30]

The dowry system may have been essential to social cohesion, but hostility toward *uxores dotatae* is manifest.[31] Particularly telling are the reports of Cato's speech *De dote* (Gell. *N.A.* 10.23.4) and of his opposition to wives owning separate property in the context of the debate about the *lex Voconia* of 169 B.C., which restricted the rights of inheritance enjoyed by women in the top property class. He conjures the following scenario of the husband's humiliation (*ORF*³ frag. 158).[32]

principio vobis mulier magnam dotem adtulit; tum magnam pecuniam recipit, quam in viri potestatem non committit, eam pecuniam viro mutuam dat; postea, ubi irata facta est, servum recepticium sectari atque flagitare virum iubet.

[To begin with, the woman brought you a big dowry; next, she retains a large sum of money which she does not entrust to her husband's control but gives to him as a loan; finally, when she is annoyed with him, she orders a "reclaimable slave" to chase him about and pester him for it. [trans. Braund]]

This statement complements and supplements the evidence of the *fabula palliata*, which presents at least four specimens of the hated *uxor dotata*—Artemona in *Asinaria*, Cleustrata in *Casina*, Menaechmus's wife in *Menaechmi*, and Dorippa in *Mercator*. It seems clear from fragments of *fabulae togatae* that the same typology features there: from a play by Plautus's contemporary Titinius, we have the line *verum enim dotibus deleniti ultro etiam uxoribus ancillantur* [In fact, men who are bewitched by dowries make themselves slaves to their wives of their own accord] (*Procilia* 3), and from Novius's *Tabellaria* survives the line *qui habet uxorem sine dote, ei pannum positum in purpure est* [The man who has a wife and no dowry has rags set in purple] (1). Whether the *uxor dotata* was also a standard type in the *fabula Atellana* must be a matter for speculation; the odds are heavily in favor.[33]

The central point about the *uxor dotata* is that her money gives her power, spending power plus psychological power. Hence, in *Casina*, the amorous *senex*

Lysidamus bitterly describes his wife as being in charge of the household: *patiundum est, siquidem me vivo mea uxor imperium exhibit* [We have to endure this, seeing that my wife is head of the household—though I'm still alive] (409). Similarly, in *Asinaria*, Artemona is in effect the "paterfamilias" (e.g., 78–79: she behaves "just like fathers tend to"), and Demaenetus has been reduced to the position of the powerless *adulescens* resisting authority.[34] Demaenetus sold his authority (*imperium*, 87) in the household when he married his rich wife. He has no resources and therefore has to imagine defrauding his wife of the money he needs to assist his son's love affair with a *meretrix*. Plautus even has Artemona describe herself as an *uxor dotata* and pronounce threats against her husband at lines 897–98: *faxo ut scias / quid pericli sit dotatae uxori vitium dicere* [I'll make sure you appreciate the risks of vilifying a wife with a dowry]. An even more extreme case is that in *Menaechmi*, where the wife is described as a *portitor* [customs officer] (117).[35] Perhaps the supreme manifestation of the power of the *uxor dotata* is her locking her husband out of the house, which happens at *Menaechmi* 668 (cf. 963: *domum ire cupio, uxor non sinit* [I'd like to go home, but my wife won't allow it]). A fragment of Afranius (*Com.* 105) seems to express a husband's outrage at such an event: *excludat uxor tam confidenter virum? / non faciet* [Can a wife lock her husband out with such assurance? She won't do it].[36] All these cases demonstrate the effects of the loss of authority by the paterfamilias.

Elisabeth Schuhmann suggests that Plautus may be involved in polemic against an increase in marriage *sine manu*, a shift away from traditional marriage *cum manu*, according to which, on her marriage, a woman passed from the legal power of her father or guardian into the jurisdiction, or *manus*, of her husband, and any property she brought to marriage passed to her husband.[37] At this period, more and more marriages were contracted *sine manu*, which left the woman in her father's power but meant that after his death she was sui juris (legally independent, with the proviso that a guardian, or *tutor*, was appointed—this being fairly notional in some cases) and could own property in her own right. If this is correct, this shift is clearly a diminution of the husband's power and authority. Not that hostility toward married women owning property in their own right is confined to the ancient world: compare the opposition to the Married Women's Property Bills of 1857 and 1870.[38]

Roman Divorce: The Double Standard Again

Just as the Roman dowry system is alien to us, so our understanding of Roman attitudes toward divorce may be deficient if we import inappropriate modern assumptions. Fortunately, there are excellent general discussions of Roman divorce among the writings of Jane Gardner, Alan Watson, Beryl Rawson, Mireille Corbier, and Susan Treggiari, and there is a particularly useful treatment of aspects of Plautus's handling of divorce by Patricia Rosenmeyer. In fact, as Treggiari points out, we know more about Roman divorce than we do about Roman marriage.[39] The crucial points are these: Divorce, like marriage, was a private matter that required "no ratification from any outside authority (such as Church or State)" and entailed no public record or private documentation.[40] According to the law, either party could end a marriage, although a woman in a *manus* marriage was probably unable to initiate divorce until much later (the second century A.D.). Doubtless her relatives could exert pressure on her behalf, and doubtless the father or guardian of a woman in a marriage *sine manu* did. In theory, then, divorce may have been easier in Roman times than in many periods since. Contrast modern Italy, where civil divorce was legalized as recently as 1970,[41] and the Republic of Ireland, where it was only made legal in the last few years and is still a process fraught with difficulties and delays.

But to say that divorce was legally possible and available to both spouses is not to say that divorce was invariably socially acceptable or available on equal terms. Wider grounds for divorce were available to men than to women. In the early Republic at least, the husband could initiate divorce on grounds including poisoning, substitution of children or keys, and wine drinking.[42] It is hard to tell what grounds were available to women.[43] Given the double standard evinced in attitudes toward adultery (already discussed), it seems overwhelmingly likely that divorce was seldom initiated by the woman. This is made especially likely given that girls were often betrothed when they were very young and were married around the age of puberty to men older than themselves, even twice their age.[44] Given the centrality of *patria potestas* (power of the father) in Roman society, it seems hard to imagine many women flouting the authority vested in the male head of household to the extent of initiating divorce proceedings.

PART 2

Divorce and Comedy: A Laughing Matter?

The evidence presented in part 1 provides a context for the treatment of divorce in Roman comedy. As I suggested at the outset, divorce is not a phenomenon intrinsically likely to feature prominently in a genre whose objective is almost invariably marriage. Yet divorce figures prominently in three of the extant plays of Roman comedy: *Amphitryo, Menaechmi,* and *Hecyra.* I argue that by making divorce crucial, these plays attempt to extend the genre of comedy.[45]

Amphitryo: A Tragicomoedia *of Adultery and Divorce*

In the prologue to the *Amphitryo* (50–59), Mercury makes the initial assertion, which is not just a joke, that this is a tragedy turned comedy—a *tragico-moedia*. This instantly marks the play as different from the usual fare of the *fabula palliata*. The most obvious difference, as Mercury points out, is the presence of kings and gods on stage (60–61). But that's not all. The play is perhaps the only place in New Comedy where the theme is adultery by a wife, as opposed to infidelity (intended, if not actual) by a husband.[46] The nearest analogues are the invented stories of adulterous passion at *Bacchides* 842–924, where a slave pretends that his young master has seduced the wife of a soldier in order to extract a sum of money from the young man's father, and in *Miles gloriosus*, where the braggart soldier Pyrgopolynices is tricked into conceiving a passion for a (fictitious) *matrona*.[47] Since the stories are invented, it seems clear that actual adultery on the part of a married woman was considered inappropriate for the genre of the *palliata*.

It is significant that Plautus takes some trouble in the first half of *Amphitryo* to emphasize the profound "harmony" (*concordia*) of husband and wife. This is expressed in very Roman terminology, for example, in the promise at lines 474–98 that Jupiter will ultimately renew the "former harmony" (*antiquam . . . concordiam*) of the marriage. Not only is Alcmena the devoted wife (e.g., 633–51), but this devotion is represented as mutual—for instance, when Amphitryo says, *quae me amat, quam contra amo* [she loves me and I love her back] (653). But Plautus creates mayhem in the marriage when Jupiter and Mercury impersonate Amphitryo and his slave Sosia to enable Jupiter to sleep with Alcmena. Amphitryo is driven to the conclusion that his wife has been seduced, and he reacts to the loss of her "purity" (*pudicitia*) with despair and fury (809–19). He suggests that he is no longer her husband—*vir ego tuos sim? ne me appella, falsa, falso nomine* [Am I your husband? Don't call me that, your liar, with your lying names] (813)—by which he must mean that their marriage is at an end.[48] For her part, Alcmena thinks that Amphitryo is trying to trick her into an admission of infidelity (*impu-dicitiai*, 820–21). What are they to do? Amphitryo considers that divorce is his only option (*numquid causam dicis quin te hoc multem matrimonio?* [Can you suggest any reason why I should not deprive you of this marriage?], 852).[49] Alcmena agrees, provided she is at fault (*si deliqui, nulla causa est* [None, if I have done wrong], 853).

This is manifestly a moment of great tension in the plot of something called a "comedy" (96). That, I feel sure, is why Jupiter immediately appears on the now empty stage to deliver his firm reassurance that Alcmena is innocent and that all will be well in the end, lest the play end half-finished (867–68). The necessity of including this divine intervention at this point demonstrates the risk that Plautus was running in choosing the theme of adultery. He is clearly trying to soothe his audience's anxieties.

The action resumes immediately with Alcmena expressing her outrage at Amphitryo's treatment of her (882–90), with a declaration that she will have to leave him unless he apologizes: *neque me perpetiar probri / falso insimulatam, quin ego illum aut deseram / aut satis faciat mi ille atque adiuret insuper, / nolle esse dicta quae in me insontem protulit* [I won't endure such false accusations of disgrace—either I shall leave him or he must apologize and swear on top that he didn't mean the things he accused me of in my innocence]. She persists in this attitude as Jupiter, disguised as Amphitryo, approaches. Unimpressed by his pleas for forgiveness, she states her intention to divorce her husband (925–30)—using, in line 928, the words of the divorce formula from the Twelve Tables.[50]

> A. ego istaec feci verba virtute irrita;
> nunc, quando factis me impudicis abstini,
> ab impudicis dictis avorti volo.
> valeas, tibi habeas res tuas, reddas meas.
> iuben me ire comites . . .
> I.   sanan es?
> A.   si non iubes,
> ibo egomet; comitem mihi Pudicitiam duxero.
>
> [A. *I refute those charges of yours with my virtuous life. Now, since I have kept myself from impure behavior, I will not subject myself to impure words. Farewell. Keep your own possessions and return mine to me. Tell my attendants to follow.*
> I. *Are you in your right mind?*
> A. *If you don't, I'll go alone with my Chastity as my sole attendant.*]

It is important to note that she is even prepared to abandon her property—namely, her own slaves—if necessary. This is the crisis point: both spouses have now declared their resolve to divorce (see fig. 2).

At this, Jupiter, pretending to be Amphitryo, withdraws the accusation of adultery: *arbitratu tuo ius iurandum dabo / me meam pudicam esse uxorem arbitrarier*

Initial situation:
Perfect marriage (*concordia*) of Amphitryo and Alcmena

▽

Obstacle:
Alcmena's alleged adultery and loss of *pudicitia*, with Jupiter disguised as Amphitryo
Threats of divorce by Amphitryo and Alcmena

▽

Resolution:
Jupiter's power to command obedience of Amphitryo

▽

Result:
Concordia restored
Birth to Alcmena of twins fathered by Jupiter and Amphitryo

Fig. 2. Plautus *Amphitryo*: a *tragicomoedia* of adultery and divorce

[I'll swear to it on any terms you choose that I believe that my wife is pure] (931–32), an oath he swears by greatest Jupiter (the latest in a whole string of humorous oaths in the play). The crucial word here is *pudicam*. This is enough to change Alcmena's mind, and she is reconciled, a situation welcomed by Sosia as the return of peace (*pax*, 957) and harmony (*concordia*, 962), words chosen to evoke the Roman marriage ideal. Amphitryo, however, is still raging to discover the identity of his wife's lover (1016). Finally, after further humiliations, he is delivered from his delusion by a deus ex machina, when Jupiter commands him to "return to your former concord with your wife Alcmena" (1141–42).

What is truly unusual about *Amphitryo* is less the appearance of kings and gods on stage than the theme of adultery, although the two forms of novelty clearly interact with one another. Adultery is, I suggest, a theme that lends itself to treatment in other dramatic genres but not in the *fabula palliata*. Two other Roman dramatic genres include the theme of adultery. In the (subliterary) mime, the favorite type was apparently the adultery mime.[51] The typical scenario is that sketched by Ovid at *Tristia* 2.497–500—"the sleek adulterer constantly makes an appearance, and the clever wife fools her stupid husband"—which can be supplemented by scenes from Horace, Juvenal, Petronius, and Apuleius that depict the adulterous wife concealing her lover in a trunk or a cupboard.[52] Adultery is also a staple theme in Roman tragedy—for example, in the stories of Agamemnon and Clytemnestra and Phaedra that feature in tragedies by Ennius and Seneca—but not in the *fabula palliata*.

How does Plautus's *Amphitryo* fit into this spectrum? Its action is set at a much higher social level than the adultery mime, and the plot relies upon mistaken identity, not upon intent to deceive. In fact, Alcmena is explicitly portrayed as an ideal wife (*examussim est optima* [she's perfectly excellent], 843). This is what makes the outcome of the play potentially tragic. Amphitryo's repudiation of Alcmena, based on a false understanding, is only averted by Jupiter's power to stage-manage the whole thing. Since the theme of adultery is one fraught with anxiety and hence, apparently, usually excluded from the *palliata*, Plautus seems to be pushing at the limits of the genre. When he has Mercury advertise this play as a tragicomedy, he is not joking. In short, I prefer to see this play as hardly conforming at all with the pattern of the *palliata* but, rather, as a hybrid between tragedy and the forms of Roman comic entertainment where adultery was a standard theme.[53]

Menaechmi: *Objective—Divorce?*

I move next to the play of Plautus that most closely resembles *Amphitryo* in its exploitation of mistaken identity: *Menaechmi*, the original comedy of errors. Although this play is in some respects close to the heart of the genre, with mistaken identity as the comic version of tragic hamartia, and although "it occupies an influential role in our image of Roman comedy,"[54] I see it as unique in the extant corpus. This is because it reverses the normal tendency toward marriage by making divorce the goal of the husband in the play and by having him actually achieve that goal. Let me indicate the extraordinary features of this play.

First of all, the central character, Menaechmus, is a young husband (he is described as *adulescens* at line 100) in an unhappy marriage.[55] Only here and in Terence's *Hecyra* do we see the early days of a marriage—and in both plays the *adulescens* is at odds with his wife but has a deep attachment to a *meretrix* who lives next door. Menaechmus's opening *canticum* presents the situation succinctly with its vivid hostility (110–22)—including criticisms of his wife, who is compared with a customs officer (*portitor*, 117); a threat of divorce (112–13, later echoed at 720 and 726); and a catalogue designed to demonstrate that Menaechmus provides for her adequately (reprised by another such catalogue at 798–801).

> ni mala, ni stulta sies, ni indomita imposque animi,
> quod viro esse odio videas, tute tibi odio habeas.
> praeterea si mihi tale post hunc diem
> faxis, faxo foris vidua visas patrem.

nam quotiens foras ire volo, me retines, revocas, rogitas,
  quo ego eam, quam rem agam, quid negoti geram,
  quid petam, quid feram, quid foris egerim.
  portitorem domum duxi, ita omnem mihi
  rem necesse eloqui est, quidquid egi atque ago.
nimium ego te habui delicatam; nunc adeo ut facturus dicam.
  quando ego tibi ancillas, penum,
  lanam, aurum, vestem, purpuram
  bene praebeo nec quicquam eges,
  malo cavebis si sapis,
  virum observare desines.

[*If you weren't a such a mean, stupid, impossible, pigheaded female, you'd
dislike anything that you see your husband dislikes. If you go on treating me
like this any longer, I'll divorce you and send you home to your father. The
fact is, whenever I want to go out, you try to stop me, call me back, cross-
question me about where I'm going and what I'm doing and what deals
I'm involved in and what I'm after and what I'm bringing and what I did
while I was out. It's a customs officer I've married, the way I have to declare
every single thing I've done or am doing. I've treated you far too indulgently.
Now I'll tell you my future policy: in return for my providing you with maid-
servants, food, woolen cloth, jewelry, household linen, and fine dresses—
everything you could possibly need—you will avoid trouble if you've any
sense and stop spying on your husband.*]

Next, in a characteristic flight of imagery, Plautus describes the hostility
between husband and wife as a state of war. For example, in talking to her
so masterfully, Menaechmus makes the declaration *pugnavi fortiter* [I fought
heroically] (129); and in stealing a dress from his wife, he asserts, *avorti praedam
ab hostibus nostrum salute socium* [I have captured some booty from the enemy
for the benefit of my allies] (134), which renders his *meretrix* (mistress) his
ally. This use of martial imagery in a marital context is unusual.[56]

The next exceptional feature occurs during the series of misunderstandings caused by the arrival of Menaechmus's twin brother. At the start of act
5, Menaechmus's wife, a typical *uxor dotata*, meets her husband's twin and
starts to row with him, thinking he is her husband. He is astonished at this
and proceeds to abuse the *matrona* and her father to their faces, which I suggest breaks the rules of the *palliata* in a shocking way. The *matrona* is disgusted
and declares her intent to live without a husband (720–21) and to get a divorce:
non, inquam, patiar praeterhac, / quin vidua vivam quam tuos mores perferam [I

tell you I'll not put up with it any longer. I'll get a divorce rather than endure your behavior] (725–26). She then summons her father, in order to complain to him, and asks him to take her away (780–82), by which she must mean dissolve the marriage.[57] The scene ends with Menaechmus's twin pretending to be mad and threatening physical violence, against these people who are, as far as he is concerned, two total strangers making incomprehensible accusations at him (835–75).

Finally, after a long recognition scene comes the extraordinary conclusion to the play: not marriage, but divorce. When, for the first time, both brothers are on stage together, Menaechmus's twin proposes that they both return to their own country, Sicily. Menaechmus agrees to this immediately—which must entail his divorce from his Epidamnian wife. At first sight, perhaps, Plautus seems to have broken with the usual integrative tendency of New Comedy. But, in fact, reintegration is shifted to a different sphere. The reunion of the separated twins, the chief goal of the play, can only be achieved through the divorce of the Epidamnian twin (see fig. 3); that is, Menaechmus's fantasy of divorce becomes a means of achieving his twin's goal of the reintegration of the original family.

This reintegration works not just on the familial level but also in the psychological sphere. As Erich Segal shows, the twins have divided between them the spheres of work and play (*industria* and *uoluptas*), and as Eleanor Leach demonstrates in her discussion of the alter ego theme in the play, the two brothers present two aspects of a single, more rounded personality.[58] Now that the twins have been reunited, they cannot be separated again—and they have clearly made staying in Epidamnus impossible. So they must return to Sicily. Therefore Menaechmus proposes to sell all his possessions in auction the next week. The slave who finishes the play by announcing the auction throws in a final, climactic item: "For sale—one wife, too, if a buyer can be found" (1160). This closing joke signifies Menaechmus's de facto divorce,[59] brought about by his simply departing.

These extraordinary features make the play unique. Instead of the usual reintegration of the members of a divided society at the close, Plautus opts for the reintegration of the primal Sicilian family, a choice that inevitably entails disruption, including divorce, to life in Epidamnus.[60] An awareness of Plautus's closural choice provides an additional explanation for the unique setting of the play. Epidamnus is usually—and rightly—explained as a country where the normal rules of social engagement are suspended.[61] But the exotic location suits a nonconformist finale and makes it a dispensable location, one that the central characters can depart from with impunity. By contrast, a play set in Athens, like the majority of the plays of New Comedy, might be expected

Initial situation:
Brother from Sicily seeks to be reunited with his long-lost twin
Brother in Epidamnus longs for divorce

▽

Obstacles:
Ignorance of twin's location and identity
Twin's marriage and other duties at Epidamnus

▽

Resolution:
Recognition of twins
Divorce of twin in Epidamnus

▽

Result:
Twins are reunited
Divorce of twin in Epidamnus

Fig. 3. Plautus *Menaechmi*: objective—divorce?

to conclude with a finale that reinforced the rules of the genre. *Menaechmi* breaks the rules in its treatment of marriage and divorce, and like *Amphitryo*, it may be seen as an experiment by Plautus testing the boundaries of the genre of the *palliata* in this area.

Hecyra, *or How to Avoid* Discidium

Perhaps the most extraordinary of all experiments in *palliata* is Terence's *Hecyra*.[62] Because the plot is particularly complex, this must be demonstrated by a fuller and closer reading of the text than was required for the plays previously discussed; for the same reason, I provide not one but two representations of the plot (figs. 4 and 5), corresponding to the pre-play plot and the plot presented in the play itself.

Hecyra begins where most other comedies leave off, in the months immediately following the marriage of a young man to an eligible young woman.[63] A slave from the young man's household provides a full narrative early in the play of how Pamphilus came to marry Philumena (115–94), which shows how this play presupposes the regular plot of New Comedy before it even gets going (see fig. 4). Despite being head over heels in love with the *meretrix* Bacchis, the *adulescens* Pamphilus finally agreed to his father's insistence that he get married. The marriage to his neighbor's daughter was initially not consummated, and Pamphilus wanted her to return to her family—that is,

Before the play:
Imperfect marriage of Pamphilus and Philumena

▽

Obstacle:
Pamphilus's feelings for *meretrix* Bacchis

▽

Resolution:
Transfer of Pamphilus's affections from Bacchis to Philumena

▽

Result:
Perfect marriage

Fig. 4. Terence *Hecyra*, or how to avoid *discidium*

he wanted the marriage to be terminated—but he had no reason to divorce her himself, because she had committed no fault. Then, observing how patient his new wife was, he gradually transferred his affections from Bacchis to his wife. At this point, Pamphilus was sent abroad on family business, and his wife was left in the house with his mother. At first, the two women got along very well, but as time passed, the wife refused even to see her mother-in-law and finally returned home to her own mother. It is at this point, after this lengthy preamble that occupies much of act 1, that the action of the play commences.

Act 2 commences with Pamphilus's parents bursting onto the stage in the middle of a row. Terence devotes the entire act to a portrayal of marital disharmony among the older generation. The first words Pamphilus's father, Laches, utters are a condemnation of the entire female sex—*quod hoc genus est, quae haec coniuratiost!* [what a tribe this is, what a conspiracy!] (198)—establishing his bigoted disposition. He asserts that mothers-in-law and daughters-in-law are like-minded in hating one another (201), then he criticizes his wife, Sostrata, for the way she has alienated their son's bride and the bride's family. He even threatens divorce (*tu hinc isses foras*, 222)—like Amphitryo (cf. Plaut. *Amph.* 852), though in different circumstances. Alone on stage, Sostrata then delivers a soliloquy (275–80) in which she laments how unfair it is that all wives are hated by their husbands and worries about how to establish that she is not at fault, given the general hostility toward mothers-in-law (*ita animum induxerunt socrus / omnis esse iniquas* [people take it for granted that all mothers-in-law are unkind], 277–78). Terence so far offers a reprise of the standard treatment of an established marriage in Roman comedy.

Initial situation in the play:
Desire of Pampilus and his father, Laches, to maintain/retrieve this perfect marriage

▽

Obstacles:
Separation caused by mother-in-law Sostrata
Alienus puer
Pamphilus's alleged affection for Bacchis

▽

Resolution:
Sostrata removes herself from situation
Bacchis removed herself from situation
Pamphilus is realized to be father of Philumena's child

▽

Result:
Marriage saved
Child born to its parents

Fig. 5. Terence *Hecyra,* or how to avoid *discidium*

Act 3 commences with Pamphilus's return home to hear the news of the rupture between his wife and his mother, an obstacle to the continuation of his marriage. But when he goes to visit his wife, he discovers a much worse obstacle: she is heavily pregnant, and not by him, as we learn from his soliloquy (361–408). This puts him in a similar position to that of Amphitryo. However, he learns that the pregnancy is the result not of adultery on the part of his wife (as Amphitryo believes) but of that typical pre-play event in New Comedy, rape by an unknown assailant. Not surprisingly, despite his feelings for his wife, he declares that it would not be "right" (*honestum*) to take her back (403–4). But he is now faced with the difficult situation of needing to explain the breakdown of the marriage without revealing the real reason, which would ruin her reputation. In desperation, he accounts for the "rift" (*discidium,* 476)[64] by alleging that his wife and mother do not get along—something that will of course be readily believed by his father, Laches—and by declaring that filial devotion trumps conjugal affection (485–92). The act ends with both of the fathers in a state of vexation: the bride's father insists that Pamphilus either take her back or return the dowry so she can be married to someone else (501–2, 508–9), and Pamphilus's father vents his anger on his wife (510–15). Terence has clearly set before us the obstacles to the repair of the marriage.

Act 4 starts by providing a reprise of the bad marital relations in the older generation, this time by presenting a row between the bride's parents,

Phidippus and Myrrina, which balances the row between Laches and Sostrata in act 2. Like Laches, Phidippus imagines his wife to be a mean-spirited mother-in-law. The accusations he hurls at her reveal that he believes that the fault for the breakdown of the marriage is entirely hers (529–35). After Phidippus has left, Myrrina delivers a soliloquy expressing her misery (566–76), which balances the similarly wretched soliloquy by Sostrata earlier.

At this point, the obstacles to the repair of the marriage seem overwhelming (see fig. 5): both fathers think their wives are exhibiting the classic mother-in-law syndrome; the *adulescens* himself is unwilling to take back a wife who has been made pregnant by some other man. We can see that Terence has replaced the usual plot structure of obstacles to achieving marriage with a plot structure that makes the repair of the broken marriage the goal of the play. That is his first major innovation, a striking variant on the usual goal in New Comedy and, of course, precisely the same goal as in *Amphitryo*. How is Terence to achieve this repair?

Instead of opting for a simple deus ex machina, as Plautus does in his *tragicomoedia Amphitryo*, Terence characteristically offers a much more human and humane solution, which comes in two stages. In the first, he demonstrates that Sostrata, the mother-in-law of the play's title character, is a generous, long-suffering individual who is prepared to sacrifice her own happiness and comfort to restore her son's marriage. Sostrata tells her son that she plans to withdraw to the country so that her presence does not impede his marriage (577–600). But the removal of that obstacle cannot affect the other, namely, Pamphilus's continuing reluctance to raise an *alienus puer* [another man's child] (649), by which Terence makes Pamphilus his own, interiorized "blocking character."[65] The agent of the happy ending is the *meretrix* Bacchis, in the final act.[66] First, she visits Myrrina to convince her that the relationship between Pamphilus and Bacchis is over (754–60); second, as she explains in a soliloquy (816–50), she realizes that Pamphilus is after all the father of his bride's child, because he committed the premarital rape.

To achieve the necessary and desired goal, Terence has overturned the standard stereotypes of not one but two stock figures—the nasty mother-in-law and the mercenary *meretrix*. The unorthodox nature of these two female characters compounds the degree of experimentation in this play. But that is not all. Terence's final innovation is to allow the story of the secret of the paternity of Philumena's child to remain with Pamphilus and the women—his mother, her mother, and Bacchis. It is the normative tendency of the anagnorisis for all the relevant facts to become common knowledge to all the characters of a play, but at the end of *Hecyra*, the two *senes*, Laches and Phidippus, along with the slave Parmeno, are left in the dark. Terence tells us this explicitly at lines 866–67: *placet non fieri itidem ut in comoediis, / omnia omnes ubi resciscunt* [I'd rather this weren't like in comedies where everyone finds out about everything].[67]

If we are right in thinking that the *Hecyra*'s lack of success on its first two productions (as graphically described in the two prologues, lines 1–5 and 29–42)[68] was generated by the play itself rather than external events, it is tempting to suggest that these massive innovations with the standard formula of the *palliata* were crucial. It looks as if Terence set out to explode the myth that the young lovers in the *palliata* get married and live "happily ever after," by bringing on stage obstacles that can occur *after* marriage.

CONCLUSION

Let me return to the paradox I presented at the start of this chapter: in the *fabula palliata*, marriage is presented as objective for the younger generation and as torture for the older generation, husbands and wives both. The situation facing men with regard to marriage was succinctly articulated by the second-century censor Macedonicus when he said that men have difficulty living with wives but cannot manage without them. In the first part of this chapter, I have argued that in the *fabula palliata*, the positive features of wives and marriage are eclipsed by negative features. This can be explained by the different kinds of marriage represented in comedy. The marriages between young people are generally represented as love matches, whereas the established marriages often involve an *uxor dotata;* that is, they are matches made for the sake of money and in which the husband's authority is diminished.

In the second part of this chapter, I moved to the question of divorce, which is a major theme in three surviving plays: *Amphitryo, Menaechmi,* and *Hecyra.* All three are highly unconventional. In the case of *Amphitryo,* Plautus explicitly marks the play as an experiment by describing it as a *tragicomoedia.* While this term has usually been taken, following Plautus's cue, to refer to the presence of kings and gods on stage, I believe it is of wider and deeper import. What makes *Amphitryo* significantly different is its themes of adultery and divorce. What seems unprecedented is Amphitryo's rage at Alcmena's *impudicitia* with a rival and Alcmena's decision to leave Amphitryo because of his lack of trust in her. The resulting tension requires reassurance in the middle of the play and a deus ex machina at the end. In the case of *Menaechmi,* the experiment consists of the switch of the goal of the play from marriage to divorce. The play presents a clash of two worlds, the world of Epidamnus and the world of Sicily. This clash is resolved by dissolving an unhappy marriage in order to achieve the reintegration of the original Sicilian family. In the case of *Hecyra*, the experiment consists of an exploration of a new marriage that seems doomed to end in divorce because of insuperable difficulties in the relationship between the new bride and her mother-in-law. The play's initial similarities with the situation in *Menaechmi*—a young man in an unhappy marriage—give way to a situation that more closely resembles that of *Amphitryo*, where the birth of another man's child (admittedly not precisely the adultery of *Amphitryo*) jeopardizes the marriage. Terence's innovations include refiguring the standard negative stereotypes of the mother-in-law and the *meretrix* as generous and intelligent characters and leaving all the men in the play (barring the *adulescens* himself) in the dark at the end. This amounts to a considerable disruption of the norms of the *palliata*.

The essential difference from the rest of the surviving examples of the *fabula palliata* is that instead of making marriage or sexual union the objective of the play, these three plays all focus on a marriage that is already in existence.[69] In each case, the dramatist puts that marriage under pressure by bringing the specter of divorce close, in effect shifting the goal from achieving marriage to retrieving it. This is done twice through mistaken identity plots, in *Amphitryo* and *Menaechmi*, and once, in *Hecyra*, through ignorance and misunderstandings.[70] In *Amphitryo* and *Hecyra* the marriage is saved, but only thanks to a virtual or real deus ex machina, whereas in *Menaechmi* the marriage is actually dissolved. Although the novelty of the *Hecyra* on these grounds has long been acknowledged, I do not believe scholars have recognized that Terence's experiment had in some respects been anticipated by Plautus. In different ways, all three plays break the rules of *palliata*—which suggests to me that the genre had difficulties accommodating the theme of divorce. All three plays, I conclude, are experiments that press at and perhaps even rupture the boundaries of the genre.

Postscript: Divorce, Dowry, and Adultery in a Normative Play

In this brief postscript, I want to consider the treatment of the themes of divorce, dowry, and adultery in a play that does not strain at the boundaries of the genre as do the three plays that comprise the focus of this chapter. The fact that these themes are not central to the plot of Plautus's *Miles gloriosus* as a whole but are associated with a classic "blocking character" seems to confirm my argument that they are accommodated in the *palliata* only with discomfort.

Plautus's *Miles* conforms to the norm of a boy overcoming obstacles to get his girl, with the character of the *miles gloriosus* providing the chief obstacle to Pleusicles' union with Philocomasium, who is in the soldier's possession.[71] Pyrgopolynices is, of course, a classic "blocking character." The themes of adultery and divorce are intertwined in a scheme invented by the other characters as part of a larger strategy to deprive Pyrgopolynices of Philocomasium, by having him fall for another woman instead. The soldier is told that the (fictitious) "wife" of the *senex* Periplectomenus has fallen desperately in love with him. The slave who is masterminding this scheme arouses the soldier's interest by singing the woman's praises. When the soldier asks about her marital status, he describes her as *et nupta et vidua* [married and not] (964), a paradox he explains by saying that she is a young woman married to an old man (965) and ready to divorce her aged husband (970). Then we see a *meretrix* being coached to play the part of the infatuated *matrona* (1158–73): she is to pretend that she has divorced her husband (1164–65) and that she has been able to stay in "her" house because it is part of her dowry, thus avoiding any hesitation on the soldier's part about entering another man's house (1166–68): this "*matrona*" is clearly another *uxor dotata*.[72] Finally, at 1276–80, the charade is acted out. When Pyrgopolynices is invited by her maid to move in with the *matrona*, he is initially horrified at the idea: *egon ad illam eam quae nupta sit? vir eius me deprehendat* [Go to a married woman's house? And let her husband catch me there?] (1276), but when he is told that she has divorced her husband because of her passion for him—and here Plautus inverts the terminology for a man divorcing his wife (*quin tua causa exegit virum ab se* [But she has already turned her husband out because of you], 277)—he is persuaded, and he immediately seeks a way to rid himself of Philocomasium to clear the way for this potentially lucrative new relationship.

When Pyrgopolynices goes inside to consummate the affair with the *matrona*, he immediately gets his comeuppance at the hands of the *senex* Periplectomenus, who is here made the agent of both comic justice and Roman morality, since he is supposedly the husband of the fictitious *matrona* and would therefore, according to Roman law, have the rights of the wronged husband.

Accordingly, the final act of the play is an exhibition of the punishment of the would-be adulterer. He is threatened with castration (1398–99) and then flogged, both procedures that might have been regarded by a Roman audience as appropriate punishments for adulterers.[73] In his choice of this form of closure, then, Plautus restores the moral norms and brings about a change of heart in the blocking character. This is demonstrated clearly in Pyrgopolynices' final words, which offer a highly moralistic condemnation of adultery (1436–37).[74]

si sic aliis moechis fiat, minus hic moechorum siet,
magis metuant, minus has res studeant. eamus ad me. plaudite.

*[If other adulterers were treated like this, there would be fewer of them, and
they would be more wary, and their appetite for such affairs would be less.
Give us your applause.]*

This play, then, offers an instructive counterweight to the three plays discussed more fully earlier in this chapter. In contrast with the experimental
elements in *Amphitryo*, *Menaechmi*, and *Hecyra*, *Miles* confirms the view that
the *fabula palliata* tends to work toward the union of the young lovers. The
relegation of the themes of divorce, dowry, and adultery to the subplot that
overthrows the blocking character confirms my argument that these themes
are not comfortably accommodated within a normative example of the *fabula palliata*. That is why *Miles* ends on such a resoundingly moralistic note,
with the condemnation of men who commit adultery.[75]

Notes

1. The question of the advisability of marriage was by no means confined to comedy.
It was a staple theme in the schools of rhetoric throughout antiquity, as is evident in a
poem such as Juvenal *Satire* 6, which is deeply enmeshed in the rhetorical tradition (see
Braund 1992). I decided from the outset not to engage in issues of comparison between
Greek and Roman comedy, which tend to distract from a full-frontal analysis of the
Latin plays as dramatic entities in their own right. For those interested in the full Greco-
Roman picture, see most recently the exhaustive analysis of scenes of dispute in New
Comedy in Scafuro 1997. It will be obvious that I endorse the kind of view held by Saller
(1991), who sees that Roman comedy can provide valuable evidence for understanding
Roman culture (see esp. 99–104). Wiles (1989, 45) sees New Comedy not as escapism
but as an expressive reflection of social issues and values.

2. Beare 1950, 120–28, provides a wonderful overview.

3. The mime apparently ousted the native *fabula Atellana* as the afterpiece on festival days (thus notes Fantham in *OCD*[3]). It is difficult to know if this shift involved a
displacement or an incorporation of the subject matter of the *Atellana*. Whether or not
the *Atellana* also utilized marriage as a central theme is harder to ascertain, although the
report in Bieber 1961 (160) of an *Atellana* called *Nuptiae* is a welcome hint.

4. Frye 1957, 163–86, esp. 163–65, 180. One major difficulty with Frye's approach
is that he dehistoricizes comedy, obscuring, e.g., differences between Greek and Roman
New Comedy, on which see n. 5 following.

5. Cf. Wiles 1989: e.g., "All the works of New Comedy (with one exception) tell the
same basic story" (31); "In all the extant Greek texts, the plots end with marriage" (33).
Wiles (1991, 31–32) rightly distinguishes between the emphases in the Greek and Roman
plays, noting that Roman comedy offers sexual gratification as an alternative objective to marriage.

6. Frye 1957, 165–66. In Plautus's *Rudens*, even the pimp Labrax is integrated through Daemones' dinner invitation at the end; E. Segal (1987, 165) notes that this is unusual.

7. On the close relationship between these two plays, see Handley in his edition of *Dyskolos* (1965, 12, 17–19): it looks like Menander is Plautus's original. In *The Merchant of Venice*, the girl's father is actually overdetermined in his isolation by being not just a miser (usurer) but also a Jew—as David Konstan observed to me, comparing also Marlowe's *The Jew of Malta* and Gauthier's *La Juive de Constantine*.

8. Konstan 1983, 33–46.

9. See Konstan's discussion of the marriage code (1983, 18–19); likewise Wiles 1989, 37.

10. In Terence's *Hecyra*, the wife has already returned to her mother as the action begins; sometimes the wife involves her father in her dispute with her husband, as happens in *Menaechmi* (discussed later in this chapter) and at *Mercator* 784–88, when Dorippa thinks her husband is entertaining a call girl and feasting; both of these are cases of the *uxor dotata* (discussed shortly) attempting to assert herself. The theme occurs in the Roman *fabula togata*, too—e.g., in Afranius's *Divortium* (e.g., Afr. Com. 47–49 [*dotem ne repromittas*], 52–54, 62–64); in his *Simulans*, where a father forces his daughter to leave her husband; and in his *Vopiscus*, which features a husband whose wife has left him (e.g., Afr. Com. 371 [*homo mulierosus*]; 372–74, including the word *morigeram*; 376 [*excludat uxor tam confidenter virum?*]; 378–82, including the word *morigeratio*). See Beare 1950, 123.

11. Bettini 1991. Wiles (1991, 32–33) pinpoints some of the difficulties of Bettini's approach, which do not affect my argument here.

12. Fredershausen 1912, 234–35, has a complete list of references to divorce in Plautus and Terence.

13. Significantly, Bettini (1991) chooses this play as the first and basic tool for exposition of his interpretation of Plautus.

14. E.g., the last lines of Plautus's *Trinummus* describe marriage as *miseria* (1185). Cf. Wiles 1989, 41, on Plautus: "Pleasure is incompatible with the married state"; "There is a presumption that at every turn the average married male wants to escape from the clutches of his wife into the arms of a prostitute."

15. So one of the words for marriage, *matrimonium*, implies. In Treggiari's words (1991, 5), "*matrimonium* is an institution involving a mother, *mater.*" Comedy itself bears explicit witness to this. Cf. Plautus *Aul.* 148–50: *liberis procreandis—/ ita di faxint—volo te uxorem / domum ducere*; *Capt.* 889: *liberorum quaerundorum causa ei, credo, uxor datast*; *Miles* 682: *nam procreare liberos lepidumst onus*. So does tragedy (e.g., Ennius *Scen.* 126W, 136W). See Treggiari 1991, 5–13. The story of Spurius Carvilius's divorce (Gell. *N.A.* 4.3.2) underlines how essential to marriage procreation was, with the oath that *uxorem se liberum quaerundum gratia habiturum*. For a discussion of some of these passages, see G. Williams 1968, 372–73.

16. On the social functions of Roman marriage, see Gardner 1986, 31. Cf. Corbier's 1991 discussion of divorce and adoption, which she sees as strategies, alongside marriage and the dowry system, used by the Roman elite with the aim of "regulating the circulation of women and wealth" (76).

17. This speech was "reperformed" in its entirety by Augustus in the Senate (see Liv. *Per.* 59; cf. Suet. *Aug.* 89.2, which describes it as the *oratio de prole augenda*; I owe these references to Barchiesi [1988] 1997). The sentiment is of course much older than

that; it is "the most ancient 'joke' on record," according to E. Segal (1987, 23). Burchill (1999, 161) offers a comic feminist reprise on the same lines: " 'The trouble with men . . . is that we don't *want* them but we *need* them.' 'I thought the trouble was that we don't *need* them but we do *want* them.' "

18. Fantham's translation (1994, 263).

19. Shelton 1998, 54–55. For fuller discussion, cf. Corbier 1991, 50–51; Treggiari in Rawson 1991, 38–41; Gardner 1986, 57 (for Augustus's legislation whereby a woman convicted for adultery was debarred from remarrying); Scafuro 1997, 235–38.

20. The speech is put into the mouth of a female slave, which makes me unsure how to read it: does this mean that the complaint can easily be dismissed by the male members of Plautus's audience? On the *univira* wife, see G. Williams 1958, 23–24; Lattimore 1942, 296 n. 251.

21. G. Williams's discussion (1958, 19–22, 28–29) of *morem gerere, morigerus*, and *morigerari* is essential.

22. J. Phillips (1985) persuasively argues that the use of padding associated with tragic performances produces a source of visual humor that invites double entendres around the ideas of *voluptas* and *virtus*, especially in Alcmena's soliloquy (*Amphitryo* 633–53). This view runs counter to the virtual unanimity of critics who see the character of Alcmena as "noble, dignified and very sympathetic" (Costa 1965, 91, citing this very passage).

23. G. Williams (1958, 18, 22) is probably right to attribute these lines to Cleustrata; in any case, as Williams says, they are "a parody and reversal of some ritual instruction given to the bride by the *pronuba*."

24. Gratwick's text (1993).

25. Comedy includes a few glimpses of ideal wives. E.g., at the opening of Plautus's *Stichus*, the young sisters who miss their absent husbands refuse to allow their father to remarry them; and in Terence's *Andria*, Pamphilus praises the woman he loves as ideally suited to him (694–97).

26. Schuhmann 1977, 56–59, gathers some of the cases. Vivid examples include *Trinummus* 51–65, described by Duckworth (1952, 284) as "perhaps the *locus classicus* in Plautus for the attitude of husbands towards their wives"; *Miles* 679–80; and *Casina* 319–20.

27. In his isolation from the community, Periplectomenus resembles the antisocial misanthropes mentioned. This makes him ripe for restoration to a role proper to his age and dignity at the end of the play, by his assumption of responsibility for punishing the *miles gloriosus* for his adulterous designs on a married woman (discussed later in this chapter).

28. Plautus's emphasis on female extravagance may reflect the *lex Oppia sumptuaria* of 195. See Schuhmann 1977, 52; Konstan 1983, 44.

29. Konstan 1983, 33–46, esp. 41–43.

30. Konstan 1983, 43; see also Watson 1967, 2–6. We need to remember how the Roman dowry system operated, since there is nothing comparable in contemporary British/North American society, though it still exists in modern Greece. According to Gardner's helpful account (1986, 97–116), although there were evidently changes through time, it seems that at our period, the dowry was essentially a contribution to the running expenses of the husband's household. Technically it was part of the husband's property, but in effect he only had the temporary use of it, and he had a duty to

maintain its value, since the woman (or her father) had the right to recover all or most of it in the event of divorce, a right established in a celebrated legal case in 230 B.C. (so notes Gratwick [1993] on Plaut. *Men.* 766–67).

31. See Schuhmann 1977, esp. 53–55.

32. Cf. Gell. *N.A.* 17.6.8–10 for a paraphrase. I found these references in Gardner 1986, 72; see also 79 n. 16.

33. Gratwick's comment in his edition of Plautus's *Menaechmi* (1993, 29) suggests that he takes this view.

34. So argues Konstan (1983, 50).

35. What particularly galls Menaechmus is his wife's vigilant watch over his movements; see Segal 1987, 45–46. Comedy turns a virtue into a defect.

36. A wife's abuse of the power over the house keys was apparently a particularly Roman concern; see Schuhmann 1977, 61 n. 79.

37. Schuhmann 1977, 65; cf. Wiles 1989, 41.

38. See Gardner 1986, 79 n. 17.

39. Treggiari in Rawson 1991, 31. In what follows, I rely on the discussions of Corbier (1991), Treggiari (in Rawson 1991, esp. 46), and Gardner (1986, 81–95). The fullest account is that of Treggiari 1991, 435–82. Watson (1967, 29–31, 48–53) draws some important distinctions between *cum manu* and *sine manu* marriages. Rosenmeyer 1995, on the divorce formula in Plautus, includes a helpful bibliography.

40. Treggiari in Rawson 1991, 36.

41. Treggiari (in Rawson 1991, 45) has some fascinating snippets of comparative material from different centuries and places.

42. See Plut. *Rom.* 22.3, with Gardner 1986, 83. See also Scafuro's discussion of grounds for divorce (1997, 309–12).

43. Treggiari (in Rawson 1991, 38) uses the unspecific phrase "matrimonial offences."

44. See, e.g., Shelton 1998, 37.

45. One important point beyond the scope of this chapter is the extent to which the genre bending for which I argue here was anticipated in the Greek plays from which Plautus and Terence drew their raw material and inspiration; both Costas Panayotakis and David Wiles have urged this point to me strongly. I believe Plautus's plays reflect or respond to changes in Roman society, but I would not wish to deny that the anxieties addressed in them may have been just as relevant to the society that fostered Greek New Comedy. David Wiles (personal communication) is surely right to say that "the aesthetic basis of the *palliata* is to keep playing Rome off against Athens and refract the one through the other."

46. So notes E. Segal (1987, 171–91, esp. 188: "the only adultery that is consummated on the Roman stage in all of Roman comedy is in the *Amphitryo*"); however, Segal accommodates the play to his view of comedy and does not regard it as atypical (172). Bettini (1991, 44) remarks that "l'adulterio femminile" is "un tipo di tragressione cui non siamo affatto abituati," something of an understatement. Konstan (1994, 149) rightly says that "female adultery has no place in the genre."

47. See Scafuro 1997, 233, on *Bacchides*. Konstan (1994, 148–49) acutely connects these passages with the constraints on the expression of eros by a woman in New Comedy.

48. Sosia's reaction to this line, delivered in an aside (814), suggests that Amphitryo might well feel himself unmanned by his wife's infidelity.

49. On line 852, see Rosenmeyer 1995, 208 n. 21, referring to Treggiari 1991, 350–53. Scafuro (1997, 234–35) convincingly reads this as resort to a domestic tribunal.

50. The traditional formula was probably *tuas res tibi habeto*. Rosenmeyer (1995, 213–15) acutely points out that this formula was primarily intended for use by husbands, and she explores the ramifications of this in Alcmena's slight alteration in the formula from imperative to subjunctive.

51. This is discussed by Reynolds (1946) and McKeown (1979).

52. Hor. *Sat.* 1.2.127–34, 2.7.53–63; Juv. *Sat.* 6.44, 6.237–38, 8.196–97; Petr. *Satyr.* 97.1–99.4 (see Panayotakis 1995, 130–35); Apul. *Met.* 9.5–7, 22–29. See Panayotakis 1995, 132–33 n. 31.

53. Cf. Rosenmeyer 1995, 211 n. 28 (Rosenmeyer also observes that Alcmena's speech is dominated by tragic meters): "The fact that the *Amphitryo* comes closer than any other extant Plautine play to portraying divorce on stage further highlights the fine line it treads between two dramatic genres." To my mind, the treatment of adultery and divorce is more central to the play's tragicomic nature than Rosenmeyer seems to allow. It is hard to assess the significance of the evidence of the so-called *phlyax* vases, which include scenes from the Greek *phlyax* play, a type of farce prevalent in Magna Graecia around 300 B.C. and specializing in the parody of tragedy. One of these vases appears to show a dramatic staging of the story of Zeus enjoying his adulterous affair with Alcmena by climbing up a ladder to her window (see Bieber 1961, 129–46, esp. 132 and fig. 484).

54. Mücke 1987, 7. This presumably explains its prominence in Segal's analysis of Plautus (E. Segal 1987, 43–51).

55. Mücke (1987, 16) notices the play's uniqueness in this respect. We might also note that the marriage is childless and socially uneven: Menaechmus, a Syracusan, is married to an Epidamnian woman (cf. Gratwick 1993, 29–30).

56. See Schuhmann 1977, 59. Pace E. Segal (1987, 24), it is hard to see the violence of this vehement language as typical.

57. This scene reverses three other comic scenes where a father encourages his daughter to seek divorce and the daughter refuses; see Konstan 1994, 146 n. 14.

58. E. Segal 1987, 43–51. Leach (1969, esp. 30–34), drawing insightfully (31) upon Harry Levin's analysis of *The Comedy of Errors*, sees Menaechmus's twin as a manifestation of his brother's wish fulfillment.

59. If we press this comic denouement, the prospect for Menaechmus's wife is much worse than divorce: instead of being sent home to her father, she is to become a slave at auction. It is preferable, however, to see the sale of the wife as a farcical afterthought.

60. Gratwick (1993, 28–30) raises the intriguing possibility that Plautus has suppressed elements in the Greek original that account for the unhappiness of the husband—namely, that his marriage to his patron's daughter, a standard procedure in Greek practice, had been forced on him.

61. Of course, the use of a nonstandard setting is not unique; *Poenulus*, *Captivi*, and *Rudens* all take advantage of their non-Athenian settings.

62. As noted earlier (n. 45), I omit any consideration here of the extent to which Terence's experimentation might have been anticipated by his Greek model; the similarities in plot between the play and Menander's *Epitrepontes*, widely remarked in the secondary literature, offer a fruitful line of inquiry (see, e.g., Barsby 1999, 24).

63. See, e.g., Konstan 1983, 133; Barsby 1999, 23–26.

64. On the term *discidium*, see Treggiari 1991, 441: it can be used synonymously with *divortium* but is broader and can denote both temporary and permanent breakdowns in a variety of relationships.

65. So argues Konstan (1983, 140).

66. Ireland (1990, 9) rightly compares her to a deus ex machina.

67. See Konstan 1983, 140.

68. For a challenge to this view, see Parker 1996.

69. It looks as if Afranius's *Vopiscus*, in the *fabula togata* genre, does something similar, and the title of Atta's *Socrus* tends in the same direction, but it is impossible to tell how unusual this was. See Beare 1950, 123.

70. For Duckworth (1952, 148–49), *Hecyra* comes under the category of "innocent mistakes."

71. Bettini (1991) uses the play as his starting point for the exposition of his system of Plautine transformations.

72. Konstan (1994, 148–49) observes that it is not clear whether the soldier believes the woman to be divorced or not; if he thinks so, it softens the violation perceived by the audience.

73. See Scafuro 1997, 222. Scafuro also cites Plaut. *Curc.* 23–28 (*sic*: the crucial line is 30) and *Poen.* 862–63, along with Val. Max. 6.1.13.

74. Warren Smith suggests to me (in a personal communication) that it may be hard to regard this recantation as anything but a neat closural afterthought by Plautus, with an effect similar to that of a mock apology like that of the slaves at Plaut. *Stichus* 446–48 (see Segal 1987, 32).

75. This picture fits well with the contrast articulated by Charlton (1938, 277–78) between Shakespearian comedy, on the one hand, and classical comedy, on the other: because classical comedy is essentially conservative, it satirizes those who step out of line. (I owe this reference to Kiernan Ryan.)

This chapter has been delivered in various forms to the 1999 Classical Association at Liverpool and at the Institute for Classical Studies at the University of London, Yale University, the University of Minnesota, Columbia University, and Northwestern University. The responses of my audiences and of my friends and colleagues who have read the chapter in draft have improved it hugely. I am especially grateful to David Konstan, Nick Lowe, Costas Panayotakis, Patricia Rosenmeyer, Elizabeth Scharffenberger, Alison Sharrock, Warren Smith, David Wiles, and John Wilkins. Warren Smith has been a wonderful editor to work for, and I am grateful for his encouragement throughout. I also thank Maire Davies and Adam Morton. I am responsible for the shortcomings that doubtless remain.

Four

"The Cold Cares of Venus"

LUCRETIUS AND
ANTI-MARRIAGE LITERATURE

Warren S. Smith

SATIRIC TRADITION

The extraordinary attack on the passion of love that closes book 4 of Lucretius's *De rerum natura* (1158–287) seems, when read in its immediate context, a digression from the main theme of the book, which is an explanation of sensory perception. The function of the passage becomes clearer when we note that it actually arises naturally from its context and that "the theme of *simulacra* [viz., in dreams] provides a springboard for the whole attack on love."[1] Moreover, the appropriateness of the passage is enhanced by its structural and thematic parallels with many other parts of the poem, including the finales of several other books, notably books 3 (esp. 931–1094, on the fear of death) and 6 (1138–286, on the plague of Athens). It also has a kind of parallel in the controversial digression on the use of wild beasts in war from book 5 (1308–49). Each of these four passages is a sardonic demonstration of the disastrous consequences of the failure of people to follow the rational advice that the poet is impressing on the reader and of their choice to follow instead the voice of Superstition, from whose shackles Epicurus has supposedly freed humankind (1.62–65). Such passages are naturalistic glimpses of the poet's view of the world, the struggles and misery of people ruled by passion and unreason (cf. also 2.1—19), the reality of human behavior and human nature that keeps breaking in on and undercutting the masterly voice of the poet, who, especially in books 3 and 4, rebuts human folly with the anger of the satiric diatribe; indeed, at 3.931–63, the narrator, in a bold personification, is actually accompanied in his diatribe by the chiding voice of Nature herself, the incarnation of the very subject of the poem.

That passages in *De rerum natura* very disparate in subject should be demonstrably interconnected by language is a tribute to the highly vivid and original use of imagery in the poem. "In practice the wise man will not compose poems" was the dictum of Epicurus himself (Diog. Laert. 10.121), founded on a conviction that plain prose is the language that conveys truth. Some scholars have stood firm on the side of the evident convictions of Epicurus himself, making an antithesis between ideas and poetry and doubting whether it is possible to "see in the poet's imagery some clue to the larger meaning of the poem";[2] such readers take Lucretius at his own self-deprecatory word (*DRN* 1.926–50, 4.1–25) that his verse is no more than honey from the Muses, smeared on the rim of the philosophic cup to make it more palatable. In fact, we can go further and show how the poet, in a way surely not envisioned by the revered founder of his school, uses imagery to establish or reinforce connections between ideas in various parts of the poem. A careful reading of the attack on love in book 4 enables us to see how Lucretius uses the passage as one of several major stopping-off places on his survey of the irrational, using his poetry to interconnect love with other destructive forces that assault our minds and bodies, such as the hallucinations of dreams, the terrors of hell, the destructiveness of war, attacks by wild beasts, hunger and thirst, and physical disease. Each of these forces, ranging from the annoying to the deadly, daily assaults our privacy and keeps us from the peace of mind that lies open to us through the fearless reasoning of philosophy.

The Lucretian passage on love in *De rerum natura* also fits into—and is an important document in the establishment of—the tradition of the *dissuasio amoris*, such as exemplified by Ovid in *Remedia amoris* and Juvenal in *Satire* 6. Though registering a serious warning against human irrationality, a warning that integrates closely with the main theme of the poem, the passage is at the same time the most lighthearted of Lucretian asides, mixing in humor for its own sake in its presentation of a satiric scene of love-struck males. Kenney writes that "it was, it seems, Lucretius who first harnessed the power of satire and applied it to the systematic exposure of error, folly, and superstition."[3]

In his exposure of the folly of love, Lucretius stands in a long tradition that has antecedents in Hellenistic literature, such as New Comedy; yet the attack on love also shows its peculiarly Roman flavor in its amenity to Latin satire, including affinities with one of the pioneers of that genre, Lucilius.[4] The Lucretian warning against love is traditionally Hellenistic in including an attack on the financial extravagance of women (*DRN* 4.1121–41), which mirrors several attacks on marriage in New Comedy, where long diatribes against spending by wives seem to have delighted the audience;[5] at the same time, the anti-marriage theme evidently had native Italian antecedents as well, in several satires of Lucilius. Indeed, Lucretius's account of the disastrous results of the tyranny of a mistress constitutes a singularly unhumorous warning in the spirit of philosophical diatribe, which seems to involve disastrous consequences for both man and woman (*DRN* 4.1121–24).

Adde quod absumunt viris pereuntque labore,
Adde quod alterius sub nutu degitur aetas.
Labitur interea res et Babylonica fiunt,
Languent officia atque aegrotat fama vacillans.

[Add that they use up their vitality and perish of hard work, add that life is spent under the whim of another. Meanwhile property dissolves and turns into Babylonian coverlets, duties lie neglected, one's reputation totters and grows sick.]

Although the reconstruction of the themes of Lucilius's satires from the scanty surviving fragments is notoriously difficult, it is evident that his satires included attacks on luxury somewhat along the lines of his successors. In Lucilius 26.639–40, a man evidently speaks of his reasons for wanting to avoid marriage, speaking of "a wife, an unfaithful debauched household, a defiled home" and fearing the entrapment of some woman who wants to do him out of a goblet, a silver plate, a shawl, and an ivory-handled mirror.

The famous passage of Lucretius in which the infatuated lover makes up pet names to idealize the faults of his beloved (*DRN* 4.1151–70) seems to have a parallel in Lucilius 8.324–25, where the syntax is incomplete and unclear but may suggest an infatuate lover explaining away his sweetheart's too masculine slenderness by pointing to her charming personality.

Quod gracila est, pernix, quod pectore puro,
Quod puero similis.

[Because she is slender, swift; because she has a pure heart; because she is like a boy.]

The context is unknown and the syntax unclear, but a clue may come from Terence's *Eunuch* 314—the only other passage in Latin using the unusual and possibly ironic form *gracila*—where the discussion concerns girls of awkward appearance whose mothers are trying to find ways to improve them; Lucilius may be describing an attempt to find a positive side in the girl who is so slim as to be "like a boy." In his own passage, Lucretius adds to the humor and alienates the sweethearts from the reader by interjecting a series of translit-erated Greek names that the besotted lovers use to describe their women.[6] Lucilius 8.331 describes making love to a woman who is a schemer (*fictrix*), which parallels the ideas presented by Lucretius at *De rerum natura* 4.1185–91 (women hide their less desirable physical attributes) and 4.1278–87 (less desir-able women find a way to seduce men by their polished habits).

To that extent, Lucretius and Lucilius parallel each other. But the finan-cial and moral collapse of the lover as depicted in the Lucretian passage seems to have a tragic sense deeper than is found in early Latin satire or in Hellenis-tic warnings against marriage, such as Theophrastus's treatise *On Marriage* (as excerpted by Jerome in *Against Jovinian* 1.47) or the case against marriage made in New Comedy. Lucretius's satiric diatribe against love has some def-inite parallels with the more "tragic" sixth satire of Juvenal. In both Lucretius and Juvenal (*Sat.* 6.275–76), love blinds the man to the faults of his part-ner; and in both, the weakness of the man held fast in the power of love is deplored, while his need to take control over his own life is asserted. But there are important differences between the arguments of Lucretius and Juvenal. The great emphasis in Juvenal is the unnatural seizing of power by women who have silenced their male partners and made them helpless, no match for the aggressiveness of their wives. The issue in Lucretius is the power of pas-sion itself, which blinds men to reality, rages out of control, and leads to the death of reason.

The men in Lucretius are empowered with the secret to stay free of the unwanted consequences of passion: avoid entangling relationships; avoid love (*DRN* 4.1073–76); the pleasures of sex will still be available. It is not entirely up to the men, however; if women were completely passive, the poet's strat-egy might have a good chance of success, but women as well are motivated by the passion of love (*nec mulier semper ficto suspirat amore* [It is not always pretended love that makes a woman sigh], 4.1192), and even an unattractive woman can set her sights on a man and accustom him to live with her (4.1278–82). Many commentators seek to find an optimistic tone to the finale of book 4, in which some men finally succumb to the power of love;[7] but such a reading of the passage is unconvincing. The final lines report the triumph of love, which has already been exposed as a great evil, full of troubles even when it is successful (4.1141–42); but at the end of the book, thanks to the designs of a determined woman, love makes its way into a man's heart like a torture treatment by the constant pounding of small blows or the dripping of water (4.1283–87). The image of the dripping water hollowing out a rock has a positive connotation in a parallel passage in Ovid, where it describes the persistence of a male lover who is eventually rewarded when the woman gives in (AA 1.475–76). Lucretius, who, like Ovid, is speaking from the perspective of the man, is depicting the reverse situation, the success of the woman who is trying to win over the reluctant man, with whom the male reader identifies and sympathizes. More important, in Lucretius, such verbs as *tunditur*, *vincitur*, and *labascit* suggest the moral and spiritual collapse of a man who is unable to resist the stratagems of a woman, even of uglier shape. The verb *tundo* is used in *De rerum natura* 4.934, where it describes the assault on men's bodies by blows of air, from which men must be protected by their skin; compare also the weakening and tottering of the *anima* by fear in 3.154–60, resulting in the victim's faltering and final physical collapse.[8]

LOVE AND DREAMS

On one level, as I have argued, the attack on love in Lucretius's *De rerum natura* 4 fits into the tradition of satiric attack on the foolish behavior of lovers and the excesses of women. But for the philosopher, a more serious point is close at hand. The world of superstition, which causes countless evils and once terrorized humankind, is the tyrant against whom mankind is asked to revolt, *tantum religio potuit suadere malorum* [so vast is the evil that superstition has persuaded us to do] (1.101). But this tyrant over human minds can have more than one shape. The superstitious world has a paradigm in the world of dreams that assails us at night, as analyzed in 4.962ff. Lucretius forces the connection between the two concepts on us by using the same word for dreams, *somnia*, to describe the vain imaginings of superstition that undercut reason: *somnia quae vitae rationes vertere possint* (1.105).[9] These hallucinations of superstition include the fear of torture after death, with which priests and poets terrorize us, because we fail to see that there is a limit (*finem*, 1.107) to our troubles on earth. Dreams also haunt and do harm to the man who is guilty of a crime, since they may prompt the hitherto undetected criminal, rendered helpless in sleep, to blurt out a confession that will be overheard by the authorities (5.1158–60). It was also through dreams that men had their first visions of the gods (5.1169–82), visions that proved to be the beginning of human unhappiness (*o genus infelix humanum*, 5.1194), once humans began to ascribe great powers to these deities and to worship them.

The discussion of dreams that Lucretius introduces into book 4 is in turn a prelude to the account of the lover, the man held in the grip of passion. The association comes from an explanation of the *simulacra* that fly abroad at night and can bring about hallucinations of attack by a panther or lion (5.1015–17), of death or falling (1020–24), of thirst (1024–25), of urination (1026–29), and, finally, of sexual arousal and ejaculation in a young man when he dreams of beautiful bodies (4.1030–36). Lucretius tends to associate dreams with "obsessive effort or emotion"[10] and thus naturally associates them with the act of love. After discussing dreams, he moves to the nature of sexual arousal (4.1037–57) and finally to a full-blown attack on the folly of love (4.1058ff.). Love is a natural enough association in Lucretius in close context with a discussion of sleep and dreams, which in turn introduces the topic of thirst and animal attacks. In 1.34 Mars himself had been shown helpless and overcome by love while lying in Venus's embrace; the lover, as is obvious from his ludicrous behavior, is cowed and controlled by a force he cannot understand, as though he were, like his unfortunate ancestors, still trembling under the vain threat of divine punishment. Sexual appetite, because of its insatiability, is indeed the "most formidable enemy of the Epicurean,"[11] and Venus mocks us with images as we constantly strive to fill an insatiable desire (4.1101).

The incompatibility of dreams and reason is a literary and philosophical commonplace,[12] and in this poem the concept is implied as early as 1.104–5, where the frightening warnings uttered by prophets are said to include the *somnia* that may overthrow *verae rationes*. Our perception of the beloved's body consists in a film of fine atoms that is continually thrown off from it. These atoms produce images for which the Greek word is εἴδωλον; Lucretius characteristically renders this word as *simulacrum* but also uses such variants as *imago, effigies,* and *figura,* as Sedley has shown.[13] The phenomenon of *simulacra* of the beloved—experienced either when awake or in the form of dreams—is responsible for the production of love but also leads to the dissatisfaction that is bound to result from it. We can absorb food and drink into our bodies, but our possession of the beloved's body never goes beneath the surface (4.1094–96).

> Ex hominis vero facie pulchroque colore
> Nil datur in corpus praeter simulacra fruendum
> Tenuia: quae vento spes raptast saepe misella.
>
> [*But out of the appearance and fair complexion of a human being nothing is granted [to come] into the body except the enjoyment of fine images: and this wretched little hope is often snatched away by the wind.*]

Sexual desire may be kept under control if its true function as "merely a state of physical disequilibrium awaiting correction, just like hunger or thirst,"[14] is recognized, but we allow it to get far beyond that and to pass over into a state of hallucination, a kind of obsessive madness. All our passion is an illusion threatening to seize control of us, truly on the level of a dream or of the fruits of Tantalus, who, in a detail of his myth (not mentioned by Lucretius), snatches at fruits above his head that the winds continually blow away. Thus we consume our lives in the pursuit of dreams as Venus mocks us with images of the beloved (*simulacris ludit amantis*, 4.1101).

TORTURES OF HELL AND
ASSAULTS BY WILD BEASTS

Lucretius includes in *De rerum natura* the theme of the control of passion over our lives, in the explanation in book 2 of the mythological tortures of hell as an allegory corresponding to the mental and emotional tortures present in the real world. Already in the first prologue to book 1, however, the picture of Mars lying helpless in the embraces of Venus, ready to do her bidding, is used as a clear testimony to the powers of love (32–40), though love there exercises a positive power in bringing about peace. There is no redeeming side effect to the passion that eats away at our insides, like the ghostly vultures haranguing Tityos (3.984–94).

Nec Tityon volucres ineunt Acherunte iacentem
Nec quod sub magno scrutentur pectore quicquam
Perpetuam aetatem possunt reperire profecto.
Quamlibet immani proiectu corporis exstet,
Qui non sola novem dispessis iugera membris
Obtineat, sed qui terrai totius orbem,
Non tamen aeternum poterit perferre dolorem
Nec praebere cibum proprio de corpore semper.
Sed Tityos nobis hic est, in amore iacentem
Quem volucres lacerant atque exest anxius angor
Aut alia quavis scindunt cuppedine curae.

[Nor do winged creatures assault Tityon lying in Acheron, nor surely can they find anything to dig for in that great breast for all eternity. Let him lie forth with no matter how vast an extent of body, let him be assigned not only nine acres for his limbs to stretch out but the globe of the entire earth. Still, he will not be able to bear pain for all time or always provide food from his

own body. But Tityos is here with us, [he] whom, lying in love, the winged
creatures wound, and painful anguish eats him away, or cares split him apart
by some other passion.]

In the "allegorical interpretation" of the eating away of Tityos's liver
by "winged creatures" as the figurative equivalent to someone writhing in
the grip of love, the physicality of the scene becomes not so much more
hypothetical and metaphorical as more real, more immediate: a creature,
no matter how huge, could not supply matter out of his liver forever for the
birds to eat, but a man "lying in love"—that is, tossing and turning on his
bed with passion—can indeed go on indefinitely being tortured by passion.
The *cura* and *dolor* that accompany love, singled out again in 4.1067, can
indeed create an internal wound that will only grow as it is nourished
(4.1068–69).

> Ulcus enim vivescit et inveterascit alendo
> Inque dies gliscit furor atque aerumna gravescit . . .

> *[For the wound comes alive and becomes chronic by feeding, and day after*
> *day the madness grows and the trouble weighs you down . . .]*

These passages underline Lucretius's warning against the passions of love
as an internal cancer that is exacerbated by the eating away by "winged creatures"—vultures in the case of Tityos, but in the comparison, probably Cupids,
loves that flit about us. Thus we are assaulted by love inwardly and outwardly.[15]

Wild beasts of various kinds, including vultures, wild boars, and especially
lions, are prominently featured in *De rerum natura*, notably in book 5 in the
accounts of primitive man, but elsewhere as well. They are either taken from
myth or seen as real terrors, obstacles to human progress. To Lucretius, who
is "an inveterate anthropomorphizer, writing about the phenomena of nature
in living human terms,"[16] the beasts are invariably used as primitive forces
pitted against the rational will of humankind; more specifically, they are powerful symbols for the poet of raw, irrational power out of control, usually working against the positive forces of civilization. Philosophers often associate
animals such as bulls, boars, serpents, and lions with pure, raw, unbridled feeling; thus Seneca, for example, quite naturally takes his examples of rage in
De ira (1.1.5) from the animal world.

> Non vides ut omnium animalium, simul ad nocendum insur-
> rexerunt, praecurrant notae et tota corpora solitum quietumque

egrediantur habitum et feritatem suam exasperent? Spumant apris
ora, dentes acuuntur adtritu, taurorum cornua iactantur in
vacuum . . .

*[Don't you see how in the case of all animals, signs give a warning that
they are rising up to do harm, their whole bodies depart from their usual rest
and they increase their own fierceness? Boars foam from the mouth, they
sharpen their tusks by rubbing, bulls toss their horns in the air . . .]*

And yet, Seneca adds, animals lack reason (1.3.3–4), so their hostile behavior can be ascribed to impulse, madness, wildness, or attack, but not to *ira*,
which requires a rational process—a desire to exact revenge—and so is found
only in humans. Thus the aggressive animal becomes an example of violent
but purposeless raging, of pure undirected feeling.

The uselessness of aggressive beasts and even the threat they pose to human
prosperity are taken for granted in Lucretius. In *De rerum natura* 5.218–19, the
mere existence and nurturing of the "awful tribe of wild beasts, enemies of the
human race," is included in a list of reasons that the universe cannot have been
made for us by divine power, and in 5.870 their destructiveness is contrasted
with the "usefulness" of domestic beasts.[17] The "winged creatures" that assaulted
Tityos were an example of such an animal symbol of destructiveness; another
mythological rationalization occurs in book 5, where the labors of Hercules
(5.22–54) against various monsters are disparaged as being incomplete and
having only limited effect, since many animals still endanger us as they roam
throughout the world (5.39–42). As before, the myth has really been introduced mainly to serve the poet's intention to introduce a warning related to
the corrosive effects of lust, in which the anxious man is split apart by sharp
desires, cares, and fears (5.43–46), along with a host of other needless troubles.
In 3.295–97 lions are taken as prime examples of creatures who "boil up in
wrath," ready to "burst their breasts with roaring" (cf. 3.741–42). In 6.194–203
the winds imprisoned in clouds are compared with wild animals imprisoned in
cages, pacing up and down and roaring to get out, until the winds shatter the
clouds and send forth flashing lightning, thus indicating the ability of the beasts
to escape and overpower the civilizing forces of society.[18]

The picture of primitive mankind in book 5 includes a vivid picture of an
attack by wild beasts on early humans as they cowered in their caves (982–87).

Sed magis illud erat curae, quod saecla ferarum
Infestam miseris faciebant saepe quietem.
Eiectique domo fugiebant saxea tecta

Spumigeri suis adventu validique leonis
Atque intempesta cedebant nocte paventes
Hospitibus saevis instrata cubilia fronde.

[No, they had more of a concern because the generations of beasts often made rest dangerous for those wretches. Cast out of doors, they fled from their rocky shelters at the arrival of a foaming boar or a powerful lion, and trembling in the dead of night, they surrendered to the cruel guests their resting places lined with foliage.]

The attack by savage predators on the unsuspecting cave people in the dead of night sounds like a nightmare version, suddenly become all too real, of the *curae* and vain worries that disturb their rest as they toss on their beds (1.104–6, 133–35); life may be "one long struggle in the dark" (2.54), but normally its terrors can be driven away by the clear light of reason. The assault by wild animals on unsuspecting primitive humans is also a symbolic reminder that the dangers of the dark can be too great for human reason alone to combat.

The attack by the animals is described in hair-raising language that recycles some of the violent phrases in book 4 about the deleterious effects of passion on the lover (4.1119–20).

Nec reperire malum id possunt quae machina vincat:
Usque adeo incerti tabescunt vulnere caeco.

[Nor can they find any device to overcome this evil; so continuously do they waste away in doubt, stricken by an unknown wound.]

So in the case of the victims of the animal attacks, the ripping out of the primitive man's intestines recalls the assault on Tityos, the old figure from myth, by winged creatures, introduced as part of the comparison between his condition and the torments of a lover. At the same time, primitive man's desperate rushing from the cave while "stretching his shaking hands over the awful open wounds" (5.995–96) and his ignorance of how to treat the deadly wounds (like the lover's inability to cure his own passion), makes them even more horrifying by its emphasis on the victim's helplessness (5.998–99).

Donec eos vita privarant vermina saeva
Expertis opis, ignaros quid vulnera vellent.

[Until the cruel torments separated them from life, bereft of any aid, not knowing what wounds wanted]

"The penetrability of our bodily boundaries"[19] makes us very open to assault.

The passage in book 5 about the unsuccessful attempt to yoke wild beasts to chariots in war puts us in the midst of a pitiful and hopeless attempt to tame the wild and unmanageable (1308–14, 1322).

> Temptarunt etiam tauros in moenere belli
> Expertique sues saevos sunt mittere in hostis.
> Et validos partim prae se misere leones
> Cum doctoribus armatis saevisque magistris
> Qui moderarier his possent vinclisque tenere,
> Nequiquam, quoniam permixta caede calentes
> Turbabant saevi nullo discrimine turmas.
> . . . .
> Morsibus adfixae validis atque unguibus uncis.
>
> *[They even tried out bulls in the service of war, and attempted to send savage boars against the enemy. And sometimes they sent strong lions in advance with armed trainers and savage teachers who could govern them and hold them back by chains, in vain, since warmed in the midst of bloodshed, they broke up the squadrons without any distinction, . . . fastening on them with strong bites and powerful claws.]*

The nightmare scene of the supposedly tamed beasts raging out of control in the heat of battle takes us back to the plight of the lovers in book 4 (1073ff.) who, at the very moment of gaining possession of their love, harm the bodies of their partners—frantically, in the midst of their *rabies* (1083), assaulting them with bites as if they wanted to rip some part off the other's body or absorb themselves into it totally. The lover has himself become a wild beast, unable, like the lions, to control himself or his actions by curbs, because madness lies at the heart of his action; *rabies* and *rabidus* are most often used in Latin of animals and are always so used by Lucretius except for their application to the lovemaking of humans in 4.1083 and 1117. The analogy with the wild beasts continues at 4.1121–40 as the lover tries to satisfy his partner by turning all his wealth into luxurious jewelry and silks and holding lavish banquets, "but all in vain, since from the midst of the fountain of charms rises up something bitter to choke him even among flowers, as when his own conscience chances to bite back on him." The depth and subtlety of the psychology here are striking. The attempt to indulge the affair to the point of mad spending causes a guilty reaction that chokes and bites back on him like a wild beast that he has attempted to control.

In 2.604–5 Lucretius reports that the Greeks depicted the Great Mother with wild beasts yoked to her chariot, but he quickly reminds us that this is a pleasant fantasy that can have no place in reality (2.644–45), since the gods live remote from earthly affairs. Similarly, in the case of the experiments by primitive men, having once asserted them, Lucretius himself, who, it has been suggested, was influenced in his strange vision by the spectacle of *venationes* he had witnessed in the arena,[20] expresses a doubt that the harnessing of wild beasts to chariots ever really happened in this world (5.1341–46). This may suggest that the poet is not indulging in personal speculation but refuting the theory of a rival philosopher.[21] In any case, he has included the passage despite its dubious historical value, using the insane chariot harnessing of dangerous animals to make the wider moral point about the inevitable spread of the violent and irrational and the self-destructive consequences of unleashing the wild beasts that attack their own masters. There is also a parallel here with his earlier doubts that there is really a Tityos or Tantalus incessantly being tortured in the lower world; but the tortures of those who are held in the grip of love are real and intense enough to compensate for the unreality of the myths.

MILITARY ANALOGY

In the passage of *De rerum natura* beginning at 4.1045, the assault on the body adopts a new set of metaphors, no longer the eating away of the body by predatory birds, but a military assault in which the two lovers seem to engage each other on the battlefield. In 1049–57 the attraction one feels toward a beautiful body is compared with falling toward a wound; the blood spurts out in the direction of the blow from the shafts of Venus that has struck us (*unde icimur ictu*, 1050). This shocking image prepares us to receive the onslaught of love with the fear we might have from an assault of the enemy. Every lover is a warrior, as in Ovid's famous phrase *Militat omnis amans* (Amores 1.9.1), though in Ovid's more logically balanced poetic conceit, the amatory "enemy" is the husband when he is incapacitated by sleep (1.9.25–26). When Lucretius uses military metaphors to describe lovemaking, he is interested not so much in tactics as in raw hand-to-hand combat; his overall intention is strongly suggested by his account of the mating of horses (5.1073–77), when the stallion "rages, struck by the spurs of winged Love," and rushes out, snorting, to battle (*ad arma*), not to confront an enemy or rival, but to mate with the mares.

Like horses, like humans—in the heat of passion, a man desires to toss his bodily moisture (*iactans . . . amorem*, 1054; and, with a play on words, *iacere umorem*, 1056) toward the body that is the source of his arousal. Yet what has precipitated this attack is a phantom, the *simulacra*, or filmy images, that have been tossed at us from the other person or that remain present in the mind (*praesto simulacra tamen sunt*, 1061), haunting us, long after the departure of the beloved. Such an image is an illusion, like the *somnia* (vain fears) at 3.1048 that tempt us to imagine and dread the supposed evil of death.

The person so sexually aroused imagines that his *cupido* is the precursor of *voluptas*, the ultimate Epicurean goal (4.1057). But Lucretius remains ambivalent about *voluptas* and has no patience with the greed that accompanies it, a greed that causes us to ever crave new pleasures and cling to life as he had already concluded in book 3 (1076–81). It is likely also that his view of lovemaking as a wild, uncontrolled activity bordering on violence would cause it to seem, in his view, incompatible with the peaceful seclusion that is the goal of the Epicurean.

The military paragraph (4.1037–57) about the nature of lovemaking as an assault leads into the satiric passage that openly attacks the passion of love (4.1058).

Haec Venus est nobis; hinc autemst nomen amoris . . .

[This is our Venus, and this is the name we give to love . . .]

The line has a double meaning: here, it says, is where Amor—that is, Cupido—gets his name (desire leads to love); but also, here is what we call love (giving a noble name to a passion that will lead to nothing but pain). Lucretius strips away the myth to reveal its hidden meaning "for us," using language that recalls the explanation of the tortures of hell in book 3 (*sed Tityos nobis hic est*, 3.992).[22] The goddess of book 1 could pacify the god of war, who lies helpless in her bosom, "overcome by the eternal wound of love," though even this gentle scene, as the quoted phrases show, is the aftermath of a military victory. In book 4 we get a clearer idea of how Venus scores her victories, since she has become a more aggressive goddess, one who uses her consort's weapons (*Veneris . . . telis*, 1052) and under whose control lust itself is turned into an assertive weapon, transformed into "love" that causes pain and heartache. In fact, this complex contradictory nature of Venus is well established in love poetry as part of a tradition that Lucretius's double portrait is only reflecting (cf. Horace *Ode* 1.19.1 [*mater saeva Cupidinum*] and 4.1–2, where the poet begs Venus to stop stirring up wars for him). Venus and her unruly son, even when they are seen as peaceful, always have an imperious side that demands nothing less than total submission ("I am your new booty, Cupid, and stretch out my conquered hands, submissive to your laws," Ovid *Amores* 1.2.19–20).

Though he does not invent this destructive Venus, Lucretius is determined to take away her power by exposing her, by driving out her aggressive persona that gets a grip on its victims. "This is our Venus" implies that we have sunk to the level of a sham love, of which the fruit is *cura* rather than *lepor*. Though longing to cast off bodily fluid (*iacere umorem collectum*, 4.1065), we find that a drop of Venus's sweetness has trickled into our heart, leading to cold care (*successit frigida cura*, 1060).[23] As is appropriate in a context dealing with the visions of dreams as images that bombard us from without, the image of the beloved becomes implanted in our heart, and her name rings in our ears. The lover must begin to fight back by removing himself from the images and the food of love (*sed fugitare debet simulacra*, 1063)—a concept picked up by Ovid in *Remedia amoris* (*ante oculos facies stabit . . .* , 583–84). The lover is encouraged not to fight against the sexual urge itself but to indulge it by divorcing it from love; cast the seed into some other body than the beloved, any one (*DRN* 4.1065). The idea of a sexual surrogate to avoid romantic entanglement is an old one. The orator Lysias, in the speech attributed to him in Plato's *Phaedrus* (231–34), pleads for the advantage of a nonlover over a lover as a sexual object; Archilochus turns to Neobule's sister when he was rejected by Neobule, whom he loved (see, further, Horace *Serm.* 1.2.116–116; Ovid *Rem. amor.* 401).

Part of what Lucretius finds so dismaying—so symptomatic of *rabies* (4.1083)—about the sex act is that it is not easy to assign lovemaking to a specific conscious motive; it seems to lack a purposeful goal. It is clear that the lover desires the beloved, but because of the wild and uncontrolled nature of the sex act, exactly what he wants from her is not so easy to define (1077).

Fluctuat incertis erroribus ardor amantium . . .

[The lovers' passion ebbs and flows doubtfully here and there . . .]

Violence, rather than kindness, seems to be included in the act and perhaps even to serve as the very basis for it. Hence the poet seeks to probe the meaning and psychology of his own metaphors. The lover bites his partner; he seems to want to wound or even rip off bits of flesh from the body of his beloved (*dentis inlidunt*, 1080). Thus the act of lovemaking involves the boundary violation and threat of invasion and mutilation that the poem repeatedly associates with the attacks of wild beasts and with death itself, the ultimate boundary violation.[24] But we cannot actually enter completely inside the body of our partner, if that is what we really want—like the frustrated lovers described by the fictional Aristophanes in Plato's *Symposium* (192–93) who want to merge with the creatures who once formed their other halves.

SICKNESS OF MIND AND BODY

A Traditional Image

It is an old tradition, going back to Sappho, that compares falling in love to the onset of a disease. In a well-known poem (frag. 31 Lobel-Page), Sappho lists a series of symptoms including heart palpitations, near blindness, aphasia, a broken tongue, a burning in the limbs, roaring in the ears, sweat, shivers, paleness, and a near-death experience. Catullus's imitation of Sappho in his poem 51, in which the narrator falls in love with Lesbia, repeats many of these symptoms and adds a lament that the sufferer is being destroyed by *otium*. Lucretius himself seems to imitate the Sappho passage, not in the discussion of love, but in an explanation (*DRN* 3.154–60) of how the *anima* can be thrown into turmoil by extreme fear (with symptoms including sweat, paleness, a broken tongue, blindness, and deafness). The description of the onset of love in *De rerum natura* 4.1068–69 is similar but more general.

> Ulcus enim vivescit et inveterascit alendo,
> Inque dies gliscit furor atque aerumna gravescit . . .
>
> [*the open sore quickens and grows habitual by feeding, day after day the madness grows and the sickness grows heavier . . .]*

Here the open sore takes us back to Tityos and his liver, while the addition of *furor* shows that the disease is of both mind and body.

One of the most powerful weapons working to the advantage of love in our struggle against it is that once we are vanquished by it, all is lost; when allowed to catch hold, it will recur incessantly. It is possible to get relief from hunger and thirst, but after the act of love, there is only a short pause before the *rabies* and *furor* are back (4.1116–17).

> Parva fit ardoris violenti pausa parumper
> Inde rediit rabies eadem et furor ille revisit . . .
>
> [*There is a pause in the violent passion for a while, then the same madness and passion pay a return visit . . .]*

No remedy can be found to lessen the inexplicable disease of lovers (1120).

> Usque adeo incerti tabescunt volnere caeco.
>
> [*So constantly do they waste away, in doubt about their unknown wound.]*

The lovers are suffering from a gangrenous condition that anticipates the plight of the victimized cavemen in 5.983ff., who lie huddled and groaning in their dwellings, holding their hands over their wounds after the beasts have ripped apart their bellies, with no clue about how to help themselves (*expertis opis*, 998).

Thus, falling in love involves an *ardor* that easily shades over into *rabies* and *furor*. The connection between these terms becomes a commonplace in Latin literature and almost inevitably suggests tragic themes—as, for example, in Juvenal's *Satire* 6.647–51, where the point is made that the passion of tragic heroines wipes out their reason and is even a mitigating circumstance for their crimes. This is consistent with the Stoic slant of Senecan tragedy, where the combination of madness and passion results in the bloody crimes of a Medea or Phaedra (e.g., *Medea* 157; *Phaedra* 112). In general in Latin literature (e.g., in love poetry or epic), *furor* is more often associated with female passion than male (cf. Ovid *AA* 1.341–43; Virgil *Aen.* 4.101; Proper. 1.13.20). In Lucretius, with his emphasis on men's responsibility for their own behavior, there is a different slant: it is the men, not their partners, who are possessed by *furor* and bring the consequent troubles on themselves. As he ends a love affair, the man stands appalled as the consequences of his action unfold before him: he sees his cash converted into fine clothing and jewelry (4.1123, 1125–30), is forced to live under the domination of a mistress (1122), and ends up consumed with a nameless sense of unhappiness that eats away at him (*remordet*, 1135) and finally drives him to such paranoia that he is suspicious even at the suggestion of a smile on his lover's face (the word *risus* ironically closes the paragraph, at line 1140).

Thirst

The Epicureans, keenly aware that the exaltation of pleasure as the highest goal would have a tendency to mislead, tried hard to counteract their reputation as mere voluptuaries by emphasizing the need to keep sexual desire under control; the great achievement by Epicurus, as described in *De rerum natura* 6.25, is to put a limit on desire and fear (*et finem statuit cuppedinis atque timoris*). We see this slant in the pro-Epicurean argument devised by Lucretius's contemporary Cicero in the first book of *De finibus*. Torquatus, Cicero's Epicurean interlocutor, is allowed (despite Cicero's own aversion to Epicurean ethics) to make an eloquent defense of Epicurus's understanding of pleasure as the absence of pain. *Cupiditates enim sunt insatiabiles* [Indeed the desires are incapable of satisfaction], Torquatus argues (1.13.43), and they are capable of destroying either an individual or a whole country. The foolish man who puts no check on his desires will inevitably discover the frustration of all his aspirations.[25] Lucretius, as much concerned with presenting a vividly satiric picture as with arguing a point, focuses primarily on the illusion and self-deception of the sex drive. Rather than attaining satisfaction, the lover finds his desire further inflamed through the sex act.

Thus too much thirst is poetically equated with greed and unnatural longing. For example, in *De rerum natura* 3.1082–84, the greedy clinging to life and constant search for new pleasures is compared with "a constant thirst for life with mouth forever agape." Lines 867–76 of book 4 have already explained the psychology of hunger and thirst in very Epicurean—that is, immediate and physical—terms: hunger requires the propping up or reparation of a building that has fallen into disrepair, and thirst requires the quenching of heat—indeed, the putting out of a fire—inside our bodies (871–73).[26]

> Glomerataque multa vaporis
> Dissupat adveniens liquor ac restinguit ut ignem,
> Urere ne possit calor amplius aridus artus.

> [*The many bodies of heat that have gathered together, confronting our stomach with a bonfire, are broken up by the arrival of liquid that quenches them like a fire.*]

From this, the step to the fires of love soon after in the same book is a short one, creating a natural association between physical thirst and lustful desire. The flame of love creates a great thirst that continually returns, unquenchable (1097–102).

> Ut bibere in somnis sitiens cum quaerit et umor
> Non datur, ardorem qui membris stinguere possit,
> Sed laticum simulacra petit frustraque laborat
> In medioque sitit torrenti flumine potans,
> Sic in amore Venus simulacris ludit amantis
> Nec satiare queunt spectando corpora coram . . .

> [*Like a thirsty man when he wants to drink in a dream and moisture is not supplied to enable him to put out the heat in his limbs, but he chases after images of water and struggles in vain and thirsts while he drinks in the middle of a roaring river, thus in love Venus plays with the images of the lover, and they can't be satisfied by gazing on the nearby body . . .*]

As before, there are affinities here with the satiric tradition. It is natural enough for a satirist like Horace to speak of a man in the grips of love as being wracked by thirst (*Serm.* 1.2.114–15), and as a good Epicurean, he points out that a thirsty man has no need to drink out of a golden cup; that is, he should not seek an affair, such as with a married woman, which will have unpleasant consequences. Finally, in the long account of the Athenian plague in book 6, it is significant that unquenchable thirst is a telling sign of the disease, which causes victims to hurl themselves into rivers and fountains (1172–77).

The Plague

Clearly the account of the plague in *De rerum natura* 6—in the longest descriptive passage of the poem, coming at its climax and ending abruptly—pulls together many of the themes from the poem about human folly, and out-of-control disease is (as I have already argued) an appropriate symbol for human lust. Torquatus, for example, Cicero's Epicurean defender, makes the connection between lust and disease explicit: *Animi enim morbi sunt cupiditates immensae et inanes divitiarum, gloriae, dominationis, libidinosarum etiam voluptatum* [Vast and empty desires for riches, glory, power, as well as [desires for] sensuous pleasures, are diseases of the mind] (*De finibus* 1.18.59). The image carries over into satire, where the childish behavior of lovers is often compared with sickness. Thus in Horace's *Sermones* 2.3.247–64, the childish behavior of grown men who fall in love and, in particular, the indecision of the *exclusus amator* are likened to madness. As an example of a satire that, like the depiction of the plague in Lucretius's sixth book, climaxes in the death of a satiric foil to score a moral point, the third satire of Persius includes the picture of an overindulgent man who ignores his doctor's advice and falls dead of a stroke in the baths (cf. Lucretius's warning at *DRN* 6.799–801); when Persius's narrator denies that this example applies to him (3.107–9), he is reminded (with an easy transition from physical sickness—itself brought on by overindulgence—to moral degeneration) that his own heart palpitations, brought on by the sight of money or a pretty girl, are a likely sign of incipient madness.

The attack of the plague is already anticipated after Lucretius, by the end of book 5, has moved humankind forward to its flourishing in the very summit of civilization (5.1457), presumably alluding to the achievements of classical Athens. At the start of book 6, these same enlightened Athenians, now specifically named (6.2), provide support to suffering humankind (*mortalibus aegris*); but later in book 6, the Athenians will be laid low by the plague. The description of the plague has been imitated in part from Thucydides' *Peloponnesian War* (but exaggerates and expands on Thucydides' version of the

Athenians' moral degeneration in time of crisis),[27] and it is often pointed out that Lucretius describes an affliction that devastated the city before the birth of Epicurus, who might have been able to help combat the plague by giving the citizens mental enlightenment (such as is summarized in 6.9–42). This interpretation is weakened, however, by Lucretius's failure even to mention, let alone emphasize, the pre-Epicurean setting for the plague; he simply introduces it as having happened "once" [quondam] (1138). Nor is it clear how the teaching of Epicurus, which, according to 6.11, presupposed that life had been established securely for mortals, would have assuaged the suffering of the plague victims. Critics doubt whether the lengthy account of the plague as it stands is an appropriate ending for the poem, and many think that Lucretius, had he lived, would have revised it. Among those who are convinced that a revision was intended, Dalzell argues that the plague "knows no cure" and that human remedies, including medicine, are helpless before it; thus "it would be a strange point on which to conclude a poem which proclaims the victory of man over fear and circumstance."[28] Likewise, Sedley, in his recent study, is convinced that "Lucretius must have intended to rework the plague passage and to make its moral explicit." I do not find such logic compelling. Sedley contrasts the horrors of Lucretius's description with Epicurus's own cheerful optimism in the face of his painful death, but his argument seems incomplete; Sedley offers no parallels from De rerum natura itself as evidence of any Lucretian tendency to close such passages with "philosophical serenity."[29] On the other side, Minadeo cites the ending of the poem as befitting the essence of a nature that, in Lucretius, is "raw, wild, full of violent motion and furious change," and he cites, as a parallel in miniature with the De rerum natura, Ode 1.4 of that other great Epicurean poet Horace—an ode that "begins with references to Spring and Venus and ends with moral reflections on the inevitability of death."[30] W. R. Johnson finds the ending grimly helpful, with a message unaffected by the dating of the plague before the lifetime of Epicurus. He writes that "the truth of Epicurus cannot save us—nothing can—from the truth of our mortality," but he maintains that "if we can learn to ponder the truth in its most dreadful aspect," we may have learned what Lucretius is really saying to us.[31]

The other masterpiece among Latin epic poetry, the Aeneid, also ends negatively, with a violent death, the murder of Turnus by Aeneas—"clos[ing] the Aeneid with a feeling of sorrow and bewilderment, as the emphasis centres not on the triumphs of Aeneas but on the tragedy of Turnus' death."[32] It seems to me an evasion of the gloom of that ending to speculate that Virgil might have changed it if he had been given time to make final revisions in his poem. In the case of Lucretius, we find that the plague at the end of the poem is used almost surrealistically, as the symbol of the sweeping away of reason, of moral calamity in any age; it is a touch paralleled in satire by the indulgent man's stroke at the end of Persius 3 (explicitly meant as a symbol for his moral degeneration) or by the shipwreck of the unenlightened man that we watch from afar in *De rerum natura* 2.1–2. Most important, the somber endings of Lucretius's books 2 (decay of the world), 3 (triumph of death and of human anxiety), and 4 (triumph of love despite attempts to overcome it), which offer no such uplifting moral principle, hardly support the theory that Lucretius would have found a way to counteract the negativism of the plague description in book 6.

The plague, described like an army, is a foreign invader, arising deep within Egypt and making an assault on the people of Athens (*DRN* 6.1141–43).[33] The poet lists symptoms of burning heat (1167–69) that accompany the plague, internal wounds and wasting away of bodies (1200–1202), and the uselessness of religion—all the holy shrines of the gods are piled high with corpses (1272). Elsewhere in the poem, such afflictions had been most characteristic of fear of death, greed in acquisition of possessions, and assault by lust. The mental anguish—the mental sorrow and fear—that accompanied the plague is also like that of the lover (*anxius angor* [the anxious dread], 1158; *perturbata animi mens in maerore metuque* [the mind was thrown into confusion in grief and fear], 1183).

The passion of love carries on, assaulting its victims as inexorably as the Athenian plague, with a kind of insatiable madness. Likewise, the irrationality produced by the fear of death provides a striking parallel for the unreasoning destructiveness of love; both are inescapable and seemingly all-powerful. Book 6 of *De rerum natura*, coinciding with the end of the poem itself, ends appropriately with a meaningless destructive act, as men fight to lay dead bodies on a funeral pyre and "shed much blood" (6.1285) over who will be first. The plague, spread unchecked and allowed to grow out of control, itself as inevitable and all-consuming as the force of love, has wrought its devastation unchallenged by all efforts of kindness, medicine, or religion to stop it.

Notes

1. R. Brown 1987, 81.
2. Kenney and Clausen 1982, 215.
3. Kenney 1971, 11.
4. See Murley 1939.
5. Cf. Plautus *Trinummus* 235–75; *Aulularia* 436–536; *Miles* 685–715.
6. See Sedley 1998, 57–58.

7. E.g., R. Brown (1987, 57) writes, "the ugly images of the diatribe against love ultimately give way to the themes of reproduction and conjugal affection."

8. See, further, R. Brown 1987, 89–90, where Brown qualifies his earlier statement, noting that the reference to repeated blows "has a distinctly ironic ring."

9. See R. Brown 1987, 71–72.

10. R. Brown 1987, 84.

11. Dudley 1965, 122.

12. Cf. the use of *somniare* (to dream) in the sense of having foolish ideas (*OLD*, [1983] s.v., 3a–c).

13. Sedley 1998, 39–42.

14. R. Brown 1987, 14.

15. See Kenney 1971.

16. West 1969, 32.

17. See C. Segal 1990, 161–62.

18. See West 1969, 54.

19. C. Segal 1990, 111.

20. See McKay 1964, 125–26.

21. This is implied by W. H. Rouse and M. F. Smith (1982, 482–83).

22. See R Brown 1987, 54.

23. The language here seems an apt description of the chill that overcomes Lucretius's contemporary Catullus in his poem 51, when the narrator's longing for Lesbia is succeeded by a realization of the destructive power of *otium*, the "free time" that causes our minds to wander in pursuit of love.

24. See C. Segal 1990, chaps. 5–7.

25. Cicero's answer to this in *De finibus* 2.9.27 is that we ought to deliver a deathblow to our vices, not merely limit them.

26. See Godwin 1986, 26.

27. See Commager 1957; Bright 1971; Sedley 1998.

28. Dalzell 1996, 160.

29. Sedley 1998, 165.

30. Minadeo 1969, 30.

31. Johnson 2000, 31.

32. Williams 1973, 2:509.

33. See C. Segal 1990, 110.

Five

Marriage and Gender in Ovid's Erotodidactic Poetry

Karla Pollmann

In aliena uxore omnis amor turpis est, in sua nimius. Sapiens vir iudicio debet amare coniugem, non affectu—nihil est foedius quam uxorem
amare quasi adulteram.

*[Every love toward the wife of another man is shameful; toward one's own
wife, excessive love is shameful. A wise man must love his wife with judgment, not with affection—nothing is more unseemly than to love one's
wife like a mistress.]*

This statement by Seneca the Younger[1] (first century A.D.) expresses
an attitude toward marriage that can be called characteristic for the
Rome of the late Republic and the early empire. Marriage was considered to
be a legal institution that would guarantee the continuation of the old noble
Roman families through the procreation of legitimate children and would
secure the organized passing on of their wealth.[2] Mostly, marriages were arranged
between a man and a woman of suitable families when the would-be spouses
were still children. This arrangement and the praised virtues of a husband and
a wife—"seriousness" (*gravitas*) and "sternness" (*austeritas*), respectively—did
not promote a relaxed harmonic relationship; crucial factors for a marriage

were political, social, and financial factors and certainly did not include mutual emotional attraction.

Though we know, from evidence like tombstone inscriptions and written documents, that Roman couples were often devoted to each other,[3] it was legally acceptable for the husband to have an extramarital relationship,[4] as long as it did not involve a married woman (*adulterium*) or an unmarried or widowed woman of noble birth (*stuprum*) and as long as it did not upset the marriage. Famous is Cato's dictum, paraphrased in Horace's *Satire* (1.2.32–35), that young men should go to a brothel rather than fornicate with other men's wives. Horace, however, omits mention that Cato continues this statement with the claim that the men should not stay there all the time. Porphyrio (ad loc.) writes:

M. Cato ille censorius, cum vidisset hominem honestum [Horace: notum] e fornice exeuntem laudavit existimans libidinem compescendam esse sine crimine. at postea cum frequentius eum ex eodem lupanari exeuntem advertisset, "adolescens," inquit, "ego te laudavi quod interdum huc invenires, non quod hic habitares."

[The famous censor Marcus Cato, when he had seen an honorable man [Horace: an acquiantance] coming out of a brothel, praised him, thinking that lust should be checked legally. Later, however, when he noticed him coming out of the same brothel quite frequently, he said, "young man, I praised you for coming here occasionally, not for living here."][5]

By the time of Augustus (63 B.C.–A.D. 14), it was felt that morals had declined, as many members of the upper class did not consider marriage at all or, worse, refrained from procreating legitimate children. In a kind of "back-to-basics policy," Augustus was determined to improve affairs by setting up laws against adultery (*lex Iulia de adulteriis et de pudicitia*) and encouraging marriage (*lex Iulia de maritandis ordinibus*) and procreation (*lex Papia Poppaea*), from 18 B.C. and A.D. 9, respectively.[6] For the first time, adultery became legally punishable; the penalties that it inflicted at the time of Augustus seem to have been *relegatio in insulam* and partial confiscation of the property of both the man and the woman.[7] The efficiency of these laws, which interfered to a strong degree with people's private lives, was only limited and also undermined by contrary behavior within the family of Augustus itself.[8]

In this official political climate of general moral renewal, including a clear emphasis on sexual morality, Ovid (43 B.C.–A.D. 17) wrote his erotodidactic poems: *The Art of Love* (*Ars amatoria*, in three books, around 2–1 B.C.), a poem on female cosmetics (*Medicamina faciei femineae*, only extant in fragments), and finally *The Remedies for Love* (*Remedia amoris*, in one book, around A.D. 1–2).[9] The following discussion will concentrate on the *Ars amatoria* (*AA*) and (to a lesser degree) on the *Remedia amoris* (*RA*), a group of poems that can be considered together as a unit of four books, as is reflected in the continuous use of the metaphors of a chariot race and a sea journey and also in the manner of the transmission of these works.[10]

The *AA* intends to teach how to win and keep a sexual partner and is addressed first to men (books 1 and 2), then to women (book 3), which is a bold novelty. The *RA* is addressed to both of the sexes throughout,[11] though there exists a certain imbalance, as the concrete hints of how to forget a former relationship are sometimes more practicable for men than for women. Therefore Ovid emphasizes in *RA* 49–52 that some advice serves as an analogy for female readers to follow (*at tamen exemplo multa docere potest*, 52).[12] The mythological illustrations, however, mostly focus on the behavior of women.[13] With the moral climate of his time in mind, Ovid is careful to make it clear throughout the poem that his target is not married women and unmarried noble women, only freedwomen, *libertinae*, whose social status eludes precise definition[14] (see *AA* 1.31–34; *AA* 2.599–600; *AA* 3.27, 57–58, 613–16; *RA* 386, which is reconfirmed in *Epistula ex Ponto* 3.3.49–64 and *Tristia* 2.237–52).[15] This specification of the addressee, however, is not clearly maintained throughout the text. This is primarily due to the ambiguity of terms like *vir*, *maritus*, *uxor*, and *coniunx*, which can mean "husband" and "wife," respectively, but also "lover" and "beloved," as the genre of love elegy adopted the terminology for its own purposes.[16] Thus the nature of the addressed *puellae* is ambiguous in Ovid as in love poetry in general.[17] The remark in *AA* 1.100 that chaste shamefulness (*castus pudor*, traditionally allotted to married women) is at risk in public places and the explicit mentioning of the *uxores* in *AA* 3.585 blur the boundaries even more in favor of an implicit, at least potential inclusion of married women as well.[18]

An illustrative case is *AA* 3.611–58, where the *puella* is advised how to elude her suspicious "partner," who is called *maritus* in line 611; only lines 613–16 make it clear that Ovid is here again addressing not married women (who have to obey their husbands and be guarded) but libertines. Therefore Toohey (1996, 164) is wrong in speaking about "suspicious husbands" in this context, though Ovid's amendment has something artificial about it. Moreover, Ovid's claim at *AA* 3.613–14 that wives have to accept that they are guarded by their husbands may be said "tongue in cheek," which then indeed blurs the terminological boundaries again. Also significant in this context is *AA* 2.685–86, where Ovid states that he does not like women who, while making love, think of their wool work, again a typical occupation for a

94

housewife.[19] In a mythological passage, we find an unveiled exhortation to commit adultery, when Ovid narrates the story of Pasiphae.[20]

This chapter will argue that Ovid's attitude toward adultery in his eroto-didactic poems can safely be described as ambiguous and is by no means clearly in the line of the moral expectations of the Augustan era. He touches upon the subject of marriage always in a teasing, negative manner that clearly undermines the intention of the Augustan marriage laws. It is therefore not surprising that Augustus used these poems as the official pretext when he sent Ovid into exile in A.D. 8 (see *Epistula ex Ponto* 3.3.57–58; *Tristia* 2.345–46).[21] However, the *AA* is not a sex manual in the crude and basic sense of the word but intends to teach how to refine, cultivate, and control a natural force. Unambiguous is Ovid's attitude toward (male) homosexuality, which he does not favor.[22] This is in accordance with the *lex Iulia de adulteriis et de pudicitia* (cf. Justinian *Institutions* 4.18.4) and with Roman morality (Seneca *Letters* 122.7–8; Phaedrus 4.16).

Despite Ovid's just mentioned general ambiguity on the subject of marriage, he comes back to it throughout the whole of these poems, thus giving more or less explicitly his view, as a poet, on the contrasts between marriage and a "free" erotic relationship as he wishes to teach it in his work. Moreover, the explicit double address to both men and women allows us to look deeper into the (implicit and explicit) differences Ovid sees between the two genders when it comes to an erotosexual encounter.[23]

MARRIAGE

Though the focus of Ovid's erotodidactic poetry clearly does not lie on the institution of marriage, he nevertheless touches upon this subject repeatedly in a rather negative way. That this is done only by the persona assumed by the poet and for a certain literary effect is made explicit by Ovid himself, who later, in his exile poetry, stresses his own immaculate moral conduct in these matters and emphasizes the humorous intention of his poetry (*RA* 361ff., especially 385–88; *Tristia* 2.212), which can also be understood as having a satirical thrust against the Augustan marriage code.

Ovid inserts occasionally biting remarks about the deficiencies of the marital relationships that form a great contrast to his envisaged erotic relationship. In *AA* 2.151–58 he claims that there is constant quarrel in a marriage because the law, not love, forms its foundation,[24] which is a kind of critical rephrasing of Seneca's statement quoted at the very beginning of this chapter and a critical hint at the Augustan marriage laws. In *AA* 2.373ff. Ovid advises the lover not to let his beloved know if he has a second mistress at the same time, as this would upset his first mistress and jeopardize the continuation of the relationship. However, Ovid does not wish to restrict the lover to one single woman, as this could be hardly demanded of her partner even by a young bride (*vix hoc nupta tenere potest*, 388). Legally, a wife could not expect a husband to be faithful to her and could not sue her husband for adultery; he could be charged for *stuprum* or *adulterium* only by the father or the husband of the daughter or wife with which the adultery was committed.[25] By connecting closely the marital and extramarital relationships, Ovid assimilates them both here as if marriage displayed a comparable pattern of behavior, not as if it were on a different legal, social, and, in particular, moral level. Moreover, he states that infidelity could be regarded as something unjust (*censura*, 387; *culpa*, 389) both in a free and in a married relationship, as a kind of moral claim beyond legal fixation. When he allows the addressed men to get around that in their pursuit of free erotic adventures (*ludite*, 389), this means indirectly that married men do not really behave better toward their wives than the "immoral" adventurers depicted in the *AA*. Here one can feel a light, but nevertheless painful, satirical sting against the Augustan marriage code, a sting we encounter repeatedly in the *AA*.[26]

In *AA* 2.534ff. the perspective changes. Here the lover should overlook generously that he has a rival with his *puella*, and he should not try to control either her correspondence or her coming and going. This is something that even husbands concede to their wives (*hoc in legitima praestant uxore mariti*, 545). Again married life is taken as an illustration—or in this case, a model—for extramarital behavior, as if the two could be justly compared. Instead of claiming that the two form an unbridgeable contrast, Ovid blurs the differences. It is unmentioned what these married women do when they go in and out of the house uncontrolled, but by inference from the immediate context, it is more than likely to be adultery. The rather blasé attitude of this passage is reinforced in lines 597–98, where it is conceded that husbands are entitled to control the (secret) correspondence of their wives—if they think it necessary (*si iam captanda putabunt*, 597). Even though the following two lines again confirm that Ovid is only interested in extramarital relationships, the abrupt change in lines 595–600 makes it clear that Ovid does not seriously recommend marital devotion to either party of a couple.

Similarly uneven is the line of argument in *AA* 3.483ff. Here Ovid advises women to answer secret love letters of their lovers in such a way that the letters cannot be used as evidence against the women themselves. Ovid begins in 483–84, . . . *quamvis vittae careatis honore, / est vobis vestros fallere cura viros* [though you are lacking wedlock's honored ties, you are just as keen to trick your lovers]. The point lies in the "though"—it means that married women are keen to trick their husbands anyway.[27] A more bitter aspect of marriage is mentioned in *AA* 3.585–86 (*hoc est, uxores quod non patiatur amari: / conveniunt illas, cum voluere, viri*), where Ovid states that wives do not enjoy the love of their husbands, because these can have sex with them whenever they want. Again the "superior" mistress is played off against the married woman, who is at an obvious disadvantage because she cannot employ any means to incite and maintain the affectionate love of her husband (as in Lucretius 4.1274–77). Ovid here makes a clear distinction between sex as a functional means of procreation and conjugal duty and sex as a fulfilled erotic relationship where the mutual attraction of the partners is the main criterion.

Apart from these "realistic" critical sideswipes at contemporary Roman married "bliss," Ovid uses myth in particular to scorn the institution of marriage and to expose some of its drawbacks. Here it becomes especially clear that he sees the discrepancy between the static quality of (ideally only one) marriage and the dynamic quality of (varied and multiple) erotic attractions as a problem, which he suggests should be solved in favor of the latter. Emblematic of his attitude is his destruction of Penelope as the mythological prototype of female conjugal constancy in *AA* 1.477: "you will conquer Penelope herself, if you only persist [sc., in attempting to seduce her]." This is consistent with *AA* 1.101–39, where Ovid uses the legend of the rape of the Sabines to illustrate the "technique" of how to catch a woman.[28] Regarding the self-awareness of the Roman Empire, this episode had achieved an elevated status as the necessary action in order to secure the continuation of the newly founded city of Rome (Livy 1.9), and it formed an important part in Augustan ideology.[29] It was emphasized explicitly that though the abduction of the women had taken place illegally, this had been compensated for afterward by the legalization of the Sabine women, who became lawfully married wives to the Roman men and were given Roman citizenship. In *AA* 1.130 Ovid flippantly alludes to that incident when he makes the Roman kidnapper console his crying booty with the words "What your father is to your mother, I will be to you" [*"quod matri pater est, hoc tibi" dixit, "ero"*]—as if this were the normal way of winning a wife. Ovid undermines ironically the whole ideological construct by claiming that this action illustrates as an *aition*[30] his own advice of how to find a suitable mistress, where clearly no lawful marriage is envisaged. He claims that the mechanisms of "wooing" are the same in the present and the past, as it is taking place at both times in the theater, which has always been a dangerous place for beautiful women (*scilicet ex illo sollemnia more theatra / nunc quoque formosis insidiosa manent*, 1.133–34). The difference is merely that the environment and the methods of "seduction" are more refined nowadays than they used to be in the past.

The idea of refined cultivation of heterosexual contact is central in Ovid's erotodidactic poems. To make this plausible, Ovid inserts a cosmology and a creation myth (including a *Kulturentstehungslehre*) in AA 2.467–88, thereby following the habit of didactic poetry in general, with particular reminiscences of Hesiod's *Theogony* (116–33) and Lucretius's *De rerum natura* (5.1011–457).[31] To understand the function of this section, it is important to have a look at its context: the lover learns from Ovid how to deal with his mistress's distress after it has been caused by himself; in AA 2.459–60 sex is said to be the appropriate "medicine" to resolve her anger, which is repeated after the creation myth in 2.489–92.[32] The creation myth itself serves as an illustration for this advice by establishing sex (*blanda voluptas*—the term stems from Lucretius *DRN* 4.1263) as the great civilizing force.[33] It had already been classified as *one* civilizing factor in Lucretius's *De rerum natura* (5.1011ff.), but Lucretius focused more on its negative side of having physically weakening effects, whereas Ovid shows its positive, psychologically soothing effect. Moreover, in contrast to Lucretius, sex advances in Ovid to be the *only* civilizing factor. Furthermore, he states that humankind did not need a teacher for making love (*quid facerent, ipsi nullo didicere magistro; / arte Venus nulla dulce peregit opus* [they learned what to do without any teacher; Venus accomplished the sweet task artlessly], AA 2.479–80), which is therefore reestablished as a natural force. Implicitly, this determines the function of the AA—as I said earlier, not a sex manual in the crude and basic sense of the word, but a work intended to teach how to refine, cultivate, and control a natural force.[34]

As I already mentioned, the cosmology and creation myth are closely linked in Ovid with practical advice for the contemporary reader of the AA. Thus the remote, timeless character of the myth is removed and is brought into direct relationship with the present world. Ovid claims that he is able to prescribe a cultivated usage of a natural driving force like *blanda voluptas* as a refined tool in an erotic relationship. As a teacher, he can show how to transform a primitive natural energy into a healthy medicine (*medicamina*, 489), thus productively channeling its beneficial effects. Looking at the line of Ovid's argument, the point here is not so much one of irony or parody and degradation of the originals;[35] rather, Ovid's aim is to integrate the civilizing effect of this force (477–78) in his didactic program and to transform it into a helpful peace-creating tool in a relationship. The original cosmological horizon is thus "domesticated" and bound into a private individual relationship. The myth is cut down, as he emphasizes only the peace-bringing effect of sex and omits its other aspects—for example, procreation, which would have been more in the line with Augustan ideology. Characteristic of the whole of the *AA* is this reversion of perspective and values by twisting many phenomena in such a way as to serve the poem's didactic aim to teach a successful sexual relationship.

Two notorious adulterous couples in myth are Mars and Venus and Helen and Paris. Ovid alludes to both of their stories repeatedly in his erotodidactic poetry. The mentioning of the human adulterers Paris and Helen is sometimes rather ornamental and too short to allow for moral analysis (*AA* 1.54, 685–86; 2.6, 699; 3.253, 759); it is here more due to poetic convention that allows for mythological stock examples. In such an erotic context, such allusions seem to risk almost invariable misunderstanding; thus Ovid is "politically correct" in calling Helen a bad woman (*AA* 3.11) and a concubine (*paelex*) of the already married Paris.[36] Twice, however (in *AA* 2.359–72 and *RA* 773–76), he defends her behavior. From as early as Stesichorus, to whose palinode[37] Ovid alludes in *AA* 3.49, the status of Helen had been ambiguous, and she had already been defended by Gorgias in his *Enkomion of Helen* (meant as a rhetorical jest: Helen is not reproachable because she was captivated by love and persuaded by words), by Euripides in the *Helen* (following Stesichorus in declaring that it was not the real Helen but her image that committed adultery), and by Isocrates in his *Enkomion of Helen* (Helen's act even had the positive consequence that the Greeks took united action against the barbarians). But the way in which Ovid excuses or even approves of the lovers' behavior (*AA* 2.365) is unprecedented.

The context of the passage in *AA* 2.359–72 explains that a brief separation can intensify lovers' feelings for each other but that a woman neglected too long will turn to a new lover. This is illustrated by Helen, who had been neglected by Menelaus—therefore it is clearly his fault that Helen turned to Paris. Moreover, even Menelaus himself, like any other man, would have done the same if he had been in Paris's situation (366). Helen just seized the opportunity provided by Menelaus himself (*quid, nisi concilio est usa puella tuo?* 368; *usa est humani commoditate viri*, 372),[38] and Paris reacts appropriately (*non rusticus hospes*, 369; as always in Ovid's erotodidactic poetry, *rusticitas* means "lack of sophistication").[39] So both Helen and Paris are characterized by Ovid as being cultivated and refined—so to speak, an ideal representation of the amorous couple, which is the didactic goal of Ovid's poetry. They form a sharp contrast to the incapability of Menelaus (*stupor*, 361), which is repeated in a similar way in *RA* 773–76 (especially Menelaus's characterization as *lentus* [sluggish] in 774, for which one can compare Ovid *Heroides* 3.22, where Briseis accuses Achilles' wrath of being *lenta*—i.e., he is neglecting her sexually and does not have enough passion to kidnap her back).[40] First, Menelaus had neglected Helen by departing for Crete and leaving her behind on her own.

Only after he had realized the love of his rival did his own love rekindle. Thus his care for Helen loses some of its credibility.

In neither of these passages, naturally, does Ovid ever raise the question of the legal relationship between Menelaus and Helen as a married couple; he replaces it with a relationship of failed erotic commitment. In the legal sense of Augustan times, Paris and Helen were clearly guilty, but Ovid measures them according to his own standards: Helen is innocent (*Helenen ego crimine solvo*, AA 2.371); it is all Menelaus's fault. So Ovid's erotic precepts aim at least implicitly at replacing the official legal precepts of how to organize a "correct" heterosexual relationship.

On the divine level, adultery is committed by Mars and Venus. Again I will ignore the rather brief allusions to the couple's relationship in, for example, AA 1.406[41] and RA 160. However, the couple's story is narrated at length in AA 2.561–92. Its epic model is the well-known story from Homer's *Odyssey* (8.266–366), but in Ovid the story is used to illustrate a didactic point, a *fabula docet*.[42] It serves to support Ovid's advice (explicitly uttered in AA 2.555—60) that a lover should never be eager to catch his beloved with a rival lover and expose them—the embarrassment of the caught couple will increase their mutual love and moreover remove the secrecy from their further action (cf. the German saying "Ist der Ruf erst ruiniert, lebt sich's gänzlich ungeniert" freely, "once your reputation is ruined, you can live with no embarrassment"). The humorous and witty elements of this passage have been analyzed in detail;[43] for our purposes, it is enough to emphasize that again the story is reinterpreted within the framework of Ovidian erotodidactic "morality": Sol should not have told the cuckolded Vulcan about his wife's infidelity (advice that is fixed as a general rule in AA 2.601ff.);[44] he should instead have asked Venus for the same favor (575). This must be understood as a mythologically disguised invitation by Ovid to commit adultery.[45] Furthermore, Vulcan should not have exposed the couple in flagrante to public ridicule, a ridicule described in AA 2.581–85 in great detail, an emphasis already found in the Homeric model (esp. Od. 8.325–32); the incident is dramatized in Lucian's *Dialogues of the Gods* (21; cf. 17). Therefore it is no wonder that Vulcan regrets his rash deed now (AA 2.591).

Most noteworthy, however, is Ovid's idea of the Roman virtue of *pudor/pudicitia* (missing in both Greek versions), which he defines as a kind of discretion due to which the couple first conceals their adulterous affair (AA 2.571—72) but that is not necessary anymore after their public exposure (590). This concept is utterly incongruent with the official Roman doctrine: to display *pudor/pudicitia* does not mean to cover up adultery; it means to refrain from committing it at all.[46] This is of course a slap in the face of Augustus's endeavor to restore these values (cf. the title of the *lex Iulia de adulteriis et de pudicitia*). In a scathing way, Ovid confronts here the intended (or rather, enforced) Augustan ideal and the opposite reality. Moreover, Ovid may intend here a literary sideswipe as well, by emphasizing that Mars and Venus committed adultery most uninhibitedly after their exposure—as it has been described in beautiful detail by one of Ovid's predecessors within the genre of didactic poetry, Lucretius, who, at the beginning of his *De rerum natura*, uses the imagery of the love between Mars and Venus as an allegory for the procreative powers of nature.

GENDER

It can be observed in all masculinocentric cultures that the destabilization of marriage (as a socially desirable form of heterosexual cohabitation) by erotic turmoil is explained with the misogynist view that women are at the root of this evil and that women alone bear the responsibility for the working of the institution of marriage by staying faithful to their husband only. Therefore it seems appropriate to analyze how Ovid treats and evaluates both of the genders in and out of wedlock, an aspect of his argument that suggests itself even more because of the two addressees of the poems.

It is crucial to bear in mind that Ovid originally intended only to write the *AA* in two books solely directed toward men.[47] In 1.617–18 we find a sudden apostrophe to the *puellae*. Ovid had just been pointing out that anybody pretending to be in love risks, easily, finding himself suddenly really in love. Ovid continues (617–18), *quo magis, o, faciles imitantibus este, puellae: / fiet amor verus, qui modo falsus erat* [Oh, therefore the more, girls, be friendly to those who pretend to be in love: the love that has only been a fake will become true]. Either these lines were part of the original two-book version, which would make it clear that Ovid intended female readers as well, or they were inserted later, when he added, due to public female demand (2.745–46), a third book addressed to the *puellae*. As already mentioned, the *RA* is intended for both sexes. It is a bold novelty that Ovid juxtaposes advice for male and female readers, as the topic of how to catch a lover was dealt with in different literary genres for each sex if we look at the "serious" models for Ovid in this respect. The male sphere had its place in philosophical treatises, written mainly in the Platonic tradition, stemming from Plato's *Phaedrus*. It aimed at a homosexual erotic relationship with strong philosophical elements. Heterosexual eroticism was dealt with in sex manuals, where, as far as we can see from the few extant fragments,[48] rules were listed by a fictitious female prostitute explaining how a woman could please a man sexually, which included various different positions during sexual intercourse (which we find also in AA 3.771–88). For the AA, Ovid selected elements out of these two kinds of erotic literature and confined them strictly to the heterosexual sphere. The RA has its sources mainly in philosophical writings and rhetorical stock examples.[49] So here again we can observe Ovid's ambitious aim to integrate various heterogeneous literary traditions in his erotodidactic poetry.

In part, the gender differences here are therefore due to the different traditions the author is following. So the *figurae Veneris* (positions in sexual intercourse) are only enlisted in AA 3.769–808, which is meant for women, and there is no male equivalent to be found.[50] In AA 1.281–82 it is stated that women feel erotic passion more strongly than men and that they can be driven beyond the normal by it (*parcior in nobis nec tam furiosa libido; / legitimum finem flamma virilis habet* [in us the lust is more restrained, not so out of control; male passion stays within legal boundaries]); the point is illustrated by various mythological examples. Compare also AA 1.341–42: *omnia feminea sunt ista libidine mota; / acrior est nostra plusque furoris habet* [all these crimes were stirred up by female lust; it is sharper than ours and has more fury]. The claim of general validity is moderated only slightly by 1.344: *vix erit e multis, quae neget, una, tibi* [scarcely one woman out of many will say no to you]. The idea of excessive *libido* as a female vice is topical.[51] It can be characterized partly as a male fantasy, partly as a projection (a male vice attributed to the opposite sex as a kind of scapegoat), but to the extent that there was an actual heightened libido, this may have resulted from the relatively limited possibilities that society granted for women to be sexually active.

In Ovid this charge becomes strongly modified by various aspects. First, he needs *two* books for men in order to instruct them sufficiently how to seduce women, while women need only one book of instruction to achieve the same with the opposite sex. If female libido would be truly so excessive, one would expect that not much subtlety were needed by the interested male. Second, in AA 3.87 the poet urges women not to be sparing with their erotic affection (*gaudia nec cupidis vestra negate viris*). If women needed such advice, their libido does not seem to have operated automatically on every occasion. Third, in AA 3.31–32 Ovid explains that often women are wronged by men, in which case it is the man's fault if the relationship goes wrong (*saepe viri fallunt, tenerae non saepe puellae / paucaque, si quaeras, crimina fraudis habent*). Again mythological examples serve to illustrate Ovid's point. Interestingly, one heroine, Medea, is used both here and in the examples in book 1. In AA 1.335–36 Ovid focuses on Medea's horrible murder of Creusa, whom her husband Jason wanted to take as his new wife, and of her own children fathered by Jason, in order to revenge her husband's unfaithfulness. In AA 3.33–34 the focus lies on Jason's unfaithful behavior against Medea, the mother of his children. So Ovid is not one-dimensional in his evaluation of the genders and shows both sides of the coin. Again we can also see his implicit demand for reciprocity of (at least seeming) devotion in a successful relationship. His ability to use the same myth and elaborate on its different aspects shows his rhetorical training and is displayed by him in his other poetry, too. The most famous object for this technique is the aforementioned Helen, who could be depicted in good or in bad terms. Fourth, we find the constant topic that violence against women should be avoided by all means (AA 1.667–68, 717–18; 2.179–80), which implies that male libido, too, can have a tendency toward excessiveness.

Other differences in gender behavior are ascribed by Ovid to different social rules and conditions for men and women, as he perceives them. As women are inhibited by their *pudor* (shamefulness), it is the task of the men to take the initiative in the heterosexual approach.[52] Moreover, women have less opportunities and fewer locations to display their physical beauty in order to catch a lover (AA 3.381ff.): while men can visit various public places for physical exercise, women are restricted for the most part to temples and theaters. While men should avoid getting too drunk at a dinner party, because this impairs their abilities to seduce a woman (1.589—600), women have to avoid excessive drunkenness or falling asleep on such occasions, because otherwise they risk indecent treatment and rape by the other sex (3.765–68). That women are vain and delighted when their physical beauties are praised (AA 1.623–24; RA 409–10) is not mentioned to have a male equivalent.

Most significant for our question, however, are the numerous instances where Ovid stresses the equality of the sexes in the erotic war, as expressed programmatically in AA 3.3: *ite in bella pares* [go to war on equal terms]. He postulates that men and women should enjoy sex equally (2.682ff., 725–28; 3.793–94), and he shows a singular interest in female pleasure and satisfaction during sexual intercourse (2.719–22), an interest otherwise rare in classical authors.[53] It is something the man has to care about, while the woman is never urged to do the same for the man. That Ovid emphasizes equal pleasure for both sexes in 3.793–94 is very important because it follows directly after the list of *figurae Veneris* where the physical characteristics of women are emphasized. But lines 793–94 add the aspect of feeling that has to be satisfying for women as well; therefore the accusation of Parker (1992, 95–97) that Ovid turns women into objects is inexact. This is not altered by AA 3.797–806, where Ovid demands that even if women—sadly enough—cannot enjoy sex, they should at least pretend to have pleasure in a credible way. It is obvious from the context, however, that these women are not forced but have sexual intercourse for the sake of material advantages.[54]

In this context must also be seen AA 1.663–708, where Ovid says that women like it when men force themselves upon them, which implies, for example, that a woman means "yes" when she says "no" (665). However, this is not meant as a request for justified rape. The whole section is embedded into the general context of erotic play, with means like simulated tears on the male side (659–60) that serve to make the encounter successful. It is clear for both sides anyway that there is prior mutual agreement. In the following lines, Ovid stresses that the man should yield when he meets true dislike and rejection (715ff.). In general, Ovid demands that women should not be stereotyped according to prejudices (3.9f.; cf. 1.755f.). As they are all different individuals, each woman has to be dealt with on a case-by-case basis.

Repeatedly the right of women is proclaimed to remunerate on equal terms if they had been wronged by men (AA 3.461, 491). In the same way as Ovid helped men to be able to cope with the natural female resourcefulness (1.419ff.) he also helps women to make use of natural male weaknesses (3.577ff.). Certain techniques can be employed on both sides, like displaying an amiable personality (2.107–44, 3.499–524), simulated tears (1.659–60, 3.677; cf. Petronius *Sat.* 17.2 and Juvenal *Sat.* 6.273–74, where this is a female device only),[55] and simulated love in general, though men have to work harder to convince women than the other way round (for men, see AA 1.615ff., 2.287ff., 2.311ff.; for women, see 3.673: *facile est*). Analogous precepts refer to external appearance, though here women have to work harder than men (AA 1.523, 3.101–250; *Medicamina faciei femineae*). Again Ovid's position is unusual as he emphasizes the legitimacy of cosmetics and does not despise it, as happens frequently in the pagan and Christian tradition (e.g., Lucretius *DRN* 4.1123–32; Pliny *Natural History* 33.12.40; Manilius 5.518–19; Juvenal *Sat.* 6.457–64; Prudentius *Hamartigenia* 264–76). In general the external appearance of women is more important than that of men, a point to which I shall come back later. Further devices employed by both sexes are performances in singing or reciting poetry (maybe one's own) if one has got the talent (2.273–86, 3.311–80), mimicking facial expression (2.145ff., 3.49ff.), certain behavior at a dinner party (1.525–630, 3.749ff.; cf. *Amores* 1.4), and the writing and answering of love letters (1.437ff., 3.467–98).

On a more general level, even more can be said about Ovid's pleasingly equal treatment of the sexes. In traditional sex manuals, it is always the woman who is instructed. It has rightly been criticized that this turns her into an object, makes her functioning and calculable.[56] In Ovid the very fact that men are also part of his *Ars* relativizes the instrumental function of women, because men are now subdued to certain precepts as well. The exclusion of alternatives, the restriction of behavioral patterns, and the avoidance of surprises in each other's demeanor apply to both parties.

Roughly speaking, one can indeed observe that for Ovid the emphasis in male seductive strategy lies more on the psychological side. Both to win and to maintain the favor of a woman, the man must (besides giving material gifts) think of promises (and how to use them), flattery, attention (but the right one) when the woman is sick, the need for persuasiveness, tolerance, patience, (seeming) humbleness and an accommodating nature, the avoidance of jealousy and criticism—indeed, a hard program for Mr. Right. Obviously Ovid does not take such patterns of behavior for granted in his male fellows, as he finds it necessary to make such a list. The female psyche and personality are thus implicitly pictured as a complex and subtle mechanism that demands careful and cunning treatment on the male side in order to guarantee success.

The male psyche seems to be less complicated: it is more important for a woman to look advantageous, which is enabled by the right choice of dress, makeup, and hairstyle, legitimate and reasonable means of allurement that are not condemned morally. If we sum up this complementary information, we can conclude that according to Ovid, there exists an apparent contrast between simple male psychology, which reacts positively to pleasant optical signals and is otherwise undemanding and easy to handle, and the obligation for men to exercise complex psychological courtship in order to be successful with the opposite sex; there is also the contrast that women, who are obviously endowed with such an intricate internal structure, are asked not to show any direct sign of it but to display relatively simple, mostly bodily aspects of interhuman communication. So women's (psychologically speaking) simple exterior and complex interior are matched by the simple psychological interior and (seemingly) subtle exterior of men when it comes to a heterosexual encounter. Ovid never comments on this phenomenon explicitly, but his insight into psychological and cultural standards of humankind is revealed in the different focus he chooses in AA 1 and 2 in contrast with book 3.

At this point, a further observation, one that goes partly beyond Ovid's ideas, may be allowed: in a way, men are urged to improve their conduct, manners, education, and/or social (nowadays also financial) position when they strive at conquering a woman. This pursuit can even be sublimated by activities like composing, writing poetry (like Ovid himself) out of love, and can thus become a cultural force in its own right. Naturally, when men leave the sphere of heterosexual relations, they are still able to display these or other sorts of skills in different areas of society. Men may then even forget about the psychological pattern they display toward women. This means, in concrete terms, that if men, for example, improve their intellectual or financial abilities in order to be able to woo a woman successfully, they can still take advantage of these improvements when they turn to other spheres of society. Seen on a general level, this means that men are urged, encouraged, or even forced (depending on the individual perception) to work on themselves and develop further substantially—or at least make it seem so—in a way that can give them a stronger position in society in general.

For women, there is a different mechanism: they are asked to reduce their complex interior (which is implicitly defined as complex by the fact that it is so complicated for men to conquer women) and to show a relatively simple and restrained surface toward the opposite sex. In a male-dominated society where male standards prevail in most—especially public—areas, this means that there is no scope or place where women actually can display their internal complexity and richness in an adequate way, apart from a very limited domestic sphere. Their improvement in hairstyle, makeup, and clothing will practically never grant them a strong, independent social position outside the relationship with their lover. The final goal of all female endeavor is always to please a male human being on a limited scope; that is, women have no other function for men except in the sphere of eroticism and sexuality. If a society (as it happens frequently in masculinocentric ones) refines the heterosexual encounter to the erotosexual dimension, then it is understandable and makes sense (at least from a male-centered point of view) to define women as—or accuse them of—having stronger and uncontrollable libido, as this is the sole perspective from which they are perceived anyway. If there is in women any energy, personality, or subtlety that wishes to break forth in the public sphere, it has to concentrate on fields of exercise in the narrow erotosexual sphere, which allows for a spectrum from the ridiculous via the pleasant to the perverse.

CONCLUSIONS

The AA and, to a lesser degree, the RA show signs of satirical exposure of certain weaknesses or patterns of behavior when it comes to heterosexual relations.[57] Already the *vera canam* [I will sing true things] in AA 1.30 announces that this poetry is based on facts, not fiction. This is also a claim of the genre of satire (cf. esp. Juvenal *Satire* 4.35: *res vera agitur* [a true tale is being told]). Then, in AA 1.29, the poet claims to be experienced (*peritus*) and maintains that the motivation for his work is experience (*usus opus movet hoc; vati parete perito* [experience motivates this work: yield to the experienced bard]). This claim is repeated at the end of AA (*si qua fides, arti, quam longo fecimus usu, credite: praestabunt carmina nostra fidem* [if you have any faith in the art that we have composed after long practice, believe it: our poems will offer you trustworthiness], 3.791–92), where the poet's own experience warrants the credibility of the content of his poetry. The claim is singular in the tradition of didactic poetry. Ovid's experience is of course proved by his earlier *Amores* and serves to replace the traditional divine inspiration for poetry.[58] Moreover, this is a hint at the theory of the *ars* (*techne*): a didactic work has the aim to present a body of knowledge, which is thought to be useful for humankind, as a teachable system.[59] In the case of Ovid, this is erotosexual love, which is a particular challenge as Amor, a semi-personified deity, is considered to be untamable (*ego sum praeceptor Amoris* [I am professor of Love], 1.17; *et mihi cedet Amor* [and Love shall yield to me], 1.21, a contrasting answer to Virgil *Eclogues* 10.69, *omnia vincit Amor; et nos cedamus Amori* [Love conquers all; let us also submit to Love]; *et quod nunc ratio est, impetus ante fuit* [what was previously an impulse is now a system], *RA* 10).[60] Ovid masters this ambition by conflating the genres of love elegy and didactic poetry. Ovid's bold claim is that he will not tell about his personal suffering and the basically uncontrollable experiences in erotic matters, as one would do in traditional Roman love elegy. On the contrary, he intends to transform the phenomenon of falling in love, which had previously been considered irrational and incalculable, into systematic, teachable precepts that could be applied successfully by his readers in present-day Rome, in a rational way and under elimination of the risks and suffering that can come with love. This means the end of the traditional Roman love elegy, whose concern was the mystic side of love and where the poet displayed an existential affliction that was beyond his control. Nevertheless, the AA and RA owe a lot, of course, to the genre of love elegy.[61]

In the *AA*, contemporary social and political realities—like the theater, a slave woman, and even the triumph of Caesar—are transformed into means to achieve the aim of winning a sexual partner. This transformation in itself has a satirical edge to it, which is enhanced by the light and funny tone of the work as a whole and by the sideswipes at not-so-ideal aspects of heterosexual relationships, especially marriage. The heaviest blow against the traditional view of eroticism and sex (which had been reenforced under Augustus) is that Ovid changes their teleology. To put it simply, Augustus says that sex has to be subordinated under the overall concept of a good upper-class Roman citizen, by the means of marriage (with certain strictly refined licenses for the male part of the population), within which you are expected to function in a certain way. In comparison, Ovid says that one should subordinate being a Roman citizen to the pursuit of a fulfilled sexual relationship outside (or rather, in sharp contrast to) marriage and should therefore make optimal use of all possibilities present-day cultivated Rome offers, thus even enhancing its cultivation. The satirical point of Ovid's "doctrine of salvation" as it is taught in *AA* is that he intends to replace marriage by erotic relationships that he finds much more recommendable. This satirical focus was clearly seen by Juvenal, who—especially in his sixth satire—uses many Ovidian motives from the *AA*, but with a completely different satirical intention; that is, he deplores the breaking down of the institution of marriage.

In a way, both Augustus and Ovid aim at channeling sex as a force difficult to control, but they do so with completely opposite approaches. Illustrative is the comparison with the didactic poet Lucretius, who in this respect is more on one line with Augustus. While Ovid described sexuality as the civilizing force of humanity that is refined and cultivated by him in accordance with the cultivated Rome of his day in general, Lucretius diminishes the positive side of sexuality and tries to subordinate it to state duties. While in Ovid the *figurae Veneris* serve to enhance the pleasure of the couple during the act ("sex should be fun"), in Lucretius (*DRN* 4.1030–1287, esp. 1264–67) the position during sexual intercourse has to enhance fertility and improve the success of conception ("sex should be fertile").

When it comes to marriage and gender, Ovid maintains a critical—in many ways, untraditional and unconventional—point of view by claiming the symmetry of the sexes, their equality in the erotic battle, and by justifying their use of appropriate means in pursuit of this end. He does all this with a twinkle in his eye, which nevertheless does not diminish the critical elements and human insights contained in his work. How should one teach unteachable love better than in a pleasant, entertaining, and distanced manner, and who else could have coped with this task better than Ovid?

Notes

The Latin passages are quoted from Ovid after the second edition of E. J. Kenney ([1961] 1994). The English translations are my own.

1. Seneca frag. 14 (Haase 1898, 3:84–85).
2. See Treggiari 1991, 83ff.
3. See Treggiari 1991, 245–47; Dixon 1991.
4. See Treggiari 1991, 215–16.
5. See Treggiari 1991, 300–301.
6. See Marquardt [1886] 1980, 75–80.
7. See Stroh 1979, 324; Treggiari 1991, 277.
8. See Stroh 1979, 351.
9. For the dates of these poems, see Döpp 1992, 106–7; Kenney 1990, ix.

10. See Küppers 1981, 2530–32; A. A. R. Henderson 1979, xvii–xviii.
11. See Lucke 1982, 40.
12. See A. A. R. Henderson 1979, 42; D. Jones 1997. Imprecise is Lucke 1982, 37 n. 11.
13. See Lucke 1982, 40 n. 24; Downing 1999.
14. See Kenney 1990, xxii. Parker (1992, 104) translates *libertinae* too narrowly with "prostitutes," though this is what they often were.
15. See Stroh 1979, 349.
16. See Stroh 1979, 333–34.
17. See Kenney 1990, xxii.
18. See Toohey 1996, 159–61.
19. See Stroh 1979, 344ff.; Giebel 1999.
20. See AA 1.310; Stroh 1979, 347.
21. For the whole issue, see Thibault 1964.
22. See Brandt [1902] 1991, ad loc.
23. See Boberg 1999.
24. See Stroh 1979, 345; Toohey 1996, 165.
25. See Treggiari 1991.
26. See Wildberger 1998, 274–77.
27. See Stroh 1979, 346.
28. See Steudel 1992, 174–75; Toohey 1996, 165–66.
29. See Döpp 1992, 114–15.
30. See Miller 1983, 34.
31. See Steudel 1992, 38–39, 42–57.
32. See Janks 1997, ad loc.
33. See Sharrock 1994, 230–32; Döpp 1992, 108–12.
34. See Küppers 1981, 2546–50.
35. See Steudel 1992, 57.
36. *RA* 458. See Lucke 1982, 115–16.
37. *PMG* 192 Page; for the reconstruction of its content, which is only extant in fragments, see Kannicht 1969, 26–41.
38. See Stroh 1979, 347.
39. See Steudel 1992, 108–9.
40. See Döpp 1992, 95–96.
41. See Hollis 1977, 106.
42. See Stroh 1979, 348; Steudel 1992, 188.
43. See Steudel 1992, 183–89.
44. See Steudel 1992, 188.
45. See Stroh 1979, 347–48.
46. See Holzberg 1990; Wildberger 1998, 274–77.
47. See A. A. R. Henderson 1979, xii–xiii.
48. See Parker 1992.
49. See A. A. R. Henderson 1979, xvi–xvii.
50. See Myerowitz 1985, 135–36; Ramirez de Verger 1999.
51. See Hollis 1977, 91. Cf., e.g., Propertius 3.19; Petronius *Sat.* 110.6–7; Juvenal *Sat.* 6, esp. 53ff., 115–32, 279–79; Phaedrus *Appendix* 11, 15.
52. *AA* 1.709–14. See Brandt [1902] 1991, xiv.

53. See Parker 1992, 96.
54. Contra Dalzell 1996, 160–61.
55. See Holzberg 1997.
56. See Parker 1992.
57. See Stapelton 2000, (introduction).
58. See Haye 1997, 80–81; Kenney 1990, xxi; Döpp 1992, 108; Steudel 1992, 196.
59. See Parker 1992, 101.
60. *Ratio* here means "system," not "logic" as Toohey (1996, 171) believes.
61. See Kenney 1990, xix; Dalzell 1996, 132–64.

Six

Advice on Sex by the Self-Defeating Satirists

HORACE *Sermones* 1.2, JUVENAL *Satire* 6,
AND ROMAN SATIRIC WRITING

Warren S. Smith

The literary and artistic consciousness of the Romans could not imagine a serious form without its comic equivalent. The serious, straightforward form was perceived as only a fragment, only half of a whole. . . . As in the Saturnalia the clown was the double of the ruler and the slave the double of the master, so such comic doubles were created in all forms of culture and literature.
—M. M. Bakhtin, *The Dialogic Imagination*

THE MARRIAGE JOKE

The Greek and Roman comic traditions embraced the marriage joke early and ubiquitously and took a firm, unequivocal stance. Susarion of Megara, of uncertain date but, according to tradition, the "inventor" of Greek Old Comedy, told "the world's oldest joke" in a famous fragment.

κακὸν γυναῖκες, ἀλλ᾽ ὅμως, ὦ δημόται,
οὐκ ἔστιν οἰκεῖν οἰκίαν ἄνευ κακοῦ.

[*Women are evil, but still, my neighbors,*
   one can't live in a home without some evil.][1]
There are similar observations in Semonides' memorable poem comparing
wives with animals (seventh century B.C.), which proclaims, at the culmi-
nation (96–98) of the rogue's gallery of types of wives, "Yes, Zeus made this
greatest pain of all: women."[2]

The theme was to have widespread literary repercussions and was appreciated by no audience more than the Romans, who—in comedy, satire, and
incidental witticisms—came up with endless variations on Susarion's marriage joke, often emphasizing not so much the "evil" of women as the
inability of men to live with or stay faithful to them. Thus in Plautus's *Asinaria*, Argyrippus, carousing with his father, Demaenetus, engages in a dialogue form of the joke with the old man, transparently setting him up to deliver
his punch line with its not-so-subtle double entendre.

> Argyr.   Quid ais, pater?
>   Ecquid matrem amas?
> Dem.   Egone illam? Nunc amo, quia non adest.
> Argyr.   Quid cum adest?
> Dem.   Perisse cupio.

> [Argyr.   Tell me father, don't you love mother at all?
> Dem.   Me love her? Yes, I love her now, because she's not here.
> Argyr.   And when she is here?
> Dem.   Death is what I long for.]

A somewhat subtler form of the joke, but with the same surprise sting at the
end, is Cicero's story in *De oratore* 2.278 about the Sicilian who, when told
by a friend that his wife had hung herself from a fig tree, replied, *Amabo te,
da mihi ex ista arbore quos seram surculos* [Please give me some shoots from that
tree to plant].

The Roman versions of the marriage joke certainly do not absolve the man
of all guilt. Part of the resulting laughter is that men know that marriage is an
"evil" yet still feel they cannot do without it. In other words, men are not
mere innocent victims of the troubles in store if they choose to live with
women; they knowingly bring them on themselves. This sets up a dichotomy
that we can see as peculiarly Roman and characteristic of satiric writing. Thus
Lucilius (644–45), the pioneer Roman satirist, concludes:

Homines ipsi hanc sibi molestiam ultro atque aerumnam offerunt:
Ducunt uxores, producunt quibus haec faciant liberos.

*[Men bring this trouble and annoyance on themselves of their own accord.
They marry wives and produce children for whose sake they do all this.]*

The fault may be on the part of the man who is incapable of loving even an excellent wife for an entire lifetime. This is the point of a poem attributed to Petronius.

Uxor legitimus debet quasi census amari.
    Nec censum vellem semper amare meum.[3]

*[A wife should be loved like a fortune got legally.
    But I would not wish to love even my fortune forever.]*

If the Romans, as Bakhtin argued, saw a comic side to every issue, balancing and coexisting with the serious, how much more inevitably is the comic aspect likely to receive prominence when the discussion is about sex. Discussions of sex certainly lend themselves easily to satiric treatment, because the sex drive puts otherwise levelheaded people in situations where they act ridiculous. If sober argument will not deter them from the distractions and disappointments of courtship, a snapshot of their laughable behavior may do so. One obvious way to highlight the absurdity of such behavior is to describe it in terms or in a manner purposefully elevated, merging the sublime and the absurd, incongruously creating the mood of a high genre in describing a low-life situation. There is a psychology to the use of such incongruous juxtaposition, which we can see more clearly in the case of philosophers, whose intention is not to write humor but to make us see sex for what it is, a slightly repulsive and ridiculous, if necessary, activity. Such an intention is apparent in the case of a Stoic such as Marcus Aurelius.

As in the case of meat and similar eatables the thought strikes us, this is the dead body of a fish . . . or of sexual intercourse, that it is merely internal attrition and the spasmodic ejection of mucus.[4]

As it was with the Stoics, so it was with the Epicureans: Epicurus equated love with sexual desire and literally brought it down to earth by arguing that it is not "heaven-sent" (Diog. Laert. 10.118). Likewise, Lucretius follows his master Epicurus in arguing that the great power of "Venus" is nothing more than an urge to ejaculate (*DRN* 4.1058–72).[5]

CLASS WARFARE: NOT SEX BUT SOCIAL STATUS

With such precedent in the "higher" genres for a deflation of the worthiness of sexual passion, it is not surprising that there is a recognizably similar strategy in the opening of Horace's second satire, the "satire on sex."

> Ambubiarum collegi, pharmacopolae,
> Mendici, mimae, balatrones, hoc genus omne
> Maestrum ac sollicitum est cantoris morte Tigelli.
> Quippe benignus erat.
>
> *[The worshipful companies of flute girls, the peddlers of potions,*
> *mendicants, mime actresses, buffoons, and all of that ilk*
> *are sadly distressed at the death of Tigellius, the singer.*
> *He was so generous!]*

The opening lines of this satire comprise "a mock-heroic opening, in which the most unusual three-word hexameter, the exotic words *ambubiae* and *pharmacopolae*, the alliteration with *b*, *p* and *m* and the asyndeton combine to give the list of mourners a solemn, impressive ring, which is undermined by the sleazy nature of its constituents."[6] The lines might seem to play off the grandiosity of a Pindaric opening, such as that to the second Olympic ode (ἀναξιφορμίγγες ὕμνοι etc.), as Horace paints an ironically broad canvas in giving us a cook's tour not, in the Pindaric manner, of gods and heroes but of disreputable characters, while introducing us to one of the seedy sides of Roman life. Indeed, the refined, sophisticated Horace of his mature poetry hardly seems recognizable in the crude language and blunt, pragmatic advice of the second satire. Coffey tried to find in this a redeeming feature by writing of the poem, "Its ethics are base, but at least it is free from hypocrisy."[7] Adulterers are celebrated in the opening lines as though they were heroes, winners in the sexual Olympics. The poem will be stark and use coarse language, and one of the speakers will even be the penis himself. Horace, as narrator, concedes that the sex drive must be satisfied, but that does not mean that the needs of the body must be glamorized. This satirist wants to force the lowliness, homeliness, and vulgarity of the sex drive on us, to force us to see it for what it is, so he uses down-to-earth language and makes the act as unglamorous as possible.

Before examining Horace's second satire in more detail, let us consider the other noteworthy Roman satire on women and sex, namely, Juvenal's famous sixth satire, with its warnings against association with women and the dangers of marriage. This poem, the longest and most prolix of all Latin satires, projects an attitude much darker than that of Horace on the issue of man's relationship with women. The sixth satire has a theme that could fit comfortably into either the Stoic or the Epicurean tradition. But Duff's reference to Menippus also applies to Juvenal: "What . . . Epicureanism attempted through gentle teaching, Menippus attempted through jests and gibes"[8]—though Juvenal's "jests" have a grimness and desperate edge that can hardly be described as humorous. This satire finds a special resonance in the Roman literary heritage in part because it displays a kind of jaded nostalgia for the past and for the *mos maiorum*, its epitome having come at some distant period when Stoic reticence was thought to have prevailed.

The satire begins, at least ostensibly, with nostalgia (6.1–3).

Credo Pudicitiam Saturno rege moratam
In terris visamque diu, cum frigida parvas
Praeberet spelunca domos . . .

[I believe Chastity lingered on earth under King Saturn and was seen for a long time when a chilly cave provided small shelter . . .]

This opening, like that of the second satire of Horace, combines solemnity with a comic overtone, in this case by pretending to treat a theme (the impossibility of marriage today) on a grand and epic scale, pushing the period of chastity back to the age of primitive human (cf. Horace *Serm.* 1.2.21–22). But while the ancient prevalence of fidelity and chastity seems clearly preferred, Juvenal's cave people are decidedly lacking in epic grandeur, sounding more like the rude savages—ignorant of government and the common good—described by Lucretius in *De rerum natura* 5.925–1104 (cf. esp. 958–59). The appeal to nostalgia both recalls and debunks epic, suggesting both Lucretius and Hesiod's *Theogony* 123–25, where Eros, who "overcomes the minds and wise counsels of gods and men," is one of the first creations (Juvenal's humorous take on this, at *Sat.* 6.21, is that adultery is *anticum et vetus*). A wide perspective is needed when one paints a broad canvas—that is, treats such a universal theme.

The make-believe solemnity of the opening is also an appropriate introduction to a satire of almost monstrous length, 670 lines, filling the entire second book of satires all by itself. Some see in this sheer length a reflection of a personal character flaw on the part of Juvenal, namely, a "genuine personal misogyny" that throws the poem out of control, causing the satirist to lose attention to structure "as his mind suggested more and more topics to him."[9] Such attempts to read personal motives and neurotic quirks between the lines of a poem are always risky. I have suggested elsewhere, however, that if criticism of women and marriage is a character flaw, it is a peculiarly common one, shared by many who write on the topic of the prospect of marriage. It is an obsessive trait shared by satirical writers as remote from each other as the Epicurean Lucretius and the ascetic Christian semi-hermit Jerome, both of whom have a similar tendency to ramble on at length and give the appearance of letting their emotions control them when they are discussing the explosive issue of sexual relationships with women.

We can recognize the traditionally Roman themes of Juvenal's misogynistic satire when we compare the presence of many of them in Horace's *Ode* 3.6, a somber, patriotic poem that would hardly be singled out by many critics as an important source for these satiric themes. We can set the themes from Horace's *Ode* 3.6 and Juvenal's *Satire* 6 (in one instance supplementing it with Juvenal *Sat.* 1) side by side.

Horace *Ode* 3.6	Juvenal *Satire* 6
(17–18) today corruption has stained marriage	(298–300) our sinful age has learned foreign luxury
(21–22) young women learn Ionic dancing	(320–26) wives dance obscenely
(22–24) they are educated in unchastity (*artibus*)	(232–34) mothers educate girls in infidelity (*docet . . . docet*)
(25) the wife seduces men when the husband is drunk or pretends not to notice	(116; 1.56–57) the wife's adulteries are when the husband is asleep or pretends to be drunk
(30) the wife will even have sex with a tradesman (*institor*)	(331–32) the wife will have sex with slaves, water carriers, donkeys
(33–36) in the days of Hannibal, there was patriotism and fidelity	(287–93) there was no adultery when Hannibal was at the gates

Even this small sample provides a clear indication that many of Juvenal's themes did not reflect a great social upheaval in the role of women between the time of Horace and his own time; his laments about the degeneration of chastity often were not inventions of his own but standard poetic topoi, which he was free to borrow, expand, and exaggerate—in effect using material very similar to that found in this "Roman ode" of Horace, but deflecting the stern moral lesson and exaggerating the farcical humor that is already implicit in

Horace's material. Nothing could illustrate more vividly the easy compatibility of the warning against women and marriage with traditional Roman moral values.

At the same time, the characters who open Juvenal's sixth satire, the cave-wife and her acorn-belching husband, who would be so out of place in the sophisticated world of Propertius's Cynthia or Catullus's Lesbia, are bizarre—even if chaste—figures, totally alien to the everyday world of Juvenal and us, his readers, where, the satirist insists, adultery is common and widespread. Hence there is the comic deflation, the implication that a trip in a time machine back to the origin of the world is necessary in order to find a society where chastity is common—and it remains in doubt whether chastity was common even then, a doubt implied by *credo*, the very first word of the poem. (Part of the joke is that Juvenal's fat and even "shaggy" wife, extolled as a model of chastity, is an alien creation who would be less than a desirable choice for a sex partner anyway.) When the universality of adultery is finally affirmed (*Sat.* 6.21), it is *anticum* and *vetus*. The religious solemnity is blatantly ironic; infidelity has become a holy sacrament.

The wife's respect for her husband was central to the Roman ideal of marriage. Cato, in *De agricultura* 143, had written advice to a farm steward about how to manage his wife: *ea te metuat facito* [make sure that she fears you]. If a wife brought with her a large dowry, however, she could always claim, at least in comedy, to hold the balance of power over him and could control the management of the household (Plautus *Aul.* 489–534). Cicero recommended in *De republica* 4.6 that censors should teach men how to control their wives, though absolute rule by the husband had begun by later Roman times to break down as an ideal, to require qualifications, and to seem old-fashioned.[10] What makes Juvenal's women really a threat is that they exercise power over their husbands (cf. *iubeo*, *Sat.* 6.223; *imperat ergo viro*, 224). They have succeeded in integrating themselves completely in male society; move freely about the city (398); remain present in the room and insist on contributing when the men attempt to discuss serious issues (399–406); receive enough education that they can have the last word even in a debate on literary subjects (434–42); and have a sexual, social, and religious (540–91) life that is self-chosen and independent from their husbands. Fully in control, they emasculate their men, who are at a loss to find a strategy to wrest back the power (cf. the focus on the passivity of the husband in lines 432–33) and who are eventually rendered physically helpless by a love philter (610–13). If this role reversal typically takes place in the context of marriage, that is not necessarily because marriage itself is the target of ridicule but because the marriage relationship is the one where the women are thrown most closely together with the men and can stand toe-to-toe with them on every issue. That is why the sixth satire is a nightmare of male disempowerment. At the same time, however, the women have won a victory that lowers, rather than ennobles, them, because, while discovering liberation from men, they lack the discipline to go with it. It has rightly been observed that the search by women for equality with sexually unrestrained men posed a particular threat in a culture where, with no reliable method of birth control, female *pudicitia* was the surest guarantee of the legitimacy of the heir.[11] Equally appalling to the upper-class male, and a prominent theme in Juvenal's poem, is the fact that female sexual promiscuity represents an endangerment to the aristocratic bloodline in the production of heirs.

Thus the women's liberation in *Satire 6* is also a nightmare of class reversal. An important subtext of the sixth satire is the degeneration of the nobility, a theme treated more explicitly in the eighth satire but often lurking in the background as an issue for Juvenal in his earlier satires as well. In Juvenal's view, any deviation from the social status of one's birth can be the cause for scandal. In the first satire, where Juvenal lays out his program, two of the initial examples of behavior motivating him to write satire are Mevia, a noblewoman who fights bare-breasted in the arena (1.22), and—the reverse social scandal—a barber (even more galling, the narrator's own barber) who has risen above his lowly status and now makes as much money as the patricians (24–25). The sexual degenerates in the second satire represent a *nefas* (2.127), a social deterioration that would shame the Roman heroes of old. In the third satire, it is the *Graeculus esuriens*, the starving and social parvenu Greek, who displaces the old Roman nobility and leaves them destitute. In the fifth, a nobleman named Virro is chided for his insensitivity to the poor. The women of the sixth satire are even more insidious than the opportunistic *Graeculi*; they are degenerate noblewomen who try to drag their husbands down to their substandard behavior—though this stance is not maintained consistently throughout (in a really breathtaking example of stubbornness, in 6.161–83, Juvenal rejects as a marriage partner even a noble woman with perfect virtue, because of the probability that her very perfection would create in her a *grande supercilium*, an overwhelming haughtiness; cf. the poem by Petronius quoted earlier).

Though Juvenal may suspect that women enjoy sex more than men do (*Sat.* 11.168–69), it would not be appropriate to a Roman matron to enjoy sex too ostentatiously. The Roman satirists are agreed that the standard to which wives should adhere does not even include lascivious motions in bed with their own husbands, which an upper-class Roman would consider more appropriate for *scorta* than for *coniuges* (Lucretius *DRN* 4.1268, 1277); much less would Roman men approve the unrestrained exercise of freedom condemned by Juvenal.

In Juvenal's eighth satire, Rubellius Blandus is taken as an example of the type of men who have noble ancestors but whose behavior is shameful: "there is a contradiction between the high pretensions of his lineage (*stemma*) and his diminutive reality."[12] Much of the disgraceful activity exposed here mirrors the exposé of the women in the sixth satire (also cf. the behavior of *nobiles* described by Marius in Sallust *Jugurtha* 85.41, *in conviviis, dediti ventri et turpissimae parti corporis* [in banquets, devoted to the belly and the most shameful parts of the body]). Men such as Rubellius are subject to ambition and lust (Juv. *Sat.* 8.135); break rods on the backs of their allies (8.136; cf. the cruel wife in *Sat.* 6 [e.g., 6.219–26]); and go out to commit adultery at night, hiding their features with a Gallic cloak (*nocturnus adulter . . . cucullo*, 8.144–45; cf. Nero's nocturnal antics in disguise in Suet. *Vita Neronis* 26 and the shameful behavior of Messalina at Juv. *Sat.* 6.118: *nocturnos meretrix Augusta cucullos* [the imperial whore [put on] a hood at night]). Other scandals include nobles acting in mimes (*Sat.* 8.198; cf. 6.71–72 on female fans of *Atellanae*) and joining gladiator troops (8.199–200; cf. 6.104–5, *ludia dici / sustinuit*). Such echoes between the sixth and eighth satires are a reminder that much of the outrageous behavior held up to ridicule in the sixth satire can be and is associated by Juvenal with the male sex as well and that such passages in fact extend beyond the sixth satire as part of a wider perspective in which Juvenal condemns the degeneration of the nobility.

In the sixth satire, Postumus seeks a faithful wife, but Juvenal illustrates to his interlocutor, through a long series of examples, that there is a dearth of women available—from the upper classes in particular—as potential wives. In lines 38ff., Ursidius seeks a wife *antiquis . . . de moribus* [of old-fashioned character] (45), and she must be not only an *uxor* but a *matrona* (49). A recurring theme is that women of the nobility are tempted to have extramarital affairs with men of the lowest classes, especially actors (61–77) and gladiators (76–113). The consequent shame is summed up by the result, in which the ugly face of the noble child reveals his true begetting. The hopeful phrase *nobilis . . . infans* (81) frames the shocker, the ignoble name and profession at the center of the line, the gladiator whose adultery has both created and corrupted this innocent baby.

> . . . nobilis Euryalum murmillonem exprimat infans.
>
> [[. . . so that] the noble baby's face may reflect that of the gladiator Euryalus.]

Luxuria (293) is the enemy that has caused the old class of noble women to degenerate; they are no longer inspired by the challenge of having to repel

Hannibal at the gates. Now a matron may indeed undertake heroic deeds, but it is for a base purpose that Eppia abandons her pleading family to go on a perilous sea journey to Egypt—in order to follow her lover. He may be ugly and deformed by years in the ring, "but he was a gladiator" [*sed gladiator erat*] (110), and Eppia willingly underwent the shame of being called a *ludia* (104), a "gladiator's moll."[13]

PHYSICIAN, HEAL THYSELF

In the final analysis, the battle of the satirist, on the subject of sex in particular, always seems a losing one: the aspiring bridegroom will marry anyway; the gigolo will have his dangerous affairs; the beleaguered husband will end up bowing to the will of his wife. In the case of the powerful feeling of sexuality, intellectual arguments are at a disadvantage. The satirist is an imperfect person; he is always ready to be held up as his own most horrible example, to play both sides of the moral fence. Horace praises the advice on safe sex of the elder Cato as "divine," yet he still (at least in his satiric persona) finds it difficult to stay away from dangerous love entanglements. His imitator Persius presents himself in no better light. There is some truth in Henderson's joke that "P[ersius] renounces his body, barely retains his voice," that "with him Satire has gone 'philosophical.' "[14] The narrative voice of Persius's satires seems jerky and erratic, not projecting the distinctive view of Horace or Juvenal; but insofar as Persius's satires do project a living and breathing satiric persona, a "satirist," he is, predictably, a flawed character. In real life, Persius may well have been *frugi, pudicus* [restrained and modest], as his ancient *Vita* claims; but in the *choliambi* that precede his satires, he (or his literary persona) sounds suspiciously like a parasite, boasting of being motivated to write not by the Muses but by the demands of the belly: *magister artis ingenique largitor / venter* [the belly teaches me art and gives me talent] (10–11). Such is the low public aim of Persius as satirist, who mentions epic inspiration only to undercut it, citing the needs of his own body as inspiration, and whose ultimate answer to society's problems, unlike Juvenal's, is to withdraw from Rome.[15] Again in *Satires* 3.44–47, Persius himself is his own horrible example: in the satiric persona of a lazy and malingering student, he admits that he once feigned an eye disease to avoid having to memorize the noble dying speech of the younger Cato. Later, among the faults for which he is chided by his tutor, Persius cannot help his heart from beating faster when he catches sight of the neighbor's beautiful daughter (3.110).

With such exposés of a narrator's inconsistency, one might compare the moral unreliability of the narrators of the two Latin satiric novels. That Lucius, the narrator of Apuleius's *Golden Ass*, undergoes an actual transformation into a donkey while in the course of his narration is a sufficient commentary both on his reliability as a narrator and on the standard set by his moral behavior.[16] On the topic of women, Lucius's condemnation of "the whole female sex," which results from his misunderstanding of the behavior of the captive maiden Charite, is quickly undercut by a reminder to the reader from the narrator himself that his negative judgment is that of an ass (*asini . . . iudicio*) (G.A. 7.10).[17]

In the case of Petronius, the self-defeating satirical intent of the narrator is more controversial and harder to establish on the basis of the fragmentary evidence, but the irony is evident enough in the case of his appointed narrators—such characters as the roguish poet Eumolpus, who is accustomed to receive showers of stone as applause for his recitations (*Sat.* 90). In telling the story of the widow of Ephesus, Eumolpus makes some self-righteous comments about the morality of women, ironically calling the widow *non minus misercors quam pudica* [just as kind as she was pure] (112), but he himself, by his own account, is revealed as a disreputable and immoral character whose moral judgments are not to be trusted (see the discussion by May in chap. 7 in this volume).

The two Latin novels vividly illustrate the unreliability of the moral stances taken by the narrator in satire, while in the case of verse satire, the argument of the satirists against sexual involvement is inevitably slanted in such a way that it engages the reader in an uphill struggle against another flesh-and-blood human being who happens to be female and who has feelings, not to mention powers, of her own. A persistent woman, even without physical charm, always has time on her side, as Lucretius reminds us in the final passage of *De rerum natura* 4 (1278–87). Horace's satiric persona ends *Sermones* 2.1 on the run, with his lover's husband having suddenly arrived back from the country: the satirist has failed to heed his own advice; he has seduced a *matrona* and is caught in the act. Lucretius, at the end of *De rerum natura* 4, admits with some resignation that a woman, even one of plain appearance, will finally succeed in conquering her man by her winning ways, using a method that is compared to the waves dashing against rocks, making it sound like a kind of water-torture treatment. The wife at the end of Juvenal's sixth satire wins the ultimate coup, the death of her adversary, her husband, by first enfeebling him, then murdering him, either by poison or (if he fortifies himself against poison) by falling back on the old tragic method of an ax.

Despite these gloomy prospects, each of these satiric passages has a common purpose. It is not at all that the reforming satirist wants to deny, explain away, or teach his reader how to sublimate the sex drive; rather, he is desperate for the infatuated man to see it for what it is, a necessary, but lowly and undignified, aspect of human life (hence it is described with crude and blunt language). Adulterous sex with a married woman, a *matrona*, is anathema to Horace in the second satire because it steps too far over the bounds of propriety, but the main objection is a practical one: such adultery brings too many dangers—retribution from the outraged husband, punishment, loss of reputation. Juvenal takes the warning a step further: it will not help to dignify the relation to offer marriage to your beloved, try to turn her into a respectable *matrona*, because she will not live up to the role; she will embarrass you, humiliate you, sleep with other men, make another man your child's father, and, finally, not only take away your manhood but actually drive you insane.

To Horace, as usual, correct behavior is not unattainable if one will be reasonable. It only takes common sense to see the consequences of adultery (*Serm.* 1.2.37–38).

> audire est operae pretium, procedere recte
> qui moechis non vultis, ut omni parte laborent . . .
>
> [*It's worthwhile to hearken, you who wish misfortune on adulterers, how they suffer at every turn . . .*]

Here Horace introduces another epic parody, this time of Ennius's *Annales* (Warmington 1935–40, 471–72), with the low word *moechis* taking the place of *rem Romanam* (the Roman state) in the original. Adulterers suffer when they are caught in the act with respectable women; most people agree that they deserve it (except Galba, who is presumably a notorious adulterer). Horace's use, in the second satire, of himself as a comic example of the discomfort suffered by an adulterer caught in the act is typical of a poet who is not embarrassed to bring up his sexual misadventures for a surefire laugh as a comic theme, even when it apparently has little to do with its context. In *Sermones* 1.2.82–85 Horace "very stupidly" waits up for a lying girl who has promised to come to him, then he has a wet dream that stains his bedclothes. In 2.3.235 Damasippus chides Horace for his *mille puellarum, puerorum mille furores* [thousand mad passions for both girls and boys]. The poet satirizes himself even more unsparingly, and in blunt detail, in 2.7, where his slave Davus complains, "You are the slave of another man's wife while Davus goes after a mere prostitute" (46–47). Davus even types his master's adultery as a *peccatum*, a "sin," implying that in this affair, Horace can make no evasion about having been seduced, because he himself is the *corruptor* (63) of the adulterous matron.

So Horace emphasizes that adultery by a man has unpleasant consequences for the perpetrator, whether the pangs of a guilty conscience or of actual physical punishment. The alternative, the second satire insists, is to have affairs not with *matronae* but with freedwomen: *Tutior at quanto merx est in classe secunda / libertinarum dico* [but how much safer are dealings with the second class, I mean freedwomen] (1.2.48–49). Here it appears we have reached a "golden mean" between married women and prostitutes. But this alternative is no sooner introduced than made the subject of a warning: it is just as easy to be obsessed about freedwomen as *matronae*. This is proven by the example of Sallustius, who takes the permission to pursue this class of women and goes to extremes, constantly chasing after freedwomen: his behavior is better than the adulterers, but he has the same disease—that is, *insanit* [he is crazy] (49). To lose your good reputation or to fritter away your father's property are bad in any case, warns Horace (61–62), reminding us by his examples that his advice is of most relevance to the wealthy, with whom loss of reputation and the squandering of an estate would be primary concerns. Horace's middle-of-the-road advice here is fatherly, careful, and conservative, making him sound almost like a *senex iratus* of New Comedy.[18] Indeed, Horace, according to his own testimony, is simply passing along the advice given him by his own father, whose commonsense warning against adultery he recorded in *Sermones* 1.4.109–14: in paraphrase, do not waste your fortune on prostitutes or lose your reputation by adultery with *matronae*. The emphasis is on the practical, not the setting of a high moral standard.

The problem (for Horace) with blustering like the *senex iratus* of New Comedy is that the father's conservative advice rarely prevails when pitted against the folly of youth: sons will still chase after prostitutes, get drunk and break down doors, and waste the family money. Horace's Sallustius and the other imaginary interlocutors who voice their objections in *Sermones* 1.2 (Cupiennus at line 36, Galba at line 46) are the disobedient children from New Comedy. In satire, the paradigm for the pupil who will not listen is Juvenal's Postumus (*Sat.* 6.28), an example of Roman satire's recurring dupe—given various names—who will not heed the satirist's advice and persists in his unhealthy behavior.

Certe sanus eras. Uxorem, Postume, ducis?

[You certainly used to be sane. Are you taking a wife, Postumus?]

Yes, he is, no matter what anyone says. Postumus and the other marriage-bent men in Juvenal's sixth satire tend to have unrealistic expectations about marriage, because they are unwilling to change with the times. Postumus is not prepared for a wife who will control his every move, night and day (30–37). Ursidius (38–59) not only wants a wife who will provide more than sexual satisfaction but also insists on one with *antiquos mores* [old-fashioned character] (45). Ursidius ought to know better, considering his own background as a notorious adulterer: such women are no longer to be found. Women have changed, but most men have not yet made the adjustment. Lentulus (78–81) tries to placate his wife with expensive canopied beds inlaid with tortoise-shell, but she still commits adultery with a gladiator. A few couples do seem to have resigned themselves to the new conditions. The marriage between Caesennia and her husband (136–41) seems successful, and he praises her as an "excellent" wife, but only because she has bribed him with a large dowry to permit her to have affairs. Another "successful" marriage is that of Sertorius and Bibula (142–60): he allows her spending sprees for now, but it is only a temporary arrangement; he will divorce her for another—not making the announcement himself, but cynically sending his freedman to kick her out of the house (146–48)—as soon as she shows signs of aging.

Unfortunately for most of the bridegrooms in the sixth satire, who expect a long-term loving relationship, their idealism is not easily lost. They will try to maintain outward proprieties in a marriage in the face of all the evidence, to the point of being rendered enfeebled (612) and poisoned (626) by their murderous spouses, who may even turn violently against their own stepchildren (628) or children (629–31). Such women are reincarnations of Clytemnestra, only they are even worse, because they have no "tragic passion" to justify their crimes (651).

Horace anticipates Juvenal in warning his interlocutors against approaching *matronae* as partners. The difference is that Horace's matrons are already married to other people and thus are not safe targets for seduction; Juvenal's (unmarried) women are not fit to become matrons at all—that is, to be the partners of men looking for a respectable marriage—because they are incapable of obedience and fidelity to one man alone. But the advice of the two satirists is couched in similar terms. Horace has been listening to the advice of a man's sexual organ, which bluntly protests that he seeks no *magno prognatum . . . consule cunnum* (i.e., no "cunt that is daughter of a great consul," *Serm.* 1.2.70). Here, as in Aristophanes' *Lysistrata* (most notably, in the abortive seduction scene between Kinesias and Myrrhine at lines 870–951), the penis and vagina seem to rebel against their owners, developing a life and set of desires of their own, separate from that of the man and woman who own them. This is how far Horace goes in his detachment of the sex drive from the rest of the life of its possessor, making it sound like something that can be dealt with neatly and controlled as a separate entity (though in reality it never is for very long). Horace advises the reader to listen closely to his sound advice and follow Nature herself (*Serm.* 1.2.74), who is rich in the wealth at her disposal, if we only manage it properly.

> desine matronas sectarier, unde laboris
> Plus haurire mali est quam ex re decerpere fructus.
>
> (78–79)
>
> [*stop chasing after married women, a pursuit in which you can incur more pain and misery than you can reap real satisfaction.*]

Juvenal (*Sat.* 6.47–49) also urges his interlocutor to stay away from *matronae*, but this time their unacceptability as marriage partners is at issue.

> Tarpeium limen adora
> Pronus et auratam Iunoni caede iuvencam,
> Si tibi contigerit capitis matrona pudici.
>
> [*Lie flat and kiss the Tarpeian threshold or slaughter a gilded calf to Juno if you can find an upper-class wife who will stay true to you.*]

Here *capitis pudici*, literally "a chaste head," is added to make the wife's behavior sound even more coarse (especially in contrast with the solemn religious allusions earlier in the sentence), by implying that the *matrona's* version of infidelity is to provide oral sex.

The satirists are constantly reminding us that if men are desperate for a sex partner, any one will do, male or female. Horace makes the description as clinical as he can: the point is not to enter a relationship but to have an orgasm (*Serm.* 1.2.116–18).

> Tument tibi cum inguina, num si
> Ancilla aut verna est praesto puer, impetus in quem
> Continuo fiat, malis tentigine rumpi?
>
> [*When your cock swells up, if a maidservant or household slave boy is at hand to be quickly assaulted, do you prefer to burst with lust?*]

Horace's adulterers either suffered a series of tortures after they were caught by the outraged husband or killed themselves by jumping off a roof, presumably as a preferable alternative to the torture that would inevitably follow on capture. Juvenal picks up on this idea, but his tack is slightly different. Whereas Horace warns that adultery with a matron may lead to forced suicide, Juvenal finds a way to top the old cliché and take it to an extreme in order to shock the interlocutor: in his view, forced suicide, whether by hanging or jumping off a high bridge (*Sat.* 6.30–32), is actually a preferable alternative to the nightmarish consequences to marriage; or if one still prefers to live, sleeping with a boy will be a safer alternative (33–37). The double standard is blatant in the case of Juvenal's narrative stance: the idea of a noblewoman prostituting herself with a gladiator or actor is presented as horrifying in the extreme, but as far as a man is concerned, any sort of arrangement is acceptable as long as it results in his enjoying sexual satisfaction.

One feels that the epithet "rhetorical satirist" is highly deserved in reference to Juvenal.[19] Even in the enormous sixth satire of over six hundred lines, though he is often accused of lack of focus, his focus and concentration are in some sense extreme. He keeps pounding away at the same point, holding it up to examine it from every angle. Such development as occurs in the poem is not so much a progression of ideas but a gradual unfolding of evidence. The apparent randomness of the order of much of the poem conveys the impression that the poet has at his disposal a vast, uncharted ocean of potential material, from which he can draw at will. In the short run, the arguments seem to be bogged down by non sequiturs, irrelevance, anticlimax, and abrupt change of subject. But in the long run, a trend emerges as the envisioned marriage about which Postumus had conferred with the narrator at the start of the poem gradually degenerates into a one-sided nightmare. Thus there emerges an exposure of the full horror show of marriage, gradually unfolding in little vignettes, so that comic or harmless annoyances inexorably give way to a climax that includes the wife's gradual exercise of control over her husband, using poison first to make him mentally enfeebled and eventually to kill him (though she is ready to switch to an ax if he learns to immunize himself against the poison). Far from ending optimistically, the sixth satire plods on a laborious slow circle and ends at the same hopeless point at which it began.

Horace, in a poem of seemingly much more modest format, will not content us with a simple presentation on one level. The idea of visiting a prostitute as an alternative to adultery might sound reasonable enough in the context of Horace's other warnings, but, typically, he introduces the idea only to have instant second thoughts, to see it as an extreme, to make it part of his warning: *nil medium est* (*Serm.* 1.2.28)—one man will only sleep with noblewomen, another only with a whore from a stinking brothel. Cato praised a well-known man when he saw him exiting from a brothel, for going there rather than bothering other men's wives; but are we really to believe Horace when he overpraises this opinion of Cato, calling it "divine" (32) and thus implying a mocking tone? The use of such an elevated epithet is only a reminder of its inappropriateness in a sordid context. In satire, idealism is there only to be undercut; laughter prevails. Again we return to the notion of parody with which the second satire began.

The ending of Horace's second satire shows "Horace," as satiric narrator, doing (at least hypothetically) what he has just promised us he would never do: he is caught in the act of committing adultery with a respectable woman and "flees barefoot with his tunic undone" (1.2.132), as he runs from the woman's house, with all in confusion, when her husband returns home. This ending, reminiscent of the farcical ending of a mime, is a reminder of the low company to which Horace has introduced us, as well as the narrator's inability to maintain a lofty moral stance. Such a disordered rout is after all a standard way of ringing down the curtain on a mime, where there is to be an "escape" from some threatening character, such as a cuckolded husband. A mime is also recalled by the ending of *Sermones* 2.8, where the guests "punish" Nasidienus by running off from his house without tasting his dinner, "as though Canidia had breathed on the food" (94–95). Cicero, in *Pro Caelio* 65, provides a commentary saying that at the end of a mime, in place of a proper close, there is often a chase scene. The most obvious kind of chase would have the duped husband rushing wildly around, trying to catch the lover, who has been discovered in hiding. In some cases, the lover would be caught, and there would follow a trial scene. In that case, a judge would pronounce a sentence against the adulterer, who would then make a farcical escape, perhaps accompanied by his lover, from the courtroom.[20] The reluctant Horace, on a love mission and ignominiously fleeing, is a figure we also meet in *Ode* 4.1, where (after his protests at 2.1.1–2 that he is too old at fifty to fall in love *diu / rursus* [again after so long]) our last vision of Horace in the poem is of the portly and graying poet once again enlisted in the ranks of Cupid's captives, this time pursuing a man. He is haunted by dreams of chasing Ligurinus across the lawn of the Campus Martius (and through flowing water, 4.1.40)—like some ludicrous reversal of Hector and Achilles outside the walls of Troy— running after he has vowed to stand firm and pursuing his unwilling "victim" as he himself once again becomes the victim of passion.

So no high moral position, no lofty ending, concludes Horace's second satire. There is just a reminder that *deprendi miserum est* [getting caught is a wretched business] (*Serm.* 1.2.134). Horace's goal in the conflict between the sexes is the most modest and practical of any of the satirists. As one might expect from an Epicurean, he does not, at one extreme, urge the reader to stay away from sexual relationships entirely, so as to maintain mental perspective; he believes there is a way to stay sexually satisfied without endangering oneself through adulterous affairs or actually entering into marriage. Simpler goals are, of course, easier to achieve, but Horace admits (1.2.24) that even with such lowered expectations, one is likely to go on making similar mistakes anyway.

Dum vitant stulti vitia, in contraria currunt.

[While avoiding one vice, a fool rushes to the opposite extreme.]

Notes

1. Susarion is discussed by Norwood (1931, 13–14).
2. Trans. Svarlien 1995.
3. *Poetae Latini Minores* B.xxxiv (my translation). The same joke is implicit in Juv. *Sat.* 6.166—*quis feret uxorem cui constant omnia?* [who could bear a wife who is perfect?]—where the inconsistency and unreasonableness of the narrator are exposed.
4. Aurelius *Meditations* 6.13, trans. Haines 1969.
5. See R. Brown 1987, 197, on Lucretius 4.
6. P. M. Brown 1993, on Horace *Serm.* 1.2.
7. Coffey [1976] 1989, 72.
8. Duff 1936, 7.
9. Courtney 1980, 259.
10. Cf. Treggiari 1991, 209.
11. See Rudd 1986, 195.
12. Fredricks 1971.
13. Balson, quoted by Courtney 1986, ad loc.
14. J. G. W. Henderson 1989, 113.
15. See Smith-Werner 1996, 312; Braund 1996, 16–19; Anderson 1982, 169–93.
16. See W. Smith 1972.
17. See Harrison 2000, 244–52.
18. Cf. Demea's outburst in Terence *Adelphoe* 88–97; Simo in Plautus *Pseudolus* 416–22.
19. This is argued most thoroughly and convincingly in De Decker's study (1913).
20. See, further, M. Smith 1975, on Petronius *Sat.* 78.8, where the "flight" from Trimalchio's house is "as though from a fire." See also the discussion of "flights" in mimes in Reynolds 1946.

Seven

Chaste Artemis and Lusty Aphrodite

THE PORTRAIT OF WOMEN AND MARRIAGE

IN THE GREEK AND LATIN NOVELS

Regine May

*In a discussion of adultery in the nineteenth-century novel, Tony Tanner argues:

> The bourgeois novelist has no choice but to engage the subject of mar-
> riage in one way or another, at no matter what extreme of celebration
> or contestation. He may concentrate on what makes for marriage
> and leads up to it, or on what threatens marriage and portends in dis-
> integration, but his subject will still be marriage.[1]

Marriage is one of the structuring patterns of society, modern as well as ancient.
Despite obvious differences from the modern novel, the ancient novel can be
seen to reflect the wishes and fears of its society. As the stability of society
rests on the avoidance of adultery and the procreation of lawful children, adultery and chastity, as two opposite poles of (female) behavior, can be seen as
central themes of the ancient novel.

The Greek novel comprises two subgroups. The first, the so-called ideal
romances (Chariton's *Callirhoe*, Xenophon of Ephesus's *Ephesiaka*, Achilles
Tatius's *Leucippe and Cleitophon*, Longus's *Daphnis and Chloe*, Heliodorus's

Aethiopika), portray a loving couple reunited in bliss after a string of adventures. During their trials, they display a remarkable preoccupation with chastity and the prospect of matrimonial bliss. They aim at marriage and lifelong bliss thereafter and use all their resources to preserve their chastity for one another. The issue of chastity is more loosely handled for the male protagonists, who are allowed extramarital experiences, unlike their female counterparts.[2] In the second group of Greek novels, the comic-realistic romances (e.g., the epitomized pseudo-Lucian's *Loukios, or The Ass* or the fragmentary Lollianus's *Phoenikika*), this plot is replaced by the (anti)hero's infidelity, his problems with sexuality, and changing partners. Greek novels of this kind are preserved rather fragmentarily,[3] but the two Roman novels, the *Satyrica* by Petronius and Apuleius's *Metamorphoses*, provide ample evidence for this more anti-idealistic and satirical approach.

The structure of the ideal novels, with their heterosexual couples, focuses on the ultimate attainment of matrimonial bliss, which makes the portrait of the female characters especially important. These heroines are so predominant in the plot that some scholars have suggested that women were the main intended readership of this kind of fiction.[4] In accord with the idealized and romantic world of Greek ideal novels, the heroine is a high-minded, chaste woman of noble birth whose love for her (future) husband is sincerely and deeply felt. She invites empathy, reader identification, and admiration. Her beauty and mind are so perfect that she appears rather artificial, and her characteristics are, as Del Corno (1989) has shown, attributable to a stylized use of stereotypes drawn from different literary genres, especially tragedy and comedy.[5] Frequently these heroines are compared with or mistaken for a goddess—often for Artemis, more rarely for Aphrodite.[6]

The recurring comparison of these heroines with Artemis, the goddess of chastity, serves a particular function. They are chaste to the point of obsession (e.g., Heliodorus's Charicleia), because the novels finally result in marriage and thus ultimately in the continuation of the family. Adultery and unfaithfulness by the heroine is a priori unthinkable in a story centered around marriage and (ultimately) the begetting of lawful children. On another level, this chastity and its defense give the heroines the capacity to ensure their self-identity against tyrannical rulers or other men attracted by their unusual beauty, who have the women in their power and, in this genre, commonly want to seduce them. The erotic power the women in turn have over their pursuers is mainly based on their unavailability to them.

The chastity theme is also found in Christian literature contemporary with the novel (cf., e.g., Revelation 14:4). Christian "novels" like *The Shepherd of Hermas*,[7] the *Acts of Paul and Thecla*, or the pseudo-Clementine *Recognitiones* concentrate on it in a context where religious vows prevent the heroes and heroines from having any sexual encounter. Their heroines make their chastity a symbol of their purity and the outward sign of their Christian belief.

The earliest extant novel, Chariton's *Callirhoe*, was probably written in the first century A.D., and chances are that Petronius knew it or similar romances.[8] Callirhoe, the heroine of this novel, is a remarkable character, the daughter of Hermocrates, the Syracusan general who defeated the Athenians in the fifth century B.C. . She is married to her love, Chaereas, but is separated from him and sold into slavery. She then discovers that she is pregnant with her husband's child, and in order to save the unborn baby and to ensure that it is born free, she decides to marry her master, who is deeply in love with her. This "adultery" is the pivotal event of the novel, and her dramatic and emotionally charged soliloquy when she decides on her second marriage (Chariton 2.8–9) shows clearly that it is not undertaken for fickleness or lust but simply follows from the love she bears for Chaereas, her first husband, and his unborn child. This second marriage, in which no word for "love" is ever used to describe her feelings, is a proof of her devotion to Chaereas and, ironically, her chastity.[9] When she finds her first husband again, she leaves her second one for him, thus resuming their initial partnership based on mutual love and devotion. This union or reunion of a loving couple is the final outcome of all the Greek ideal novels. Callirhoe is, however, the only heroine in the known ideal novels who commits this "virtuous" adultery. The other heroines are either faithfully married to their husbands but separated from them (Xenophon of Ephesus's Anthia) or—the majority—chaste virgins (Longus's Chloe, Heliodorus's Charicleia).[10]

Since the story of the loving couple and their movement toward marriage and fulfillment is at the center of the novel, the plot is furthered by threats to this fulfillment. In the idealistic novel, the couple's love for each other is never questioned, and the threats to their love must derive from the outside. Adultery is present as a threat, since a novel moving toward marriage "often gains its particular narrative urgency from an energy that threatens to contravene that stability of the family on which society depends."[11]

One of many interchangeable and stereotypical threats may be the presence of a rival in love, usually a rival of the heroine, who uses every possible means to get the heroine out of her way and to replace her in the hero's affections. This kind of woman is portrayed as the prototype of wickedness: her lechery and infidelity (in most instances, these women are married) are used as foils to make the heroine shine even more. There is no touch of satire in her depiction; she is a flat character, as seriously evil as the heroine is seriously good. There are only two exceptions: Achilles Tatius's Melite is a rounded and sympathetic character, and Longus's Lycainion is portrayed sympathetically. However, although these characters are exceptions in their niceness, they do not offer the serious alternative of marriage to the heroes (since both women are already married); thus they do not form a serious threat to the heroine.

Both the Potiphar motif[12] and the Phaedra motif[13] occur in these fictions as variations on the theme of threats to the hero's or heroine's faithfulness. Heliodorus, especially, makes the most of the Phaedra motif (Heliod. 1.9–10, 7.9–10): Arsake falls in love with Theagenes, the hero of the novel, and tries everything to win him over and remove the heroine, Charicleia, including trying to burn her at the stake in a fit of malice and jealousy. Arsake does not succeed, and her character is modeled closely on that of the tragic heroine Phaedra, who in several Greek tragedies[14] was driven by Aphrodite into hopeless love with her stepson Hippolytos and committed suicide after unjustly accusing Hippolytos (to her husband) of having violated her. Arsake's desperate suicide is explicitly linked to the Phaedra story by a quotation from Euripides' *Hippolytos stephanophoros*, which announces Phaedra's suicide by hanging (Heliod. 8.15).

At the end, the lovers of all ideal novels overcome dangers of this kind unscathed, and the threatening female predator is only an episodic inconvenience, only one of the story's many different retarding elements that separate the lovers and postpone their reunion, thus fulfilling a function comparable to pirates or tempests, which lead to equally episodic separations of the couple.

It is also significant for most of these novels that they are set in the remote and more glorious past of Greece;[15] the heroes are often sons and daughters of famous Greek figures of the classical period.[16] They are high-minded persons, meant for the reader's admiration—perhaps even emulation. The dangers they encounter on their way to happiness, be it tempests or adulterers, are often deadly but are always overcome due to their steadfast characters. At the end of the novels, hero and heroine are reunited with each other and their families and thus return home to their own social background and to a socially accepted way of living.

The protagonists of the comic-realistic novels are of a different mold: they are everyday people with everyday faults. Since they are not perfect and idealized heroes, the depiction of their faults is already the first step toward satirization; their worldliness makes it possible to give the narrative a satirical twist.

These characters live in the present time, not in an ideal past. Apuleius's protagonist, Lucius, claims relationship with Plutarch (Apul. *Met.* 1.2), and Petronius's antihero, Encolpius, travels through the contemporary southern Italy of the early empire. They are not of noble birth but are middle- or even lower-class individuals. Since the plot of these novels is centered not around the travails of heterosexual lovers but, rather, around the adventures of a male individual, the female characters in these novels take on different functions, and marriage is not the ultimate goal of the protagonists.

The females portrayed in the realistic novels of the Roman period are, with a few exceptions, promiscuous or generally evil and are by no means supposed to direct the readers to admiration or even emulation. The rare exceptions occur only in Apuleius—namely, Charite in the main narrative and Psyche in a very exceptional mythological inset tale[17]—and will be dealt with toward the end of this chapter. There is no central heroine in either Petronius or Apuleius (although Lucius's initiation into the cult of Isis in the *Metamorphoses* is sometimes thought to have taken over the function of the hero's union with the heroine),[18] and the picaresque heroes of both authors' stories are male and promiscuous. It is especially this promiscuity that causes the role of women to change in these novels: women occur in episodes rather than at the center of the stories. The hero has more or less important, but always only episodic, encounters with them. He meets them in one city, and forgets about them when he travels on, like an Odysseus without a Penelope waiting for him at home.

Like the down-to-earth heroes, these women are not idealized but butts of the author's humorous approach, something that is made much easier by their exchangeability. Petronius, for example, by changing the female and male partners in the sexual experiments of his hero, Encolpius, can stress a different vice in every woman through exaggeration.

Although they are protagonists in a "realistic" novel, the women of this genre are still literary creations. Just as their sisters in the ideal novel take over characterizations from highborn and high-minded heroines of drama and epic, these women are given some recognizable literary features, but features drawn from lesser—and often misogynistic—genres. For example, some female characters display adaptations of traditional misogynistic themes found in Roman satire.

The character of the novel plot also changes. There is no longer the unifying plot element of a separated couple and the telos of reunion and marriage, with the happy end of the novel reached as soon as this reunion is achieved. The plot is, however, as artificial as that of the ideal novels: it displays equal literary color, but in the realistic novels, the echoes in character description are taken not only from drama but also from lower forms of literature. This literary color of the plot is used both in the main sequence of adventures experienced by the realistic heroes and in its embellishment by added inset tales, shortish self-contained stories told to the narrator by other characters in the novel or sometimes told by the narrator himself.

Some of these tales may derive from Aristides' lost Milesian tales (or Sisenna's translation into Latin, which is lost, too).[19] The little we know about Milesian tales suggests that they were highly indecent and immoral short stories.[20] Their plots must have involved sexually explicit encounters and adultery tales, perhaps told by low-life characters. Apuleius himself claims that his novel is a string of Milesian tales, in the very first sentence of the *Metamorphoses: At ego tibi sermone isto Milesio varias fabulas conseram auresque tuas benivolas lepido susurro permulceam* [But I would like to tie together different sorts of tales for you in that Milesian style of yours, and to caress your ears into approval with a pretty whisper].[21] The inset tales in the Roman novel often deal with similar topics, so that many of its female characters are actually adulterous wives, keen on satisfying their sexual desires. In contrast with the main narrative, it is often these female characters who are the predominant persons in the inset tales.

In keeping with the bourgeois setting of the realistic novels, the characters of the inset tales are—unlike the idealized heroes of the ideal novels—everyday people: bakers, gardeners, teachers of rhetoric, who allow easy satirization. The characters are hardly individualized. A description of their profession or social status suffices to introduce them—for example, *Matrona quaedam* [a certain married lady] (cf. Petron. *Sat.* 111; Apul. *Met.* 10.19). Although they sometimes might be given names, they are types (the type of the cunning woman, the credulous husband, or the handsome lover), with only occasional hints of individuality.

These characters are therefore open enough to allow a different sort of identification: whereas the characters of the ideal novel invite admiration and thus identification of the reader with the character, the heroes of the realistic novels and the inset tales allow derisive comparison of their exaggerated character traits with people of the reader's acquaintance. They are de-individualized enough, but still possess enough characteristics, to invite comparison with "real-life" people.

A discussion of passages in the novels of Petronius and Apuleius will demonstrate the way the concept of marriage is treated in the two Roman narratives. Petronius was very likely a courtier of Nero, and his novel dates to ca. A.D. 65/66.[22] He sometimes seems to parody the ideal Greek novels,[23] because his novel replaces the chaste and devoted heterosexual couple with an unfaithful homosexual one, involved most of the time in an unstable *ménage à trois* (Encolpius and his *eromenos* Giton, plus either Ascyltus or Eumolpus). These lovers, too, undergo various temptations, as well as tempests (to which, however, they invariably try to succumb) and apparent deaths. But it is also obvious that the Greek ideal novel is not the only genre parodied in the *Satyrica*.[24] The wrath of Priapus that pursues the unfortunate Encolpius[25] with impotence is appropriated from the epic wrath of Poseidon or Hera. This is significant since the idealistic novels derive some of their structure from Homer's *Odyssey*, which ends in the reunion of Odysseus with his chaste wife, Penelope. Petronius stresses, rather, the other aspect of the *Odyssey*, namely, Odysseus's erotic involvement with Circe and Calypso, whose love for him forms a threat to Odysseus's return but only delays it temporarily. Already in the *Odyssey*, the contrast between the faithful wife and the "other women" is brought out. In Petronius, as far as we can tell from the fragments, there seems to have been no final reunion with a faithful and waiting wife; instead, the stress is on the episodic encounters.

There is hardly a genre that is not used in the *Satyrica*,[26] and Roman satire,[27] as it is featured by Petronius's contemporary Persius and later by Juvenal,[28] is especially evident in his depiction of his female characters. Thus the Circe episode (*Sat.* 126–141.1), besides being modeled on the obvious *Odyssey* parallel[29] (the witch and goddess Circe keeps Odysseus enthralled and absent from his home and wife for one year in book 10 of Homer's *Odyssey*), also features some of the typical attitudes criticized in Juvenal's misogynist sixth satire. Circe, who has fallen in love with the hero, Encolpius (who is pretending to be a slave), sends her maid Chrysis out to invite him to an erotic encounter. Chrysis disparagingly describes her mistress as wanton, a woman who falls in love only with slaves, actors, or (worse than that) gladiators.[30]

Nam quod servum te et humilem fateris, accendis desiderium aestuantis. quaedam enim feminae sordibus calent, nec libidinem concitant, nisi aut servos viderint aut statores altius cinctos. harena aliquas accendit aut perfusus pulvere mulio aut histrio scaenae ostentatione traductus. ex hac nota domina est mea: usque ab orchestra quattuordecim transilit et in extrema plebe quaerit quod diligat. (*Sat.* 126.5–7)

[*As for your admission that you're a slave with no pretensions, that's precisely why you fire my lady's passion, and she's on heat. The fact is that scum rouses some women; they don't feel randy unless their eyes are on slaves or public employees with their tunics hitched up. Some get excited at the arena, or it could be with a grimy muleteer, or with someone disgracing himself as an actor, making an exhibition of himself on the stage. My mistress is one like that; she vaults over the first fourteen rows in front of the orchestra, and looks for a lover from the dregs of society.*][31]

Ego adhuc servo numquam succubui, nec hoc dii sinant, ut amplexus meos in crucem mittam. viderint matronae, quae flagellorum vestigia osculantur . . . (*Sat.* 126.9–10)

135

[I've never knuckled under to a slave yet. Heaven forbid that I should ever see any intimate of mine strung up! Slaves are a job for the married women; they go in for kissing the traces of the whip . . .]

These features are common disparaging themes of satire used against women, but Encolpius does not take the warning of her maid and the lesson of his own (otherwise vast and readily applied) literary knowledge.[32] He sees Circe as the paragon of female beauty (*mulierem omnibus simulacris emendatiorem. nulla vox est quae formam eius possit comprehendere* [no statue could match her perfection, no words could do justice to her beauty], *Sat.* 126.13–14), and he compares her to a goddess (*per formam tuam te rogo ne fastidias hominem peregrinum inter cultores admittere. invenies religiosum, si te adorari permiseris* [It is I who must beg you by that beauty of yours not to disdain to accept this foreigner among your votaries. You will find me a devout follower, if you permit me to prostrate myself before you], *Sat.* 127.3).

Encolpius's comparison of Circe to a goddess is significant. Not only is this a reminiscence of the goddess Circe in the *Odyssey*, but it can also be taken as a comic parody of the Greek novels: their heroines are of such beauty that their onlookers confuse them with statues of goddesses or the goddess herself, most often the personification of chastity, Artemis. Petronius does not specify which goddess Circe is to resemble, although by comparing her mouth to that of Praxiteles' Artemis statue (*osculum quale Praxiteles habere Dianam credidit, Sat.* 126.16), Encolpius links her to the goddess of chastity. The intertextuality with the Greek novels raises the comic contrast between the expected chastity and the realistic promiscuity this woman is going to display. When Circe is described as something she is so blatantly not, and when she immediately sets about disproving Encolpius's sentimental dreams about idealized women, she not only dispels these dreams as unrealistic but also presents the whole female race as unable to live up to this kind of idealization in real life.

Encolpius's initial response is thus only the natural one expected of the hero of an ideal romance, but it is completely inadequate for the protagonist of Petronius's realistic novel. The continuation of the encounter between Encolpius and Circe also inverts the allusion to the Greek novels. There is no swearing of eternal fidelity to each other (although Encolpius is willing to give up his *eromenos* Giton for her, albeit only temporarily; cf. *Sat.* 127–30), and the theme of chastity is also turned into its opposite, because the couple immediately sets about consummating their mutual attraction, without even a pretense of marriage.

When, however, due to the curse of Priapus, Encolpius proves to be impotent, Circe turns out to be sarcastic and even cruel. In a letter to him, she compares his impotence with death and stresses her ability to find other lovers without any problems or qualms of conscience (*Sat.* 129.5–7, 9).

> Quid tamen agas, quaero, et an tuis pedibus perveneris domum; negant enim medici sine nervis homines ambulare posse. narrabo tibi, adulescens, paralysin cave. numquam ego aegrum tam magno periculo vidi: medius [fidius] iam peristi. quod si idem frigus genua manusque temptaverit tuas, licet ad tubicines mittas. . . . nam quod ad me attinet, non timeo ne quis inveniatur cui minus placeam. nec speculum mihi nec fama mentitur.

> *[I am writing to inquire about your health, and to ask whether you were able to arrive home on your own two feet. Doctors say that people who lose their sexual powers are unable to walk. I warn you, young man: you may become a paralytic. No sick person I have ever set eyes on is in such grave danger. I swear that already you are as good as dead. If the same chill gets to your knees and hands, you can send for the funeral pipers. . . . As for myself, I have no fear of encountering any man who will find me less attractive than you do. After all, my mirror and my reputation do not lie.]*

Revengeful, sexually promiscuous, and faithless, Circe is far from the ideal heroine of the Greek romance. Her lechery links her, rather, with the stereotypes of Roman satire on women.[33] Marriage with a woman of this kind would, even if intended, be impossible for the hero, and this satirical portrait of Circe as an epitome of the contemporary Roman woman is unlikely to predispose any reader toward marriage.

Women are always portrayed negatively in the *Satyrica*. Quartilla and Tryphaena represent the type of the lecherous woman often criticized in Roman satire. Quartilla and Oenothea, the two priestesses of Priapus, are satirized as dishonest women who hide their sexual desires behind a thin curtain of religiosity (*Sat.* 17, 137; cf. Juv. *Sat.* 6); again, they display their promiscuity in a sexual episode involving the hero, Encolpius. Quartilla never speaks of marriage before trying to have intercourse with Encolpius, and the farcical "wedding ceremony" she organizes between the boy Giton and her prepubescent slave girl Pannychis, as described by Encolpius, shows that she does not respect any social or religious aspect of marriage (Petron. *Sat.* 26).

> consurrexi ad officium nuptiale. iam Psyche puellae caput involverat flammeo, iam embasicoetas praeferebat facem, iam ebriae mulieres longum agmen plaudentes fecerant thalamumque incesta exornaverant veste, cum Quartilla [quoque] iocantium libidine accensa et ipsa

surrexit correptumque Gitona in cubiculum traxit. sine dubio non repug-
naverat puer, ac ne puella quidem tristis expaverat nuptiarum nomen.
itaque cum inclusi iacerent, consedimus ante limen thalami . . .

[I got up to play my part in the ceremony. By now Psyche [sc., Quartilla's
servant] had draped a marriage veil over the girl's head, and the Tumbler was
leading the way with a marriage torch. The drunken females formed a long
line, clapping their hands; they had adorned the bridal chamber with lewd
coverlets. Quartilla was roused by the lecherous behaviour of the sportive
crowd. She sprang up, grabbed Giton, and dragged him into the bedroom.
The boy had clearly offered no resistance, and the girl had not blanched fear-
fully at the mention of marriage. So they were tucked in, and they lay down;
we seated ourselves at the threshold of the chamber . . .]

By dressing the seven-year-old Pannychis in all the accoutrements of a
proper wedding, as symbolized by the flame-colored veil and the wedding
torches (a proper element even of the "wedding" of Psyche in Apul. *Met.*
4.33), Quartilla parodies the time-honored institution of marriage as well as
its ceremonies. This "wedding," the only one in the *Satyrica*, is not a proper
one but only a staged affair, which uses the right props but not the right ideology. On the contrary, it involves two children in parody of the wedding rites,
eagerly watched by the voyeuristic adults. Together with the ceremony, the
ideology behind marriage is turned upside down, and it is the women who
take the active part in this parody: Quartilla and her maid dress the girl, who
is herself not the modest bride of the tradition but keen on the consumma-
tion of the wedding rites; it is the women who lead the wedding procession
and drag Giton, the "bridegroom" (who, however, follows not unwillingly),
into the marriage chamber. Encolpius is left as the observer of the "ceremony,"
neither applauding nor criticizing it. The men are debauched, too, but more
implicitly so. The women are portrayed as more active, even predatory, in
their promiscuity and contempt for the marriage ceremony.

A more refined approach to the characterization of the female can be found
in the well-known story of the Widow of Ephesus, an inset tale told by the
traveling poetaster Eumolpus (*Sat.* 110.6–8).

ne sileret sine fabulis hilaritas, multa in muliebrem levitatem coepit
iactare: quam facile adamarent, quam cito etiam filiorum obliviscteren-
tur, nullamque esse feminam tam pudicam, quae non peregrina libidine
usque ad furorem averteretur. Nec se tragoedias veteres curare aut
nomina saeculis nota, sed rem sua memoria factam . . .

*[[Eumolpus] refused to allow the happy atmosphere to dissolve without some
story-telling. So he launched a lengthy attack on women's fickleness, remarking on the readiness with which they fall in love, and the speed with which
they cease to think even of their offspring, and claiming that no lady is so
chaste that she cannot be driven even to distraction by lust for some outsider.
He said that he was not thinking of those tragedies of old, nor of names familiar to earlier generations, but of an incident which occurred within his own
recollection.]*

The story is intended to illustrate especially the latter part of Eumolpus's claim,
the fact that women are all shameless and can be driven into *furor* (frenzy) by
their love for a mere stranger. *Furor* is of course a key word for frenzied women
from Virgil's Dido to women like Phaedra or Medea from contemporary Senecan
tragedy, all of whom fall in love too easily and accordingly wreak havoc for
themselves and sometimes for the ones they love.[34]

Eumolpus's story does not, however, illustrate the *furor* that he claims
women would be driven to by their dangerous love. The widow's sagacity, as
will be seen, is cold reflection about how to keep her lover alive; her portrait,
although highly satirical, reflects not frenzy but only fickleness. *Furor* and the
tragic portrait of vicious female characters are different: Eumolpus claims that
not only the heroines of tragedy, of days long gone by, but also normal, "everyday women" are dangerous. The portrait of the evil female antagonists of the
Greek novels (the Phaedraesque characters of the stories of, e.g., Xenophon
of Ephesus), set in the more heroic past, is now extended to that of any contemporary woman on earth. Shamelessness, Eumolpus claims, is inherent in
the nature of all women, there is no differentiation into "good" or "bad" women.

The widow's story (*Sat.* 111–12) is very well known in its own right,[35] and
a short summary will suffice: The husband of a highly virtuous woman dies.
She buries him in a vault, where she, too, stays—determined not to leave his
body but to starve herself to death. She is highly admired for this by the townspeople, as *singularis exempli femina* [so unique an example] (*Sat.* 111.3) and
solum illud . . . verum pudicitiae amorisque exemplum [an authentic example of
chastity and love] (111.5). A soldier, who had been commanded to guard cru-
cified robbers in the neighborhood, is made curious by the light in the vault,
which is kept alight by the widow's maid. He approaches the vault and, with
some help from the maid, manages to persuade the beautiful widow, who resists
at first, to take some nourishment and finally to sleep with him. This "second marriage" goes on for three days, *non tantum illa nocte, qua nuptias fecerunt*
[not merely on that night's celebration of their union [lit. "marriage"]] (*Sat.*
112.3). Then the soldier discovers that one of the bodies he was to guard has

been stolen from its cross, and he now fears he will be put to death himself. The widow, however, is unwilling to lose her second husband so soon: *mulier non minus misericors quam pudica "ne istud" inquit "dii sinant, ut eodem tempore duorum mihi carissimorum hominum duo funera spectem"* [But the woman's sense of pity matched her chastity. "The gods must not allow me," she said, "to gaze on the two corpses of the men that I hold most dear"] (*Sat.* 112.7). So she helps the soldier to put her dead husband's body up onto the cross instead.

This woman is well known for her chastity, the main virtue of a Roman wife. She is married and willing to remain *univira*[36] (another Roman ideal) after her husband has died—and even to follow him to the grave.[37] She is, in short, the idealized image of a Roman wife, so ideal that when she has decided to starve herself to death in her husband's tomb, she attracts spectators on pilgrimage to see her *pudicitia*. At first sight, then, she is the Roman mirror of the Greek novel heroine, who is gazed at for her goddesslike beauty that even results in pilgrimages to see her. Similarly, the widow's wish to die after her husband's death by the dramatic means of starving herself is reminiscent of the suicidal feelings uttered by Greek heroines whenever they believe that their beloved is dead. If this were an ideal Greek novel, her chastity would be maintained. Since, however, this is a Roman novel (and, furthermore, very likely a Milesian tale),[38] an informed reader will expect that she will easily succumb to temptation.

Her chastity, however, another trait linking her with the likes of Callirhoe, is not going to last long: when wanting to die *univira*, the widow doth protest too much. Although she is portrayed in such an ideal way at the beginning of the story, she soon gives in to the soldier's blandishments and is not only unfaithful to her dead husband but also goes much further in her betrayal, by suggesting hanging his body on the cross in order to save her newly found lover. Without any qualms, she substitutes the living "husband" for the dead one and professes a similar affection for both of them (*duorum mihi carissimorum hominum* [the [two] men I hold most dear], *Sat.* 112.7), not distinguishing between her lawful marriage and this sudden erotic attraction. This scene gains even more poignancy when the intertextuality with the Greek novels is considered.

It is remarkable that the tryst between the matron and her soldier is called a *nuptias*, a "wedding," although it does not resemble a legitimate wedding at all.[39] The idea of marriage, as in the children's wedding discussed earlier, becomes a mere farce; the word *nuptias* becomes only a euphemism for sexual intercourse. This turn of phrase is not unique,[40] but in a story about a wife who is renowned for her matrimonial chastity, it is rather telling.

This fickleness of the woman who was admired for having precisely these virtues of a Roman wife is intended to prove Eumolpus's initial point that no woman, no wife, will ever remain faithful to her husband. He does not go so far as to speak against marriage in general; he speaks only against the characterization of women. Indeed, he is very much in favor of marriage when it serves his own purpose of securing a rich wife (and more important, her money) for himself later on in the story,[41] despite claiming that in his eyes there is no single virtue in a woman that warrants marrying her.

Eumolpus, who, in telling the story of the Widow of Ephesus, displays some self-righteous criticism of women, has already touted himself (in his introduction) as wanton and promiscuous, when telling the story of the Pergamene Boy (Sat. 85–87), which is also presumably modeled after a Milesian tale and is in many respects its equivalent. Thus the narrator of the story is himself a disreputable and promiscuous character, and by telling a tale about his own sexual depravity before telling one about the depravity of women, he also disqualifies himself as a proper judge of morality.[42] In addition, he tells the story to a party of people that includes the woman Tryphaena, who has evidently committed adultery with the hero, Encolpius, in a lost part of the novel. She blushes but at the same time caresses the neck of the young boy Giton, Encolpius's eromenos (erubescente non mediocriter Tryphaena vultumque suum super cervicem Gitonis amabiliter ponente [Tryphaena blushed to the roots of her hair, and leant her cheek affectionately on Giton's neck], Sat. 113.1), which shows her debauchery, although the story has hit home. Her husband (if that is what he is), Lichas, is not pleased by the story—any more than by what he sees his wife doing: At non Lichas risit, sed iratum commovens caput, "Si iustus" inquit "imperator fuisset, debuit patris familiae corpus in monumentum referre, mulierem affigere cruci" [But Lichas, far from laughing, shook his head angrily and said: "If the governor had done the right thing, he would have replaced the husband's body in the tomb, and strung the woman up on the cross"] (Sat. 113.2). His reaction is indignation, but not so much at the widow's lack of faithfulness as at the desecration of her husband's body. However, this self-righteous moralizer has apparently also had sexual relations with Encolpius[43]—again in the lost part of the novel—and thus himself is no proper judge of a woman's chastity.[44]

Petronius, then, on the whole pictures women generally as unfaithful and unvirtuous individuals. This criticism is, however, explicit: they are either clearly portrayed as evidently promiscuous and despising marriage (Quartilla)—even openly professing this themselves (Circe in her letter to Encolpius)—or explicitly described as shameless and unfaithful by male characters within the plot (Eumolpus's Ephesian widow). Sometimes it is claimed that the text in the story of the Widow of Ephesus is open to ambiguous interpretation,[45] since the reader has to decide whether the widow's actions are justifiable or not. She is called a *prudentissima femina* [very resourceful woman] by the author when she decides to put her dead husband on the cross—clearly an ironic comment meant to direct the reader toward seeing her fickleness. The Widow of Ephesus loses her ambiguity through the context and becomes an exemplum for the promiscuity of the female of the species.

Petronius's male characters are not much better. By having an adulterous old man tell the widow's story, Petronius leaves us the opportunity to judge him as well as her. Eumolpus reveals himself as a lecher in his story about the Pergamene Boy, and Encolpius is interested in any homosexual or heterosexual offer he gets. There is a gradual difference, however, between the women, who are explicitly called unfaithful, and the men, whose depravity is more implicit—left for the reader to find out through their actions and stories—and not directly labeled as depravity or promiscuity. No character in Petronius's story explicitly criticizes the loose behavior of the men, while deprecatory remarks about the women abound. This is more than just a "double standard":[46] not only do the men escape the narrator's criticism for their adulteries, but the women are also explicitly called lecherous and generally portrayed as much more depraved. It is the women (Quartilla, Circe) who try to seduce the men. The men (Giton, Encolpius) more or less passively give in to the wiles of the females, thus leaving the main "guilt" for the adultery with the women, who even "seduce" the men by force if that is what it takes (Quartilla).

The females come out worse in Petronius's characterizations. Thus he does not need to openly argue against marriage. In line with the explicit criticism of women, marriage is derided and degraded—for example, when women themselves take the lead in abusing the whole ideology of Roman marriage by turning it into a farce.

The second extant Roman novel is the *Metamorphoses* by Apuleius (A.D. ca. 125–ca. 180). In this novel, the hero, Lucius, is accidentally transformed into an ass by witchcraft. His own story is not without meetings with women, almost all of whom are evil and promiscuous.[47] The first married woman he meets, Pamphile, the wife of his host Milo, is both a dangerous witch and an adulterous lover of young men. She has the ability to force young men into her power with the help of love incantations and makes ample use of it.[48]

The main criticism of women in the *Metamorphoses* is found in the inset tales, especially in the latter half of the novel. Already in the first book of the novel, however, two evil and rapacious witches with uncanny erotic and magic power over men appear. The tale of Socrates and his "lover," the witch Meroe (*Met.* 1.6–19), who first induces him to abandon his wife and home and eventually kills him through magic after he has tried to run away from her, is indicative of the portrait of most women in the novel. They are more powerful than most men and are a force with whom neither the hero nor any man should get involved at any level of relationship. If he does, it will unerringly lead first to erotic submission to her spells and then to inevitable destruction and death.

As can already be detected from the first story involving a woman in the novel, these inset tales are not always of a lighthearted tone. Some of the women in these stories turn out to be deadly monsters, and, interestingly, it is on the men with whom they had formed relations that their anger is centered. The "heroine" of the first inset tale is not Socrates' wife but his concubine. He has a wife and children at home and has still fallen victim to the witch's powers (cf. *Met.* 1.7).

The married woman Pamphile, whom the hero encounters shortly after hearing the tale of Socrates, is described—and later seen to work—as a witch intent on pursuing her extramarital affairs. She is not much different from Meroe. Both women, married or not, have the same qualities as witches and adulteresses. Like the women in Petronius, both are intent on pursuing young men to satisfy their desires; but Apuleius's women are much more dangerous.

The warning of the first inset tale—that is, not to have dealings with witches, be it of a magical or erotic nature—is lost on Lucius, who is by mistake metamorphosed into an ass by the beautiful witch apprentice Photis, with whom he had some erotic encounters. During their lovemaking, Lucius compares her several times to Venus, the goddess of love (e.g., *Met.* 2.17, 3.22).

As the narrator turned ass journeys through the Greek world, he is able to hear several stories about adulterous women presented in book 9 of the *Metamorphoses*. Lately, these stories have been explored as foils for the situation of Lucius,[49] but they can also stand on their own as portraits of married women who indulge in adultery. The initial negative characterization of women is also, in a less deadly sphere, extended to the portrait of "normal," everyday wives, who do not deal in witchcraft but are still lecherous and cunning when they want to achieve their promiscuous aims.

During the course of book 9, the narrator and his own story drop into the background. Instead, he tells us the sequence of adultery tales, starting off with the most famous one, the "tale of the tub" (*Met.* 9.5–7). The pretty wife of a poor laborer is just enjoying herself with her lover when her husband comes home unexpectedly early from work. She hides her lover in a tub, but her husband tells her that he has sold the tub for five denarii. She cleverly tells him that although she is always at home, chastely spinning wool for their upkeep, she has still managed to sell the same tub for seven denarii. In fact, she claims, the buyer is just now inside the tub, inspecting it. The husband, very pleased with his cunning wife, bids "the buyer" to come out of the tub and, in answer to the latter's request, eagerly offers to clean it himself. While the husband is inside the tub, the wife leans over its lid and tells him which places to clean, and her lover takes advantage of her stooping position. The cleaning and the lovemaking go on until both "tasks" are completed. Then, having received the seven denarii, the unsuspecting husband even carries the tub to the lover's house on his back.

This consummately told adultery story is the only one in Apuleius where the adultery of the wife has no negative consequences for any of the participants; thus it bears some parallel to Petronius's tale of the Widow of Ephesus. The husband is poor[50] but given seven denarii for his tub, which enables him to continue living; the lover escapes rather cheaply, since seven denarii is not a large sum, and he gets away with his life and, more important, with his pleasure fulfilled. The wife has the best deal of all: not only does she get the seven denarii (since she looks after her husband's household), but she also manages to satisfy her desire and keep her husband unsuspecting.

The characters are only very roughly sketched, as undefined as the landscape and time of the story.[51] The husband is, above all, poor, but he later turns out to be of infinite naïveté and simplicity, too,[52] when he unwittingly turns into his wife's pimp. The wife, despite being thin (*tenuis*) like himself because of poverty, is still "notorious as the last word in lasciviousness" [*postrema lascivia famigerabilis*] (Met. 9.5)—desiring and lustful although she is hungry. No reason is given for her adultery, unlike for that of the widow in Petronius. Her encounter with her lover is casual; no emotion or affection is expressed. This lack of feelings on her part makes her a rather unsympathetic character.[53] The tryst between the woman and the conventional "impudent lover" [*temerarius adulter*] is described not in any affectionate terms but matter-of-factly, in a conventional crude metaphor, *Veneris conluctationibus* [Venus' wrestling match] (9.5.2).[54] Furthermore, she seems to have been in similar situations before, since she reacts in cold blood as a *mulier callida et ad huius modi flagitia perastutula*, someone "who was bright and experienced in misconduct of this kind" (9.5.4).[55] This is apparently not her first adulterous encounter; her lover is perhaps one among many.

In her attack on her husband for coming home too early and lazily, the wife describes herself as the stereotypical chaste Roman *matrona*, whose ideal life is expressed by the phrase *domum servavit, lanam fecit* [she guarded the house and made wool]. Her more elaborate version—*ego misera pernox et perdia lanificio nervos meos contorqueo, ut intra cellulam nostram saltem lucerna luceat* [And here I am all night and all day wearing my fingers to the bone by spinning wool, so that we can at least light a lamp inside our tiny hut] (9.5.5)—even stresses that she obeys these Roman customs under more difficult conditions than most women, thus being even more virtuous than them. Then she ruthlessly goes on to contrast her own *pudicitia* with the voluptuousness of her neighbor Daphne, who, she maintains, spends her time with her lovers. (During all this time, her own lover is hidden in the *dolium*.) This insistence on her virtue and dignity is continued when the adulterer calls her by her dignified title *mater familias* (9.7.1). By insisting on the typical Roman virtues while blatantly not obeying even the basic rules, she disqualifies herself of this title. Apuleius thus portrays her as both confidently alluding to the virtues many Roman wives were so proud of that they had them chiseled onto their tombstone and sinning against them at the same time. This betrayal of Roman conjugal values is most obvious when the wife has sex with her lover as she bends over the rim of the *dolium: maritum suum astu meretricio tractabat ludicre* [she . . . made sport of her husband like a clever prostitute] (9.7.6). This phrase neatly links the two contradictory traits of her character: although she is married and on the surface pretends to be virtuous, she behaves like a *meretrix*,[56] and, furthermore, she not only betrays her husband but derides him, too. This latter behavior culminates in her suggestion that her husband should carry the *dolium*, the means of her latest adultery, to her lover's house, thus humiliating her unsuspecting husband as much as possible.

In comparison to the Widow of Ephesus, who succumbs to a "natural" desire to live and love on after her husband's death, this woman is more hard-hearted and cruel to her husband. Within the *Metamorphoses*, however, this story is comparatively lighthearted, since no one is dangerously hurt by the woman's adultery. As an introduction to the complex of adultery tales in books 9 and 10, it does not at all prepare the reader for the ever increasing cruelty of the female protagonists of the later tales.

The other adultery story of book 9 (14–31) is more complex, ultimately consisting of three separate stories intricately woven into each other. The characters of the main actors are more elaborately drawn but are even more black-and-white than in the preceding story. The husband, a baker, is *bonus alioquin vir et apprime modestus* [a good man in general and extremely temperate], but the narrator explains that *pessimam et ante cunctas mulieres longe deterrimam . . . coniugem* [he had drawn as mate the worst and by far the most depraved woman in the world], into whose mind all sins flow together as if into *quandam caenosam latrinam* [some muddy latrine] (*Met.* 9.14). Her character is one of the vilest Apuleius has described: she is *saeva scaeva, virosa ebriosa, pervicax pertinax, in rapinis turpibus avara, in sumptibus foedis profusa, inimica fidei, hostis pudicitiae* [cruel and perverse, crazy for men and wine, head-strong and obstinate, grasping in her mean thefts and a spendthrift in her loathsome extravagances, an enemy of fidelity and a foe to chastity]. Upon hearing the story of an old woman about a young man's fabulous dexterity in things adulterous, she is inspired to give up her present lover (9.16–21) and start a relationship with the successful and clever lover of a friend of hers. The adulterer is duly invited to visit her (9.22). Before they consummate their relationship, the baker returns unexpectedly early from visiting his friend the fuller and tells his wife the story of the fuller's wife's adultery and how the adulterer was caught and punished by the fuller (9.23–25). He is genuinely disgusted by the behavior of the fuller's wife, who, as he says, *pudoris ut videbatur femina, quae semper secundo rumore gloriosa larem mariti pudice gubernabat* [was usually, it seemed, a woman who preserved her chastity and always enjoyed a fine reputation for virtuous management of her husband's hearth] (9.24), but he is equally troubled at the fuller's intention of killing the adulterer and harming his wife. He manages to keep the fuller from becoming a murderer by separating the couple.

The baker's wife, when told by her husband about the fuller's wife's adultery, hypocritically attacks the loose morals of her fellow adulteress (*Met.* 9.26).

Haec recensente pistore iam dudum procax et temeraria mulier verbis execrantibus fullonis illius detestabatur uxorem: illam perfidam, illam impudicam, denique universi sexus grande dedecus, quae suo pudore postposito torique genialis calcato foedere larem mariti lupanari maculasset infamia iamque perdita nuptae dignitate prostitutae sibi nomen adsciverit . . .

[As the baker told this story, his wife, bold and impudent as always, kept cursing and damning the fuller's wife as faithless and shameless and a great disgrace to the entire sex: she had disregarded her chastity, trampled under foot the bond of the marriage bed, stained her husband's home with the scandal of a whorehouse, and exchanged the dignity of a married woman for the name of a prostitute.]

In her attack, she ironically makes clear that this adultery of one woman shames the whole female sex. Since, however, she is an adulteress herself, the statement becomes universally true; all women, even the ones protesting their innocence, are universally portrayed as failing and adulterous, and the condemnation is even more credible since it is spoken by a woman herself.

With the help of Lucius the ass, who had been maltreated by the baker's wife, the baker then discovers that his own wife has hidden an adulterer under a vat. Lucius steps on the young adulterer's fingers (9.27), and the baker rapes the adulterer to avenge his destroyed marriage: *mulieres appetis atque eas liberas, et conubia lege sociata corrumpis, et intempestivum tibi nomen adulteri vindicas?* [what are you up to . . . chasing after women—and free women at that—breaking up properly sanctioned marriages, and claiming the name of adulterer before your time?] (9.28). This is a rather unexpected solution to the baker's marriage problem. In describing the fuller's wife's affair, he tries to show some understanding of her, since *occulta libidine prorumpit in adulterum quempiam* [[she] has burst out with a secret passion for some lover] (9.24). Although he files for divorce from his own wife, he does not have the furious fit that the fuller had; he allows the adulterer to live—punishing him with humiliation—and leaves his wife alive, too. Unfortunately, the baker's wife is not as urbane as he thinks she is, and in addition to being an adulteress, she is also murderous: she finds an old witch who helps her to have an apparition kill the baker (9.29–30). It seems that the baker's belief in leniency with adulterous wives was misguided, since this is ultimately responsible for his death.

Apuleius uses a comparable device to Petronius in more explicitly influencing his reader's perception of the women toward a negative view. The same woman described with the strong adjectives of *Metamorphoses* 9.14 (quoted earlier) is ironically called *pudica uxor* (9.22; cf. 9.28) or *uxor egregia* (9.23) by the narrator, a pattern that is repeated again and again to enhance the sarcastic portraits of women of this kind: for example, the murderess of *Metamorphoses* 10.23 is called *egregia illa uxor*.

The women in book 10 become even more vicious; they unscrupulously try not only to commit adultery but also to kill the whole family of their husbands for revenge. The evil stepmother in *Metamorphoses* 10.2–12, whose story is meant to evoke the Phaedra tragedies, is driven by jealous love for her stepson into poisoning her family, who only survive because the doctor who is to supply the philter gives her a narcotic instead. The sister-in-law in *Metamorphoses* 10.23ff. manages to murder five innocent members of her family out of unjustified jealousy.

No wife in these stories is virtuous. They all either manage to keep up the impression (as in the *dolium* story) or are finally found out after indulging in vice for quite a while (as are the fuller's and baker's wives) while seeming virtuous before. This insistence on women who seem something else than what they are indicates that universally all women, especially wives, are depraved and interested in adultery.

All these women in Apuleius are not only adulterous; they are far more vicious than the women in Petronius, who represent only one single vice. The woman of the *dolium* story is also heartless, and the baker's wife is a murderess in the bargain. All in all, they are much more dangerous, and adultery is not their worst vice but a connecting motif that all these women share. Adultery is the common and detectable denominator for all other sins.[57]

Apuleius thus takes the pessimistic view of women even further than does Petronius. The adultery tales of book 9 and 10 of the *Metamorphoses* show an ever-degrading view of the female of the species, and the adultery tales become even more atrocious as the novel proceeds. From the "tale of the tub,"[58] where the duping of the gullible husband is told as if the adultery of the wife were the just punishment for his stupidity, to the needless cruelty and viciousness of the evil stepmother and murderess of five in book 10, the women become more and more dangerous, the endings of the tales more and more unhappy, until they dissolve in absolute annihilation of whole families. Thus, toward the end of book 10, the reader is left with the impression that all women are vicious and that any marriage is going to result in the husband's and his household's death.

It is important, however, that Apuleius does not only portray unvirtuous married women. He also has two counterexamples, Psyche in the inset tale (or, rather, *mise en abyme*) "Cupid and Psyche" (*Met.* 4.28–6.24) and Charite (4–8.15). The marriage of Cupid and Psyche is the only happy one in the whole novel, with a happy ending symbolized by the only child born in the whole *Metamorphoses*, their daughter Voluptas (6.24). Yet even Charite, who in many respects portrays a "realistic" spin-off of the virtuous heroine of the Greek ideal tale (and another Dido),[59] is overcome by *furor* when she has to avenge her dead husband on her second suitor, who is responsible for her husband's death.[60] Psyche, too, is unaccountably cruel to her two sisters, when she contrives their deaths as a revenge for their jealous efforts to destroy her marriage with Cupid.[61] Even these two heroines, at first glance virtuous, *univirae*, and faithful wives, are dangerous when provoked. Most of the more realistic marriages are doomed to dissolution by adultery, which is always instigated by the wife, never by the husband. This dissolution is sometimes even accompanied by the murder of the husband.

In Lucius's world, there seems to be no happy marriage, except perhaps that of Cupid and Psyche, which, however, happens on the level of an inset tale and, what is more, in the divine sphere of myth, as a marriage between a mortal maiden and a god. This is intended to foreshadow the union of the hero with the goddess Isis in book 11 and thus has quite a different function. Indeed, Lucius, restored to his human form by Isis, voluntarily becomes her devotee and vows eternal chastity (*Met.* 11.19), in stark contrast to the preceding stories of promiscuity and adultery, his own and those of others. On the human level, by the time the reader reaches the end of book 10, the general idea of marriage in Apuleius is that there is an ultimate breakdown of affection. Women are unreliable and murderous, and the belief in the all-encompassing evil of the female of the species drives Lucius into wishing for a nonsexual union with the goddess Isis.[62]

The treatment of chastity and adultery in the ancient novels is of a manifold nature. The Greek ideal novels, set in an ideal past, focus on marriage as their aim. Thus chastity has an intrinsic value in itself, and their larger-than-life, highborn and idealized heroines succeed in preserving it until their fulfillment in marriage. Adulterous tendencies are associated only with the antagonists, among whom the women are especially determined and vicious, but only episodic characters who never offer a real threat to the heroine or her lover.

In Petronius, women are revealed as very ungoddesslike, cruel and lustful, unchaste and disrespectful of marriage ideology. His Widow of Ephesus is intent on pursuing her pleasure and proves that Greek ideal heroines do not survive into the "real world" of the Roman fictions. His male characters, too, take marriage lightly, and nothing is left of the high-minded union of equals as portrayed in, for example, Chariton's *Callirhoe*.

Marriage, especially as an embodiment of Roman virtues, is not to the fore in Petronius's story. His married female characters (e.g., the Ephesian widow and Tryphaena), although professing to be virtuous, have no inclination to be so in reality. Thus marriage is implicitly negated as a telos, both for the hero and for the diverse women he encounters on his way. The challenge offered by the sentimental plot in the Greek ideal novels is answered by their opposite: these women are not *univirae* and chaste but promiscuous and adulterous. The Roman ideals connected with the idea of marriage are ridiculed. Marriage has lost its symbolism and meaning and thus need not be pursued at all.

In Apuleius, the women's disrespect for marriage is further enhanced in the adultery tales. It becomes ubiquitous, and its actors become less sympathetic than even the characters in Petronius. The wives commit adultery in a casual way and, as it seems, on a regular basis. No love is involved, which might give an excuse in, for example, the case of the Widow of Ephesus. Many adulterous women in Apuleius are even more dangerous: they use witchcraft to lure their helpless male victims into sexual relations, without leaving them the chance of refusal. When confronted with resistance or discovery, they often turn to murder. Unlike the antagonists in the Greek novels who do not succeed in murdering the object of their jealousy (i.e., the heroine), they mostly do succeed, turning into poisonous mass murderesses. Men, who are in Petronius's novel implicitly largely on the same low level as the women, often turn into innocent victims in Apuleius. In the *Metamorphoses*, adultery is not the ultimate vice; it is just a signal of the often even more dangerous vices of the women. With a few exceptions who foreshadow Isis and are either shaped after Greek ideal novels (Charite, Cupid and Psyche) or on the divine level of the gods (Cupid and Psyche again), this novel portrays nearly ubiquitous misogyny.

The full range of the ancient novel portrays two ultimate contrasts, the idealized chaste and goddess-like woman, on one side, and the satirized promiscuous adulteress, on the other. The difference between the two opposites derives from the individual novelist's concept of his society and his own agenda in portraying it: love and marriage can be a glorified goal and basic element of a working social structure; but the ultimate dissolution and satirization of the concept of marriage can be a sign of an overall pessimistic view on contemporary society.

Notes

1. Tanner 1979, 15.

2. Cf. Ach. Tat. 5.26–27; Longus 3.17ff. Male chastity was very unusual and believed to be impossible in the Greek world; cf. Heliod. 10.9, with Morgan 1978, ad loc. This seduction of the male protagonist serves to stress that he is irresistible and equally godlike in beauty, and as is made explicit in the case of Daphnis, it gives him the necessary sexual education.

3. See fragments with translation in Stephens and Winkler 1995.

4. See Egger 1988 and 1994, 263 (with further literature), for a critical assessment.

5. For an analysis of Heliodorus's heroes with respect to their characterization through tragedy and comedy, see Paulsen 1992.

6. For a heroine as beautiful as a goddess, often as Artemis (goddess of chastity), see Heliod. 1.2.6, 1.7.2, 2.33.3, 5.31.1; Chariton 1.1.2; Xen. Ephes. 1.2.7; Longus 4.33.3–4. In the Roman novel, cf. Psyche in Apul. *Met.* 4.28 (Venus). Only the married Callirhoe has the binary nature of being mistaken for both Artemis and Aphrodite, but as the *maiden* Aphrodite before her marriage and as Aphrodite "proper" after she has given birth. Psyche is mistaken for Venus for reasons of plot, since she is to cause the goddess jealousy. It is made clear in the text, however, that Psyche is a maiden, too. On Psyche and Venus, see Schlam 1978, 98.

7. See Hilhorst 1998 on erotic features in this "novel."

8. The dating of the Greek novels is a notorious problem; see Bowie and Harrison 1993, 160. For Chariton's date, see, e.g., Plepelits 1976, 4–9; Plepelits (29–30) also discusses the reference to a "Callirhoe" in Persius *Sat.* 1.134 as a possible reference to the novel. Ruiz-Montero (1991) pleads for a slightly later date of the late first or early second century A.D.

9. A good characterization of this exceptional heroine is that by Kaimio (1995, with further literature).

10. Achilles Tatius's Leucippe is a more problematic case. There is more sexuality, generally, in this particular novel, which in some ways ironically plays off the mentality of the ideal novel; see Goldhill 1994, 66–102. Leucippe, its heroine, is only accidentally still a virgin throughout the novel, since her mother surprises her with her lover

Cleitophon just before they consummate their love, and Leucippe in the later part of the story quite unaccountably decides that she only wants to resume this physical relationship when she is married to Cleitophon.

11. Tanner 1979, 4.

12. In the Potiphar motif, the hero refuses to sleep with his master's wife, and because of this she accuses him of trying to rape her (cf. Genesis 39).

13. An excellent recent discussion of the recurring Phaedra motif can be found in Zimmerman-de Graaf 2000, 417ff. (with further literature).

14. These include, among others, two tragedies by Euripides and one by Sophocles. See Barrett [1964] 1992, 253ff.

15. This is a common feature in the Second Sophistic. See Bowie 1977.

16. Examples are Callirhoe's father, Hermocrates of Syracuse, and the Persian king Artaxerxes in Chariton; *Parthenope and Metiochus* features the daughter of Polykrates of Samos.

17. Byrrhena, Lucius's "aunt," is sometimes included in the list of "good" women in the *Metamorphoses*, but her relation to the hero is at least problematic. It has its cruel aspects, since she does not try to avert his public humiliation at the Risus Festival in *Metamorphoses* 3. Harrison (1997, 58–59) even argues that Byrrhena, a foster sister of Lucius's mother, is sexually attracted to the young Lucius, which would put her into the same category as the other promiscuous women (cf. Schlam 1978, 97, for a more kindly view of her). Plotina, mother of ten and faithful to her husband (*Met.* 7.5–8), occurs only in a story of lies told to robbers. On the irony of this situation, see Lateiner 2000, 323–24.

18. See, most recently, Lateiner 2000.

19. The fragments are collected in Buecheler 1912, 264–65.

20. Our scanty knowledge of this genre is conveniently collected in Harrison 1998.

21. Translations from Apuleius are by Hanson (1989). It is to Apuleius, not to Sisenna, that Renaissance allusions to Milesian tales refer. E.g., Juan L. Vives (*The Office and Duetie of an Husband*, trans. Thomas Paynell [London, ca. 1558], fol. O7r) refers to *Milesiae fabulae, ut Asinus Apuleji* [Milesian tales like Apuleius's Ass] (quoted from the handout of an unpublished paper by Robert Carver, the abstract of which is Carver 2000).

22. For an elaborate discussion of the evidence, see Rose 1971; Walsh 1970, 244ff.

23. The first to have proposed this approach is Heinze (1899), followed by Walsh (1978). The approach is criticized, e.g., by Sullivan (1968, 93ff.).

24. See, e.g., Sullivan 1968, 91–98, 189ff., for the literary patterns evoked in the *Satyrica*.

25. Cf. *Sat.* 139: *me quoque per terras, per cani Nereos aequor / Hellespontiaci sequitur gravis ira Priapi* [I too, o'er lands and hoary Nereus' seas, / Am hounded by the heavy wrath of Priapus, / Who haunts the region of the Hellespont] (trans. Walsh 1996). See Sullivan 1968, 92ff., for a critical assessment.

26. See Courtney 1962, 86. In the *cena Trimalchionis*, Petronius humorously uses the Platonic *Symposium* and Horace's *Satire* 2.8 (*cena Nasidieni*) as foils for his story.

27. Cf. Sullivan 1968, 116: "Satirical topics in Petronius are numerous: there is satire on religion, superstition, legacy hunting, bad taste, and love; there are satirical sketches of libidinous women, corrupt and drunken priestesses, a lecherous and importunate poet, and of course the great portrait of Trimalchio."

28. For a comparison between Petronius and Juvenal, see Sandy 1969, to which this discussion is partly indebted.

29. See esp. Adamietz 1987, 1995.

30. Cf., e.g., Juv. *Sat.* 6.71ff. (for actors), 103ff. (for gladiators and the attractiveness of their scars for women; cf. Mart. 12.58), 279 (for slaves).

31. Translations of Petronius are by Walsh (1996).

32. This is a recurring motif in the *Satyrica*. Cf. Conte 1996, 91ff., on this scene.

33. See, e.g., Sullivan 1968, 123; Bowie and Harrison 1993, 161. Coccia (1989, 131, 139) sees Circe and, indeed, all the women in the *Satyrica* more as symbols for female corruption in all the structures of Petronius's society than as literary creations.

34. See Huber 1990, 12.

35. See Huber 1990; Sullivan 1968, 219 n. 2; Grisebach 1889.

36. See Rudd 1990, 154ff., on *univiratus* and Dido, who also promises to remain faithful to her dead husband and does not manage to do so. There are many obvious echoes of Virgil's Dido in the widow (see Huber 1990)—e.g., "marriage" in a cave or vault, the servant girl quoting Anna's speech to Dido to her mistress, etc.—but a closer comparison is beyond the scope of this chapter.

37. See Huber 1990, 15–16 with n. 19, on women committing suicide after their husband's death and for further literature. For heroines in Greek novels wanting to commit suicide under similar circumstances, see Kerényi [1927] 1964, 10, 142, 168, 188. See also Pecere 1975, 54–55.

38. The location of her story in Ephesus as well as its nature point to this genre; see Harrison 1998, 67.

39. This again is reminiscent of Dido's attitude toward her relationship with Aeneas; cf. Virg. *Aen.* 4.172: *coniugium vocat, hoc praetexit nomine culpam* [She calls it marriage, with this word she covered her guilt].

40. Cf., e.g., Plaut. *Cist.* 43–44; *Rhet. Her.* 4.34: *cuius mater quotidianis nuptiis delectabatur* [whose mother delighted in daily weddings]; Iustin. 31.6; and the farcical "wedding" of Giton and Pannychis in Petron. *Sat.* 25–26.

41. Cf. also his "adventures" with the children of Philomela (*Sat.* 140).

42. On Eumolpus as an old lecher, see, e.g., Beck 1979, 249ff.; Huber 1990, 53; Conte 1996, 104ff. (with further literature).

43. Cf. *Sat.* 105.9: *Lichas, qui me optime noverat . . . accurrit et nec manus nec faciem meam consideravit, sed continuo ad inguina mea luminibus deflexis movit officiosam manum et "salve" inquit "Encolpi"* [Lichas, who knew me in and out, also raced forward; . . . He didn't bother to examine my hands or face, but trained his eyes directly on my lower parts, extended a formal hand towards them, and said: "Greetings, Encolpius!"]

44. It has to be kept in mind that the novelists (Petronius and Apuleius) are men, brought up in the double standard of their times, and the satire against women in these novels is seen from a male perspective. For an analysis of the male satirist behind female characters in satire, see J. G. W. Henderson 1999, esp. 196, 201.

45. See Huber 1990, 50.

46. On the double standard, see Stone 1977, 501–5; Thomas 1959, esp. 195: "unchastity, in the sense of sexual relations before marriage and outside marriage, is for a man, if an offense, none the less a mild and pardonable one, but for a woman a matter of the utmost gravity."

47. Cf. Konstan 1994, 126: "In general, passionate love is represented as a violent and destructive fixation, it is also especially associated with women."

48. Cf. *Met.* 2.5: *Maga primi nominis et omnis carminis sepulchralis magistra creditur* [She is considered to be a witch of the first order and an expert in every variety of sepulchral

incantation]. Similar phrases are attributed to Meroe (*Met.* 1.8) and Photis (3.15). On the relations between these characters, see Schlam 1978, 96.

49. See Bechtle 1995; Tatum 1969.

50. This is already stressed in the introductory sentence, with *lepidam de adulterio cuiusdam pauperis fabulam* [an amusing story about the cuckolding of a certain poor workman] (9.4) and later, *Is gracili pauperie laborans fabriles operas praebendo parvis illis mercedibus vitam tenebat* [Toiling in lean poverty, this man kept alive by doing construction work for a small pay] (9.5).

51. See Mattiacci 1996, 121–22, on the barren landscape reflecting the loneliness of the actors. This story resembles the typical plot of adultery mimes (cf., e.g., Juv. *Sat.* 6.41ff.), in which the characters are not individualized either.

52. When he came home unexpectedly, he "mentally commended his wife's virtue" [*laudata continentia*] (9.5) for locking the door, revealing an attitude that is obviously wrong and naive.

53. Cf. Mattiacci 1996, 123 (my translation): "tutto si riduce ad un occasionale incontro di sesso, che ben si accorda del resto con la sintetica e negativa caratterizzazione della donna" [everything reduces itself to a casual sexual encounter, which also agrees well with the artificial and negative characterization of the woman].

54. Cf. *Met.* 2.17.5, 5.21.5; Mattiacci 1996, ad loc. Similarly, the actions of the adulterer are rather stealthy: *statim latenter inrepit eius hospitium* [immediately an impudent lover slipped secretly into his [the workman's] lodgings] (*Met.* 9.5.2). The description of the husband's house as a *hospitium* is a homely characterization that enhances the negative impression of a breach of faith.

55. Similar terms used of her throughout the novella portray her in a similar way, as clever but depraved: *aspero sermone* [with a bitter tirade] (9.5.4); *e re nata fallaciosa mulier* [The tricky wench was equal to the occasion] (9.6.1). Cf. *astu meretricio* at 9.7.6 (discussed in the next paragraph in text).

56. Note that the manner in which this is completed is described most crudely: *ille pusio inclinatam dolio pronam uxorem fabri superincurvatus secure dedolabat* [The pretty lover boy then leaned the construction worker's wife down on top of the jar, bent over her back, and tinkered with her at his ease] (9.7.5). The passage is full of sexual innuendo and vulgarisms. Cf. Mattiacci 1996, ad loc.

57. I thus hold a more pessimistic view than Carr (1982), who argues that similarities between Juvenal and Apuleius are meant to cause laughter and provide entertainment.

58. This story was famously used by Boccaccio in the second story of the second day of the *Decameron*.

59. On the characters of Charite and Psyche as inspired by Virgil's Dido, see, e.g., Harrison 1997, 62–67; parallelisms in their marriage are analyzed by Papaioannou (1998).

60. See Schlam 1978, 100.

61. See W. S. Smith 1998 on "Cupid and Psyche" as a mirror of the novel and on Psyche's cruelty.

62. See Lateiner 2000, 323–24. This union with Isis has also been analyzed as ironic— e.g., famously by J. Winkler (1985). It is, however, beyond the scope of this chapter to discuss the "seriousness" of book 11 and Lucius's union with Isis. For the present purpose, it suffices to realize that Lucius's absolute devotion to Isis and resulting chastity is contrasted with the ubiquitous adultery of the preceding ten books.

Eight

Dissuading from Marriage

JEROME AND THE ASCETICIZATION OF SATIRE

Elizabeth A. Clark

Although satire is sometimes considered a tactic of social reform,[1] Jerome's satirical approach to marriage aims not to reform the institution but to warn Christians—especially Christian women—away from it entirely.[2] Christian devotees, presumably already "reformed," are here shamed and coerced into lives of supererogatory renunciation. Jerome employs traditional satiric techniques to press a decidedly nontraditional agenda, the creation of an ascetic hierarchy that produces "distinction" and "difference"[3] among practitioners of Christianity. Indeed, Jerome's most bitter complaint against his opponent Jovinian centers on the latter's erasure of the very distinction among Christians that Jerome seeks to promote.[4]

Jerome's satirical sketches are traditional in several respects. As I shall detail in this chapter, he quotes from and alludes to the writings of Roman satirists. His cast of characters—the dandies and legacy hunters—also strikes a familiar note. Moreover, only when Jerome writes in a satirical vein are his representations of women vitriolic, a characteristic common to the genre;[5] in his nonsatirical compositions, he often praises women.[6] Like earlier satirists, he yearns for the "good old days" when simple virtues allegedly prevailed.[7] He, too, masterfully deploys the satiric techniques of exaggeration, construction of a fictive adversary, and mimicry of opponents' voices; he depicts his satiric targets through diminutive and demeaning adjectives and nouns.[8] Like Lucilius in particular, Jerome merges satire and invective in scathing attacks upon his opponents.[9]

Three distinctive features nonetheless distinguish Jerome's satire from that of his classical predecessors. First, Jerome attacks not stereotypical "pagan" characters but his fellow Christians. In fact, Jerome rarely bothers with the foibles and wrongdoings of particular contemporary "pagans" at all,[10] although he can cite the virtues of (usually earlier) "pagans" as shaming devices for Christians of his own day. It is Christian deviants—"deviants" from Jerome's highly ascetic point of view—who bear the brunt of his scathing ridicule. Thus Christian, not "pagan," dandies and legacy hunters are deemed doubly deserving of mocking censure, given their supposed religious commitment. Likewise, the *cinaedus* appears in new dress as the wanton priest or monk who relies on his presumed sanctity to storm the houses of society ladies.[11]

Second, Jerome's satire targets not human vanity, greed, lechery, and viciousness—so scathingly detailed in "secular" satire—but home, family, *pietas*, and other institutions and virtues to which many Romans, judging from the extant literature, would have paid at least lip service. Despite his disclaimers to the contrary, Jerome scoffs at marriage as tantamount to sexual sin, encourages children to defy their parents for the sake of ascetic renunciation, and mocks any expressed yearnings for offspring. Such views did not endear him to many of his contemporaries, not even to Christians—although they ensured his place in the corpus of antimatrimonial propaganda produced in later centuries.[12] Jerome's transformation of classical satire to a new, highly asceticized, Christian register is striking.

Third, Jerome's ascetic campaign gains force not only by his adaption of lines from classical satire but also by his pilfering of material—shamelessly and usually without acknowledgment—from Tertullian. Thus Jerome does not himself originate many of the satiric motifs by which he seeks to dissuade his coreligionists from marriage. Nonetheless, the two intervening centuries that separate Jerome from his North African predecessor had witnessed a notable devaluation of marriage; ascetic ideals flourished as the empire was progressively "Christianized." As asceticism became the dominant discourse of late ancient Christian writers[13]—if not the dominant practice for all Christians—mere restraint in sexual matters was deemed to be an inadequate response for those who desired to obtain the perfection of the angels. Thus Tertullian, although praising lifelong virginity, aims his sharpest attack at second marriage. Jerome, to the contrary, transposes Tertullian's critique to denigrate first marriage: a decisive "heightening" of ascetic fervor is here evident. How Jerome creates ascetic "distinction" is the theme I wish to explore in this chapter. I will proceed by noting Jerome's debt to previous satirists, show how he adapts the satiric mode for his own ascetic aims, and conclude by demonstrating how Jerome borrows and intensifies the ascetic rhetoric of his Christian predecessor Tertullian.

JEROME'S SATIRIC PREDECESSORS

Jerome represents himself as dubiously linked to the Latin satirical tradition: he aligns himself with Juvenal, Horace, and Lucilius,[14] yet he vehemently disclaims the association ("I am no satirist"; "I write only plain prose, not satire").[15] Although Jerome's apparent indecision could plausibly be ascribed to his sense that vindictiveness is unbecoming to Christians,[16] his disclaimers themselves arguably constitute a trope by which he seeks to parade his sincerity.[17]

If we judge from his usage, Jerome's knowledge of the Latin satirists varied. He quotes Horace most frequently, citing verses not only from the *Satires* (*Sermones*) but also from the entire Horatian corpus; Horace appears to be Jerome's favorite Latin poet after his beloved Virgil.[18] Next stands Persius— Wiesen counts sixteen citations;[19] Courtney and Adkin add others[20]—whose biting wit was readily appropriated by Jerome for his own polemics. Last, Jerome directly cites one or more verses each from Lucilius and Juvenal.[21] Nonetheless, since recent scholars argue that Juvenal was reappropriated earlier in the fourth century than the late fourth-century date previously posited, Jerome may have had some acquaintance with his works.[22]

Jerome adduces the Roman satirists to quite diverse ends. He, like other early Christian writers, finds no incongruity in citing "pagan" authors to enforce "Christian" values. Thus Jerome quotes verses from Horace to encourage more intensive study of the Bible,[23] to warn against the Pelagian belief that humans can be free of sin,[24] and to poke fun at his own wordiness.[25] He cites lines from Persius (while removing their satiric bite) to suggest that God knows his esteemed correspondent "inside out."[26] Frequently Jerome mocks his opponents' writing or speech by allusion to or citation of a satirist's words.[27] Jerome does not, however, deploy verses of Roman satire to expose "the lurid sickness of the pagan camp," as Charles Witke suggests was a useful function of such satire for later Christians.[28]

Most significant for the present discussion, Jerome cites earlier satire to advance his ascetic agenda. As David Wiesen notes, Jerome can "adopt the sentiments and sometimes even the diction of the pagans in his censure of the contemporary world," while infusing it with a novel Christian spirit.[29] The satirists' mocking critique of their contemporaries' "morality" was easily appropriated by Jerome to criticize Christians of his time who appeared less devoted to ascetic renunciation than he. For instance, Lucilius's description of the donkey eating thistles ("like lettuce to the lips") provides Jerome with an apt description of his hometown bishop and the latter's associates, who care more for their bellies and riches than for spiritual things—not fit mentors, he fears, for his sister in her new commitment to ascetic renunciation.[30] Against the anonymous opponent who criticized *Adversus Iovinianum* at Rome, Jerome directs menacing threats taken from Horace: this buffoon should be wary of Jerome's attack, should "flee from him, he has hay on his horns."[31]

Jerome frequently reproaches the deviant teaching of his adversaries through an assault on their literary abilities. Borrowing phrases from Persius, Jerome mocks the inelegant grammar or overly inflated rhetoric of his anti-ascetic opponents. Thus he lampoons Jovinian by alluding to a character of Persius, a centurion who although "smelling like a goat," nonetheless critiques philosophers' words that "balance on jutting lips."[32] Again quoting Persius, Jerome mocks Jovinian's verbosity: "even mad Orestes swears he's gone mad."[33] Likewise, he ridicules the style of the unnamed opponent of *Epistulae* 50 via a reminiscence of Persius: no doubt the monk would feel flattered to have a hundred curly-haired schoolboys pore over his text.[34] Once more citing Persius, Jerome mocks the "Onasus" of *Epistulae* 40, who despite his unattractive nose, aspires to be "son-in-law of kings and queens, to have girls fight over him, and [to have] roses sprout up everywhere he steps."[35]

Jerome also cites Persius to garner more direct support for his ascetic agenda. Thus the Roman "mob" who, Jerome predicts, will fault a young woman's ascetic renunciation includes those who parade their "fat paunch."[36] The purple-cloaked nurses and maids who recite drivel to encourage a young widow to remarry are caricatured in lines by which Persius mocks effeminate poets who pompously declaim at dinner parties for the benefit of the glutted, drunken "sons of Romulus"; note here the sex change that renders Persius's male poets as Jerome's nurses and maids.[37] Most pointedly, Jerome borrows Persius's description of hypocritical Romans who slosh themselves in the Tiber "to sluice off the remains of the night" before they offer fervent morning prayers for riches and legacies, to caricature those Christians who believe that, with a cursory washing, they may remove the pollution of sexual intercourse before receiving the Eucharist.[38]

To denigrate enemies and advance the ascetic cause, Jerome also employs two pieces of satiric writing not derived from these earlier Latin poets. Jerome's designation of his opponent (and former friend) Rufinus of Aquileia as "Grunnius Corocotta Porcelli" occurs frequently in his writings during and after their dispute over "Origenism."[39] Jerome's caricature of Rufinus as "Porky the Grunter" alludes to the late Latin minisatire "The Testament of the Pig." Here, the porcine hero, M. Grunnius Corocotta, unable to escape the grasp of the cook, leaves his solemn testament.[40] Rufinus's literary production, Jerome implies, descends to the same level as "The Testament of the Pig" and other popular farces. By allusion to "The Testament of the Pig," Jerome satirically mocks Rufinus's style: Rufinus had better hire a grammar master before he turns a hand to Latin composition! In this one chapter of *Apologia contra Rufinum*, Jerome also cites Horace three times and alludes to Juvenal,[41] which suggests that his mockery of Rufinus is aimed as satire.

Another piece of satiric writing that Jerome appropriates from a previous writer is his lengthy quotation from "Theophrastus" in *Adversus Iovinianum* 1. Jerome prefaces his citation with many examples of sexual chastity drawn from Greek, Roman, and "foreign"—as well as biblical—history to prove that virginity, widowhood, and (at the very least) "single marriage" were highly prized even among non-Christians.[42] The sources for these chapters of *Adversus Iovinianum* have been much discussed, albeit without firm conclusion. In 1915 Eduard Bickel posited that Jerome may have derived much of his material from Porphyry's citation of Plutarch's *Gamika paragellmata*. Since some of the writings Jerome names as sources (treatises by Aristotle and Seneca on marriage, in addition to Plutarch's work)[43] are not extant, the attempt to trace his sources has been unsuccessful.[44] Although Jerome's extract names (mythological) women mentioned in Juvenal's *Satire* 6, Courtney concludes that the resemblances are "mere commonplaces." Arguing that there is no provable link between Juvenal and Seneca on these points, he notes that Juvenal's antimarital stance accords better with the sentiment of the remarks of "Theophrastus" than does Seneca's more favorable assessment of marriage.[45]

Most puzzling, however, is Jerome's long citation in *Adversus Iovinianum* 1.47 from the diatribe of "Theophrastus" against marriage. Since there is no corroborative ancient evidence that the Aristotelian philosopher Theophrastus wrote a treatise against marriage, considerable skepticism has attended Jerome's claim. Recently, Ralph Hanna III and Traugott Lawler have posited, albeit tentatively, that Jerome simply made up the *ecloga Theophrasti*. Jerome's alleged historical references, they conclude, are for the most part imaginative reconstructions from the generally shared "common knowledge" of educated Romans.[46] Bickel, in contrast, argues that the material in Jerome's *ecloga Theophrasti* was derived from Porphyry and Seneca and that, in any event, traces of Latin authors in the excerpt preclude attributing the piece tout court to a Greek writer.[47]

Whatever the sources of this section, the passage Jerome ascribes to Theophrastus is one of the most scurrilous ancient depictions of the disadvantages of marriage for the "wise man"—and note the female sex of the intended audience. Even on the unlikely chance that the wife turns out to be "good and agreeable" (a possibility briefly and grudgingly conceded: she would be a *rara avis*),[48] so much woe attends even the best marriage that the wise man should avoid it; reliable friends or relatives of proven character are more deserving heirs. This depiction from "Theophrastus" of greedy, complaining, jealous, vain, domineering, and adulterous wives—women who cannot be "tried out" before marriage—is doubtless offered as a contribution to the ancient philosophical debate as to whether the wise man should marry.[49] Whatever virtue the wife may appear to possess is here more darkly interpreted: if she is beautiful, she will find lovers; if she chastely bears the husband's children, he suffers tortures along with her. Yet as Wiesen and others have noted, the extract does not well suit Jerome's desire to warn women away from marriage; presumably, a different catalogue of marital woes would have been preferable for a female audience,[50] a point that may count against the arguments of those who posit that Jerome simply "made up" this diatribe of "Theophrastus."

Jerome so skillfully borrows from his predecessors' compositions that Hagendahl goes so far as to label him a "plagiarist."[51] Yet Jerome does not confine his "borrowing" to "pagan" writers; he weaves citations from and allusions to biblical and earlier Christian writings into his new, asceticizing composition.[52] His pirating of ascetic themes and exempla from Tertullian in particular—a topic to which I shall return—provides an especially vivid example of how Jerome skillfully recast earlier Christian writings to raise the stakes for ascetic renunciation. Jerome does not, however, lack originality; he composes his own satiric sketches to advance his rigorously ascetic agenda, and to these I next turn.

JEROME'S SATIRICAL SKETCHES

difficile est saturam non scribere . . .
—Juvenal *Sat.* 1.30

Jerome's satirical portraits of lax clergy and dissembling renunciants ably advance his ascetic agenda.[53] Likewise, his scathingly witty depictions of matrimony aim to dissuade girls from contracting marriage or to warn widows against a second union. The nuptials Jerome claims to have witnessed in Rome (of a couple "from the dregs of the people") in which the groom had already buried twenty wives and the bride had seen twenty-two husbands stand as a striking counterexample to the lives of sexual and marital renunciation to which he called his Christian audience.[54]

Whether Jerome knew Juvenal's sixth satire, with its stinging mockery of matrons' imagined foibles, remains undecided.[55] That he often attempts to dissuade *women* from marriage, however, gives his satiric portraits a different "bite" from those of his "pagan" predecessors, who ostensibly aimed to frighten *men* away from matrimony through their depictions of adulterous, greedy wives.[56] In this respect, the *ecloga Theophrasti* contained in *Adversus Iovinianum* 47 stands closer to the tradition of earlier misogynist satire than do Jerome's sketches of married life in his letters to women, in which he elaborates the woes of marriage from the wife's perspective.

Moreover, dissuasions to marriage can be found in all periods of Jerome's writings; they are not limited to the years in which he waged his fierce literary battle with Jovinian (392–93). Perhaps surprisingly, Jerome's famous *Epistula* 22, written to Eustochium on "the virgin's profession" and dated to 384, does not dwell at length on the difficulties of matrimony as a dissuasive device, perhaps because Eustochium had already made her decision for lifelong virginity. To be sure, Jerome praises Eustochium for "fleeing Sodom" (i.e., marriage),[57] and he reminds her of her widowed sister Blaesilla's unhappy fate. His concern is both to warn Eustochium against "falling" (as have so many pretended virgins)[58] and to assure her that she is not "spouseless" but has Jesus as her ardent bridegroom.[59] Although Jerome here briefly denigrates marriage (as suitable only for those who "eat their bread by the sweat of their brow," whose "land brings forth thorns and thistles," who wear the "coats of skins"— all references to the punishments attending the first sin in Eden),[60] he explicitly denies that his aim is to recount its drawbacks.[61] He suggests that if Eustochium desires a full catalogue of the vexations of marriage, she might read his *Adversus Helvidium*, supplemented by the writings of Tertullian,[62] Cyprian, Bishop Damasus, and Ambrose. The only specific marital "vexation" Jerome names in the midst of this disclaimer carries, significantly, sexual resonance: wives cannot "pray always" as Paul enjoins (1 Thess. 5:17), since the sexual act precludes a life of constant prayer. (The hidden intertext prompting Jerome's claim is 1 Corinthians 7:5, Paul's advice that married couples should "deprive one another [sexually] . . . for prayer.")[63]

Indeed, when we follow Jerome's advice to Eustochium and turn back to *Adversus Helvidium*, probably written in 383, we find a highly satirical depiction of the matron's lot. Jerome takes his cue from Paul's mention of the "anxieties" of marriage in 1 Corinthians 7:32–34. How might these "anxieties" be elaborated? I cite Jerome's sketch in *Adversus Helvidium* 20.

Do you imagine that there is no difference between the woman who is free night and day for prayer, free for fasts, and the one who at her

husband's approach makes up her face, prances about, fakes her flatter-
ies? The virgin behaves so as to appear more ugly; she will wrong her
appearance so as to obscure her handsomeness. But the married woman
paints herself before the mirror; abusing herself, she tries by artifice to
acquire a greater beauty than she was granted by birth. Next come the
clamoring children, the noise of the household, the little ones waiting
for her attention and her chatter; there is the adding up of costs, the
preparation for future expenses. On the one side, the cooks, armed for
their task, rip into the meat; on the other, there is the murmuring throng
of weavers. Meanwhile it is announced that the husband has arrived
with his friends. Like a swallow the wife flits about to inspect the house.
Is everything in place? Is the floor swept clean? Are the cups adorned
[with flowers]? Is the meal ready? Tell me, I ask you, where amidst all
this can there be any thought of God? Can these be happy homes? Where
is there any fear of God amidst the beating of drums, the noise of the
pipes, the tinkling of lyres, the clash of cymbals? The hanger-on glories
in his humiliation. The public victims of men's lusts are brought in, the
scantiness of their attire the target of shameless eyes. The miserable wife
must either rejoice in this—and die; or take offense—and her husband
is pricked to a quarrel. *There* are dissentions, the seeds of divorce. Or
if you find some home where such things don't happen—that would be
a *rara avis!* Yet even here, there is the care of the house, the raising of
children, the needs of a husband, the correction of the slaves: these
things call us away from the thought of God. . . . For so long as the debt
of marital intercourse is paid, perseverance in prayer is neglected.

Having tried his hand at satirical composition in the 380s, Jerome stood
well armed for his attempted refutation of Jovinian. Probably in late 392 or
early 393,[64] Jovinian (we gather from Jerome's rebuttal) argued that after
morally upright Christians had passed through the baptismal laver, nothing
would distinguish virgins and widows from matrons.[65] His view directly countered Jerome's affirmation of ascetic "distinction," that the hundredfold harvest of the parable of the sower (i.e., virgins) excelled the sixtyfold harvest of
the widows, which in turn surpassed the thirtyfold harvest of the married.[66]
Nearly the whole first book of *Adversus Iovinianum* attacks Jovinian's attempted
demotion of consecrated virginity and widowhood to the level of marriage—
or, from Jovinian's perspective, the elevation of marriage to the same rank
as virginity.

Jerome begins in characteristic fashion, faulting his opponent's barbarous
style and language.[67] He brandishes his own educational credentials with witty

assistance from Horace and Persius,[68] followed closely by citations from or allusions to Plautus (thus relegating Jovinian's tract to the realm of comedy), Virgil, Heraclitus, and the Sybilline oracles.[69] Throughout the treatise, Jovinian's abilities as a writer are the target of attack: Jerome claims that he had barely "hoisted sail" before the torrent of Jovinian's words swept him out to sea.[70] Yet Jerome argues that since even the brazen Jovinian does not dare to alter or replace the words of Scripture, Jerome himself will proceed by way of scriptural argumentation so that his opponent cannot claim that he was "overwhelmed" by Jerome's rhetorical skill rather than by the truth of his arguments.[71] Here, as elsewhere, Jovinian is slandered as the "Epicurus of Christianity"[72]—a denigration surprising only in that Jerome later concedes that Epicurus himself taught that wise men rarely marry (and that he advised a vegetarian diet).[73]

Taking care to distinguish his exaltation of virginity from the views of "heretics" such as Marcion, Mani, and Tatian,[74] Jerome, in *Adversus Iovinianum*, elaborates Paul's teaching on marriage and virginity in 1 Corinthians 7. Assisted by misogynist sentiments borrowed from the Book of Proverbs,[75] he presses Paul's words to enjoin an even more rigorous renunciation than did the apostle.[76] Jerome notes Paul's hope that the Corinthians, by eschewing marriage, might avoid "tribulation in the flesh" (1 Cor. 7:28), and he sarcastically comments: "We in our inexperience might have thought that marriage at least offered the joys of the flesh. But if the married must suffer 'tribulation in the flesh,' the very point that we might have imagined to be their only source of pleasure, what else is there to marry for . . . ?" Yet, Jerome adds, this is not the place to revel in "rhetorical commonplaces" about the difficulties of marriage; this topic he has already broached in *Adversus Helvidium* and (interestingly, given his former disclaimer) in his letter to Eustochium.[77] Throughout this and the following chapters of his exposition, Jerome pirates without acknowledgment the arguments of Tertullian, a point to which I shall return.

Throughout *Adversus Iovinianum*, purity is associated with the state of sexual abstinence; only those who so abstain may devote themselves to prayer (cf. 1 Cor. 7:5). Jerome unabashedly interprets 1 Peter 3:7 (husbands should "give honor to their wives, the weaker vessels") to mean that they should "abstain from marital relations."[78] Acknowledging that Paul tolerates, but does not recommend, second marriages for widows (1 Cor. 7:39–40), Jerome adds, more darkly, that it is nonetheless preferable for a woman "to prostitute herself with one man rather than with many."[79] "In view of the purity of the body of Christ," he archly claims, "all sexual intercourse is unclean."[80]

Two points are here worthy of note. First, while much of Jerome's witty denigration of marriage in *Adversus Iovinianum* 1 is borrowed from Tertullian, the acerbic invective of his own devising is directed largely against the writing style and personal characteristics of his opponent. Thus it is not just Jovinian's views that Jerome attacked; Jovinian himself is subject to mockery. Although, according to Jerome, Jovinian claims to be a monk, he dresses smartly and eats well. Sleek and plump, Jovinian resembles a bridegroom—so, Jerome argues, why not align practice with theory by marrying?[81] Imitating earlier satirists' mockery of "parasites," Jerome depicts Jovinian with many hangers-on, fellows who are no strangers to the curling iron, whose elegant coiffure and ruddy cheeks signal to Jerome their porcine status: Jovinian (Jerome concludes) must be feeding these "pigs" to make pork for hell! Joined to these round-bellied, well-dressed parasites are the crowds of Jovinian's virgins who, in Jerome's slanderous denigration, mimic Dido in naming their state (i.e., of sexual relations with men) "wedlock" so as to "veil their fault."[82] Chanting Jovinian's words—most likely those of 1 Timothy 2:15 ("they shall be saved through childbearing")—the women avow that God wishes them to become mothers. According to Jerome, the noble and wealthy with good reason embrace Jovinian, for if he had not come, "drunks and gluttons could not have entered Paradise!"[83] Jerome's sarcastic sketch does not obscure the "reality" he likely faced: many Roman Christians, including wealthy aristocrats, faulted his renunciatory strictures as excessive. More congenial to them was a brand of Christianity that more warmly espoused "family values."[84]

A second point also warrants note: although *Adversus Iovinianum* is aimed at a male opponent, much of its antimarital rhetoric could with a minimum of readjustment be recast to dissuade women from marriage. Nonetheless, a decisive difference remains: when Jerome writes to advise men against marriage, he reverts to a misogynist rhetoric borrowed from "pagan" writers and Old Testament wisdom literature that accords ill with his praise elsewhere of women's piety and abilities, not to speak of his supportive association with women such as Paula, Eustochium, and Marcella.[85] Here, his denigration of women correlates strongly with the type of literature on which Jerome relies for his argument; when he writes to or about his Christian women friends in his own voice, his praises of them are frequently extravagant.

Adversus Iovinianum 1.28 furnishes an instructive example of Jerome's antimarital admonition to men. Claiming that the uxorious Solomon spoke from experience when he uttered such lines as "It is better to dwell in the corner of the housetop than with a contentious woman in a common household" (Prov. 21:9, 25:24), Jerome also appeals to an aphorism of an earlier Roman orator, Varius Geminus: "The man who does not quarrel is a bachelor." Jerome elaborates this antimarital rhetoric with an a fortiori argument: if wives become proud and contemptuous of their husbands when they share equally in a household, how much more, he concludes, will they become so when the wife is the richer of the two! She then becomes the mistress, not the wife, of the home, and may offend her husband at will. Even if the house is his, she drives him away with her constant nagging and chatter. Since women's insatiable desire serves only to enervate men's minds, it is no wonder that "wives" are often classed with the greatest evils—and this applies not merely to hateful wives, for any woman may turn out to be such. Yet even if the wife is loved, she is still compared by "Solomon" (Prov. 30:15,16) to a grave, to fire, and to parched earth.[86]

Such misogynist rhetoric is manifestly opposed to Jerome's frequent praise of women elsewhere in his writings.[87] Not only Christian women receive his accolades: he even praises the virtues of "pagan" women in *Adversus Iovinianum* 1.43–46, although such acclamations stand as "shaming devices" for contemporary Christians, not as recommendations for "paganism." Misogynistic expression in Jerome's writing seems firmly linked to the satiric mode he appropriates from his "pagan" predecessors.

In letters to his Roman friend Pammachius after the publication of *Adversus Iovinianum*, Jerome registers shock that readers have deemed his position too harsh. He claims that he there expressed himself more gently toward the married than had Paul and a host of earlier patristic commentators.[88] Even when he argued against marriage in his letter to Eustochium, Jerome alleges, nobody complained.[89] He argues that although his critics insinuate that his views are "Manichean," distinguishing the hundredfold and sixtyfold from the thirtyfold surely does not betoken "heresy."[90] In any event, he concludes, God rewards faith, not the sheer fact of physical virginity; otherwise, we would have to number the vestal virgins among the saints.[91] He adds that since he himself is not a virgin, his exaltation of virginity does not entail self-promotion.[92] Rather, Jerome aims to create ascetic "distinction": there is not one reward "for hunger and for excess, for filth and for finery, for sackcloth and for silk."[93] According to Jerome, the abasement of virginity to the level of marriage is Jovinian's great error.

Jerome's antimarital propaganda did not cease with his response to Jovinian, if for no other reason than that the public's negative assessment of *Adversus Iovinianum* frequently prompted Jerome to defend its themes. Three letters from the year 394—*Epistulae* 50, 52, and 54—show Jerome employing satiric topoi in his reaction to the Jovinian debate.

In *Epistula* 50, Jerome defends his ascetic position against a Roman monk (apparently known to Jerome from his, Jerome's, earlier residence in the city)[94] whom Jerome lampoons as a "home-grown dialectician, a regular of the Plautus Players," ignorant of philosophy.[95] Gaining his reputation for learned eloquence from the adulation of "feeble women," the critic thinks to over-whelm Jerome. The latter thinks it lucky for the world that the man did not take up the legal profession, for no one could ever emerge innocent from the stand if *he* served as prosecutor!

As is customary with Jerome's invectives, criticism of an opponent's style here merges with mockery of his inerudition.[96] Here, Jerome jeers that his critic's writings are incomprehensible—but maybe the Muses (if no one else) appreciate his talents.[97] To display his own learning against his oppo-nent's alleged ignorance, Jerome, in just one chapter of *Epistulae* 50, cites or alludes to Virgil, Persius, Terence, Horace, Juvenal, Epicurus, and Aristippus. Perhaps the monk's words are taken for eloquence by curly-haired schoolboys (cf. Persius *Sat.* 1.29) or by his partisans, who must resemble the parasites Gnatho and Phormio of Terence's play. Instead of spreading dark insinuations, why does the monk not argue his case in books to which Jerome can respond? Then Jerome will show that he, too, can fix his teeth into an opponent, that he, like Horace's menacing character, has "hay on his horns."[98] Jerome, as a well-educated man, has, in Juvenal's words, often "withdrawn his hand from the ferrule,"[99] and he has, like Virgil's Turnus, "launched a forceful spear."[100] Neither Jovinian's "swineherds" nor the "pig" himself will be able to frighten Jerome with their grunting.[101] Yet—and here Jerome's satiric piece acquires its rhetorical force by abandoning invective in favor of a more suit-ably Christian humility—Jerome chooses rather to emulate the one who "gave his back to the smiters, who hid not his face from shame and spitting" (Is. 50:6), who pled for his crucifiers, "Father, forgive them, for they know not what they do" (Luke 23:34). Jerome ends his attack with a witty one-liner: far from condemning marriage, he recommends that any man who is subject to night scares should take a wife so that he does not have to sleep alone.[102]

Among the notable satiric features of *Epistula* 50—addressed to a man—is Jerome's ridicule of women: their lack of education prompts them to imagine the ignorant monk wise and eloquent.[103] Jerome depicts his oppo-nent as a great favorite among virgins and widows (Jerome sarcastically inquires whether the monk teaches them to eat, drink, visit the baths, and use per-fume). With pearls of wisdom rolling from his lips, the unblushing monk frequents the houses of noble ladies. He distorts Christian teaching by sup-pressing Paul's critique of marriage and thinks to cover Jerome with oppro-brium. Equipped with an athletic physique and a forthright style of declamation, Jerome's buffoonish opponent is a great favorite among women unable to dis-tinguish wisdom from bluff.[104]

The satiric mode also prevails in Jerome's *Epistula* 52, on proper clerical behavior and likewise composed in 394. The recipient, Nepotian, a young nephew of a friend, had abandoned the military profession to become a priest. Here, Jerome warns Nepotian of the dangers that await young members of the clergy: "women" head the list of possible imperilments. Since Nepotian cannot rely on his past continence to save him and cannot count on proving more resistant to female blandishments than did David and Solomon, he needs to protect himself from contact with women. As a cleric, he should always remember that Adam lost his inheritance, his *kleros*, by the treachery of a woman. If necessity demands that Nepotian visit a widow or a virgin, he should not arrive in the company of clerics who curl their hair or dress ornately. Nepotian should neither accept little gifts from the women nor lard his speech with terms of endearment: no "sweetie pies" should cross his lips.[105] He should avoid those legacy-hunting clerics who hover around the bedsides of the aged and the ill—men who, I posit, if "de-Christianized," might be lifted from the pages of Juvenal or Persius.[106] As a "preacher of continence"—Jerome's description of a proper priest—Nepotian should discourage widows from remarrying.[107] In his closing statement, Jerome reveals that ten years earlier, he had endured great calumny for his treatise to Eustochium; he fears that his present letter will receive the same response, even though he has not "named names" and has reproached no one personally.[108]

A third letter, *Epistula* 54—to Furia, a young widow contemplating remarriage—also dates from 394 and contains themes similar to those Jerome rehearses in *Epistulae* 50 and 52. Here, Jerome's sarcastic depiction of his anti-ascetic opponents rests in uneasy tension with his fawning adulation of Furia and her distinguished family, descended from Camillus. The fact that Furia's brother was the husband of Eustochium's (now dead) sister Blaesilla gives Jerome an appropriate entrée to remind Furia with what hostility his ascetic agenda was greeted in Rome. Although men will shake their fists at him, raving as "the angry Chremes,"[109] and although a "mob of patricians" (perhaps including Furia's father?) may roar against him, he will defend himself against any allegation of "heresy."[110] Here, in a letter to a woman, men are ridiculed for their failure to endorse Jerome's ascetic agenda.

Despite Jerome's disclaimers, there is little doubt that he in fact wishes to disengage Furia from her father, whom he represents as desirous for a grandson. Jerome quotes to her Psalm 45:10–11, "forget your people and your father's house, and the king [here, Jesus] will desire your beauty," and he reminds her that she is not "his to whom she has been born, but his to whom she has been born again."[111] Jerome can scarce restrain his satiric bent, even at the risk of insult to Furia's aristocratic parents: does her father, Jerome asks, fear the extinction of the Camillan line if she does not produce a little tyke to crawl upon his chest and drool down his neck?[112] The servant women who will (in Jerome's imagination) urge Furia to remarry are mocked with lines of Persius (*Sat.* 1.32–35).[113] Likewise, matrons' makeup and alleged love of finery are ridiculed,[114] as are the now familiar curly-haired stewards and handsome footmen.[115]

The foregoing, however, is merely Jerome's rehearsal for the satiric depiction of second marriage in *Epistula* 54.15. Here Jerome mocks the motivations of young widows who allege their feminine incompetence as reason for a second marriage: this shameful pretense, he argues, obscures their real desire, sex. "No woman marries to avoid sleeping with a husband," Jerome baldly charges. If Furia is not motivated by sexual desire, why should she "play the harlot" just to increase her wealth (i.e., by seeking a husband's help in managing her finances)? In a chilling economic calculus, Jerome asks Furia why she would put an uncertain (monetary) gain before a sure loss of self-respect?

Jerome next rehearses the problems of second marriage, especially the problems faced by women who remarry. The husband, seeking to inherit her money, will feign illness to elicit from her a goodly portion. Depicting the problems occasioned by merging the children of various marriages, Jerome borrows (with acknowledgment) the motif of "the cruel stepmother" from the topoi of rhetoricians, comic poets, and writers of mimes. How can any possible benefits accruing from a second marriage compensate for these problems?[116] Significantly, Jerome ends his exhortation to Furia with a recollection of *Adversus Iovinianum*: she can there read how he bested Jovinian's defense of second marriage. Jerome ends his letter with one last pointed quip: "Think every day that you must die, and you will never again think of marrying."[117]

Although in the letters and treatises here discussed, Jerome borrows verses or motifs from earlier satirists, he shows himself proficient in reshaping the genre's thematic to suit his own ascetic ends.[118] Like his predecessors, Jerome parades a cast of stock characters who serve as the butt of his mockery, but they now are put on stage to encourage—or to shame—Christian audiences toward lives of supermeritorious sexual renunciation, to the achievement of ascetic "distinction." To this end, *Adversus Iovinianum* retains a central place for Jerome years after the original controversy had abated.

TERTULLIAN REDIVIVUS

While Jerome's use of Tertullian to advance his own ascetic aims has long been well documented,[119] Pierre Petitmengin has more recently noted that Jerome's references to Tertullian cluster in his writings that date to 393–97, a fact that Petitmengin relates to Jerome's composition of *De viris illustribus* 53 (on Tertullian) just a few years earlier.[120] I would add to Petitmengin's hypothesis: since Jerome composed *Adversus Iovinianum* in 392 or 393, he had reason then and in the years shortly thereafter to defend his antimarital rhetoric by citing his predecessor Tertullian, whose writings constitute a virtual archive of satirically ascetic propaganda. Moreover, that Tertullian was conversant with the Latin satirical tradition and employed its devices and themes has often been acknowledged; his treatise *De pallio* is sometimes singled out as an especially good example of the satiric style.[121]

Jerome indeed derives much of his antimarital rhetoric in *Adversus Iovinianum* 1 from Tertullian. Chapters 7–17 and some examples of noble "pagans" at the book's end borrow from Tertullian's *De monogamia* in particular.[122] Moreover, a long section of Jerome's *Epistula* 123, to Geruchia, is similarly derived from Tertullian's *De exhortatione castitatis*, *De monogamia*, and *Ad uxorem*. Motifs from Tertullian also abound in other of Jerome's ascetic writings, such as *Epistula* 22.[123] Nonetheless, despite these (usually unacknowledged) appropriations, Jerome drives Tertullian's arguments and examples in a more stringently ascetic direction: now, it is not "monogamy" that is encouraged but lifelong sexual abstinence.[124] How Jerome both borrows and recasts Tertullian is the theme of this section.[125]

Adversus Iovinianum provides the fullest example of Jerome's appropriation of Tertullian's arguments. Like Tertullian, Jerome depends heavily on Paul's teaching on marriage and virginity in 1 Corinthians 7. Although Jerome here derives some interpretive motifs from Origen,[126] many of his arguments and examples are taken directly from Tertullian—but with additions that heighten their ascetic import.

Tertullian's *De monogamia*, on which Jerome relies heavily (but which he elsewhere proclaims to be a heretical book)[127] mines the opening verses of 1 Corinthians 7. According to Tertullian, 1 Corinthians 7:1, "It is good for a man not to touch a woman,"[128] implies that since it is "not good" to touch, it is evil, "for nothing is contrary to good but evil." Paul, Tertullian notes, "permits" marriage—but anything for which "permission" must be granted is not an absolute good. Likewise, when Paul writes, "It is better to marry than to burn" (1 Cor. 7:9),[129] the very comparison of marriage with something evil (i.e., burning) suggests that even the "better" is not a true good. Yet, Tertullian concedes, "it is better to lose one eye than two."

Tertullian's interpretation of Paul, however, does not press the biblical text in as rigorously ascetic a direction as does Jerome. For example, Tertullian notes that Paul's preference for celibacy appeals to the worries that marriage entails, the "caring for a spouse" (1 Cor. 7:32–34): practical problems, not innate pollution, are here the issue. Moreover, Tertullian asserts, although the Paraclete could have preached the "annulling of marriage," he did not; rather, as "Comforter" (John 14; Rom. 8:26), the Paraclete demands not absolute continence but only "single marriage."[130]

On some points, Jerome's exposition of 1 Corinthians 7 merely follows Tertullian's. Jerome repeats Tertullian's argument that if it is "not good to touch a woman," it must be bad, for there is no opposite to "good" but "evil."[131] Likewise, according to Jerome, Paul's claim that it is "better to marry than to burn" (1 Cor. 7:9) shows that marriage stands in contrast to an evil, not to something absolutely good; and what is counted as merely the lesser of two evils is suspect. Nonetheless, Jerome concludes, it is better to lose one eye than both.[132] Jerome lifts these points directly from Tertullian.

Jerome's exposition, however, lends a more sinister cast to the evaluation of marriage. First, he notes that Paul did not write, "It is good not to take a wife"; rather, he wrote, "it is good not to touch a woman," implying that even a touch could endanger a man. Momentarily abandoning Paul, who apparently did not provide sufficient documentation to prove why it was "bad to touch," Jerome summons up verses from Proverbs to bolster his interpretation: women "hunt for the precious life" (6:26) and cause young men to lose their reason (6:23, 7:7); "can a man take fire in his bosom and his clothes not be burned?" (Prov. 6:27). Men, Jerome continues, should rather "flee" from women, as Joseph escaped the clutches of Potiphar's wife (Gen. 39:13); for Jerome, Joseph serves as a model of sexual abstinence, not merely, as for Tertullian, a model for the once married.[133] Moreover, claims Jerome, when Paul writes, "Let each man have his own wife" (1 Cor. 7:2), he does not encourage unmarried Christian men to wed but only concedes that men already married when they become Christians may keep their spouses. Yet how much better would it be, says Jerome, if these previously acquired wives were now treated as "sisters."[134] Last, whereas Tertullian asserts that the Holy Spirit is now, in his time, reinstituting the law of "one marriage," Jerome understands the Paraclete to proclaim the message of virginity.[135]

Jerome's reasoning is clarified in his exegesis of 1 Corinthians 7:5, a passage Tertullian does not comment on in *De monogamia* but touches on in *De exhortatione castitatis*:[136] marriage is to be avoided because of the polluting quality of sexual intercourse. Jerome makes much of Paul's recommendation that married couples "separate for prayer," since marital relations hinder prayer and (according to Jerome) disallow the reception of the Eucharist. Jerome again appeals to an intertext to strengthen his argument: since Paul elsewhere commands Christians to "pray always" (1 Thess. 5:17), Christian couples might best never engage in sexual relations. Moreover, argues Jerome, when "Peter" (1 Pet. 3:7) enjoins husbands to give honor to their wives as "the weaker sex," he means that they should abstain from sexual relations.[137] Jerome further claims that if the married couple separates sexually for prayer, they will "taste the sweets of chastity" and desire to commit themselves to perpetual abstinence.[138] Last, the "present distress" that Paul lists as a reason for continence—usually interpreted by modern exegetes to signal Paul's expectation of the world's end—means for Jerome the "distress" of pregnancy and childbearing; he cites as justification Matthew 24:19: "Woe unto those who are with child and give suck in those days."[139] Although Tertullian elsewhere asserts that the sexual act is the same in marriage and in "fornication," a maxim adopted by Jerome,[140] it nonetheless appears that Jerome's devaluation of marriage is imbued with a far stronger antisexual animus than is Tertullian's.

Exegeses of the opening chapters of Genesis by Tertullian and Jerome likewise afford an instructive contrast. Citing the Genesis creation story in *De monogamia* 4, Tertullian notes that God made one woman for the first man, taking one of his ribs to make one (and only one) "helper"; God then pronounced that "the two"—not three or more—should be made "one flesh" (Gen. 2:21–24). Continuing his exposition of Genesis, Tertullian observes that Lamech's digamy is the next post-Edenic sin after Cain's fratricide.[141] The flood (Gen. 6) having punished both sins, monogamy was restored among Noah and his sons. Even in the ark, Tertullian claims, the animals—"unclean" as well as "clean"—entered "two by two" (Gen. 6:19–20), signaling that God willed "monogamy" for all creatures.[142] Moreover, according to Tertullian, the first Adam was a monogamist in the flesh; the last Adam, Christ, although unwedded, was a "monogamist in spirit," faithfully (albeit allegorically) united to his one wife, the Church (cf. Eph. 5:22–32).[143] Genesis 1–6 thus provides considerable exegetical ballast for Tertullian's promotion of "monogamy."

Jerome likewise turns to Genesis to build his case in *Adversus Iovinianum* 1.14–15, but the Genesis to which *he* appeals favors complete sexual abstinence. Like Tertullian, Jerome notes that God made the one rib of Adam into one wife, so that two—not three or four—could be "one flesh." He appropriates Tertullian's example of Lamech, who divided the "one flesh" with two wives. Cain's murder of Abel occasioned a "sevenfold" vengeance (Gen. 4:15), but plural marriage brought forth a penalty "seventy times seven" (Gen. 4:24), and the differing magnitudes signal differences in guilt, Jerome claims. Jerome also cites Tertullian's example of the first Adam as a monogamist, the second Adam as unmarried,[144] but he elaborates this theme to different ascetic purpose. Although Jerome repeats Tertullian's claim that Christ, in the flesh, was a virgin but was married once (to the Church) in the spirit, he argues that Christ's love for the Church, which renders it "without spot or wrinkle" (Eph. 5:25–27), implies that human husbands should likewise love their wives "without spot," that is, asexually.[145] Moreover, he claims, since Christian women are part of Christ's body, they are *his* ribs, not those of any human male;[146] such rhetoric accords well with Jerome's frequent claim that virgins are "brides of Christ."

For Jerome, moreover, worthy of note is not Adam and Eve's monogamous marriage, their being "one flesh," but their virginal status at creation. Virgins they were made, and virgins they were intended to stay, since only after the first sin and their expulsion from Eden did they marry, according to Jerome's construal of Genesis 1–4. As Christians, Jerome maintains, it is into Christ's virginity that we are to be "born again," a virginity in which "there is no male and female" (Gal. 3:28).[147]

Tertullian's biblical examples of chaste coupling receive further demotion in Jerome's rendition. In several instances, Jerome reconstrues the symbolic message of the biblical examples so that they advocate not chaste marriage, as they did for Tertullian, but celibacy. On Noah's ark, according to Jerome, it was only the *unclean* animals who boarded two by two—the single ones entering by sevens, an odd number that signals "cleanness."[148] In addition, Jerome insists that Noah and his sons separated from their wives while on the ark, a figure of the Church; only when they descended to the life of "the world" were they joined in (sexual) pairs.[149]

Likewise, Jerome heightens, whenever possible, the ascetic resonance of other biblical stories cited by Tertullian. Whereas for Tertullian, Moses exemplifies the man married once, for Jerome, the married Moses represents "the Law" (in contrast to the Gospel); that not Moses but the virginal Joshua was allowed to enter the Promised Land contains a lesson for later Christians.[150] While Tertullian emphasizes that priests can be married only once, Jerome argues that no priest may engage in sexual relations with his wife during the time of his priesthood, since (according to Jerome) the injunction that a bishop or a deacon is to be the "husband of one wife" (1 Tim. 3:2, 12) refers only to the time "before he was elevated to the priesthood."[151]

Jerome's penchant for appropriating Tertullian's examples sometimes leads him slightly off his course. Tertullian concludes *De monogamia* with a catalogue of "pagans" who upheld the notion of "one marriage," a catalogue doubtless intended to shame Christians of his own era.[152] Thus Dido (who preferred to "burn rather than marry," in an outrageous pun on 1 Cor. 7:9) and Lucretia (who killed herself rather than live with the stain of rape on her marriage) are held up as exemplars. The wives of various pagan priests who could marry only once and those women who maintained total abstinence for specified periods of time, such as the vestal virgins, are also praised by Tertullian.[153] At the end of *Adversus Iovinianum* 1, Jerome repeats some of Tertullian's most memorable examples—Dido (lauded via Tertullian's pun "she preferred to burn rather than to marry"), Lucretia, and the wives of various pagan priests.[154]

Jerome seems not to notice that they do not entirely fit his purpose, the advocacy of complete and lifelong abstinence.[155] Logic here has succumbed to Jerome's desires to prove chastity's universal appeal and to shame laxer Christians through the praise of "pagan" marital continence.

Jerome's *Epistula* 123, to Geruchia, is a second work that borrows heavily from Tertullian's treatises *De exhortatione castitatis* and *Ad uxorem*, as well as from *De monogamia*. Since Geruchia is a widow, Tertullian's rhetoric against remarriage here suits Jerome's purpose well. Jerome recites Tertullian's argument that since priests are chosen from the ranks of the laity, laymen are bound by the law of "one marriage" that holds for priests.[156] He summons up "pagan" examples of those married once, in a list nearly identical with that in *De monogamia*.[157] Tertullian's distinction between what God "wills" and what God "permits" is repeated and applied to the question of second marriage.[158] The "clean" and "unclean" animals of Noah's ark ingeniously become, in Jerome's interpretation, the "unmarried" and the "married."[159] Tertullian's "one rib, one wife" witticism is again repeated, as are his appeals to "two" (not more) "in one flesh" and to Lamech, who, by his digamy, "divided" woman. The comparison of the first Adam, monogamist in the flesh, with the second Adam, monogamist in spirit, is likewise rehearsed.[160] The polygamy of the Old Testament patriarchs is explained away by the "difference in times" between that era and the Christian present.[161] That these and similar motifs were stock-in-trade arguments that Jerome borrowed from Tertullian for his own purpose, his creation of ascetic "distinction," is suggested by their recurrence in several other treatises and letters.[162]

That Jerome derives much of his antimarital rhetoric from Tertullian seems evident. Moreover, like Tertullian, Jerome borrows from the "pagan" satiric tradition to encourage Christian virtue and disclaims such association with "pagan" writers in the very act of appropriating them. Tertullian famously and rhetorically had asked, "What has Athens to do with Jerusalem?"[163] In writing to Eustochium, however, Jerome replaces Tertullian's urban periphrasis with a literary one: "What has Horace to do with the psalter?"[164] Given Jerome's mixing of satire and Scripture in his antimarital polemic, the answer, arguably, might be "Much."

☙

Notes

The following editions were used for Jerome's works: for *Adversus Helvidium* and *Adversus Iovinianum*, *Patrologia Latina* 23; for *Apologia contra Rufinum*, *Sources chrétiennes* 303; for *Epistulae*, *Corpus Scriptorum Ecclesiasticarum Latinorum* 54–56. The edition used for

Tertullian's works was *Corpus Christianorum, Series Latina* 1–2. The chapter and section numbers in Jerome's treatises and letters here cited are taken from the Latin texts and occasionally differ from those found in modern translations.

I thank Warren Smith, Gregson Davis, and Randall Styers for helpful editorial comments, and I thank Alan Cameron for some useful bibliographical suggestions.

    1. Rudd (1986, 28) argues that this is a mistaken understanding of satire. Wiesen (1964, 249–50, 252–53), however, understands Jerome to believe that satire has a "reforming purpose."

    2. As is well rehearsed in all general books on Roman satire, satire as a poetic genre came to an end before the time of Jerome, although various satirists continued to be read with avidity in his era. Jerome's satiric sketches, then, do not represent a genre of literature but, rather, convey the biting, mocking attitude characteristic of classical Roman satire. Juvenal was experiencing a renaissance by the later fourth century; Horace had remained part of the standard school curriculum and hence was well known to those who had enjoyed a literary education. See Wiesen 1964, 1–5; Adkin 1994 (for Juvenal); and n. 45 in the present chapter. As shall become clear in my discussion, Jerome's diatribe against marriage is marked by a strong antisexual tone.

    3. The terms are used in the sense given by Bourdieu ([1979] 1984).

    4. It is notable that Jerome rarely attacks "pagans," saving his satiric critique and invective for his fellow Christians; see Favez 1946, 211–13, 225–26.

    5. Here, Jerome stands in uneasy tension with his satirical predecessors, whose antimarital and antifeminist propaganda was of a piece; when writing satirically, Jerome tends to follow this pattern, but otherwise, he does so less predictably, women often being praised while marriage is nonetheless denigrated. Momigliano (1966, 476–77) reminds readers (in a critique of Wiesen's *St. Jerome as a Satirist*) that it is equally important to locate those situations/topics for which Jerome did *not* indulge in satiric writing and to attempt to ascertain the reason for his reticence.

    6. See Clark 1979b for an extended discussion of the ways in which Jerome praises and promotes his (celibate) women friends amid his denigration of marriage and women in general.

    7. Cf., e.g., Varro *Gerontodidaskalos*; Juvenal *Sat.* 11. Jerome even appeals to the "pagan" past for examples of morality that in his era seem lacking: see *Adversus Iovinianum* 1.41–46 and his apostrophe to ancient, "purer" Rome in 2.38. See Wiesen 1964, 20–25, for other examples of Jerome's appropriation of this theme. (It is worthy of note that the classical satirists would sometimes denigrate the simplicity of the distant past, with its acornbelching primitives [Juvenal *Sat.* 6.9–10; cf. Wiesen 1973, 482; Rudd 1986, 201–2; Courtney 1980, 262].) In his commentary on Juvenal, Courtney (1980, 25) notes that each generation of satire writers tended to put the beginning of "corruption" later, with the result that the "life-style of early Rome" seemed "to last far later than in fact it did."

    8. For examples of Jerome's use of diminutives, see Wiesen 1964, 53–54, 76, 85–88, 134. A good example of satiric mimicry can be found in Jerome *Ep.* 22.13.

    9. For satirical invective directed against Rufinus, see Jerome *Ep.* 57.4, 84.8, 125.18; the prefaces to his commentaries on Jeremiah, Ezekiel, and (book 10 of) Isaiah; *Apologia contra Rufinum*. Vigilantius receives the next most vicious treatment; see *Contra Vigilantium* 1, 3–4, 6, 8, 13, 15. John of Jerusalem, Helvidius, and Pelagius also are the objects of invective in the treatises Jerome directs against them.

10. A notable exception is Jerome's mockery of Vettius Agorius Praetextatus and Fabia Anconia Paulina in *Ep.* 23.2, 39.3.

11. Although G. M. H. Murphy (1966, 322–24) scores Jerome's lack of satiric originality, I shall argue in this chapter that Jerome uses the satiric mode to accomplish quite new Christian purposes.

12. See Hanna and Lawler 1997, 19: over 150 nearly complete medieval copies of *Adversus Iovinianum* survive. For the fate of *Adversus Iovinianum* in the early Middle Ages, see Laistner 1952, 250.

13. For an extended discussion of this phenomenon, see Clark 1999.

14. Jerome *Ep.* 50.5, 117.1.

15. Jerome *Ep.* 22.32, 40.2. In *Ep.* 22.28, Jerome expresses his alleged worry that his language sounds more like invective than admonition: . . . *ne videar inuehi potius quam monere.*

16. See Wiesen 1964, 258–61. Fontaine (1988a, 336 n. 27) notes other allusions to Persius in Jerome's *Ep.* 14 to Heliodorus, adding to Hagendahl's list (1958, 284).

17. For similar rhetorical moves, see Horace *Serm.* 1.4.39–40; Juvenal *Sat.* 1.79. Jerome also attempts to convince readers of his abandonment of pagan authors by recounting his famous dream in which, at the Judgment Seat, he was accused of being a Ciceronian, not a Christian; he alleges that he subsequently renounced his reading of "pagan" works (*Ep.* 22.30).

18. See Hagendahl 1958, 281, 284: there are perhaps forty-five passages from Horace in Jerome's writings, quite evenly distributed throughout all periods.

19. Wiesen 1964, 9.

20. Adkin 1994, 71–72, also citing a suggestion by Courtney. See Jerome *Ep.* 52.12.2 (cf. Juvenal *Sat.* 6.304), Jerome. *Ep.* 22.29.4 (cf. Juvenal *Sat.* 13.241–42).

21. Lucilius 1299 Marx (1904–5), cited by Jerome in *Ep.*7.5 and alluded to (possibly from a reference by Cicero?) in *Apologia contra Rufinum* 1.30; Juvenal 1.15 (*Et nos saepe manum ferulae subduximus*), cited in *Ep.* 50.5 (with *subtraximus* for *subduximus*) and 57.12.2 and probably alluded to in *Apologia contra Rufinum* 3.6 and 1.17.

22. See Cameron 1964, 363–77, citing evidence from the *Historia Augusta*; Adkin 1994, 69–72; Fredericks in Ramage, Sigsbee, and Fredericks 1974, 169; Knoche [1971] 1975, 153; Coffey [1976] 1989, 122.

23. Jerome *Ep.* 58.11, citing Horace *Serm.* 1.9.59–60.

24. Jerome *Ep.* 133.1, citing Horace *Serm.* 1.3.68–69.

25. Jerome *Ep.* 6, citing Horace *Serm.* 1.3.1–3.

26. Jerome *Ep.* 58.7, citing Persius *Sat.* 3.30: *ego te intus et in cute novi.*

27. Thus he mocks the anonymous opponent of *Ep.* 50.5 or Rufinus's need of grammar instruction (*Apologia contra Rufinum* 3.6, 1.17), citing Juvenal *Sat.* 1.15.

28. Witke 1970, 269. Here Jerome shows himself in a different position from Tertullian, who frequently attacks "pagan" mores and practices. Doubtless the Christianization of the empire in the two centuries between Tertullian and Jerome reduced the need for such constant polemic.

29. Wiesen 1964, 6.

30. Jerome *Ep.* 7.5, citing Lucilius 1299 (Marx 1904–5): *similem habent labra lactucam asino carduos comedente.* See discussion in Hagendahl 1958, 102 n. 4; cf. Jerome *Apologia contra Rufinum* 1.30.

31. Jerome *Ep.* 50.5, citing Horace *Serm.* 1.4.34. The reference perhaps alludes to the practice of tying hay to the horns of dangerous oxen to warn passersby of danger: see Plutarch *Crassus* 7 for this explanation.

32. Persius *Sat.* 3.82 (*Atque exporrecto trutinantur verba labello*), cited in Jerome *Adversus Iovinianum* 1.40. Jerome also cites this line in *Ep.* 40.2 to describe an opponent.

33. Persius *Sat.* 3.118 (*non sani esse hominis non sanus iuret Orestes*), cited by Jerome in *Adversus Iovinianum* 1.1.

34. Jerome *Ep.* 50.4, probably alluding to Persius *Sat.* 1.29–30 (*ten cirratorum centum dictata fuisse / pro nihilo pendes?*).

35. Jerome *Ep.* 40.2, citing Persius *Sat.* 2.37–38 (*hunc optet generum rex et regina, puellae / hunc rapiant; quidquid calcaverit hic, rosa fiat*), with the subject of the attack changed to the second-person singular ("you").

36. Jerome *Ep.* 38.5, citing Persius *Sat.* 1.57: *pinguis aqualiculus*. Shortly thereafter, they could complain of Blaesilla's death, apparently hastened by excessive ascetic renunciation: see Jerome *Ep.* 39.

37. Jerome *Ep.* 54.5, citing Persius *Sat.* 1.32–33, 35: *hic aliquis, cui circum umeros hyacinthina laena est, / rancidulum quiddam balba de nare . . . eliquat* [Jerome has *perstterpit*] *ac tenero subplantat uerba palato*. That the poets are depicted as effeminate may encourage the gender slide.

38. Jerome *Ep.* 49(48).15, citing Persius *Sat.* 2.16: *noctem flumine purgas*.

39. See, e.g., Jerome *In Isaiam* 12, *prologus*; *In Hiezechielem* 10; *In Hieremiam* 4.61.4; *Ep.* 125.18. The controversy raged especially fiercely from 399 into the opening years of the fifth century.

40. In this farcical piece, the pig, after bequeathing acorns to his father, wheat to his mother, and barley to his sister, whose nuptials he regrets he will not live to see, designates to whom his various body parts should be left (including his *musculos* to the cinaedus, and his "claws" to matrons). M. Grunnius Corocotta dates his testament to the year in which Clibanatus ("Mr. Breadpan") and Piperatus ("Mr. Pepper") held the consulship. The pig also requests a monument with gold letters to be erected in his honor so that his name will be remembered. Conceding his inability to write *manu mea*, Grunnius dictates his inelegant testament to a scribe. A spoof on the Roman testamentary habit, the piece is mentioned explicitly by Jerome in *Apologia contra Rufinum* 1.17 (Jerome complains that Rufinus might as well learn doggerel from the crowd that guffaws at "The Pig's Testament," since books written by know-nothings find plenty of readers). The text of "The Testament of the Pig" can be found in Buecheler 1895, 241–42.

41. Cf. Juvenal's *manum ferulae subduximus* (*Sat.* 1.15) and Jerome's *ferulae manum subtraximus*.

42. By citing both biblical and "pagan" sources, Jerome probably hopes to convey the notion that there is a universal consensus regarding the topic; see Hagendahl 1958, 155.

43. Jerome *Adversus Iovinianum* 1.49. Assessing the possibility of Seneca's lost *De matrimonio* as a source for Juvenal's *Satire* 6, Courtney (1980, 252) concludes that scholars can posit no more than "the existence of an inherited stock of misogynistic themes."

44. It is unclear if such treatises ever existed. Jerome's appeal to Greek sources, some of which were never put into writing (such as some alleged "writings" of Pythagoras), provided a grounds of attack for Rufinus, who recognized that Jerome was bluffing: see Rufinus *Apologia contra Hieronymum* 2.7 and Jerome's reply in *Apologia contra Rufinum* 3.39.

45. Courtney 1980, 259–62. Courtney concludes (261) that Jerome's one true reference *(rara avis)* may have been derived from Persius; otherwise, Jerome seems to have known little of Juvenal.

46. Hanna and Lawler 1997, 8–9, 26–27, 231–58. Despite these editors' helpful tracing of possible sources for Jerome's construction of the *ecloga Theophrasti*, they appear unappreciative of Jerome's skillful rhetoric and deft use of both biblical and philosophical argumentation in the *Adversus Iovinianum*. Thus Jerome is said to come off "very badly indeed" as a biblical interpreter (21), and to be "animated by a nearly neurotic horror of female sexuality" (18).

47. Bickel 1915, i–xii. For a discussion of the sources, see Courcelle 1948, 60–62; Hagendahl 1958, 150–56; Wiesen 1964, 153–58 (Wiesen thinks Jerome inserted his reminiscences of Juvenal into the *ecloga Theophrasti*).

48. This is perhaps an allusion to Persius *Sat.* 1.46, although the phrase may have been a commonplace by Jerome's time.

49. For references to some earlier discussions of the topic, see Wiesen 1964, 113–15.

50. See Wiesen 1964, 158, 164–65. Jerome supplies plenty of antimarital ammunition for women in his various letters to them, especially *Ep.* 22 and 54. Jerome and other church fathers were adept at "gender-bending" biblical texts to suit their ascetic purposes, as I have shown in detail in Clark 1999.

51. Hagendahl 1958, 147–48. The term is here used somewhat anachronistically, for to incorporate allusions to and citations of earlier literature into one's own writing was the mark of an educated person; to be obliged to reveal all one's sources might imply disdain for the educational level of a writer's audience. "Intertextuality" is a key feature of late ancient Latin literature, in which unidentified echoes of Virgil and other writers abound.

52. See Hagendahl 1958, 136–37; Adkin 1992, 135.

53. See, e.g., *Ep.* 22.13, 28–29; 52.6; 128.3; 125.6, 10, 16; 117.7, 9; 130.18; *Adversus Iovinianum* 2.36.

54. Jerome *Ep.* 123.10.

55. Given a previous generation's understanding of satire as embodying "realistic" portrayal, it probably should not surprise us to find such sentiments as the following by Knoche ([1971] 1975, 148): "Satire 6 is the greatest female character study coming from antiquity"; "a host of individual scenes are presented in which the weaknesses and the vices of the women of Rome are revealed." Whether Juvenal aims *Satire* 6 primarily at "women," at "marriage," at "husbands," or at "gender" has been the subject of considerable debate; for a variety of opinions on the subject, see Knoche [1971] 1975, 148; Coffey [1976] 1989, 127; W. S. Smith 1980, 329–31; Anderson 1982, 274–75; Rudd 1986, 201–3; J. G. W. Henderson 1989, 94–96.

56. Note Rudd's comment (1986, 205) that "it is significant that in the whole of Roman satire no man is ever criticised for being false to his wife."

57. Jerome *Ep.* 22.2; the allusion is to the escape of Lot and his family from the destruction of Sodom in Genesis 19. See also Tertullian *Ad uxorem* 1.5 and *De exhortatione castitatis* 9.

58. Jerome *Ep.* 22.13–14.

59. Jerome *Ep.* 22.16, 25, 41.

60. Jerome *Ep.* 22.19.

61. Jerome *Ep.* 22.2. Nonetheless, Jerome here cannot refrain from mentioning a few: pregnancy, screaming babies, jealousy of rivals for the husband's attention, problems of running a household.

62. Jerome here (*Ep.* 22.16) mentions Tertullian's (lost) treatise *To a Philosophical Friend*, probably also the reference in *Adversus Iovinianum* 1.13. For the possible contents of the treatise and its use by Jerome, see Barnes 1971, 250–53.

63. Jerome *Ep.* 22.22.

64. See Haller 1897, 1 n. 1; Opelt 1973, 37.

65. Jovinian, as cited by Jerome in *Adversus Iovinianum* 1.3.

66. For examples of this image, see Jerome *Ep.* 22.15, 48(49).2–3, 66.2, 123.9.

67. As Warren Smith astutely notes (1997, 131–32), Jerome's bombast at the beginning of the *Adversus Iovinianum* fades as the treatise proceeds, suggesting that Jerome sensed that his attack on Jovinian would win fewer converts to his own position than he had hoped.

68. Horace *Ars poet.* 139 ("The mountains labor; a poor mouse is born"); Persius *Sat.* 3.118 ("That he's gone mad, even poor Orestes swears").

69. Jerome *Adversus Iovinianum* 1.1, citing Plautus *Pseudolus* 1.1.23; Virgil *Aen.* 10.640. Jerome's alignment of satire with comedy also is evident in *Ep.* 50.1, his mockery of the unnamed monk, "a regular of the Plautus Players," who has attacked his *Adversus Iovinianum*. Hagendahl (1958, 269–70) finds only one trace of Plautus in Jerome's writings prior to 393; the references fall mostly into the period 393–402, suggesting that this is the era in which Jerome was reading (or rereading) Plautus.

70. Jerome *Adversus Iovinianum* 1.3; the "hoisted sail" topos is also found in Juvenal *Sat.* 1.149–50.

71. Jerome *Adversus Iovinianum* 1.4.

72. Jerome *Adversus Iovinianum* 1.1; see also 2.36. The name *Epicurus* was simply a code word for those who pursue pleasure.

73. Jerome *Adversus Iovinianum* 1.48, 2.11.

74. Jerome *Adversus Iovinianum* 1.3.

75. These are discussed later in this chapter, under "Tertullian Redivivus."

76. A good example of Jerome's pressuring of Paul's meaning comes in his discussion of 1 Cor. 7:5, on the couple's (sexual) separation for prayer. According to Paul's teaching, the couple should then come back together again so that "Satan" will not tempt them to stray elsewhere; according to Jerome, the short periods of respite from marital sex should prompt them to adopt it as a perpetual mode of life (see discussion later in this chapter, under "Tertullian Redivivus"). Likewise, Jerome interprets the "present distress" of 1 Cor. 7:26 (usually now taken to mean Paul's expectation of the world's end) to connote pregnancy and childbearing (*Adversus Iovinianum* 1.12).

77. Jerome *Adversus Iovinianum* 1.13.

78. Jerome *Adversus Iovinianum* 1.7.

79. Jerome *Adversus Iovinianum* 1.14.

80. Jerome *Adversus Iovinianum* 1.20. John Opelt's otherwise useful essay (1993) is marred by his assumption that Jerome believed Adam and Eve to be married (although without sexual relation) in the Garden of Eden (11)—against the evidence of, among other places, *Adversus Iovinianum* 1.16—and by his attempt (21) to "improve" Jerome's view of marriage by citing only part of Jerome's words on the topic from his *Commentary on Ephesians*.

81. Jerome *Adversus Iovinianum* 1.40.

82. Jerome *Adversus Iovinianum* 2.36, citing Virgil *Aen.* 4.172.

83. Jerome *Adversus Iovinianum* 2.37.

84. For Roman resistance to the extreme forms of ascetic renunciation proposed by Jerome, see Hunter 1987, 45–64; K. Cooper 1996.

85. For a discussion of the seeming disjunctions between Jerome's complaints about women in general and his praise of his women friends, see Clark 1979a.

86. Jerome *Adversus Iovinianum* 1.28.

87. See, e.g., Jerome *Ep.* 24, 38, 45, 77, 108, 127 (esp. 127.5), and the prefaces to book 1 of his *Commentary on Galatians* and to his *Commentary on Zephaniah*.

88. Jerome *Ep.* 48(49).3; 49(48).3, 11. Jerome claims that he is merely a commentator on Paul, not a "dogmatist on my own account" (*Ep.* 49[48].14).

89. Jerome *Ep.* 49(48).18. Jerome contradicts this point in *Ep.* 52.17.

90. Jerome *Ep.* 49(48).2.

91. Jerome *Ep.* 49(48).6.

92. Jerome *Ep.* 49(48).20.

93. Jerome *Ep.* 49(48).21.

94. Earlier scholars posited that the monk might be Pelagius, a view now refuted by Duval (1980, 525–27). The critic is identified as a monk in *Ep.* 50.3.

95. The similarities between Plautus's comedy and satire is noted by Ramage, Sigsbee, and Fredericks (1974, 10). See n. 69 in the present chapter for Jerome and Plautus.

96. See Opelt 1973, 177–80.

97. Jerome *Ep.* 50.1–2.

98. Horace *Serm.* 1.4.34.

99. Juvenal *Sat.* 1.15.

100. Virgil *Aen.* 12.50.

101. Whether Jerome here intends an allusion to "The Testament of the Pig" is unclear.

102. Jerome *Ep.* 50.4–5. Jerome's witticism may be derived from Cicero *Pro Caelio* 15.36: Cicero impugns the moral character of Clodia, his client's former lover who now brings a charge against his client. To serve as her representative in court, Clodia wants her youngest brother, a man who (according to Cicero's counterattack) is especially prey to "idle terrors of the night" when his sister is sleeping with some fellow. If the allusion is intentional, the moral smear may carry over to Jerome's critic. Fredericks notes the use of epigrammatic phrases as especially characteristic of Juvenal; Martial's epigrams had put "the sting in the tail" (Ramage, Sigsbee, and Fredericks 1974, 137, 167). On Jerome's polemical use of antithesis, see Opelt 1973, 169.

103. Jerome *Ep.* 50.1, 5.

104. Jerome *Ep.* 50.3–5.

105. Jerome *Ep.* 52.5. Jerome conveniently forgets that he has accepted small presents from women (see *Ep.* 31, 44). Even Pope Damasus could be accused of being a "tickler of ladies' ears" (*matronarum auriscalpius*). See *Quae gesta sunt inter Liberium et Felicem episcopos*, CSEL 35,4; Fontaine 1988b, 177–92.

106. Jerome *Ep.* 52.6. Cf. Juvenal *Sat.* 1.37–39; Persius *Sat.* 2.15–16.

107. Jerome *Ep.* 52.16.

108. Jerome *Ep.* 52.17.

109. This is a reference to a deceived (and deceiving) father in Terence's *Phormio;* cf. Horace *Ars poet.* 94.

110. Jerome here (*Ep.* 54.2) alleges that he does not quote the verse "Let the dead bury their dead" (Matt. 8:22) to promote separation of ascetically minded children from their parents. According to Clement of Alexandria (*Stromateis* 3.4.25), Marcion cited the verse to promote ascetic renunciation based on a hatred of the Creator.

111. Jerome *Ep.* 54.3–4.

112. Jerome *Ep.* 54.4. Furia's father may have been Quintilius Laetus, prefect of the city of Rome in 398–99: see A. H. M. Jones et al. [1971] 1980, 492–93.

113. Jerome *Ep.* 54.5, quoted in n. 37 in the present chapter.

114. Jerome *Ep.* 54.7.

115. Jerome *Ep.* 54.13. Jerome seems literarily obsessed with curly-haired stewards; they reappear in his warnings to Salvina (*Ep.* 79.9).

116. Jerome *Ep.* 54.15.

117. Jerome *Ep.* 54.18.

118. On Jerome's mixed genres and plurality of styles, see Fontaine 1988a, 337–38.

119. In 1895 Harnack had already counted more than fifty references and posited that Jerome knew probably eighteen of the now extant Tertullianic writings and seven of the lost works (Harnack 1980, 256, 270–74). For more recent studies, see Micaeli 1979, 1985; Petitmengin 1988; Adkin 1992.

120. Petitmengin 1988, 46. Petitmengin notes (47) that there is only one citation of Tertullian of any length that is exact (Jerome *In Danielem* 3.9.24, citing Tertullian *Adversus Iudaeos* 8.9–13, 15–16); beyond the explicit references can be counted many other borrowings and reminiscences.

121. See, e.g., Weston 1915, 17–24; Wiesen 1964, 13–14; Ramage, Sigsbee, and Fredericks 1974, 174. Cf. Sider 1971, 120–21. *De pallio* is Tertullian's defense of the pallium, the garb of philosophers, as the appropriate dress (rather than the toga) for Roman males.

122. *De monogamia* is usually taken to be the most "rigorous" of Tertullian's treatises on marriage, dating to his Montanist period. Harnack's famous line "rigorism is not Montanism" (1904, 2.2.273) still should provide a cautionary word. Jerome's borrowings from *De monogamia* in his *Adversus Iovinianum* are noted by Schultzen (1894, 492–93). For a discussion of Tertullian's views on marriage and virginity that emphasizes their anti-Marcionite dimensions, see Tibiletti 1969, 71–93.

123. See esp. Adkin 1992 for some verbal borrowings and reminiscences of Tertullian in *Ep.* 22.

124. Adkin (1992, 134) speaks of Jerome's borrowings from Tertullian as enhancing the "rhetorical effect": indeed they do, but in the direction of creating a sharper distinction between married and celibate Christians.

125. That Jerome quotes from Tertullian frequently is evident (see, e.g., his use of Tertullian's *De ieiunio* throughout *Adversus Iovinianum* 2, as well as in *Ep.* 22.10 and 55.2). Although Jerome recommends some of Tertullian's treatises to Eustochium (*Ep.* 22.22), he also has sharp words against Tertullian. Thus Tertullian is said "not to be a man of the church" (*Adversus Helvidium* 19), while in *Comm. Titum* (on 1:6), Jerome declares that *De monogamia* is "a heretical book." It is also startling how few of Tertullian's writings—writings attested elsewhere in Jerome's corpus—are mentioned by Jerome in *De viris illustribus* 53. What is the reason for Jerome's short list? Perhaps he cribbed a good portion of this work from Eusebius, who is not generally well informed about

Latin authors. Micaeli (1979) provides a useful catalogue of word parallels that demonstrate Jerome's borrowings from Tertullian, but he does not show how Jerome appropriated Tertullian's phrases for his own, more rigorous, ascetic arguments (with one exception: in *Ep.79.7*, Jerome changes a reference to Tertullian so that it contains the phrase *despumat in coitum*, thus adding a cruder tone to Tertullian's words [Micaeli 1979, 428–29]).

126. These include, namely, the elision of marriage and celibacy with slavery and freedom, uncircumcision and circumcision, in 1 Cor. 7:18–14, used by Jerome in *Adversus Iovinianum* 1.11. See Origen's commentary on 1 Cor. 7:18–20.

127. Jerome *Comm. Titum* (on 1:6).

128. Most modern commentators understand that Paul quotes the Corinthian ascetics, who argue against the propriety of marriage. On this reading, Paul is seen to agree in theory with the Corinthians but to concede marriage in practice in the next verses.

129. Tertullian takes the "burning" to portend the fires of punishment, contrary to most ancient and modern commentators, who see a reference to fires of lust.

130. Tertullian *De monogamia* 3.

131. Jerome *Adversus Iovinianum* 1.7.

132. Jerome *Adversus Iovinianum* 1.9.

133. Cf. Tertullian *De monogamia* 6.

134. Jerome *Adversus Iovinianum* 1.7.

135. Tertullian *De monogamia* 3, 14; Jerome *Adversus Iovinianum* 1.39. To be sure, Tertullian also praises abstinence; see *Ad uxorem* 1.3, 6.

136. Tertullian *De exhortatione castitatis* 10.

137. Jerome *Adversus Iovinianum* 1.7.

138. Jerome *Adversus Iovinianum* 1.12. Jerome conveniently overlooks Paul's next words, that the couple come together again so that "Satan" will not tempt them to stray elsewhere. In *De exhortatione castitatis* 10, Tertullian claims that Paul urges temporary separation for prayer so that couples may know what is *always* profitable. If carnality impedes the work of the Holy Spirit in first marriage, "how much more" it does in second marriage. The recommendation thus stands as an aspect of Tertullian's argument against remarriage, not against first marriage.

139. Jerome *Adversus Iovinianum* 1.12. Tertullian is one of the few church fathers who retained the sense of the imminence of the world's end, especially in his later years, when imbued with Montanist convictions.

140. Tertullian *De exhortatione castitatis* 9; Jerome *Adversus Iovinianum* 2.24.

141. According to the text of Genesis 4:23–24, Lamech's sin lay in killing a man who had wounded him—that is, exacting excessive vengeance—about which he then boasted to his two wives. Tertullian makes the "sin" to be the plural marriage.

142. Tertullian *De monogamia* 4; *De exhortatione castitatis* 5. See n. 154 later in this chapter.

143. Tertullian *De monogamia* 5.

144. Jerome *Adversus Iovinianum* 1.14.

145. Jerome *Adversus Iovinianum* 1.16. For Jerome, *castitas* usually denotes "no sex," whereas in classical Latin it more often denotes the virtue and fidelity of a married woman (Horace *Odes* 3.24.23; Tacitus *Annals* 1.33).

146. Jerome *Adversus Iovinianum* 1.10.

147. Jerome *Adversus Iovinianum* 1.16.

148. Jerome *Adversus Iovinianum* 1.16. In *Ep.* 36.1 Jerome refers to a treatise by Origen titled *On the Clean and Unclean Animals*, which he implies Tertullian translated into Latin. No such treatise of Origen is extant, either in Greek or in Latin. The portion of Origen's *Homily 7 on Leviticus* (4–7) that pertains to the clean and unclean animals relates to Hebrew food laws (Origen gives a "moral" interpretation); likewise, Tertullian's *Adversus Marcionem* (2.18.2) mentions the Levitical food laws. In neither case is "sex" the issue. For a discussion of Jerome's reference in *Ep.* 36.1, see Petitmengin 1988, 45–46.

149. Jerome *Adversus Iovinianum* 1.17.

150. Tertullian *De monogamia* 6; Jerome *Adversus Iovinianum* 22. Cf. Num. 27; Deut. 34; Josh. 1. Jerome assumes that Joshua was virginal since the texts pertaining to him do not mention a wife. Some of Jerome's exegesis appears to derive from Origen's *Homilies on Joshua* (1.1, 2.1, 17.2).

151. Tertullian *De monogamia* 7; Jerome *Adversus Iovinianum* 1.34–35.

152. In *Ad uxorem* 1.6 and *De exhortatione castitatis* 13, Tertullian claims that pagan chastity is false because it is inspired by the devil; on this argument, the rhetorical force of examples of chaste pagan women would be considerably devalued.

153. Tertullian *De monogamia* 17. Cf. *De exhortatione castitatis* 13; *Ad uxorem* 1.6.

154. Jerome *Adversus Iovinianum* 1.43, 46, 49.

155. Adkin (1992, 133) remarks (in writing of *Ep.* 22.13.1) that "inappropriateness of the argument" sometimes provides "convenient verification that it has been borrowed from elsewhere."

156. Tertullian *De exhortatione castitatis* 7; Jerome *Ep.* 123.5.

157. Jerome *Ep.* 123.7, 13 (Dido and Lucretia). Cf. Tertullian *De exhortatione castitatis* 13; *De monogamia* 17; *Ad uxorem* 1.6–7.

158. Jerome *Ep.* 123.6. Cf. Tertullian *De exhortatione castitatis* 2; *De monogamia* 3; *Ad uxorem* 1.3.

159. Jerome *Ep.* 123.8, 11. Cf. Jerome *Adversus Iovinianum* 1.16; Tertullian *De monogamia* 4.

160. Jerome *Ep.* 123.11. Cf. Jerome *Adversus Iovinianum* 15; Tertullian *De monogamia* 4; Tertullian *Ad uxorem* 1.2.

161. Jerome *Ep.* 123.12; Tertullian *De exhortatione castitatis* 6.

162. Thus "one rib, one wife" reemerges in Jerome *Ep.* 79.10, and the notion that Jesus was a virgin in the flesh and a monogamist in the spirit recurs in *Ep.* 49(48).9. Other Tertullianic motifs that reappear in Jerome's writings include the notion that the fate of Sodom may overtake Christians who are marrying and giving in marriage at the end of time (Tertullian *De monogamia* 16; *Ad uxorem* 1.5; cf. Jerome *Ep.* 22.2, *Adversus Iovinianum* 16) and the idea that the "sowing" of reproduction has been done so that the "harvest" (of cutting it down) can take place (Tertullian *Adversus Marcionem* 1.29; *De exhortatione castitatis* 1.2, 6.3; cf. Jerome *Adversus Helvidium* 21; *Adversus Iovinianum* 1.16; *Ep.* 123.12).

163. Tertullian *De praescriptione haereticorum* 7.

164. Jerome *Ep.* 22.29. Jerome also cites 2 Cor. 6:15, "What accord has Christ with Belial?"

Nine

Change and Continuity in
Pagan and Christian (Invective)
Thought on Women and Marriage
from Antiquity to the Middle Ages

Barbara Feichtinger

Moreover, it is the peculiar glory of your family that from the days of Camillus few or none of your women are recorded as having known a second husband's bed. Therefore you will not be so much deserving of praise if you persist in widowhood, as you would be worthy of execration if you, a Christian, failed to keep a custom which heathen women observed for so many generations.[1]

So, in his fifty-fourth epistle, *De monogamia*, addressed to the Roman aristocrat Furia, Jerome cites pagans as models for his Christian addressee. In doing so, he enters into an intellectual (semi)alliance with paganism that seems at odds with his usual combative asceticism.[2] On closer examination, however, it becomes clear that Jerome often incorporates elements of pagan *dissuasio matrimonii* in his discussions of marriage and that he is neither the first nor the last of the Doctors of the Church to do so.

Why, then, did Christians turn to the traditions of ancient misogamy or to pagan ideals of monogamy and cultic virginity when looking for arguments in favor of their ascetically motivated skepticism toward marriage? One could cite the continuing influence of ancient modes of thought and ways of life, from which Christians could not have entirely emancipated themselves even if they had wished to do so, or the desire for legitimization through precedent.[3] But that alone is not a satisfactory answer. First, it is clear that on other occasions, Christians were perfectly capable of breaking with pagan traditions if it seemed opportune to do so; this would seem to indicate a conscious strategy on their part. Second, classical arguments for and against marriage were not simply taken over but underwent a complex process of adaptation, whose causes, conditions, and manifestations are worthy of examination—not least as preconditions for the development of medieval misogamy.

CLASSICAL MARRIAGE AND MISOGAMY

The ancient world, with its patriarchal structures, was characterized by a view of marriage that made distinctions according to gender. For religious, economic, and social reasons, married life was usually the only alternative for a free woman.[4] Unmarried women were the exception and were treated with suspicion;[5] they were seen as pitiful creatures.[6] Men had more room for maneuver and greater freedom of choice (aside from the social imperative of assuring the continuation of the family). There was, especially among men of high social standing, a desire to avoid the troublesome obligation of supporting a family and an unwillingness to marry that might be linked to the existence of prostitution, homoeroticism, or a philistine desire for independence. Skepticism toward marriage could even be felt in republican Rome, where the cult of the family played an important role. Gellius (1.6.2) mentions a comment by Q. Metellus Macedonicus, who says, "If we could get on without a wife, Romans, we would all avoid that annoyance; but since nature has ordained that we can neither live very comfortably with them nor at all without them, we must take thought for our lasting well-being rather than for the pleasure of the moment." For this reason, official measures for making marriage compulsory were primarily directed at men who were unwilling to marry;[7] but even in early times, when asked to promulgate marriage laws, Solon replied that women were a heavy burden.[8]

This differentiation between the genders led to a situation in which the ideal of successive monogamy, of *univira/monandros*, as a branch of classical discourse on marriage and in the context of *pudicitia* and *fides*, was only applicable (with unimportant exceptions)[9] to women.[10] Paradoxically, *univira* became increasingly important during the late Republic and early empire, at a time when marriages among the upper classes were particularly short-lived (due to divorce).[11] Christianity, therefore, found in place a basic aversion toward the remarriage of women and was able to reinterpret it according to its own ideas—and eventually apply it to men.[12]

Classical pro- and anti-marriage discourse has three main characteristics: a strict concentration on the male perspective;[13] emphasis on procreation as the (sole) purpose of marriage;[14] and a close link with normative misogyny,[15] the stereotypes of which can be traced in an unbroken line from Hesiod's warnings against women to the late high points of the ascetic philosophical movements of the empire.[16] Although positive opinions of marriage and wives can be found,[17] texts are dominated by cynical voices. The Roman satirist Lucilius, for example, is of the opinion that, for the unmarried, everything in life seems good, for the married, everything bad; one can tolerate marriage for the sake of the children, but only as a wealthy man.[18]

Ridicule, irony, and hyperbolic satire seem to be elements of central importance when men in the ancient world deal with the distorted images of the unavoidable[19] inconveniences of married life. On the one hand, many of the poetical genres used in classical marriage discourse—the invective song, the epigram,[20] satire, and comedy[21]—tend to convey a humorous view of affairs, even if the humor threatens, on occasion, to turn to sarcasm, as when Hipponax of Ephesus, the sixth-century composer of invectives and begging songs, says: "Two days of a woman are full of pleasure: the day when she is married and the day when she is carried out—dead."[22] On the other hand, there is an ambivalent view of marriage in the works of philosophers, who are detached[23] or understanding about the inevitability of human weakness,[24] though they, too, on the whole, despite differences of tone, see a wife as a handicap for a philosopher.[25] Marriage was incorporated critically into the systems of the Hellenistic philosophical schools and related to their conceptions of human happiness. The Cynics took a skeptical attitude toward marriage (Diogenes exhorted philosophers not to marry),[26] the Neoplatonists an ascetic one.[27] Epicurus also explicitly spoke out against marriage and procreation, since for him they were simply a burden to the philosopher.[28] Philosophers of the Peripatetic school—especially Theophrastus—were in favor of a reduction of passion in marriage, corresponding to their general theory of the reduction of emotions. Only the Stoics were on the whole convinced of the public and private necessity of marriage. From Antipater of Tarsus (third century B.C.) to Musonius Rufus and Hierocles of Alexandria, the Stoics sing the praises of marriage as an ideal form of *humanitas*.[29] But Cynical-Stoic diatribe, with its elements of σπουδογέλοιον, was a rich source and fund of complaints against marriage[30] on which the Doctors of the Church in the East and West could abundantly draw.[31] Epictetus's statement of the incompatibility of married life with a philosophical way of life anticipates the admonitions of the Christian *patres* to remain free from the claims of the family for the sake of God.

> But in such an order of things as the present, which is like that of a battlefield, it is a question, perhaps, if the Cynic ought not to be free from distraction, wholly devoted to the service of God, free to go about among men, not tied down by the private duties of men or involved in relationships which he cannot violate and still maintain his role as a good and excellent man, whereas, on the other hand, if he observes them, he will destroy the messenger, the scout, the herald of the gods that he is. For see, he must show certain services to his father-in-law, to the rest of his wife's relatives, to his wife herself; finally, he is driven from his profession, to act as a nurse in his own family and to provide for them. To make a long story short, he must get a kettle to heat water for the baby, for washing it in a bath-tub. . . . [32]

Both the close links between misogamy and misogyny and the element of satirical mockery in the works of poets and philosophers are a result of the works' pragmatic social function and the nature of their intended addressees. The patriarchal social system of the ancient world, with its gender segregation,[33] produced literary forms that were addressed from man to man, despite the existence of female readers and authors. Literature was primarily a medium for men to reflect on the world and on themselves. Texts pro and contra marriage are therefore statements by men on women and life with them. Their misogynistic tone has a double function in relation to its addressees: it is directly addressed to men and serves to reassure them of their dominance; indirectly, it is addressed to women, with an implicit exhortation to them to accept their inferiority and the norms that govern it. With an emphasis on philosophical argumentation, these texts underpin the social freedom of a privileged class of men by emphasizing the differences in status between men and women. Their prominent misogynistic elements are a reaction to the social and political consequences of liberalizing tendencies that improved the financial situation of women. A certain economic prosperity in urban society is a necessary prerequisite for a negative attitude toward marriage (a farmer struggling for his existence cannot do without his wife). Such attitudes came to the fore with particularly misogynistic undercurrents—for example, in Juvenal's satires on women—at the very times when the increasing freedom, power,

influence, education, and financial independence of wives threatened to desta-
bilize the patriarchal system.

Antigamous literature in the ancient world had a dual function—as propaganda for endangered norms and values and as entertainment. Its philosophical argumentation served as propaganda in favor of the values of an
intellectual and social elite (the minority that could at all afford to remain
single). Furthermore, in the *mundus perversus* of hyperbolic satire, the distorted misogynistic images and the sarcastic generalizations of the *dissuasio
matrimonii* underpin social norms and lead to increased conformity in society. Laughter—in particular, the *iocari et delectare* that accompanies satirical
misogynistic discourse on marriage—has a noteworthy function in this context. Men's collective laughing at women—which goes well beyond the inherent amusement men sometimes display toward each other—clearly bonded
and strengthened them, while at the same time excluding women and objec-
tifying them. Women could only join in two awkward circumstances. They
could distance themselves from the object of ridicule, thus breaking the pha-
lanx of female solidarity: by laughing at the nonconformist behavior of other
women, they confirmed and accepted stereotypical norms. Or they could
identify themselves with the object of ridicule, feeling that they were themselves being ridiculed and, in so doing, accepting the role of the ridiculed,
inferior object. Given their social freedom, men were able joyfully to utter
lamentations about the burden of having a wife and children, only to cling
unrelentingly to the social indispensability of marriage as the basis of male
dominance. Ancient misogamy and misogyny therefore acted as a safety valve
that, as might be expected, rarely called marriage into question by presenting alternative models for society as a whole. Consequently, like all social
satire, it contributed in the end to the reform and maintenance of the exist-
ing hierarchical social system.

EARLY CHRISTIAN MISOGAMY

Early Christian misogamy differs in many ways from the situation just described.
First, sexual abstinence, which had only been of peripheral importance in
classical marriage discourse, came to play a central role.[34] For early Christian ascetics, sexuality represented the situation of fallen humanity;[35] marriage was no longer a divine institution.[36] Second, the successive monogamy
required by the New Testament not only altered the hitherto morally unim-
peachable status of divorce[37] but also led increasingly to a *dissuasio matrimonii secundi* following the death of a partner. In the following period,
Manichaean dualism and Encratite movements, as well as eschatological

tendencies, transformed the general resistance to second marriages and remarriage into a general rejection of marriage for the "true" Christian.[38] Third, the eschatological and ascetic tendencies in early Christianity led to a fundamental and wide-reaching reinterpretation of the classical Platonic and Aristotelian inheritance: the concept of (collective and individual) immortality through marriage and procreation was transformed by the ascetic movements into the concept of immortality, or eternal life, through the renunciation of procreation.[39] Procreation as an aim of marriage therefore lost its importance for some time to come. Fourth, early Christians were deeply preoccupied by the question of how to reconcile eschatological concerns with a meaningful existence within the social conditions of the time.[40] It was no longer a question of choosing between the joys of life as a bachelor and the expensive boredom of married life; rather, one chose between eternal bliss and the futility of earthly life, denying marriage the self-evidence that it had maintained largely untouched throughout antiquity.[41] Celibacy was no longer a positive or negative exception; it was the anticipation of heavenly angelic life and, as such, normal for a "true" Christian. Fifth, the gender-specific weighting in favor of a male-biased misogynistic misogamy was to a considerable extent abandoned as women, due to their early commitment to the Christian faith, increasingly became the direct addressees. Additionally, it became possible, thanks to ascetic tendencies, for women freely to choose celibacy, while the ideals of chastity and faithfulness were also applied to men. Consequently, the close links between misogamy and misogyny became looser, and both tendencies took on new, distinctive functions.

The apostolic pioneer of Christian *dissuasio matrimonii* was St. Paul.[42] He combined Jewish sexual rigorism[43] with an eschatological indifference toward marriage as the institution of a transitory world and justified his preference for celibacy Christologically—Christ demands undivided devotion.[44]

Both the ideal of successive monogamy and the rejection of marriage in favor of ascetic abstinence represented an unprecedented provocation for the family-centered ancient world and led to the accusation that Christians were socially intolerable misanthropists who lived *contra naturam*. The roots of the references to legitimizing pagan *exempla*, which Tertullian was one of the first to use, may well lie—especially during the persecutions—in attempts to moderate this provocativeness and gain acceptance for Christians. Nevertheless, the continued use of this strategy in the post-Constantinian period shows that the recourse to classical misogamy and misogyny also had other (sociopolitical) functions, which I will examine with reference to a comparison between Tertullian and Jerome.[45]

CHRISTIAN ADAPTATION
OF CLASSICAL MISOGAMY AND MISOGYNY:
TERTULLIAN AND JEROME

The recourse by Tertullian and Jerome to pagan traditions for the formulation of their Christian misogamy has similarities in structure and content: in their numerous statements on the subject, both authors respond to concrete cases that show that marriage and celibacy were hotly debated problems for their contemporaries. Both authors belong to the radical, ascetic wing of Christian thought and therefore come dangerously close to charges of heresy,[46] which they attempt, more or less successfully, to ward off by grudgingly accepting marriage.[47] Their views were of paramount importance for Christian asceticism.[48] Both authors aim their advice at men as well as women; both address two different groups—(ascetic) Christians directly and pagans indirectly. Both have recourse to characteristic elements of the philosophical and satirical-misogynistic branches of classical misogamy and recontextualize them, introducing new differentiations and intentions. In this respect, however, considerable differences can be seen between the two authors, resulting from their differing historical circumstances. I will confine myself to a brief summary here, since these two authors are treated extensively in Elizabeth Clark's chapter in this book (chap. 8).

In their ascetic Christian attacks on marriage, Tertullian and Jerome make reference to topoi belonging to classical marriage discourse and the misogyny closely connected to it. They thus seek legitimacy by linking themselves to tradition. The divergences between the two authors reflect clearly the changing social, political, and religious environment between the second and fourth centuries. On the one hand, Tertullian, working among the persecutions of the pre-Constantinian era, had to steer an often ambivalent and contradictory course in his use of classical misogamy, between the Scylla of annoying and provoking the pagans with a radical attack on marriage and the Charybdis of endangering the unique nature and value of Christian celibacy by connecting it too closely to pagan traditions. Jerome, on the other hand, after the establishment of Christianity as the state religion, felt obliged to defend ascetic celibacy within Christianity by using pagan misogamy, which he judged to be of continuing exemplary value. He attempted to establish his ascetic way of life in the face of competing Christian conceptions and to render them attractive, notably to the Roman aristocracy.[49]

The non-gender-specific ways of life that Christianity offered women led to a progressive weakening of the connection, inherited from the classical period, between *dissuasio matrimonii* and misogyny. It was simply not sensible to try and win women over to ascetic celibacy with misogynistic insults. Consequently, increasing reference was made to positive exempla of pagan chastity and monogamy to convince both men and women of the value of abstinence. Tertullian and Jerome now served to further the integration of Christianity by using the exemplary behavior of women to promote the acceptance of provocative (celibate and abstinent) lifestyles. Both writers use aspects of misogyny, on the one hand, to control ascetic Christian women through strict norms of behavior and, on the other, to draw a dividing line between ascetic Christian lifestyles and other ways of life that were branded as decadent. The clearly exemplary behavior of Christian women (and men), conforming to traditional pagan ideals, could thus signal to the world at large that Christians were the true representatives of a socially stabilizing value system in a decadent society. For Tertullian, this serves the purpose of safeguarding the Christian community at a time of crisis; for Jerome, the emphasis is on winning over the Roman senatorial aristocracy for asceticism. Thus these Christian authors achieved something of a coup: they managed with their stylizations to transform the originally deviant celibate lifestyle of ascetic Christian women into the norm, while maintaining and even strengthening traditional moral yardsticks.

Misogyny had served as fertile ground for classical misogamy, and it proved, once again, to be indispensable, but for different reasons, in an ascetic Christian context: it served to take the sting out of the strongly radicalized Christian *dissuasio matrimonii* by making connections possible in public discourse between endangered lifestyles and traditional values of norm and deviance, as well as hierarchical gender systems. Both Tertullian and Jerome, then, had good reason to turn to classical traditions of misogamic and misogynistic discourse.

MEDIEVAL MISOGAMY

It was, above all, Jerome's polemic *Adversus Iovinianum* that transmitted the traditional topoi of classical misogamy (in a modified ascetic Christian form) to the Middle Ages.[50] With his borrowings from Tertullian, he had created a more or less canonical model of classical-Christian misogamy. He had placed philosophical misogynistic traditions in the service of his ascetic intentions and had put them to use in a new, strained relationship to satirical misogyny, as part of his elitist ascetic propaganda. The dominance of asceticism is superseded in medieval literary discourse by three closely connected, yet individual, branches of anti-marriage literature. Alongside ascetic misogamic tracts, philosophical anti-marriage treatises and popular misogamic writings with an emphasis on misogyny became important in their own right, each with their own aims and intended audiences. Jerome's *Adversus Iovinianum*, however, remained the transmitter, authority, and exemplary starting point for the developments in all three branches of medieval misogamy.

During the migrations of the Dark Ages and in the following period, relations between men and women took many varied forms, including monogamy as well as polygamy and concubinage, which were only marginally controlled by church and state. In the course of the important reforms within the church and the limiting of the power of the nobility in the eleventh and twelfth centuries, marriage in the classical sense became reinstitutionalized, and both the church and secular powers sought increasingly to influence it. The upsurge of misogamy in literary discourse at the time can be seen as a reaction to these developments:[51] "For the church, it meant a clear enforcement of its own authority over lay marriages and insistence on celibacy for its own elite."[52]

Ascetically Motivated Misogamy

The misogamy contained in ascetic treatises written for monks and nuns is continually present in manuscripts dating from the sixth to the twelfth centuries and strongly so thereafter. As might be expected, it is, both in form and function, the most direct descendant of patristic traditions. Only the emphasis has changed, from apologetic and persuasive attempts to integrate a provocative lifestyle to the maintenance of an accepted way of life. An important branch of ascetic, monastically oriented exhortatory literature came into being, extolling the virtues of virginity, condemning marriage, and aimed at reaffirming monks and nuns in their monastic abstinence.[53] As long as ecclesiastical men and women were being addressed, the misogynistic elements in the texts remained small; when only (or mainly) men were being addressed, the presentation of distorted images of women knew practically no bounds. Using contrasting series of *exempla in malo* (examples of evil and destructive women)—less prevalent in texts addressed to women—and *exempla in bono* (examples of chaste and virtuous women), as well as panegyrics of virginity, ascetic texts affirm the divinely ordained superiority of a celibate lifestyle. Like Tertullian and Jerome before them, they often have recourse to the letters of St. Paul and discredit the pro-marriage tendencies of the Old Testament by citing specific examples of asceticism in the New Testament, lending their claims an unchallengeable authority. Remarkably, these texts are not entirely free from obscenity, although, in contrast to generally misogynistic misogamy, it tends to be scatological, rather than sexual, in nature.

One of the continuing purposes of ascetic misogamy was to distinguish the respective status within the church of ascetics and nonascetics—a clear perpetuation of the aims of Tertullian and Jerome. In the Middle Ages, the aim of drawing a demarcation line between clergy and laymen also became increasingly important. Outside the monasteries, misogamic tracts—with an increasingly philosophical emphasis—started being addressed to priests. In such cases, the perspective was limited entirely to that of a man, since only a man could hold the office. Additionally, however, there was a visible tendency to play down the radical, ascetic rejection of sexuality and procreation based on eschatological and dualistic reasoning, in favor of the rejection of marriage as a legal institution. Marriage (for priests) in itself seems on occasions to be more despised than is promiscuity. This is the point at which ascetic misogamy becomes philosophical misogamy.

Especially from the eleventh century onward, these ascetic philosophical tracts serve the purpose of enforcing celibacy for a clerical elite.[54] Whereas the church, on the one hand, was fighting against misogamic heresies and attempting to gain control over the marriage of laypeople, it was at the same time mobilizing all its forces against the marriage of priests, which was beginning to bring economic problems with it. Clerics had to be prevented from treating their benefices as private property that they could dispose of at will: the concept of the alienability of ecclesiastical lands was connected with the moral imperative of eliminating marriage among priests and abolishing simony.

Hugh of Folietto's *De nuptiis libri duo*—written in the form of a letter—is a noteworthy tract because it bridges the gap between ascetic and philosophical misogamy.[55] The treatise assumes that the reader has a knowledge of Map's *Valerius*,[56] yet its world is not that of an educated courtly elite but that of the monastery. Hugh (ca. 1100–74), who was a canon regular of St. Augustine at the Foundation of St. Lawrence near Corbie, addresses his treatise *De medicina animae*, which contains *De nuptiis*, primarily to an ascetic audience of monks. Nevertheless, the first part of the first book is an uncontaminated example of philosophical misogamy, discouraging the addressee—a "very dear brother"—from carnal nuptials; in it, the writer utilizes all the traditional arguments and examples of the genre.

The opening motif of *De nuptiis*, which takes the form of highly misogynistic thematic answers to the favorite medieval question *Quid est mulier*, is immediately underpinned by a long list of testimonies of philosophers and saintly men enumerating the burdens of wedlock. Theophrastus (via Jerome) is quoted at full length as a special authority;[57] Cicero and Socrates (via Jerome) follow as deterrent examples. Toward the end of chapter 1, Xenophon and Columella are cited as new authorities. Chapter 2 of book 1 musters scriptural evidence against marriage. While part 1 is a dissuasion from marriage, part 2 is a persuasion to take monastic vows. The work's title, organization, and exhaustive compilation of pagan and biblical sources are strikingly similar to the theme of Jerome's *Adversus Iovinianum*.

Philosophically Motivated Misogamy

Philosophical misogamy maintains the function, which it inherited from the ancient world, of distinguishing status and creating an intellectual elite.[58] It increasingly stood in the service, however, of the emancipatory secularization of intellectual elites (in the universities and at courts) that anticipated humanism, despite the fact that it relied heavily on patristic conceptions of *dissuasio matrimonii* and had to assume, given the nature of medieval education, that intellectuals and clerics would be the same people.

All the *dissuasiones* are written by educated men, very much aware of their privileged state, standing on a lofty mountaintop (as Wilson and Makowski put it) surrounded by the mist of literary and mythological allusions, indignantly surveying the vices and follies of humankind.[59] For these writers, misogamy is to a large extent an exercise in self-definition. This branch of medieval misogamy, therefore, once again restricts itself to a male perspective.[60] As in the pre-Christian ancient world, the focus shifts from celibacy to a (sexually active) life as a bachelor,[61] which is in blatant contrast to the ascetic ideal as represented by Jerome. Marriage is no longer placed in the context of threatened morality and sin, and virginity is of course no longer glorified as it was in ascetic treatises. Marriage is presented as simply being an unwise and career-damaging way of life for an intellectual elite striving for autonomy.

The treatises of philosophical misogamy, usually written in Latin prose, advise against marriage in the voice of well-intentioned friends. They are underpinned by catalogues of *exempla in malo*, taken preferably from pagan and mythological sources, which are seen as authoritative. Since only men are addressed, these texts contain absolutely no praise for women.

The earliest medieval meditations on philosophical misogamy come, not surprisingly, from the pen of Pierre Abelard, the first professional scholar of the Middle Ages. As early as his *Theologia Christiana*, Abelard emphasizes the importance of complete autonomy and the necessity of freedom from social obligations for intellectual scholars and philosophers.[62] Abelard makes a connection between financial obligations and marital burdens in the teachings of Theophrastus in *Adversus Iovinianum*, which he cites at length. He looks for and finds a precedent for his own position as an intellectual (not an ascetic) in the example of classical philosophers and Jerome's judgment (from his ascetic Christian standpoint) and transmission of them. Abelard chose a direction that was to have momentous consequences and that prefigured the developments of the Renaissance: the patristic tradition was being examined no longer for its own sake but as a legitimizing intermediary between pagan antiquity and the present, furthering the emancipation of an increasingly secular intellectual class. In contrast to the *Theologia Christiana*, which represents a basic theoretical exposition of Abelard's position, his *Historia calamitatum* is a subjectively colored text on *dissuasio matrimonii*.[63] The *Historia* was written about 1132, when Abelard was abbot of St. Gildas in Brittany and Heloise was abbess of the Paraclete in Champagne. Chapter 7 contains an autobiographical letter in a consolatory style to a friend, in which Abelard enumerates the standard authoritative arguments against marriage by using Heloise—his mistress and, later, wife—as a mouthpiece. Thus the *dissuasio* is put in the mouth of a sympathetic, loving, educated, and intelligent woman, whose persona provides a convenient and effective distancing device for the author.

According to Abelard, Heloise disapproved of his marrying her for two reasons: the danger it entailed and the disgrace that was bound to result from it. Her uncle, she maintains, would never come to terms with the arrangements, and Abelard would be lost to both the church and philosophy. Once again, Jerome is the main source for the dicta of the Apostle Paul, as well as for the *sententiae* of Theophrastus, Cicero, and Seneca and for antithetical *sua voce* catalogues, which are modeled on *Adversus Helvidium* and Jerome's *Epistles* 22 and 54.

> To say no more of the hindrance of the study of philosophy, consider the status of the dignified life. What could there be in common between scholars and wet-nurses, writing desks and cradles, books, writing tables and distaffs, stylus, pens and spindles? Or who is there who is bent on sacred or philosophic reflection who could bear the wailing of babies, the silly lullabies of nurses to quiet them, the noisy horde of servants, both male and female; who can endure the foul and incessant degrading defilement of infants?[64]

Once again, the authority of the Doctor of the Church is called upon to set the *dissuasio* in a philosophical and pagan, rather than patristic, framework and to advocate freedom and dignity rather than asceticism. The extent to which Abelard's *dissuasio matrimonii* differs from Jerome's aim of ascetic abstinence is illustrated by Heloise's argumentation in favor of free love, which is influenced by *amour courtois* and Ovidian conceptions of love. She refuses to marry Abelard, making clear that she would much prefer to be called his mistress—even his whore—than his wife, so that her charm, not marital chains, would tie him to her.[65] The absence of both catalogues of bad wives and exempla of pagan virgins are a testimony to the internal consistency of the text.

One of Abelard's most talented students at Montagne Sainte Geneviève, the Englishman John of Salisbury, who became secretary to Theobold, archbishop of Canterbury (whose court was also frequented by Peter of Blois), also expressed his views on—or, rather, against—marriage, in book 8 of *Policraticus de nugis curialium et vestigiis philosophorum* (1159).[66] John's dissuasion from marriage, under the title "The Annoyance and Burdens of Wedlock according to Jerome and other Philosophers,"[67] is embedded in his list of capital vices, in which he criticizes (courtly) lasciviousness and counsels moderation in all things. The title itself makes clear that clerics and philosophers are seen as being the same people and that the author is attempting subtly to balance philosophy and asceticism, celibacy and virtue in general.

John's explicit borrowings from Jerome's misogamy, despite their seeming congruence, bear witness to a certain amount of adaptation. Jerome justifies his recourse to pagan philosophers and exempla with reference to the stimulus and integration they provide in the face of the disturbing failure of Christian regulations.[68] John, however, sees pre-Christian traditions as real alternatives for his readers, who seem to be put off by Christian rigor and asceticism.

> In this respect [that the burdens of marriage detract from the freedom of the philosopher] the whole chorus of serious philosophers are in agreement, so that those who are repelled by the strict doctrine of Christian religion, may learn chastity and virtue from the pagans.[69]

In the Christianized Middle Ages, it was no longer a question of winning recognition for or defending ascetic or celibate lifestyles (as long as they remained within the bounds of orthodoxy). Instead, philosophers and clerics had to be presented with alternative forms of nonascetic celibacy. Jerome secularizes misogamy, freeing it from the highly ascetic context of antiquity.[70] In imitating the "Theophrastus" section of Jerome,[71] John makes fun of those who are so obtuse as to take on the burdens of marriage more than once;[72] John shifts the emphasis of his misogamy from the supposed sinfulness of marriage to its stupidity, turning from Jerome's critique of the institution itself to a critique of the misuse of marriage and poor behavior within marriage (which John attributes especially to women).[73] He makes it clear that only unmarried (though not necessarily chaste) philosophers and clerics can be sure of avoiding public humiliation due to their indiscreet wives.[74] Whereas Jerome cites as an *exemplum in bono* the virtuous Bibia, who did not complain of her husband's bad breath because she thought all men smelled like that, John uses a similar argument for the opposite purpose, introducing the type of the embarrassing, emasculating wife into the misogamic canon via the exemplum of the wife who openly calls her husband's virility into question.[75]

The public image of the cleric within courtly etiquette clearly took on considerable importance, as cleric-philosophers sought a suitable image for themselves. After mentioning the famous examples of the wives of Cicero, Phillipus, and Socrates (handed down by Jerome), John quotes verbatim the story of the Widow of Ephesus from Petronius's *Satyrica*, introducing it with a borrowing from Juvenal's sixth satire.[76] He then once again cites Jerome as an authority legitimizing the statements of Petronius. All this is aimed at upgrading the moral status of educated clerics by condemning the poor behavior of women. John, as a serious churchman, an older man, and a man imbued with strong moral principles, may, with his renewed connection of misogamy and misogyny, have been protesting against the specific atmosphere of—as well as the irritating background of new ideas from—the English court, which was patronized so lavishly by Queen Eleanor and in which troubadour poetry and courtly love flourished so richly.

Walter Map's *Dissuasio Valerii Rufino ne ducat uxorem* (1180–90)[77] was one of the most widely disseminated and widely used works of philosophical misogamy.[78] Not unlike John of Salisbury, Map included this epistolary pamphlet in his collection *De nugis curialium*, a work criticizing the court of King Henry II, whom Map admired for his education, eloquence, courtly cultivation (*facetia curialium*), cosmopolitan elegance, and intellectual wit.

Map's *Valerius* is probably the rhetorically most perfect *dissuasio* in the antigamous tradition and follows Quintilian's model closely.[79] In it, the author chooses the persona of a certain well-meaning Valerius, who writes to his (red-headed) friend Rufinus in an urgent attempt to dissuade him from marriage. The exposition of the letter is reminiscent not only of Juvenal's sixth satire (which also associates marriage and death),[80] but also of the letter of Abelard's Heloise, which it also resembles in its use of the metaphors of elegiac and courtly love (reminding one of Andreas Capellanus's *De arte honeste amandi*) and in its opposition of love and marriage (*uxorari tendebat, non amari*). The method of documentation is the favorite medieval device of *frequentatio*, a rhetorical figure designed to bring scattered references together to elaborate a principle.[81]

There is no need to insist upon the great similarity to Jerome, especially in light of the fact that the letter was originally attributed to him (Migne lists it as *Ep.* 36 in *PL* 30). There are, however, significant changes. As with John of Salisbury, misogamy and misogyny are linked, and examples are reinterpreted misogynistically. For example, Map lists parts of the canonical catalogue of virgin births—traditional *exempla in bono*—to prove that neither age nor high walls can protect a maiden's virginity: "a virgin verging on old age and eminent in repute for chastity, at last by a vision of Apollo conceived and bore Plato."[82] This statement about Perictione is a verbatim quote from Jerome's *Adversus Jovinianum*, where she is used as an *exemplum in bono* to exemplify the Christlike virgin births of antiquity. *Valerius*, however, transforms the incident into an *exemplum in malo* to demonstrate women's incapacity to resist a lover. The exempla almost invariably end with a final apostrophe applying the moral of the paragraph to Rufinus himself. Thus the ancient illustrative example is turned into a genuine medieval exemplum, complete with moral and application. Map's lengthy apology for his use of pagan exempla is worthy of note in this connection.

> My Friend, are you amazed or are you, the rather, affronted, because in my parallels I point out heathen as worthy of your imitation, idolatries to a Christian, wolves to a lamb, evil men to a good. . . . I know the superstition of the heathen; but . . . the unbelieving perform very many things perversely; nevertheless they do some things which, although barren in their case, would in ours bring forth fruit abundantly.[83]

Map argues that all the advantages of Christianity are worthless if people (men) turn their back on philosophy for the sake of marriage and become animals ("I do not wish thee to be the bridegroom of Venus, but of Pallas!").[84] He then emphasizes the interest of the pagans, who are of course disadvantaged in comparison to Christians, in (philosophical) education and cultivation.[85] Despite heavily biblical language, the emphasis has clearly changed from ascetic abstinence to philosophical *humanitas;* pagan antiquity is recognized more and more in its own right as an integral part of education for the cultivated court and clergy. Map's increasing distance from the ascetic intentions of Tertullian and Jerome is underlined by his absolute lack of reference to St. Paul's statements on marriage. All this suggests that the *Valerius* was written for the school and the learned at court, rather than for the monastery. For the budding young scholar and the educated courtier, the *Valerius* provides a wealth of classical and mythological allusions, a witty and clever use of language, a wealth of ironic and enigmatic passages, and a fine rhetorical model. Its considerable success justified its methods.[86]

Map presents a whole set of new dissuasive exempla, most of which are included in the misogamic canon for the first time. Essentially—as Wilson and Makowski emphasize—Map takes a dim view of marriage and women while, at least in theory, exalting love. Thus his treatise can be read as a counter-gospel of courtly love. The ironic use of the iconography of courtly love in the setting of his poem would have raised expectations among his audience that they were about to be presented with a genuine romance, but Map presents instead an inverted eulogy of courtly ladies, cataloguing a remarkable multitude of wicked women. At the same time, he claims to be attacking marriage, not love—thereby providing a convenient camouflage for his attacks on women. In Map's *dissuasio*, a contemporary misogamic preoccupation (*amour courtois*), an ancient theme (philosophical misogamy), and a timeless satirical topos (misogyny) are conflated. As such, the work had a demonstrably large and lasting appeal for a wide audience.[87]

Both John of Salisbury and Map included their *dissuasiones* in works criticizing the court of Henry II. Map, the younger man, finds different shortcomings—too much ambition and too little polish. Even the Muses, he argues, refuse to frequent so uninspired a court. His criticism, therefore, is less moral and more urbane than that of John of Salisbury. The differences between John's and Map's treatments might also, of course, reflect a change of situation: in 1173 Eleanor supported the rebellion against her husband by their eldest son and was subsequently imprisoned in Winchester Castle. Consequently, the pronounced emphasis of Map's *dissuasio* on the wicked and potentially destructive effect of women is hardly surprising, especially in view of the fact that Map was one of King Henry's particular favorites.[88]

Peter of Blois's *dissuasio matrimonii*, which is included as the seventy-ninth letter *ad R. amicum suum* in his (successfully) published correspondence,[89] is inconceivable, both in its title and in many details, without Map's *Valerius*. There are also biographical similarities: Peter of Blois was a Frenchman by birth, but he spent most of his adult life in England, first in the service of the archdeacon of Salisbury, then under Archbishop Richard. In 1182 he was made archdeacon of Bath. Like John of Salisbury and Walter Map, Peter was associated with the court of Henry II. Peter's letter is unusual for several reasons. First, it is a *post facto dissuasio*, because the addressee is already married. Second, Peter is the first medieval misogamic writer to refer to Juvenal's sixth satire as a canonical text on the vices of women and wives. Third, no scriptural arguments are found in the letter; the dissuasive arguments are directed toward a professional scholar and are entirely philosophical, historical, and rhetorical. Fourth, and most important, Peter is original in his incorporation of exemplary material into the Theophrastus fragment.[90] Peter's work of philosophical misogamy creates a paradox: although its innovative use of Theophrastus was only possible through the intermediary of Jerome, its end result is as different as possible from the ascetic Christian perspective of the Doctor of the Church.

Andreas Fieschi's treatise *De dissuasione uxorationis* is a witty and elegant, if somewhat conventional, example of the continued reception of Map's *Valerius*. It also confirms as canonical the establishment of a (largely nonascetic) philosophical misogynistic tradition, which saw Pallas Athene as the only woman appropriate for the members of the secular and clerical elite of the time.[91]

Popular Misogynistic Misogamy

It was in the aggressively satirical elements of misogynistic misogamy, rather than in philosophical treatises, that the desire to control women socially and keep them in check survived and resurged. This tendency had already been present in early antiquity and had reemerged in late antiquity—with altered and more limited aims—as part of the dissemination of Christianity and asceticism. Its resurgence in the Middle Ages may have been a reaction to the economic prosperity and relatively high social status of women of all classes.[92] In the final analysis, misogamy was transformed in this context into little more than an integral part of misogyny.

The background for this upsurge of misogynistic marriage literature, which now could be written without even a nod in the direction of religious values, was supplied by a change in the cultural climate around the middle of the thirteenth century. At this time, medieval Europe reached its demographic peak and was moving in the direction of urban market economies and secularization. Works filled with humor, wit, and biting satire replaced exhortations to perfection. Gone, too, was any mention of the possibility of the spiritual equality of the sexes (achieved through sexual abstinence) that had been stressed by the ascetic tendencies of early Christianity. In the face of altered economical and social conditions, the misogynistic discourses of the end of the thirteenth century accompanied and promoted the ousting of women from public life and positions of power. This decline in genuine female influence was supported by two factors: first, by an excessive veneration of the ideal woman, culminating in the cult of the Virgin, which seems to have fortified the belief in the moral and social dangers of women of flesh and blood; second, by a misogynistic discourse of derision, reflecting Juvenal's caricatures of the relatively emancipated, financially independent, and powerful women of imperial Rome, which revived stereotypical images of the female body and biological functions, their moral instability and general inferiority. These theories were "scientifically" legitimized by the rediscovery of Aristotle's theories.[93] Even holy women were suspect—thirteenth- and fourteenth-century monastic "reform" for convents involved provision for stricter supervision by male superiors and stern rules of enclosure.

In the context of Augustine's teachings connecting the Fall and sexuality—concepts central to medieval theology—marriage, as the legal setting for the sexual act, remained ambivalent. The unavoidable closeness of marriage to the sins of the flesh led to a corresponding rigor in the sphere of canon law, which began, during the twelfth century, to establish itself alongside theology as a discipline in its own right. The growth at this time of rigid antisexual positions strongly suggests the existence of vigorous conflicts during the development of marital canon law and the establishment of marriage as a sacrament, with its concomitant economic problems.[94]

Popular misogamy at this time can therefore be read both as a parody of the excesses of canonical marital casuistry perpetrated by the educated elite and as a medium for expressing social change. It not only anticipates the downfall of courtly culture and the rise of the cities but also mirrors the strategies within society for depriving women of power resulting from altered economic conditions, as well as representing the emancipation of the masses from the clerical monopoly on literature.

Although the genre contained considerable potential for innovation and explosive social comment (the personae of late medieval satires subvert by ridicule the ideals of the two dominant classes—in this case, the aristocracy and the clergy), popular misogamy, which was increasingly being turned into misogamic misogyny, remained faithful to common themes and conventional literary traditions. The misogynistic basis for the guessing game involving the question *Quid est mulier* can be found not only in the usual ancient sources but also in great quantities in the sermons and other works of ecclesiastical writers, the popular genres of the vernacular, and the Latin *comedia elegiaca*.

The existence of numerous vernacular texts suggests that the genre had a broad public appeal.[95] This public would include laity and clerics, the educated and uneducated. As in classical satire, men are the direct and women the indirect addressees.

The texts, usually in verse form, work by inverting values, demonstrating their illusory nature. Their argumentation is supported not by biblical or classical authority but by the (hyperbolically distorted) experience of a normal man.

So much misogynistic literature with a misogamic content was produced between the thirteenth and fifteenth centuries—for example, the *Couplets sur le mariage* or the *Chanson de mal mariage*—that it is difficult to make a representative selection.[96] The thirteenth century produced the anonymous treatise *De conjuge non ducenda*, whose setting seems to be a modernization of the setting of Walter Map's *Valerius*. Instead of the anti-marriage advice of a friend, a number of well-meaning angelic personae are presented, who may represent John Chrysostomos, to whom several spurious antifeminist works were ascribed in the twelfth century; John the Evangelist; John the Apostle; Peter of Corbeil (Petrus de Corbolio), the arch defender of the celibate and chaste ideals; or Laurentius of Durham, to whom the *De conjuge* has been mistakenly attributed. They advise against marriage, presenting the full array of misogynistic motifs and prejudices. The thematic accusations against women are all-inclusive: all nubile women are under attack, as is the institution of marriage.

As a text of general misogamy, the *De conjuge* is in full methodological, ideological, and topographical agreement with the prototype of this branch of misogamy, Juvenal's sixth satire, even though it contains clear traces of the ascetic Christian filter through which the genre had passed since late antiquity. Nevertheless, the poem lacks any direct mythological, literary, or scriptural allusions. The limited literary and biblical echoes are paraphrased but not identified. Thus the poem would have appealed not only to an educated audience that would appreciate and enjoy the text's ironic subtleties and complex scriptural echoes but also to a bourgeois audience that could enjoy the topography and the coarse obscenities without any understanding of the subtleties. All of these observations suggest that the author was consciously trying to project a persona less educated and of lower social class than himself. A full-fledged satire in the general Juvenalian misogamic tradition, *De conjuge* ridicules both celibate and marital propaganda while playing to contemporary prejudices.

The *Roman de la rose*, not only one of the most widely disseminated and influential vernacular poems of the Middle Ages but one that justified Jean de Meung's long-lasting reputation as a savage misogynist, puts all of its misogynistic and misogamic statements into the mouths of unsympathetic characters (the Jaloux, La Vieille), stock figures of medieval comedy delivering stock tirades. Juvenal, Valerius Maximus, Theophrastus (quoted entirely), and Ovid are the predecessors of the *Roman*, but parts of the Abelard-Heloise correspondence are used to underpin the misogamic arguments. In the *Roman*, the canon of arguments of philosophical misogamy is closely connected to misogyny in general and to personal complaints on the vices of women.

Similar qualities can be found in the *Matheoli lamentationes*, an enormously long Latin work of the thirteenth century by a clerk named Matheolus, who was unfrocked for bigamy (i.e., for marrying a widow) and laments his misfortune in four books containing 10,508 half-lines of alternately rhymed verses. It is one of the most bitter and certainly the longest tirade against women and marriage, pronouncedly eclectic and learned, making use of the whole topography of the misogamic canon, yet claiming to rely on personal experience rather than authority.

One of the last genuine works of medieval general misogamy, the *Quinze joyes de mariage*, is an anonymous satire from the turn of the fourteenth century (between 1372 and 1461). The framework of the satire is a prayer to the Virgin Mary enumerating her fifteen joys, a *persuasio* to moral improvement through reflection and imitation. Conversely, the *Quinze joyes de mariage* is a *dissuasio* from marriage by means of a meditation on and contemplation of the miseries of married life. It is not an ostensibly learned work. The catalogues of mythological, historical, and biblical exempla are missing.

Eustache Deschamps's *Miroir de mariage* remains, in its content, more faithful to the philosophical and ascetic traditions of misogamy. However, it breaks new ground formally in its use of the *altercatio*. The *Miroir* is a debate weighing the advantages and disadvantages of the married state. False friends—Desir, Folie, Servitude, Faintise—present the addressee, Franc Vouloir (a personification of free will), with the usual arguments of laymen and clerics in favor of marriage; at the same time, Repertoire de Science, as a true friend, counsels against worldly marriage in favor of spiritual marriage, borrowing extensively from Theophrastus's *Liber aureolus* and Jerome's *Adversus Iovinianum*. His use of a letter is reminiscent of both Map's *Valerius* and Hugh of Folieto. Misogynistic elements are used extensively, but the argumentation is essentially elitist: marriage is appropriate neither for scholars (*miles scientiae*), nor for knights (*miles armati*), nor for clergymen (*miles christiani*); others, however, may submit to the necessity of marriage in order to ensure the survival of the human race. Deschamps's work anticipates the fifteenth and sixteenth centuries, both in its form as an *altercatio* and through its use of allegorization, which transforms the traditional dispute *an vir ducat uxorem* [should a man take a wife?] into a psychomachia between reason and the emotions.

Finally, the prologue to the "Wife of Bath's Tale" in Chaucer's *Canterbury Tales* can be included in the category of general misogamic satire, defined as a dissuasion by inversion employing everyday specificity, exemplary documentation, and current misogynistic topoi presented by an experienced persona. In addition to her full use of the general misogamic canon, Dame Alice also manages to incorporate into her speech the standard arguments of the philosophical and ascetic branches of misogamy in a masterfully ironic way, which not only incriminates her but ridicules the arguments of the misogamic canon. Dame Alice's prologue is a *dissuasio* disguised as a *persuasio*. The tone of her speech is one of sustained irony, and her method of argumentation is the systematic inversion of the aristocratic and ecclesiastical models of marriage, augmented by three categories of well-known misogamic arguments: the ascetic, the philosophical, and the general corpora.

Particularly interesting is the treatment of Jerome's polemic *Adversus Iovinianum*, which is the main source for the first part of the Wife of Bath's prologue (lines 1–130): Alice uses Jovinian's well-known exempla and arguments in favor of marriage in the form of an inversion of the ascetic misogamic canon. She herself turns out to be the stock female character of the ascetic misogamic canon: Dame Alice is the personification of the *ardens corpus* [burning body] accusation hurled at wives by preachers of asceticism. Like most competent misogamic writers, she takes quotations out of context and disregards parts of quotations that do not suit her immediate purpose. In this speech, she uses the ironic inversions of arguments of ascetic misogamy, while at the same time personifying the canon's topography. The traditional accusations made against women are turned into subtle survival techniques in the battle of the sexes in a period when women were despised. In the prologue to the "Wife of Bath's Tale," which masterfully combines a satire on and a topology of the three distinct strains of medieval misogamy, the long tradition of misogyny and misogamy involving the pointed ambivalence of values seems to take on a new quality.

CONCLUSION: MEDIEVAL MISOGAMY AND COURTLY LOVE

The individual branches of medieval misogamic discourse—ascetic, philosophical, and popular misogamy—not only have much in common with each other (indeed, individual texts often mix the various genres). Each is also linked, in its own specific way, to the concept of courtly love.[97] This is only possible because a skeptical attitude toward marriage is an integral part of the code of courtly love, which idealizes extramarital love.

In ascetic misogamy, the conception of spiritual love was enlarged by contemporary ideals of courtly love and etiquette. At the same time, the poetry of courtly love was eliminating, with the help of ascetic-Platonic ideas, any erotic traces that might have been left over from its classical roots (in particular, Ovid). This reconciliation of spiritual and courtly love (which of course never lost their basic differences) led to the use of almost identical images in courtly love lyrics and poetry on the Virgin Mary.

Philosophical misogamy and the concept of courtly love were aimed at similar groups of people: the clergy, scholars in the upcoming universities, and the courtly elite. Their intentions were also similar—the creation and maintenance of intellectual social elites through cultural refinement and distinction. Both the codes of courtly etiquette and philosophical misogamy involved the use of exclusive forms of expression. The texts were not translated into the vernacular but continued to be copied in Latin for the entertainment and education of the same type of educated audience for which they were written. In theory, their code of values was presented as an ideal for everyone, yet it remained deliberately inaccessible to the masses.

When elements of the code of courtly love were actually included in misogamic texts (it should not be forgotten that, apart from Hugh and Abelard, all writers under consideration were associated with the court), it was usually ironically. It would seem that John of Salisbury, Walter Map, and Peter of Blois, who were patronized by Henry II and associated with the first major European court to encourage literature propagating the courtly ideal, fill out the contemporary view of the role of women, complementing the distancing idealization of women in courtly love with elements of a distancing pejorative view of women. In both cases, an elitist group of men defined itself via hybrid concepts of the role of women, leading to or even aiming at the de facto absence and powerlessness of women.

The upsurge in misogynistic marriage satire seems, for its part, to be a reaction of the lower classes to the norms propagated by intellectual discourse. The philosophical rejection of marriage by careerist clergymen was perverted through exaggeration and generalization: not only an intellectual elite rejects marriage; everybody does so. The ascetic rejection of marriage was undermined by explicit and blunt worldliness and the idealization of extramarital promiscuity. At the same time, misogynistic marriage satire became involved, not without aggression, in the progressive takeover of married life by the church. It served to break down the almost religious worship of idealized womanhood by the upper classes: it satirized it, accused women of every possible vice, and treated them as the root of all evil.[98] In this respect, the misogynistic misogamy of the Middle Ages, which at first sight would seem to have little in common with courtly love, can be seen to complement it and share its aims. Both attempted to control and restrict female authority and influence in political, religious, and economic life by imposing a system of norms upon them. Exaggerated idealization served just as much as aggressive defamation to restrict a woman's tangible sphere of activity and her practical freedoms.

Notes

1. Jer. *Ep.* 54.1.2 (CSEL 54.466); translation by Wright (1963).

2. Elsewhere, Jerome tirelessly preaches the necessity of breaking with pagan traditions; cf. Feichtinger 1995.

3. On a formal level, the rules of classical rhetoric were certainly important in influencing the use of historical exempla.

4. Since domestic worship was to some extent in the hands of the wife and death rites were performed by legitimate sons, marriage was indispensable for the survival of the clan. In its struggle to maintain the number of citizens in the face of high infant mortality and low life expectancy, the state was aided by the censors, who kept an eye on procreation and would not hesitate to fine even older celibates or annul childless marriages, even if the couple protested and was in love (cf. Gell. 4.3.2, 17, 21, 44; *PW* 5.1244).

5. Temporary celibacy existed among female priests of Apollo and Isis (Xen. Eph. 3.11.4–5) and among vestals. The respect for virginity among pagans must be judged with care: the requirement, e.g., that the bride of the *flamen dialis* be a virgin is mentioned only in Christian sources (Tert. *Exh. cast.* 13 [CCL 2.2.1033–35]; Jer. *Ep.* 123.7 [CSEL 56.80–81]); cf. Kötting 1988, 8).

6. Terms such as *xera* or *vidua* refer to the "emptiness" of life without a husband and children. A girl who died without having married was especially pitied.

7. For the marriage laws of Augustus, see Csillag 1976; Raditsa 1980; Galinsky 1981. They notably encouraged marriages with numerous children, offering advantages in taxation (see Gai. *Inst.* 2.286; Suet. *Aug.* 34).

8. Successive monogamy may have been required for certain pagan priesthoods, since the marriage of the priest was often considered to be a *hieros gamos* (cf. Gell. 10.15, 23–24; Plut. *Aetia Romana* 50; Kötting 1957, 1018–19). But in general, Christians had no obvious role models for abstinence or monogamy.

9. See Humbert 1972. Religious rules in the ancient world opposed only the remarriage of women (see Kötting 1988, 8–11). In the Greek (and Jewish) world, women who had only been married once were not held in such high regard as they were in Rome (see Kötting 1957, 1017–18).

10. See Val. Max. 2.1.3; Funke 1965–66; Lightman and Zeisel 1977; Kötting 1988. The importance of *univira* can originally be traced back to attempts to maintain the purity of the gens and to fear of a *perturbation sanguinis*; it was restricted to the upper levels of society.

11. For the transferral of the secularized term meaning "good woman" to Christian widows, see Lightman and Zeisel 1977, 24–32.

12. See Kötting 1988, 24. John Chrysostomos, in *Ad viduam iuniorem*, points out the low regard in which the people held second marriages. Tertullian also made use of popular attitudes in the ancient world, which saw second marriages as unseemly: cf. Tert. *Monog.* 10.7 (CCL 2.1243); Hilar. *Tract. in Ps.* 131.24 (PL 9.742–43; CSEL 22.680–81); Zeno *Tract.* 1.5.4, 6 (PL 11.303–5, 311–18; CC 22.172–73 [= II.7]; 31–37 [= I.4]). For the continuing problems of the exegesis of the Letter to Timothy, see Kötting 1988, 22–23. The church of the fourth century in Asia Minor and later in the West promulgated laws against remarriage while sanctioning their being disregarded; see Basil *Ep.* 199.18, 188.4 (PG 32.717–20, 673–74). Jerome (*Adv. Iov.* 1.14 [PL 23.244]) mentions the denial of the consecrated Bread for the unmarried. See Kötting 1964; 1988, 15, 33–36.

13. Ironically enough, one of the few statements on marriage by a woman, defending and pitying the plight of her own sex, is the complaint of Medea in Eur. *Med.* 230–51.

14. Eratosthenes says that virginity is a treasure but that it would die out if practiced by everybody (*Anth. Pal.* 9.444); cf. Lucilius frag. 633, 634–35, 638–43 Krenkel. Pessimistic opinions of procreation can be found in Eur. frag. 908 Nauck, commented on by Clement of Alexandria (*Strom.* 3.3.22.2).

15. Wilson and Makowski (1990, 1–11) point out that a precise differentiation between misogamy and misogyny is essential for the understanding of medieval misogamy.

16. See Hes. *Theog.* 585–602; *Erga* 53–82. Semonides of Amorgos says mockingly that women were created, devoid of reason, from the bristly pig and other creatures (Stob. 22.193 [4.561–66 Wachsmith and Hense = frag. 7 Diehl). Whether the "Weiberjambos" of Phocylides of Milet (frag. 2. Diehl) should be placed chronologically before or after Semonides remains unclear: see Kakridis 1962; Verdennius 1968–69.

17. Cf. Homer's representation of marital affection between Hector and Andromache (*Il.* 6.407–96). Hesiod (*Erga* 702–5) says that an understanding woman is a treasure trove of virtue but difficult to find.

18. *Anth. Pal.* 11.388. Cf. Palladas on the domination of women, even of those who do not go as far as to lash out with a slipper (*Anth. Pal.* 10.55).

19. Although certain groups within society (e.g., soldiers) were not allowed to marry and there probably existed a shortage of women (see Pomeroy 1985, 102–6, 250–60), it is safe to assume that the great majority of men married on at least one occasion.

20. A collection of aphorisms by Johannes Stobaios includes the headings "marriage is very good" (4.494.2–4.512.15 Wachsmith and Hense); "it is not good to get married" (4.513.2–4.523.8 Wachsmith and Hense); and "for some, marriage turns out useful; for others it is unhealthy" (4.524.1–4.531.23 Wachsmith and Hense).

21. Aristophanes, who, e.g., in *Lysistrata* takes married life as one of his themes, provides an explosive cocktail of misogyny and positive attitudes toward women. The cynical sentences of works of New Comedy reflect contemporary ambivalence: see, e.g., Menand. frag. 578 ("Marriage, if one will face the truth, is an evil, but a necessary evil"), 59, 575–76 Körte. For skepticism toward marriage in the comedies of Plautus, see Braund, chap. 3 in this volume.

22. Quoted in Stob. 22.35 (4.515 Wachsmith and Hense).

23. The question of whether or not to get married was a favorite topic in the schools of rhetoric for training in reflective Genos. See Quint. 3.5.5–8. These rhetorical exercises find their counterpart in the Middle Ages; see Curtis 1965, 164.

24. Cf. *Anth. Pal.* 10.116: " 'No married man but is tempest-tossed,' they all say, and marry knowing it."

25. Cf. the collection of passages in Buddenhagen 1919 and the summary in Oepke 1959, 653–54.

26. See Diog. Laert. 6.29; Hübner [1828–33] 1981, 2:21; Epict. 3.22.67ff.

27. See, e.g., Porph. *Ad Marcell.*

28. Epict. 1.23.3. For Democritus and Epicurus, cf. Clem. Alex. *Strom.* 2.23.138.3 (Stählin and Früchtel 1985, 2:189). Cf. also the Sophist view of Antiphon frag. 49 Diehl; Grilli 1953, 77.

29. For the books by the Stoics with pro-marriage tendencies, see Bickel 1915. In his sixth satire, Juvenal seems to be satirizing the Stoic marriage ideal by inverting it.

30. See Oltramare 1916, 51–60. Jerome (e.g., *Adv. Iov.* 1.13 [PL 23.241]) makes clear that he is referring to a traditional topos within a genre; cf. *Ep.* 22.22.3 (CSEL 54.174–75).

31. Early examples of Christian reception of diatribes can be found in the apocryphal Acts of Thomas, in which Jesus appears in the figure of the apostle to a couple on the evening of their wedding day and gives them (successfully, of course) ascetic advice. Gregor of Nyssa, in *De virginitate*, speaks out in favor of the ascetic ideal, not only by glorifying mystically profound virginity but also (chap. 3 [PG 46.325–36]) by portray-

ing the disadvantages of marriage in a manner reminiscent of diatribe; John Chrysostomus, who also wrote a *De virginitate* in his youth, does not miss the opportunity of dealing with this theme (from a more female perspective). Neither does Gregor of Nazianzus, in his poem *Perì partheniou*. There are also extant under the name of Basil the Great two treatises on virginity (perhaps predating Gregor of Nyssa), which also mention the *molestiae nuptiarum*. See Capelle and Marrou 1957, 1003; Hansen 1963.

32. Epict. 3.22.69–71 (trans. Oldfather [1928] 1985). Cf. the analogies in Tert. *Ux.* 2.4–5 (CCL 1.388–89).

33. Free women were almost entirely excluded, especially in ancient Greece, from the symposia in which literature was created and received, as well as from theatrical performances.

34. Marriage in the ancient world was defined by consensus and procreation. The ascetic tendencies of Christianity were directed against sexuality and/or procreation, although fine dividing lines are discernible between the two. As a kind of compensation, ideas were developed (by Augustine, among others) that saw a spiritual bond between husband and wife as an integral part of marriage. For the development of Augustine's concept of marriage, see Clark 1991.

35. As Clark (1991) shows, the majority of the Doctors of the Church in the East and West believed that after the Resurrection, as in Paradise, there would be no sexuality or gender, since humans would be "like the angels." Augustine irrevocably connects earthly sexuality, which to a large extent goes against the will, with the fallen status of humanity, saying that the refusal of the limbs to obey the will is a consequence of the refusal of man to obey God.

36. Neither God the Father, nor God the Son, nor the Holy Ghost have anything similar to the married life of the ancient gods.

37. For an interpretation of this radical change, which broke both with Jewish and with pagan traditions (Matt. 19:6; Mark 10:9; 1 Cor. 7:27), see Tert. *Monog.* 9.4–5 (CCL 2,2.1241–42); *Ux.* 2.2 (CCL 1.1.384–87); Lact. *Div. inst.* 6.23.33; Clem. Alex. *Strom.* 2.145.3, 2.146.2 (Stählin and Früchtel 1985, 193). Divine right is placed in opposition to state law, which recognized marriages after divorce from or the death of the partner.

38. The attitude toward marriage inherited from the Jewish tradition, which contained few ascetic currents, was a positive one; see Oepke 1959, esp. 655–56. In the New Testament, St. Paul's emphasis on the superiority of a celibate lifestyle can largely be explained by his millenarianism, which brought with it two contrasting answers to the futility of earthly existence: libertinism (the body is unimportant, therefore one can do with it what one will) and asceticism (celibacy, abstinence, rejection of procreation). Both lifestyles put into practice the idea that all earthly circumstances were invalid.

39. Cf. Eijk 1972.

40. One of the earliest documents on the question of the integration into the community of those in favor of marriage is Ignatius of Antioch's (ca. 110) *Letter to Polycarp* (5.2); see Niebergall 1974. Certain anti-Gnostic and anti-Manichaean groups saw marriage as a divine institution and wished to place it under the protection of the church. Other groups took an attitude of tolerant indifference toward marriage as a worldly institution. Encratic movements within Christianity, however, wished to precipitate the desired end of the world through a rejection of procreation and preached a radical rejection of marriage in favor of abstinence.

41. (Successively monogamous) wedlock as the "normal state" in the ancient world had maintained throughout antiquity the status of a kind of natural law. Alternative blueprints for society existed only as myths, and even Plato's utopian marriage-communism remained a fleeting episode.

42. Still worthy of discussion is the question whether St. Paul, in 1 Cor. 7:1–16 and with his recommendations of celibacy, paved the way for an "unbiblical" asceticism or whether he saved the institution of marriage from radical ascetic attacks; see Niederwimmer 1975.

43. For the intensification of Jewish sexual rigorism, see Niederwimmer 1975, 12–74.

44. St. Paul's decision that baptism and marriage were not mutually exclusive was not self-evident; see Niederwimmer 1975, 90. A strong trend in favor of celibacy existed from the start, and the coexistence of marriage and celibacy was only a result of the process of catholicization; see ibid., 223. However, Paul's positive attitude toward marriage was—in analogy to courts within the church or the manumission of slaves— limited to an indifferent acknowledgment of its status as a necessary secular institution.

45. I have chosen Tertullian because he is the first postbiblical author to have treated the theme at length. His techniques of argumentation therefore form the basis for the structure, repertoire of motives, and topics of ascetic Christian *dissuasio matrimonii*. For Jerome as an explicit recipient of Tertullian's writings, see Petitmengin 1988; Clark, chap. 8 in this volume.

46. For Tertullian as a heretic, see Hilar. *Com. in Mt.* 5.1 (*PL* 9.942–43; *CSEL* 17.383?). See also Jer. *Contra Helv.* 17 (*PL* 23.211–12); *Adv. Ruf.* 3.12 (*PL* 23.486–88); Aug. *Haer.* 86 (*CCL* 46.336–37). Jerome caused a scandal in Rome with his radical anti-marriage polemic against Jovinian; he was only able to escape prosecution for Manichaeanism by Pope Siricius by hurriedly leaving Rome.

47. Despite his denigration of marriage, Tertullian (*Monog.* 1) emphasizes, in order to defend himself against ascetic heretics, the toleration of one marriage among the Montanists. Jerome also believed in the fundamental *bonum* of marriage: see *Adv. Iov.* 1.3, 8, 23 (*PL* 23.222–24, 231–32, 252–54); *Ep.* 22.2, 49.4 (*CSEL* 54.145–46, 355–56).

48. Positions more favorable to marriage, like those formulated in the anti-Gnostic struggle of Clement of Alexandria, paved the way for the recognition of marriage as a fully valid Christian form of life, yet in the Catholic Church, celibacy, as represented by the clergy, remains even now the ideal, the superior form of *imitation Christi*. For the continuing influence of Tertullian, see Schanz and Hosius 1959, 3:330–33. For Jerome, see Albrecht 1994, 1314–15; J. Morgan 1928; Benoit 1961. The methods used in addressing men and women would seem to be analogous. In *Ad uxorem* (1.4.3 [*CCL* 1.1.377]), Tertullian aims to counter arguments for the necessity of a husband; in *De exhortatione castitatis* (12.1 [*CCL* 2.1031f.]), he presents a similar refutation of the (seeming) necessity of a wife. *De monogamia* is addressed both to men and women. In *Adversus Iovinianum*, Jerome speaks out against marriage from a basically male perspective (1.28, 47–49 [*PL* 23.260–62, 288–94]). In his letters, he focuses to a greater extent on the position of women, even though he emphasizes that his comments are applicable to both sexes.

49. The inherent and central function of these distinctions of status are examined by Clark in chap. 8 in this book.

50. There were over 150 relatively complete copies of *Adversus Iovinianum* extant in the Middle Ages; see Hanna and Lawler 1997, 19; Laistner 1952; Wilson and Makowski 1990. For the high regard in which Jerome was generally held in the Middle Ages and on the influence of his works, see Delhaye 1951, 70–71.

51. As had been the case in late antiquity, social discourse for and against marriage in the eleventh and twelfth centuries focused on questions of orthodoxy and heresy; see Wilson and Makowski 1990, 65–68.

52. Wilson and Makowski 1990, 63. Also see ibid. for further literature on the historical background.

53. See Bugge 1975; Lucas 1983.

54. See Lea 1966; Gilchrist 1967.

55. *PL* 176.1202–18.

56. See Delhaye 1951, 83.

57. Bock's (1899) theory that Hugh used a now lost intermediary—not Jerome's *Adversus Iovinianum*—for his quotations from Theophrastus's *Liber aureolus*, which would make Hugh's treatise extremely important, has been refuted by Bickel (1915).

58. Peter of Blois (*Ep.* 79 [*PL* 207.244]) makes a clear distinction between the problems of marriage in general and the marriage of a philosopher.

59. Wilson and Makowski 1990, 106.

60. Only during the Renaissance is the ideal of philosophical celibacy also applied to women; the consequences for such women were highly ambivalent. See Feichtinger 1997a.

61. Extramarital affairs were presented as being far more desirable than marriage. Models for this can be found as early as Juvenal *Sat.* 6.42, in which Ursidius, as a *moechorum notissimus olim* [once the most notorious of the gigolos], is encouraged to preserve his unmarried and amorous state.

62. *PL* 178.1165–202.

63. The text is quoted from Monfrin 1967. A good summary of the controversial question of the authenticity of the correspondence between Abelard and Heloise can be found in Wilson and Makowski 1990, 76.

64. *Hist. calam.* 7 (Monfrin 1967, 76); translation by Muckle (1964).

65. *Hist. calam.* 8 (Monfrin 1967, 78): *Addebat denique ipsa et quam periculosum mihi esset eam reducere, et quam sibi carius existeret mihique honestius amicam dici quam uxorem ut me ei sola gratia conservaret, non vis aliqua vinculi nuptialis constringeret.*

66. The text has been edited by Webb (1909).

67. *Policrat.* 8.11 (Webb 1909, 294): *De molestiis et oneribus coniugiorum secundum Ieronimum et alios philosophos.* All translations from *Policraticus* are taken from Pike 1938.

68. Jer. *Adv. Iov.* 1.47 (*PL* 23.289): *Ut quae Christianae pudicitiae despiciunt fidem, discant saltem ab ethnicis castitatem.*

69. *Policrat.* 8.11 (Webb 1909, 296): *Concinit in hunc modum totus recte philosophantium chorus, ut, si qui Christianae religionis abhorrent rigorem, discant vel ab ethnicis castitatem.* The differences from Jerome's wordings are subtle but significant.

70. Cf. *Policrat.* 8.11 (Webb 1909, 305): *Ieronimus testis est . . .*

71. *Policrat.* 8.11 (Webb 1909, 289–99): "Similar and such were the remarks of Theophrastus. They in themselves are sufficient to explain the perplexities of the married state and the calamities that overtake its cherished joys."

72. *Policrat.* 8.11 (Webb 1909, 298–99): "Who could pity the man who, once freed from the fetters, fled back to chains?"

73. See Delhaye 1951, 77.

74. *Policrat.* 8.11 (Webb 1909, 300): "But those who philosophize, or rather clerics, are fortunate in that not one of them proves impotent or has in court been branded with infamy of this sort."

75. Cf. the anecdotes concerning unconsummated marriages at *Policrat*. 8.11 (Webb 1909, 300); see Wilson and Makowski 1990, 84–85.

76. *Policrat*. 8.11 (Webb 1909, 301–4).

77. Citations of Map are from the edition by James ([1983] 1994).

78. See Pratt 1962, 13–15.

79. See Wilson and Makowski 1990, 84–88.

80. It is nevertheless remarkable that there is no direct quotation from Juvenal's sixth satire; see Wilson and Makowski 1990, 95.

81. For a structural analysis of the lists of examples and for a convincing interpretation of the ambivalences evoked, see Wilson and Makowski 1990, 90–91.

82. *Val. dist*. 4, cap. 3 (James [1983] 1994, 155): <*Perictione*>, *virgo vergens in senium et fama castitatis privilegiata, tandem Apollinis oppressa fantasmate concepit peperitque Platonem*. All translations of *Valerius* are taken from Tupper and Ogle 1924.

83. Ibid.: *Amice, miraris an indignaris magis quod in parabolis tibi significem gentiles imitandos, Christiano ydolatras, agno lupos, bono malos? . . . Gentilium novi superstitionem, sed. . . . Plurima perverse agunt increduli; aliqua tamen agunt que, licet in ipsis intereant, in nobis habunde fructum facerent*.

84. Ibid. (James [1983] 1994, 156): *Veneris te nolo fieri sponsum, sed Palladis*.

85. Ibid.: "Or if they drove themselves with eagerness for their own arts, not with a view to future happiness, but merely in order not to have ignorant souls, what will we have if we neglect the divine page . . . ?"

86. See Wilson and Makowski 1990, 94–95.

87. See ibid., 96–97.

88. See ibid., 97–98.

89. *PL* 207.243–47.

90. See Wilson and Makowski 1990, 101–4.

91. Cf. *Diss. uxor*. 8 (Rajna 1891, 270): *Nubat tibi Pallas, amice, scilicet virtus; quia numquam solus esse poteris, si solus cum virgine virginabis*. For the full text, see Rajna 1891, 266–72. Wilson and Makowski (1990) have rightly drawn attention to the emphasis in philosophical marriage treatises on pseudo-family ties (on a metaphorical level).

92. See Wulff 1914; Neff 1900; Moore 1943; Utley 1944; Rogers 1966.

93. The credit for disseminating the Aristotelian view of woman as an imperfect male—and thus, by extension, a creature lacking in reason and morality—must to a large extent be given to Thomas Aquinas.

94. See Wilson and Makowski 1990, 119–20.

95. Examples are *Les quinze joyes de mariage* (see the edition of Crow [1969]) or Eustache Deschamps's *Le miroir de mariage* (see the edition of Rynaud [1894]). *De conjuge non ducenda* has on several occasions been translated into English and French; see Wright [1841] 1968.

96. For medieval misogyny, see Wulff 1914.

97. A short summary of research and literature on this subject can be found in Wilson and Makowski 1990, 68–69.

98. Andreas Capellanus's *De arte honeste amandi*, one of the best sources for *amour courtois*, supports the theory that an exaggerated idealization of women is often very closely connected with aggressive defamation in the code of courtly love. The palinode of the last book, *De reprobatione amoris*, includes a comprehensive battery of misogynistic topoi and scathing attacks on women.

Ten

Walter as Valerius

CLASSICAL AND CHRISTIAN IN THE *Dissuasio*

Ralph Hanna III and Warren S. Smith

alter Map's *Dissuasio Valerii ad Ruffinum* partakes of a twelfth-century craze. Antimatrimonial dissuading was a minor, if widespread, topic of contemporary Latin letters. The foundational example, of course, is Heloise's apparently conversational demonstration to Abelard of the inappropriateness of marriage to the philosophical life (see Blamires, Pratt, and Marx 1992, 88–89). And at the middle and during the third quarter of the century, examples of the genre proliferated.[1]

Map was a scholar and civil servant who secured for himself a comfortable life under Henry II of England. He lived under the income of a number of parishes given to support him as a royal clerk, and he held various offices in the diocese of Lincoln. He lived into the first decade of the thirteenth century. Not a prolific writer, in the 1170s he wrote his *Dissuasio*, a work that enjoyed a large circulation in the Middle Ages. Map himself included it in a much larger work, the *De nugis curialium*, boasting that the *Dissuasio* "pleased many, is greedily snatched up, eagerly copied, read with greatest delight" (*De nugis* 4.5). The larger anecdotal collection survives only in one manuscript and was not widely known until the nineteenth century. The *Dissuasio*, in contrast, survives in some 131 manuscripts often combined with Jerome's so-called *Liber aureolus* of Theophrastus or with other selections from Jerome's *Against Jovinian*, thereby forming a version of a book of "wykked wyves" such as so irritated the Wife of Bath (of Chaucer's *Canterbury Tales*), who claimed it was eagerly read by her fifth husband, Jankyn (prologue 669–85).

Map wrote his *Dissuasio*, probably in the 1170s, in a context already rich with antimatrimonial argument—and he inspired more of it. To take the most readily at hand examples, he certainly know both John of Salisbury's and Hugh of Fouilly's essays. Within a decade of his having written the *Dissuasio*, Peter of Blois would pillage it for his own purposes. Yet Map's effort is distinctly different from all these surrounding texts. One can immediately focus these differences by a glance at an ignored yet revelatory instance of dissuading, in this case one in fact directed at Map himself.

Epistle 24 by Gerald of Wales, Map's friend, younger contemporary, and fellow Welshman, is addressed to Map. This epistle is very easy to overlook.[2] I suspect Gerald, like Peter of Blois, responds to Map's work, rather than the other way round. But in certain respects, that is helpful: it makes the text a more pointed foil to Map's greater, if less substantial, effort.

Gerald's letter does not belong fully in the antimatrimonial arena. He certainly urges Map to forget about marriage (Brewer [1861] 1964–66, 277ff.), and he takes his ammunition in part from the Bible: for example, he follows St. Jerome, Heloise in her advice to Abelard (Blamires, Pratt, and Marx 1992, 88), and others in reading 1 Corinthians 7 selectively, turning it into an anti-marriage tract—so that, for example, "abstain from one another" (1 Cor. 7:5) is taken out of context to mean "abstain from marriage." Gerald's primary target, however, is a good deal broader, although well within the parameters of Map's work. Gerald's effort is thoroughly protreptic: he wants Map to be *sine macula* (Brewer [1861] 1964–66, 278), "without stain." Thus, along with marriage, he wants Map to give up his frivolities, his literary interests, altogether. By doing so, Gerald argues, Map will fulfill his promise and become the man he had been trained to be (he had a Paris M.A. after all)—a Christian philosopher. Map should by now, Gerald says, have sown his wild oats; consequently, he should grow up, act his age, and follow the sober life appropriate to his lofty training, *Juvenilis enim excusabilis est levitas, cum laudabilis fuerit ipsa maturitas* [for frivolity is excusable in a young man, while maturity itself would be praiseworthy] (Brewer [1861] 1964–66, 288).[3]

Reading Gerald's letter tells one a great deal more about him than it does about Map. Thus, the text highlights the achievement of the *Dissuasio* by contrast. At many moments, one can see Gerald striving, perhaps a bit leadenly, for a wit one might recognize as an imitation of Map.

Marcum igitur amodo, mi charissime, manu teneas, non Martialem, non Martianum, non Maronem; nec Marcum solum, sed et Matthaeum, sed et Lucam, sed Johannem. (Brewer [1861] 1964–66, 286)

[So from now on, my dearest friend, hold Mark in your hand, not Martial, not Martianus, not Maro; and not only Mark alone, but also Matthew, Luke, and John.]

Hanna has elsewhere pointed to the gloriousness of Map's *paranomasia* (rhyming words or wordplay);[4] Gerald plainly can hear that, but he does not quite achieve it. In some sense, he appropriately demonstrates here his own detachment from frivolities, mere verbal luster. The classical poets are all the same (*Mar-* . . . *Mar-* . . . *Mar-*)—even Martianus Capella, whom one would have scarcely thought unedifying Christian reading.[5] In contrast to such a repeated dull stroke, the Gospels open out expansively: *Marcus* does sound a bit like *Martialis*, but it is immediately varied into *amodo . . . mi . . . manu*, and beyond the further attenuated echo of *Mattheaum* follows the remainder of the evangelists.

Moreover, Gerald unabashedly argues theologically. His text, in contrast to Map's allusiveness, mainly cites. Gerald performs here as a *compilator*. In modern terms of "originality," he is responsible only for the connective tissue of his letter. Otherwise, Gerald just piles up authoritative quotations—in the main scriptural—to support his point. In essence, he relies on one traditional theological style, argument by proof-text: a statement is immediately followed by the appropriate biblical statement that justifies it. Theological learnedness is biblical absorptiveness, knowing the text so thoroughly that the immediately relevant instance springs immediately to mind.

But this is not the only form Christian argument takes in Gerald's dissuasion. Often a more antique language of Christian exegesis appears. It is thoroughly explicit at such a moment as the following reading of Isaiah 33:18–19.

Super *populum impudentem* glosat Hieronymus "gregem philosophorum." Super *non videbis*, "in ecclesia sanctorum." Super *populum alti sermonis*, "sicut Platonis, Aristotelis, Tullii facundiam et subtilitatem," quam pauci *intelligunt*; *in quo* populo scilicet, *nulla est sapientia* quantum ad Deum, qui per prophetam ait, "Perdam sapientiam sapientum, etc." (Brewer [1861] 1964–66, 274)[6]

[On "an impudent people," Jerome glosses "the herd of philosophers." On "you will not see [the insolent people]," [he glosses] "in the church of the

saints." On "a people of deep speech," [he glosses] "like the eloquence and
subtlety of Plato, Aristotle, and Cicero," which few understand. No doubt
in this people "there is no wisdom" relating to God, who says through the
prophet, "I will destroy the wisdom of the wise," and so on.]

Gerald ceaselessly argues that Virgil should have nothing to do with Christ,
that the songs of the poets are like the croaking of frogs and must be rejected
equally with pagan philosophy (Brewer [1861] 1964–66, 283), that pagan and
holy letters should remain utterly segregated.

If Map agrees with Gerald's warning against mixing pagan and holy (and
a number of modern critics have thought so), he does not write the *Dissuasio*
in that way; instead, he interweaves a riotous fabric of sources with an eye for
the colorful and humorous.[7] For example, in one passage, a sentence starting
with the exalted name of Jupiter ends in undignified mooing.

Iupiter, rex terrenus, qui etiam rex celorum dictus est pre singulari stre-
nuitate corporis et imcomparabili mentis elegantia, post Europam mugire
coactus est. (*Dissuasio* 89–91)

[Jupiter, an earthly king, who was also called king of the heavens because of
the outstanding power of his body and the incomparable elegance of his mind,
was driven to mooing after Europa.]

Map writes a masterpiece because of his equipoise. He straddles—apparently acknowledging the power of—both Mark and Martial. Utterly central
to this stance is the status of his work as pseudonymous literature—or, put
otherwise, as literary hoax (one so convincing that the *Dissuasio* is ascribed
to its true author in only one manuscript out of some sixty, and for centuries
readers ascribed the work to Valerius Maximus or Jerome).[8]

The *Dissuasio* went abroad into the world not with Walter Map's name
affixed but as authored by one "Valerius," who (though *Valerius* may also be
a pun on *Gauterus*) is someone else, perhaps a classical figure, with an urbane
style of argument. Indeed, the argumentative style of the *Dissuasio* (as will be
illustrated further in this chapter) seems presented as an alternative to the
invective that characterizes Roman diatribe satire, such as Juvenal's second
and sixth satires (which attack homosexuality and marriage, respectively) and
Jerome's *Against Jovinian* (an attack on marriage). In the *Dissuasio*, Valerius
imputes flat-footed Christian argument of the Gerald of Wales stripe to his
equally classical addressee, Rufinus. Thus Rufinus is either surprised or angry
that Map takes so many of his examples from the heathens rather than the

Bible (284–86), but his narrator wants Rufinus to be like a resourceful bee that can draw honey even from the nettle and hardest rock. This reference again cleverly combines classical allusions. First, it implies creativity of high quality, setting for Rufinus a goal as craftsman as great as Horace himself, who had famously compared his style of craftsmanship to the careful work of a bee, which, though small, draws honey from many places and does mighty works (*Ode* 4.2.28–33). Second, *urtica*, stinging nettle, was widely cited in classical literature as an aphrodisiac (e.g., Ovid *Ars amatoria* 2.417), so Map makes Valerius seem to be asking Rufinus to become the busy bee who will carefully avoid getting stung by incitements to marriage but, far from completely avoiding the pleasures of the world, will still end up rich in "honey," a reference itself rich in sensuous overtones (so long as he does not turn that honey into marriage). Equally, when Map goes on to add "so that you may suck honey out of the rock and oil from the hardest stone," he intermeshes the reference with a biblical allusion, the song of Moses praising the bountifulness of the Lord in Deuteronomy 32:13. The medium is the message: while urging Rufinus to draw on both Christian and heathen sources, Map sets the example and invokes God's blessing on the result.

This is particularly ironic, in a way that may serve as introduction to Map's Christian paganism. Map derives Rufinus's name from classical sources: Flavius Rufinus is the archcriminal in whose fall Claudian exulted, whereas Rufinus of Aquilea, his near contemporary, was the correspondent and rival of Jerome—hence, there was the false ascription of Map's treatise to Jerome. (Another allusion to Claudian underlies the title of Alain of Lille's *Anticlaudianus*, a poem about creating the perfect man, composed just after the *Dissuasio* in the 1180s.) Map's Rufinus is nominally, of course, criminal in his heterosexuality; yet he is doubly criminal in the strength of his hypocritical Christian avowals.

Thus the *Dissuasio* is redolent with classical allusion and quotation, as is Jerome's *Against Jovinian*, which is one of Map's sources, but with which he has obvious differences (on this issue, see, further, Delhaye 1951, 79–83; Hanna and Lawler 1997, 61–62). Perhaps the litmus for this stylistic behavior is the discussion of Solomon (*Dissuasio* 65–74). He is introduced as *sol hominum* [the sun of men], a touch of Christian etymologizing. But Map allows the discussion of his fall to segue neatly into a mythographic portrayal of the sun personified, Phoebus. The reference to the god being transformed into *pastor Admeti* [the shepherd of Admetus] (line 72; cf. Euripides *Alcestis* 8) incorporates into a biblical story a very appropriate pagan example of how the mighty have fallen and enshrines some serious classical scholarship (see Hanna and Lawler 1997, 204).[9]

Valerius presents himself from the opening of the epistle as the unwilling prophet of doom. But when he finally actuates this role rhetorically near the center of the work, he does not present himself as a figure like Gerald's Isaiah (by way of Jerome), a chastiser of erring Judean monarchs. Instead by a roundabout method, he takes as his model, from a pagan source, the "humble but holy" Tongillius, supposedly Caesar's soothsayer (*Dissuasio* 136–40); yet this is not the name for that soothsayer that Map had found in Suetonius but, rather, the name of an ambitious Roman who is ridiculed in the satiric tradition for using tricks to try to attract legacy hunters (Martial 2.40) and who tries to live beyond his means (Juvenal *Sat.* 7.130).

Thus, as a usual argumentative move, Valerius dissuades by eschewing the very Christian rhetoric Gerald insists upon. Map invents for his speaker what the classics might (or should) have said, allowing Valerius to voice a classical history. Indeed, Valerius is characterized as a sort of late classical yenta, someone who knows the true gossipy stories that underlie the formed literary presentations of classical texts (and some very obscure texts at that).

To take merely two examples, Valerius transforms snippets of Aulus Gellius into dramatic anecdotes. First, Gellius is the sole source for a famous antigamous oration by one Metellus; Map goes beyond the oration to record that private conversation whose learned wit gave Metellus the status to speak so compellingly (*Dissuasio* 217–22). Metellus's wit relies on twisting a recondite point in the Latin version of Aristotle's *Topics* (1.8.103b), *Talia erunt predicta, qualia subiecta permiserint* [Predicates will be such as their subjects permit], so that it refers no longer to grammar but to the necessity of a husband to be "subject" to his wife. This complex witticism indicates Map's willingness to use Parisian school training in a manner foreign to Gerald's sobriety, and Map's Valerius cannot resist doubling the joke: what Metellus actually said publicly (according to Gellius) has already been cited as a bon mot of Cato Uticensis: *Si absque femina posset esse mundus, conversatio nostra non esset absque diis* [If the world could be without women, our intercourse would not be without the gods] (*Dissuasio* 209–10). So attributed to Cato, the comment provides a wry commentary on a famous line by Lucan, *victrix causa deis placuit, sed victa Catoni* [While the gods were pleased with the victorious cause, Cato was pleased with the losing one] (*Pharsalia* 1.128). Map's suggestion is that Cato's failure to share in the opinion of the gods is enhanced by the presence of women.

Second, the anecdote involving Pacuvius and Arrius (*Dissuasio* 198–205) may rest on a meeting Gellius describes between the playwrights Pacuvius and Accius (the garbling of the latter name may be due to the recollection of a satiric story about "Attius and Tettius" in Gellius 3.16.13).[10] As for the macabre joke about the wife hanging herself from a fig tree, Map found the inspiration for part of it in a joke *(salsum)* reported by Cicero in *De oratore* 2.69.278. Thus, the status of the two figures and the exchange between them comes completely from Valerius's fictive insider knowledge of the late classical literary scene, particularly its comedy and satire.

With this sort of rhetorical move, Map creates a "classical" attitude a good deal more difficult and poised than Gerald's theological one. The *Dissuasio* does gesture at fixed bipolar opposites of a kind that Gerald would have found comfortable, opposites that would prioritize Christian over pagan, the mind over the body. There are argumentative moments that turn upon such polar pairings as *voluptas* and *veritas* (*Dissuasio* 18–20: "many persuade you to follow your desire but you have me alone as an advocate of truth"), Venus and Pallas (113–16: "bound to Venus like Mars, you will become an object of laughter; Pallas Athene was falsely rejected in the Judgment of Paris"), or *delectare*, "to delight," and *prodesse*, "to be useful" (115–16). This last pairing is itself classical: the antithesis is found in Horace's *Ars poetica* (333). But the *Dissuasio* never quite rests there.

A couple of examples may solidify the point. Unlike most dissuading, whether Jerome's late classicism or its twelfth-century resuscitations, the *Dissuasio* generally eschews invective. In fact, Valerius presents the rhetoric of invective, the reduction of someone to a butt of humor, as a subhuman activity. It is behavior ascribed to the satyrs, who in Map's version join the heavenly court to take part in the ridicule of Mars when he is trapped in Vulcan's net—a net into which Rufinus may fall if he allows himself, like Mars, to be chained to Venus (*Dissuasio* 106, 113–14). Contextually, one might think that the opposite to this half-bestial derision would be Jupiter's unfallen divine state, one of *mentis elegantia* [mental elegance] (*Dissuasio* 90–91); this state of fulfillment is in fact identical with the verbal control of the master rhetorician (cf. Valerius's use of *elegantia* as a "term of art," a standard of verbal excellence he wants to maintain in his epistle to Rufinus, at *Dissuasio* 127). Hard as it might seem to match Jupiter's *elegantia*, Rufinus will have to actually surpass it, if he does not want a woman to set him "mooing" after her the way Jupiter did after Europa.

Similarly, Valerius constantly breaks down even those most hallowed oppositions that ought to be underwriting his argument. At moments, just as Gerald sought to, the *Dissuasio* insists on the value of profit over delight. But delight itself is never far from being privileged in its own right. One example is the wonderful medieval bestiary, colorful and rich in humor, which roams through the *Dissuasio*, starting with the voices of "cranes and screech owl," which are rejected in the opening paragraph because they predict the coming of winter; instead, Map loves the lark and blackbird, which predict warmer weather (1–7). He fears that Rufinus may turn into a hog or an ass (12) or be bitten by a snake (16). Later, Valerius can suggest, rather conventionally, that Venus's rose is delightfully dangerous (214–16); yet his language equally suggests how unfortunate it is that what delights might produce sin. This problematic stance scarcely is Valerius's last word on the subject: quite incongruously, in the story of Periccion, the rose comes to be associated with chastity and its destruction; the "defloration" of its attracting *purpura* [purple flower] is both lamented and, with qualifications, extolled (279–83). Valerius may overtly urge Rufinus to imitate Cicero, *eloquencie princ[eps]* [prince of eloquence], who (in an anecdote borrowed from Jerome) would not marry again after his divorce of Terentia because he could not give equal attention to philosophy and to a wife. But Valerius is nonetheless eloquent and himself given to delight.

Thus Map's rather equivocal references to *delectatio*, "delight," are informative. They are inevitably part of the several references to springtime scattered through the *Dissuasio*, most especially the opening reference to Philomela. Although Valerius is forced by circumstances to be a bird of ill omen, he implies that he would rather be a nightingale, the bird of spring—and of sex.

More powerfully, at least three of Valerius's allegedly misogynistic "heroes" are described in terms that link them firmly to delectation. Ulysses (*Dissuasio* 32–34), Canius (179–97), and, much less explicitly, Jason (321–25) all lived the opposite of cloistered lives; Canius indeed *multarum gauderet amoribus* [rejoiced in the loves of many women]. In short, all three men personify a logic of self-conscious indulgence. All enact what is inherent in the description of Venus's flower, the rose. Each allows himself to experience woman's temptation fully—but not permanently. Ulysses *delectatus est* [was delighted] by the Sirens (as well as by Circe, a connection Map leaves implicit), but he can experience the fullness of delight because he artificially restrains himself from sin by tying himself to his (nonetheless very phallic) mast. Similarly, Canius (produced by a reference in the first of Gerald's evil Mar- boys, Martial) wins measured approval for his explanation of his reason for having many lovers: *Vices noctium dies reddunt letiores, sed tenebrarum perpetuitas instar inferni est* [The changes that night brings make the days more cheerful, but a constant darkness would be like hell] (*Dissuasio* 186–87). In his sexual athleticism, he certainly does "sin," but that very Don Juanism prevents his ever being committed to the slavery of marriage (and in this, Map follows good classical advice: cf. Ovid *Remedia amoris* 403–4, where the reader is advised to find a second lover in order to decrease his passion for the first).

Thus the *Dissuasio* rejects Gerald's dichotomies. These mainly underwrite an insistence upon the primacy of a single way of knowing, one fundamentally Bible-based and requiring the rational manipulation of the text as a vehicle for developing understanding. In contrast, Valerius imagines a more supple knowledge. For him, only through uncommitted indulgence of the prohibited, the forbidden, or the undesirable, by testing or experiencing, does one come to any mature view of virtue. He wishes for Rufinus, *semel martius fueris et non sis, ut scias quod felicitatem impediat* [If only you had been married once and were not now, so that you might know what impedes happiness] (*Dissuasio* 165–66). He claims that Cato could only achieve the wisdom that allows him to be cited as an authority by that indulgence that allows firm experiential knowledge.

> Amice, Cato non nisi sensa et cognita loquebatur, nec quisquam femi-narum
>
> *Execratur ludibria, nisi lusus, nisi expertus, nisi pene conscius.* (*Dissuasio* 210–13)
>
> [Friend, Cato said nothing except things he felt and knew, nor does anyone curse women's frivolousness unless he has been fooled, and knows it, and feels the pain.]

Like John Milton, who offers a similar argument against censorship in *Areopagitica*, Map knows this form of argument from the classics. There, it is a topic of pastoral most notably argued in Virgil's first eclogue: Tityrus's poetry has only limited value, unless he can continue to sing outside the shade "where the barren stones cover all" (*Ec.* 1.47), while Meliboeus faces an uncertain exile. That naive *puer* who still heads out to sea to court the fickle Pyrrha in Horace's Ode 1.5 thinks that she will be *semper vacuam, semper amabilem* [always free for him, always worthy of his love], in contrast to the fictive narrator of the poem, who has already hung up his dripping clothes as an offering to Neptune. From the point of view of the experienced, Gerald's theological argument constitutes what Milton would call "a cloistered virtue," one that achieves its assertive power only through experiential ignorance: indeed, like Pallas, possessing a virgin's wisdom.

While such a reading may characterize Valerius's wit, one ultimately needs to ask a question that would never arise in the case of Gerald's epistle. What purpose does this sort of writing serve? Here Map's own answer, offered as part of the framing account in *De nugis curialium* (within which he recuperated the *Dissuasio* as his own, not Valerius's), seems most persuasive.[11] In asserting authorship, Map must unveil the hoax—which, he claims, has insured the text's popularity and, indeed, its very legibility. Explaining pseudonymity (and recycling the text in a more expansive literary context) emphasized that authorial wit that Gerald found maddening about Map—and the epistle as its exemplification.

But, *De nugis* argues, the apparent classicism of the *Dissuasio* was conceived precisely to allow open-minded reading of the epistle. To have done otherwise, to have "published" the letter as his own, Map says, would have insured that it not be read. Its projected audience, twelfth-century advocates of "the ancients," would have rejected the work as merely "modern." It might only be appreciated by passing for something other than what it is and by substituting "the names of dead men in the title" for Map's own; thus Map alludes to the complaint of Horace in *Epistle* 2.1 that readers reject contemporary works and turn to what they consider "classics" because of their age.

As a rhetorical gesture, this argument resembles very closely what we have already described as one pedagogical movement of the epistle. Unlike Gerald's monotonal protreptic (a text that certainly situates itself as the product of a contemporary author that is purely derivative and imitative of established ways), Valerius the anonymous insists upon plural ways of knowing. In these terms, the work, from Map's perspective, functions as rhetorical satire of its audience. Not only does it explore and explode a current neoclassical craze, the rhetoric of dissuasion,[12] but it also comments devastatingly on the audience's inability, when left to its own wits, to distinguish the primary terms of its own literary canons of taste, "ancient" and "modern."

Further, this rhetorical satire is thoroughly consonant with the epistemological decorum that we have ascribed to Valerius's letter. Map addresses an audience prone to respond to texts in terms of external markers (e.g., the author's name and era). But just as Ulysses wants to hear the Sirens (even knowing that it is a dangerous business), Valerius's ideal reader (i.e., Walter Map) must experience the *Dissuasio* openly, without regard to its source, and must judge it on merits intrinsic to itself. In these terms, Map offers his audience a counterdefinition of "modernity." It is not the debilitated world of venerating "the ancients" that is highlighted in the explanation Map provides at the end of the *Dissuasio*. Rather, in ages to come, his book will provide the refinement that readers will have totally lost.

> Simiarum tempus erit, ut nunc, non hominum, quia presencia sibi
>   deridebunt,
> Non habentes ad bonos pacienciam. (*De nugis curialium* 4.5)

> [*It will be an age of apes (as it now is), not of men; they will scoff at their
>   present, and have no patience for men of worth.*]

The hoax of the *Dissuasio* demonstrates strikingly the power of modernity. One "modern," at least, can in fact "do classics" so well as to pass for such (even while leaving abundant clues that he is not an "ancient" at all). Not only does this act expose the pretensions of Map's contemporaries; it also shows that modernity might indeed exceed the classical past. This is not just because, as is the customary argument, it can exceed the classics because it is better; it is better because it is Christian. It can accomplish all that the classics did (well enough to be confused with them) and other things, too.

Ultimately, painful as it may be to admit it, Gerald of Wales is probably right about Map. He is a good deal too much like Valerius's character Canius, *poeta facundie levis et iocunde* [clever poet of frivolous eloquence] (*Dissuasio* 179–80). His modern classicism (which out-classics the ancients) appears born out of a severe distaste for John of Salisbury and idealizing Christian human- ism. It is much more "Chartrian," in the spirit of Bernard Silvester or Alain of Lille—or, in the native tradition, the "Nicholas of Guildford" who may have written a Philomela poem. Map, as rhetorical satirist, would surely have enjoyed the anonymous Middle English poem *The Owl and the Nightingale*.

Notes

1. See Hanna and Lawler 1997, 31–43. All citations of Map's *Dissuasio* are from the edition in that volume (121–47). Readers interested in pursuing Map's biblical and clas- sical allusions will find them presented in full in the notes to that edition (pp. 196–219).

2. See Giraldus Cambrensis *Symbolum electorum*, epistle 24, in Brewer [1861] 1964–66, 1:271–89. Translations are ours.

3. Cf. the considerably more elegant *Hanc [divinam paginam] dudum floribus viris tui subarrasti; hec in estate tua expectat ut facias uvas; huius in iniuriam non ducas aliam, ne facias in tempore vindemie labruscas* [to this page you once betrothed yourself in the flow- ering of your spring; it expects that in your summer you will bring forth grapes; do not injure this page by wedding another, lest you bring forth wild grapes in your vintage sea- son] (Map *Dissuasio* 304–7, citing Isaiah 5:2).

4. See Hanna and Lawler 1997, 52–54.

5. Martianus underwrites that moment in the *Dissuasio* that most resembles Gerald's, the appeal to marry not a woman but Christian wisdom (308–11).

6. We have adjusted the punctuation to emphasize the statement as biblical text and gloss; the Vulgate text of Isaiah reads *ubi doctor parvulorum? Populum impudentem non vide- bis, populum alti sermonis, ita ut non possis intelligere desertitudinem linguae eius, in quo nulla est sapientia* [Where is the teacher of children? You will not see an impudent people, a people of deep language, so that you cannot understand the emptiness of its language, in which there is no wisdom (our translation)]. The source in Jerome, not reproduced with verbal exactness, is to be found in *Corpus Christianorum* 73 (1973): 416.76–88; the final scriptural allusion, which Gerald adds—a form of theological "originality"—is to

Obadiah 8: *Numquid non in die illa, dicit Dominus, perdam sapientes de Idumaea?* [On that day, says the Lord, will I not destroy the wise out of Edom?]

7. See, e.g., the interpretation of D. W. Robertson, the twentieth century's mordant throwback to Hieronimian invective satire, in the headnote to his chapter on Map (1970, 223); cf. also Neil Cartlidge's nondescriptive reference (1997, 190–91) to "that misogynistic repulsion for female sexuality which is found in works like the *Epistola Valerii.*"

8. For a survey of the ascriptions, see Hanna and Lawler 1997, 60–62; see also Pratt 1962, 12–14.

9. This scholarship sits cheek by jowl with submerged materials (and it is important that they are so submerged) from a text that seeks to moralize classical myth into Christian poetry, the Carolingian *Ecloga Theoduli.*

10. Another variation on this pairing appears in Erasmus's *Adagia* 1.10.76: *idem Accii quod Titii* [Accius and Titius take alike].

11. See James [1983] 1994, most particularly 312.

12. This is argued in Hanna and Lawler 1997, 47–52, 55–59.

Eleven

Antifeminism in the High Middle Ages

P. G. Walsh

ON NOT TAKING A WIFE

*A*s an appropriate climax to the history of antifeminism in the High Middle Ages, we may instance the long poem called *De coniuge non ducenda*, which was composed about 1230.[1] In this humorous composition, the spokesman, Gawain, recounts at the outset that he fell in love with a beautiful girl and that his married friends encouraged him to take the plunge and marry her.

12   Uxorem ducere quondam volueram,
      Ut vitam sequerer multorum miseram,
      Decoram virginem, pulchram et teneram,
      Quam inter alias solam dilexeram.

13   Hinc quidem socii dabant consilium
      Ut cito currerem ad matrimonium;
      Vitam coniugii laudabant nimium
      Ut in miseriis haberent socium.

[I had once sought to marry a wife, so as to tread the wretched path of many, a handsome maiden, beautiful and innocent, a girl whom alone among all

others I loved. This was why certain friends counseled me to hasten swiftly into marriage. They praised married life effusively, so as to have an associate in their wretchedness.]

But then God sent three messengers from heaven to dissuade him from taking the fatal step. Their names were Peter, John, and Lawrence. They have been persuasively identified as Peter of Corbeil, archbishop of Sens, who died in 1222; John Chrysostom, the eloquent fourth-century bishop of Constantinople, whose sermons on occasion reflect antifeminist sentiments; and Lawrence of Durham, who wrote an antifeminist poem and condemnation of sexual passion before dying in 1154.[2] All three heavenly visitors offer similar arguments against marriage. Wives are frail, so that husbands need to toil incessantly to tend them; wives are fickle and greedy, and their lust leads them on the broad road to adultery; wives are arrogant, irascible, and spiteful, so that for men, marriage is an experience more painful than death. The poem, which extends over more than two hundred lines, ends as follows:

J22 "Quis potest coniugis ferre molestias,
Labores varios et conteumelias?
Labor et taedium restant post nuptias;
Uxorem igitur, Golwine, fugias."

J23 Post haec angelico finito nuntio,
Tactis epistoliis et evangelio,
Ipsis trahentibus me de incendio,
Respondi breviter "vobis consentio."

["Who can endure the hardships of marriage, its varied toils and insults? Toil and weariness are in prospect after marriage. That is why, Gawain, you must shun a wife." Then when this message from heaven was concluded, I put my hand on the Epistles and the Gospel, and as they dragged me out of the fire, I briefly replied: "I have come round to your view."]

Of course, the thirteenth century is by no means the end of the story. We can move forward into the fourteenth and fifteenth centuries to find similar sentiments in vernacular literature. John Lydgate's poem *Payne and Sorrow* is a direct imitation of *De coniuge non ducenda*, and the "Wife of Bath's Tale" by Chaucer continues with the tradition, citing in the prologue the formative voices of Theophrastus and Jerome, as well as Walter Map (see Smith, chap. 12 in this volume). But *De coniuge non ducenda*, in which the savagery of earlier diatribes has mellowed into a more humorous treatment, is an apposite point at which to conclude this survey of the theme in medieval Latin.

SECULAR AND PATRISTIC INFLUENCE

Earlier chapters in this book have outlined the two traditions on which the theme of antifeminism in the Middle Ages rests, namely, the secular satire in classical literature and the diatribes of the Fathers.[3]

In the twelfth and thirteenth centuries, knowledge of Greek in the monasteries and cathedral schools of the West was at best rudimentary. We are not to anticipate evocations of Agamemnon's bitter animadversions on Clytemnestra in the *Odyssey*, of Hesiod's portrayal of Pandora in *Works and Days* ("An evil thing, in which all take pleasure at heart as they embrace their own misfortune"), or of Plutarch's patronizing criticisms of some wives in his *Precepts for Marriage*.[4] Such influences from Greek literature emerge only through the meditation of those writing later in Latin, whether secular or Christian.

However, by the twelfth century, many of the genres of Latin literature of the classical period were familiar to learned clerics, who mined from them rich veins of antifeminism. There are, though, some obvious absentees who could have provided apposite fare. We hear little or nothing of Catullus's savage onslaughts on Lesbia or of her counterpart in real life, Cicero's Clodia in the *Pro Caelio*. The "Milesian" tradition, as represented in Petronius's story of the Widow of Ephesus and in the anecdotes in Apuleius's *The Golden Ass* attesting that no woman's virtue is unassailable, is not widely known.[5] And since Tacitus was the least read of the Roman historians, we look in vain for exploitation of the evil ways of Poppaea Sabina in the *Annals*, as indeed for the historian's idealization of Roman mothers in his *Dialogus*.[6]

The most influential of the genres was naturally Roman satire, and of the three leading verse satirists—Horace, Persius, and Juvenal—by far the most influential in the depiction of antifeminism was Juvenal. His sixth satire in particular was devoted to the vices of women, and what this poet of the wit wrote tongue in cheek was enthusiastically seized upon by bitter misogynists among the medieval clergy. Second in importance was Ovid. Though in his *Ars amatoria* he pretended to hold the balance between winning and keeping a man and winning and keeping a woman, the *Remedia amoris* is wholly concerned with how to get rid of the lady. Ovid's contemporaries doubtless read the poet's cynical observations on female lust with a large pinch of salt, but they were grist to the mill of medieval satirists as they compiled their catalogues of complaints against women's errant behavior. Among the historians, Sallust was the most popular in the High Middle Ages, and his celebrated depiction of the vices of Sempronia in the *Catilinae coniuratio* provided further ammunition.[7]

But the influence of the secular writers of the classical period was overshadowed by the diatribes of patristic writers. Taking their cue from the animadversions in Holy Scripture, men like Tertullian, Cyprian, and Augustine continued the developing tradition in the Greek Fathers of the idealization of sacred virginity and the inevitable corollary of advice against marriage and criticism of women who adorned themselves in order to catch the eyes of the opposite sex.[8] Among the Latin Fathers, the writings of Jerome attracted the closest attention. In particular, his *Adversus Jovinianum* (A.D. 392), composed after the monk Jovinian had argued that the married state was of equal merit and obtained equal heavenly rewards as sacred virginity, launched a ferocious attack against the message of the errant monk. He assembled citations from Scripture, on the one hand, and philosophy, on the other, to denigrate the married state and, by implication, to pillory the female sex.[9] The most celebrated among the citations was that of Theophrastus, the fourth-century pupil and successor of Aristotle as head of the Peripatetic school.

Non est ergo uxor ducenda sapienti. Primum enim impediri studia philosophiae, nec posse quemquam libris et uxori pariter inservire.

[*The philosopher should therefore avoid taking a wife, for to begin with this hinders the study of philosophy, and no one can minister to books and a wife at the same time.*][10]

Jerome appropriately appends the famous Ciceronian anecdote. It will be recalled that Cicero divorced Terentia after thirty years of marriage when they were both grandparents. (Terentia was not crushed for long; according to Jerome, she rallied so effectively that she married Sallust and later Valerius Messala before expiring at the ripe age of 103.) Cicero then married young Publilia for her money but soon divorced her, and when Hirtius offered him his sister's hand, Cicero responded with Theophrastus's observation: "It is difficult to attend to philosophy and a wife at the same time."[11]

A CLERICAL AUDIENCE

Jerome's treatise against Jovinian became very popular in the twelfth and thirteenth centuries, when a flood of antifeminist sentiment washed over a readership that was largely, if not exclusively, clerical. The question of the literature readership to which the authority of Jerome was addressed is clearly important;

we may clarify the situation by saying that in the twelfth century, there were undoubtedly laypersons, men and women, with a good knowledge of Latin, but the overwhelming proportion of educated readers were clerics.[12] A simple cleric who had not been admitted to holy orders could marry and remain a cleric, but in the Western church, the tradition had developed that those who presided over the liturgy should not marry, so those who took holy orders were opting for celibacy. Therefore, in the interest of insuring greater numbers of well-qualified ordained clergy, simple clerics were discouraged from entering the married state, for once married, they could not be ordained, and their path to a career in the church was accordingly closed.[13] This was undoubtedly a strong contributory reason for the growth of antifeminist literature in the High Middle Ages.

A perfect example of this is provided by Peter Abelard's *Historia calamitatum* (A.D. 1118), with its candid account of his love affair with Heloise and the tribulations that resulted from it. When Abelard was in his middle thirties, he won a high reputation at Paris as philosopher and theologian. Fulbert, canon of Notre Dame, pressed him to tutor his beautiful and talented niece, and the passionate attachment that ensued resulted in Heloise's conceiving and bearing Abelard's son Astrolabius. When Abelard sought to appease the infuriated uncle by agreeing to marry the girl, Heloise sought to dissuade him, since this would have foreclosed his career in the church. The arguments she advanced were based on the celebrated passage of 1 Corinthians 7 and on Jerome's treatise against Jovinian. Abelard reports her objections like this: "She said that if I did not accept the advice of Paul, nor the exhortations of the saints, with regard to the great yoke of matrimony, I should at any rate consult the philosophers, and pay heed to what was said by them or concerning them." He then reveals that Heloise had cited the testimonies of Theophrastus and Cicero as reported by Jerome.[14]

The influence of Jerome's *Adversus Iovinianum* is further exemplified in John of Salisbury's *Policraticus*, or *Statesman's Book* (A.D. 1159). John was the outstanding humanist of his day, and he is much less rabid in his views on women than are most of his contemporaries. But in an important observation, he identifies the clerics of his day with the philosophers of old, suggesting that the same arguments proposed by the philosophers for excluding women from their lives apply closely to his contemporaries among the clergy. John's learning in Latin literature allows him to reinforce the arguments of Jerome by citing the anecdote of the Widow of Ephesus from Petronius's *Satyricon* as an example of the fickleness of women.[15]

John, however, largely contents himself with exposing the hindrances caused by marriage, whereas Walter Map, writing a generation later in his *Courtiers'*

Trifles (A.D. 1182), is much more outspoken in his condemnation of women. Beginning with scriptural exemplars of their pernicious influence, he then turns to evil women in mythology and history to offer a veritable encyclopedia of unfaithful wives garnered from Ovid, Aulus Gellius, and other authorities.[16]

Almost contemporary with *Courtiers' Trifles* is the *De amore* (ca. 1185) of Andreas Capellanus, the celebrated treatise that prescribes the rules for polite living. This is an appropriate place at which to note a further factor that may have sharpened the satirical pens of men seeking to denigrate the female sex. The prominence of courtly love in the twelfth-century literature is reflected in the poetry of the troubadours, the romances of Chretien de Troyes, the contemporary Latin lyrics, and scholastic theories of love such as the treatise of Andreas. In all these, the suitor sets his lady on a pedestal high above him, adopting a quasi-religious posture before her. He offers to perform laborious deeds in her name. His total self-submission virtually amounts to idolatry. He has often a fixation about her naked form, a desire to gaze upon her and possess her. Though there is little historical evidence that the courtly love theory was ever translated into practice in the real world of the twelfth century, its widespread existence as literary fantasy offered a severe challenge to the spiritual and moral ideals that leading figures in the church sought to uphold. The reaction by some orthodox clerics was to denigrate the objects of such idolatry.[17]

The *De amore* of Andreas is composed in three books. The first two offer instruction on courtly loving in a series of dialogues, in which men of different social backgrounds are instructed on how to press their suits before women of lower and more exalted positions in society. But in the third book, there is an astonishing volte-face. Andreas launches into a full-scale condemnation of such courtly loving, urging the young friend to whom the treatise is addressed to steer clear of women. The various possible explanations for this bewildering contrast between the idealization of women in the earlier books and the scurrilous catalogue of their alleged vices in the third are not of concern here.[18] What is relevant to the theme of this chapter is the astonishing virulence of the onslaught on the female sex.

Each of the alleged vices to which women are subject is accorded a separate paragraph.[19] Avarice leads the field; women are perpetually demanding gifts, and if a man has nothing to offer, he is contemptuously reflected. Envy of the beauty and possessions of other women follows. Woman is given to slander (*maledica*). She is greedy (*rapax*) and a slave to her belly. She is fickle (*inconstans*) and always ready for betrayal. She is disobedient, and the only way of ensuring a right course of action is to tell her to do the opposite. Her arrogance is so overweening that it often breaks out in anger. She is vainglorious, like

Eve, who sought the knowledge of good and evil. She is ready to lie to obtain even the slightest advantage. She often takes to drink *(ebriosa)*. She is an inveterate chatterer *(virlingosa)* and will talk to herself in the absence of another. She is a slave to degenerate living and to lust *(luxuriosa, libidinosa)*. Finally, in her addiction to astrology and the practice of magic, she is a slave to superstition. In short, the Book of Ecclesiastes (7:27ff.) has it right: no woman is good.

Clearly this catalogue of vices is traditional, deriving, on the one hand, from the texts of Juvenal and Ovid and, on the other, from those of the Latin Fathers (especially Jerome), as well as from arguments garnered from John of Salisbury and Walter Map.

The *De amore* of Andreas provides evidence of another facet of antifeminism in the literature, if not the life, of the twelfth century. In his first book, Andreas distinguishes sharply between the deferential approach demanded for courtly ladies and the exploitation of casual sex forced upon country girls. "Should you find a suitable spot," he writes, "you should not delay in taking what you seek, gaining it by rough embraces. You will find it hard so to soften their outwardly brusque attitude so as to make them quietly consent to grant you embraces, unless the remedy of at least some compulsion is first applied to take advantage of their modesty."[20]

This theme of forcible conquest of rustic girls is also enshrined in the poetic genre of the pastourelle, or the shepherdess song, which developed out of folk tradition into vernacular as well as into Latin poetry.[21] The conventional exordium of such compositions depicts a shepherdess resting in the shade of a tree and the approach of a gallant (alternatively, their positions are reversed). A dialogue follows in which the gallant seeks to persuade the girl to have sex with him. She seeks to fend him off, sometimes successfully and sometimes not. In a pastourelle by Walter of Chatillon, *Sole regente lora*,[22] the shepherdess resists, pleading her extreme youth and the fear of a beating from her mother, but when he lays hands on her, she does not struggle further. There is a similar outcome in a well-known pastourelle in the *Carmina Burana*, *Vere dulci mediante*,[23] in which the gallant's offer of the gift of a necklace is brusquely rejected, after which he resorts to force.

4. "Munus vestrum" inquit "nolo,
   quia pleni estis dolo."
   Et se sic defendit colo.
   Comprehensam ieci solo;
   Clarior non est sub polo
   Vilibus induta!

5.   Satis illi fuit grave,
     Michi gratum et suave.
     "Quid fecisti" inquit "prave?
     Ve ve tibi! Tamen ave!
     Ne reveles ulli cave
       Ut sim domi tuta."

[*"I don't want this gift of yours," she said, "for I know that you are full of guile." Saying this, she used her staff to defend herself. I grabbed her and threw her to the ground. No more radiant creature exists under heaven, though she was clad in tawdry garments. For her it was quite oppressive, but for me satisfying and sweet. "What is this dirty trick you have played?" she asked. "Shame on you! Still, God be with you. Be sure not to disclose this to anyone, so that I may not suffer at home."*]

As I have noted elsewhere, in this account of how country girls are fair game for predatory males, it is striking that early on, the girl addresses her social superior in the respectful plural (*pleni estis*), but after his ungentlemanly behavior, she reduces him to her own social level by using the singular (*Quid fecisti?*). There is admittedly an element of playfulness about the composition (underscored by the witty rhymes), which warns us against the too ready assumption that the poet describes an actual experience or an everyday occurrence.[24] The Latin literature of this period abounds in denials by clerics who have attained respectability that the risqué compositions of their earlier days represent fact rather than playful fantasy.[25]

A LITERARY RIVALRY

When we turn to the satirical writing of the High Middle Ages, we must be similarly circumspect before condemning the antifeminist diatribes as misogyny pure and simple. In the final decade of the eleventh century and in the early years of the twelfth, a remarkable trinity of learned scholars came to prominence in ecclesiastical life in France. These scholarly clerics—Hildebert of Lavardin, Marbod of Rennes, and Baudri of Bourgueil—had steeped themselves in the writings of the satirists of classical antiquity. Employing the traditional techniques of creative imitation, they noted the targets at which Horace, Persius, and Juvenal had launched their darts, then they adapted them to the changed conditions of their Christian society.[26] A host of other would-be satirists followed who vied with each other to be seen as leading counterparts to the classical satirists. When Walter of Chatillon composed his pungent poem *Missus sum in vineam,* he ended each stanza with a line from Horace, Persius, Juvenal, Ovid, or another admired *auctor* (author). When Bernard of Cluny wrote his *De contemptu mundi,* he posed the question

> Flaccus Horatius et Cato, Persius et Iuvenalis
> Quid facerent, rogo, si foret his modo vita sodalis?
>
> [*What would Horatius Flaccus, Cato, Persius,*
> *and Juvenal do, I ask, if they*
> *Shared the life of today?*][27]

The vices of women are an attractive target, and just as Juvenal gained celebrity or notoriety by the blatant exaggerations of his indictments and the outspoken language in which they are framed, so the medieval satirists similarly wrote tongue in cheek. This is not to deny that the churchmen were pursuing a policy of discouraging their youthful charges in monasteries and cathedral schools from abandoning the celibate life. Nor does such imitation of the classical *auctores* excuse these poetic excesses in the spirit of the French proverb "Tout comprendre, c'est tout pardonner" [to understand all is to forgive all]. But it is important to grasp that as with Juvenal, so with these twelfth-century authors, the indictments and the language of abuse are stylized and not deeply felt.

Hildebert of Lavardin (ca. 1056–1133), bishop of Le Mans and, subsequently, archbishop of Tours, was the finest scholar and the most competent versifier of his age. His extant indictment of women is confined to part of a single poem, *De tribus titiis: Muliebri amore, avaritia, ambitione.* The poem was composed before 1096, perhaps while Hildebert was still archdeacon at the cathedral school at Le Mans, in which case it may have been directed toward the pupils at the school. The entire poem is only sixty-six lines, but this short composition was to have a powerful influence on the ensuing satirical tradition. Accordingly, the first section is worth quoting in full.[28]

> Plurima cum soleant sacros evertere mores,
>   Altius evertit femina, census, honos.
> Femina, census, honos fomenta facesque malorum,
>   In scelus, in gladios corda manusque trahunt.
> 5 Felix expertus exemplo femina quid sit,
>   Quique suos aliqua suffugit arte dolos.
> Femina res fragilis, nunquam nisi crimine constans,
>   Nunquam sponte sua desinit esse nocens.

Femina flamma vorax, furor ultimus, unica clades,
10   Et docet et discit quicquid obesse solet.
Femina vile forum, res publica, fallere nata,
    Successisse putat cum licet esse ream.
Femina triste iugum, querimonia iuris et aequi,
    Turpe putat quotiens turpia nulla gerit.
15 Femina tam grauior quanto privatior hostis,
    Invitat crimen munere, voce, manu.
Omnia consumens, vitio consumitur omni,
    Et praedata viros, praeda fit ipsa viris.
Corpus, opes, animos enervat, diripit, angit,
20   Tela, manus, odium suggerit, armat, alit.
Urbes, regna, domos evertit, commovet, urit,
    Unaque tot regum spem capit, arma premit.
Femina sustinuit iugulo damnare Ioannem,
    Hippolytum leto, compedibusque Ioseph.
25 Femina mente gerit, lingua probat, actibus implet
    Quo lex, quo populus, quo simul ipsa ruit.[29]

[*Though numerous factors are wont to undermine pious behavior, the trinity of woman, wealth, and distinction are causes of more profound destruction. Woman, wealth, and distinction are the kindling and the torches that ignite evils; hearts and hands they draw towards wickedness and its weapons. Blessed is the man who has come to know the nature of woman by some celebrated example, and who by exercise of some skill escapes her wiles. Woman is a frail creature, never showing constancy except in wickedness, never ceasing to wreak willing harm. Woman is a devouring flame, extreme madness, disaster unparalleled. She both teaches and learns all that is wont to hinder us. Woman is a cheap commodity, available to all, born to deceive. She believes she has prevailed when she can be the guilty party. Woman is a grim yoke, a complaint against what is right and just. She considers it demeaning whenever she performs nothing demeaning. Woman is a foe the more oppressive as the more she works in private. She entices to wickedness by gifts and voice and hand. She devours all things and is herself devoured by every vice. She plunders man and herself becomes plunder for men. She exhausts bodies, loots resources, afflicts minds; she proffers weapons, arms hands, nurtures hatreds. She betrays, harries, and burns cities, kingdoms, households; she alone bears off the hopes of numerous kings, and represses their armies. It was woman who robbed Paris of his senses, Uriah of his life, David of his devotion, and Solomon of his faith. It was woman who succeeded in condemning John to being beheaded, Hippolytus to death, and Joseph to imprisonment. It is woman*]

*who transacts in mind, commends in speech, fulfills in deeds the means by
which law and nation and she herself with them are brought low.]*

The rhetorical devices that here reflect the poet's preoccupation with the
medium as much as with the message are to become the stock techniques of
Hildebert's imitators. Repetition of *femina* (which initiates no fewer than
nine of the dactylic couplets) is repeatedly combined with alliteration (in lines
3, 5, 7, 9, and 11), and alliterative effects are introduced independently in other
couplets. Tricola are prominent throughout; it is interesting to note that
when a group of three nouns is followed in the same line by a group of three
verbs, the first verb governs the first noun, the second the second, and the third
the third (lines 19–21); a similar effect is achieved in line 4 with two nouns and
two verbs. Antithesis is another prominent feature, the artistic balance enhanced
by chiasmus at line 19. The exempla are a combination of figures from Holy
Scripture and from classical antiquity: Paris (suborned by Helen) and Hippolytus (propositioned by his stepmother, Phaedra), on the one hand; Uriah (whose
death David plotted when lusting after his wife Bathsheba), David, and Solomon
(whose apostasy was ascribed to the influence of his foreign wives), on the other.

Marbod of Rennes (ca. 1035–1123), almost equally celebrated a poet as
Hildebert, had followed a similar path of ecclesiastical advancement. Like Hildebert at Le Mans, Marbod had been archdeacon in his native town of Angers,
where he was head of the cathedral school. In 1096 he was consecrated
bishop of Rennes, and in 1102 he composed his *Liber decem capitulorum*.[30] In
this assemblage of diverse topics of the day, the third and fourth chapters are
devoted to the seamier and worthier aspects, respectively, of women.

The third chapter, entitled *De meretrice* (On the bawd), a composition
of eighty-eight lines, pays Hildebert the dubious compliment of close imitation; the entire work was addressed to him. It begins with a similarly stylized exordium.

Femina, triste caput, mala stirps, vitiosa propago,
Plurima quae totum per mundum scandala gignit . . .

[Woman, grim creature, evil stock and depraved progeny, who gives birth to
numerous scandals throughout the world . . .]

It continues in a similar strain, depicting woman as the devil's agent: "Among
the countless snares that the crafty Foe has laid over the hills and the plains
of the world, the greatest is woman; scarcely any man can escape that snare."
The hackneyed charges are laid against her: she causes enmities and disputes;

she is envious, fickle, prone to anger, greedy, a drunkard and a glutton, secretive, lustful, a liar and a chatterbox, and arrogant to boot.

A series of rhetorical questions, introducing the notorious biblical exemplars, echoes Hildebert's repetition of *femina* at the beginning of the line.

Quis suasit primo vetitum gustare parenti?
Femina. Quis patrem natas vitiare coegit?
Femina. Quis fortem spoliatum crine peremit?
Femina. Quae matris cumulavit crimine crimen,
Incestumque gravem graviore caede notavit?
Quis David sanctum, sapientem quis Salomonem
Dulcibus illecebris seduxit . . . ?

[Who urged our first parent to taste the forbidden fruit? Woman. Who compelled a father to deflower his own daughters? Woman. Who robbed the brave man of his hair and destroyed him? Woman. What woman heaped crime on her mother's crime and stained that heinous incest with yet more heinous slaughter? Who seduced the saintly David and the wise Solomon with womanly enticements . . . ?]

It is possible to justify such condemnations of Eve, of the daughters of Lot, of Delilah, and of Herodias and her daughter, on the basis of biblical judgments. But to pin the blame for David's lust on Bathsheba and for Solomon's on his wives strains all credulity. Marbod appends Jezebel and her daughter Athaliah to his biblical catalogue of guilty women.[31] Then, following Hildebert's example, he cites female reprobates from classical antiquity—Eriphyle (who was bribed with a necklace to persuade her husband, Amphiaraus, to take part in the investment of Thebes, where he was destroyed by Zeus), Clytemnestra, the daughters of Danaus, and Procne—thus attesting his assiduous reading of Ovid and classical *auctores*.[32]

After this outrageous attack on the whole female sex under the cover of the misleading title *De meretrice*, Marbod attempts to introduce a balance with his fourth chapter, entitled *De matrona*, or *De muliere bona*. In this composition of 125 lines, his argument propounds the equality of gender in nature and stresses the importance of woman's biological and social roles in society. He gives pithy sketches of courageous women in Scripture and in classical literature, offering evidence of his secular learning by citing Alcestis, Lucretia, and Arria as exemplars of faithful wives ready to forfeit their lives in selfless devotion to their husbands. Though we are conscious of an element of Ovidian opportunism in this presentation of womanly virtue as counterbalance to the cynical disparagement in *De meretrice*, this is nonetheless a striking *elogium* of laywomen in medieval society.[33] When we meet such praise of women elsewhere, it is largely addressed to women living the life of consecrated virginity, as in Abelard's correspondence with Heloise, in the writing of Hildegard of Bingen, or in the poem of Serlo of Bayeux that I must now proceed briefly to discuss.

Contemporary with Hildebert and Marbod, Serlo was, by comparison with them, a minor satirist. Born around 1050 near Caen as the son of a Norman priest, he later became a protégé of Bishop Odo of Bayeux before dying around 1120. He wrote one poem relevant to our theme, entitled *Ad Muriel sanctimonialem* (To the nun Muriel), a work whose aim was to confirm this lady, who may have been the sister of Bishop Odo, in her resolve to remain a consecrated virgin.[34] Not unexpectedly, given the prominence of the topic in the satires of his more eminent contemporaries, the poem launches an attack on married life and all its difficulties.

> Nunc de matronis cuius sint condicionis
> Audi, quaeso, parum; cum ultam noscitis harum,
> Quod sunt felices haud unquam postea dices.
> Ferrea iura subit mulier quo tempore nubit . . .
> . . . .
>
> Sit speciosa? Cito fiet suspecta marito
> Ex tenui causa, nil prorsus criminis ausa;
> Tamquam convicta sceleris feret aspera dicta,
> Nec solum verbo, sed verbere saevit acerbo.

> [*Now listen, I beg you, to a word or two on the status that married women have to assume. Once you know the nature of their lives, you will never thereafter say that they are blessed. When a woman marries, she submits to iron laws. Is she beautiful? Then she will soon be suspected by her husband on the slightest evidence, when she has indulged in no wrongdoing at all. She will endure harsh words as though found guilty of wickedness, suffering his violence not only in words but also in painful whipping.*]

Serlo then proceeds to tread his dogged path through the alleged horrors of married life, drawing on the traditional testimonies of Juvenal and Jerome to discourage the nun from any thought of abandoning the veil.

Another contributor to this knockabout disparagement of marriage and the female sex is Petrus Pictor, canon of Saint Omer. Among his satirical compositions is a poem of 246 leonine hexameters that was composed before A.D. 1120.[35]

Its title, *De illa quae impudenter filium suum adamavit*, indicates that the content is to be a narrative of an impious matron, stemming ultimately from the tragedy of Phaedra and Hippolytus dramatized in Euripides' *Hippolytus* and Seneca's *Phaedra*. As recounted here, the story is in essence that told by Apuleius in *The Golden Ass* 10.2–12. (This raises the interesting question whether the comic romance of Apuleius was in circulation in France at this date.)[36] But Petrus is not content with condemnation of the wicked matron. Halfway through the poem, he extends his topic to hurl abuse at womankind in general, incorporating phrases that evoke the earlier treatments of Hildebert and Marbod.

> Femina, terribilis draco, trux lupa, bestia vilis, . . .
> Femina, rara bona, si quae bona, digna corona.
>
> *[Woman is a fearsome snake, a harsh wolf, a cheap brute, . . . Woman, if any good woman exists, is scarcely ever worthy of a goodly crown.]*

The climax of these antifeminist tirades is reached with the *De contemptu mundi* of Bernard of Cluny.[37] Bernard was a monk at Cluny when the enlightened Peter the Venerable was abbot (1122–56). Peter encouraged the monks under his spiritual charge to devote themselves to intellectual activities in addition to the daily routine of prayer and manual work, guidance that made him at odds with Bernard of Clairvaux. But it seems doubtful that Peter would have approved of Bernard of Cluny's wholesale condemnation of the ills and follies of the world that he describes so pessimistically.

The *De contemptu mundi* is a poetic treatise of some three thousand lines, divided into three books. After contemplating the bliss of the future life in heaven by contrast with the horrors of hell, Bernard turns to the urgent need for the moral reform in this life that is required to attain that bliss. Books 2 and 3 are a systematic review of the moral laxity of the twelfth century. He examines the failings of nine representative figures in male society—bishop, king, priest, cleric, soldier, nobleman, judge, merchant, and farmer—before turning his withering gaze upon the contributions of women (2.429–598).

At the outset (2.437, 440), the entrenched monk claims that his attack is confined to fallen women.

> Daemonialia denique retia stant modo scorta
> . . . .
> Inquinat omnia turba nefaria, grex meretricum.
>
> *[In short, harlots, the devil's nets, stand at the ready. . . . That Impious crowd, that flock of whores, defiles the whole society.]*

But soon Bernard broadens his attack to embrace the entire female sex (2.445–46).

Femina sordida, femina perfida, femina fracta
Munda coinquinat, impia ruminat, atterit aucta.

[*Woman is filthy, woman is treacherous, woman is frail. She pollutes
What is clean, peers into the unholy, exhausts men's gains.*]

Though he reminds himself that his target is not "righteous women, whom I ought to bless" (2.449), but those with the mentality of a Locusta (thus evoking Juvenal *Sat.* 1.71), he soon reverts to the indictment of women en masse.

Nulla quidem bona, si tamen et bona contigit ulla,
Est mala res bona namque fere bona femina nulla.
Femina res rea, res male carnea, vel caro tota.
Strenua prodere, notaque fallere, fallere docta;
Fossa novissima, vipera pessima, pulchra putredo.
. . . .
Pro truculentia! Viscera propria mergit in undis.
Femina perfida, femina fetida, femina fetor.
Est Satanae thronus. . . . .
. . . .
Quae bona femina? Cui bona nomina? Quae bene casta?

[*Indeed, no woman is good, but if any happens to be good, an evil thing is
     good, for
Scarcely any woman is good. Woman is a thing on trial, a wickedly carnal
     thing, indeed
One wholly carnal. She works hard at betrayal, is born to deceive, is
     skilled at deception.
She is a dike unprecedented, most depraved of vipers, rottenness with a
     fair face.*
. . . .
*What hard-heartedness! She casts her unborn child into the waters.
     Woman is faithless,
Woman is foul, woman is foulness. Satan sits poised on her.*
. . . .
What woman is good? Or of good repute? Or is truly chaste?][38]

In this welter of abuse (it is clear from the rhetorical fireworks that Bernard, like his predecessors, is drugged by the sights and sounds and rhythms of his lines), the poet follows the tradition of citing biblical and classical exemplars of saintly men undone by the wiles of women. Among the hackneyed examples of Old Testament figures—Joseph and David, Solomon and Samson—Bernard additionally presents Reuben, who disgraced himself by committing adultery with his father's concubine (Genesis 35:22). Here, as elsewhere in these catalogues, the sins of the men are visited on their hapless female victims.

As we read these repetitive accounts in which each satirist appears to compete with his predecessors in the crudity of his abuse, we long for some evidence of originality and humor to lighten the tedium. This is happily supplied in a poem earlier ascribed to Alexander Neckham or, alternatively, to Anselm, under the title *De vita monachorum*, but which Manitius identifies as the *De contemptu mundi* (or *De monachis*) of Roger of Caen.[39] In the course of this long poem composed in elegaic couplets, a section is devoted to the cult of antifeminism.[40] Much of it is of a piece with the sweeping denunciations of other satirists, but there is an amusing vignette of women's beauty preparations that is worthy of Ovid himself. The passage ends with the conventional claim that the poet is not lambasting the entire female sex but that there are few to whom the indictment is not relevant.[41]

Femina, dulce malum, mentem roburque virile
    Frangit blanditiis insidiosa suis.
Femina, fax Satanae, gemmis radiantibus, auro
    Vestibus, ut possit perdere, compta venit.
Quod natura sibi sapiens dedit, illa reformat;
    Quicquid et accepit dedecuisse putat.
Pingit acu, et fuco liventes reddit ocellos;
    Sic oculorum, inquit, gratia maior erit.
Est etiam teneras aures quae perforat, ut sic
    Aut aurum aut carus pendeat inde lapis.
Altera ieiunat mensae, minuitque cruorem
    Et prorsus quare palleat ipse facit.
Nam quae non pallet sibi rustica quaeque videtur:
    "Hic decet, hic color est verus amantis" ait.
Haec quoque diversis sua sordibus inficit ora;
    Sed quare melior quaeritur arte color?
Arte supercilium rarescit, rursus et arte
    In minimum mammas colligit ipsa suas.

Arte quidem videas nigras flavescere crines;
    Nititur ipsa suo membra mouere loco.
Sic fragili pingit totas in corpore partes,
    Ut quidquid nata est displicuisse putes.
O, quos in gestus se mollis femina frangit,
    Et placet in blaesis subdola lingua sonis!
Dulcia saepe canit, componit sedula gressum,
    Ut quadam credas arte movere gradum.
Saepe auditores eius facundia torquet;
    Et modo ridendo, nunc quoque flendo placet.
Mille modis nostras impugnat femina mentes,
    Et multos illi perdere grande lucrum est.
Nil est in rebus muliere nocentius, et nil
    Quo capiat plures letifer hostes habet.
Nec nos in totum iactamus crimina sexum,
    Tempore sed nostro rara pudica manet.

[Woman, sweet evil, with her traps and charms breaks down the resolve and the strength of men. Woman, the devil's torch, comes adorned with gleaming jewels and gold and raiment, to enable her to destroy us. She transforms what nature in its wisdom has bestowed on her, for she believes that any natural gift has defaced her. She embroiders herself and bruises her poor eyes with dye, claiming in this way to make them more attractive. She pierces her delicate ears so that gold or precious stones can dangle from them. Another fasts at table and draws off her blood to ensure a ghostly complexion, for any lady who is not pale considers herself boorish. "This," she says, "is the apt and true complexion of a lover." She also stains her face with foul substances of various kinds; but why, o why, is a better complexion sought by artifice? By artifice she thins out her eyebrows, by artifice too she compresses her breasts down to vanishing point. By artifice indeed one may observe her dark hair becoming blonde; she tries to shift her limbs from their natural position. In this way she adorns every part of her frail body, so that you would think that all her natural endowments displeased her. Note into what degenerate postures woman forces herself, and her crafty tongue gives pleasure with its lisping sounds. Often she sings sweet songs and carefully orders her walk, so that you are led to believe that some artifice dictates her step. Often her eloquence disturbs her listeners, and she gives pleasure at one moment by smiling and at another by weeping. Woman assaults our minds in a thousand ways, and she regards it as a great gain to destroy many. There is nothing in the world more noxious than woman.

The death-bringing Foe has no resource by which he can trap more men.
We are not casting aspersions on the whole sex, but in our day, only the
occasional woman remains chaste.]

THE POWER OF THE TRADITION

The degree to which antifeminism had permeated the literate society of western Europe is documented by an entry in the encyclopedia of Vincent of Beauvais, who composed his massive work between 1247 and 1259. Vincent
attempted to encapsulate in his *Speculum maius* the entire range of knowledge
that was accessible to the society of his day. It was divided into three parts,
Speculum naturale, Speculum doctrinale, and *Speculum historiale,* and it filled
eighty books. Vincent drew upon about two thousand works of some 450
authors.

Astonishingly, this Christian counterpart to the elder Pliny's *Natural History* devotes a chapter of *The Mirror of Nature* to the vices of women.[42] Under
this heading, Vincent compiles judgments on the frail behavior of women
from a dozen acknowledged *auctores,* ranging from Terence to Macrobius and
the mysterious philosopher "Secundus," who is much quoted in the twelfth
century but not before. From Seneca's *Natural Questions,* he unearths "The
root of women's vices is avarice." Half a dozen passages from Ovid follow, five
from the *Ars amatoria* and one from the *Amores (casta est quam nemo rogavit,*
1.8.43). Juvenal's sixth satire is duly cited, as is Virgil's *Varium et mutabile semper femina,* though Vincent mistakenly ascribes it to book 5 of the *Aeneid,* not
book 4. The longest entry is from Macrobius's *Saturnalia,* the famous anecdote about the youthful Papirius who attended a meeting of the Roman Senate with his father. Since the discussion was confidential, he misled his mother
when she sought information about it, by telling her that the discussion had
centered on whether a husband should have two wives or a wife two husbands.
The outcome was that the matrons laid siege to the Senate house, demanding that for preference a wife should have two husbands. The purpose of the
anecdote is to characterize women as guilty of curiosity.[43]

In summary, it is clear that the classical authors exercised a powerful influence on the creative minds of the High Middle Ages as they strove to reconcile the attitudes of Ovid and Juvenal, in particular, with the changed society
of the twelfth and thirteenth centuries. Since that society was uniformly Christian in the West, the leading literary figures looked to the Christian human-
ists of the fourth century, especially to Jerome; they evoked the latter to justify
the irrational prejudices that the satirists in particular displayed toward women
other than consecrated virgins and toward the married state. The resultant

mélange of ideas was to prove a rich quarry from which the vernacular writers who came after them were able to draw in order to enliven their humorous compositions.

✒

Notes

1. The text of this poem and designation by sections follow Rigg 1983 (who is admirably informative on this poem), but the translation is my own. Cf., earlier, Raby 1957, 222.

2. As Rigg (1983, 7) indicates, no antifeminist writing by Peter of Corbeil has been identified, and it is possible that there is confusion with Peter of Blois, whose *Ep.* 79 (*PL* 207.243ff.), advice to a deacon not to abandon the path to the priesthood, is an onslaught on marriage drawing upon Jerome and Walter Map. Lawrence, prior of Durham, wrote a biblical epic entitled *Hypognosticon*, in which discussion of Solomon provokes a long condemnation of sexual passion. John Chrysostom's homilies frequently condemn women's fondness for bodily ornamentation (see, e.g., *PG* 62.98, 145, 542), so that his reputation for antifeminism became a byword in the Middle Ages.

3. See chaps. 8, 9, and 10.

4. Homer *Od.* 24.199ff.; Hesiod *WD* 56ff., 702–3 (quote is from 57–58); Plutarch *Mor.* 139A.

5. The story of the Widow of Ephesus was, however, known to John of Salisbury (see n. 15).

6. Tacitus *Annals* 13.45, 14.1; *Dialogues* 28.

7. Sallust *Cat.* 25.

8. For Tertullian's condemnation of women for elegant dress and jewelry see *De cultu feminarum* 2.6. Cyprian's *De habitu virginum* 16 and Ambrose's *De virginibus* 1.6.28–29 are similarly censorious. Augustine echoes these strictures more moderately in his *De sancta virginitate* 33–34, but in his *De bono coniugalis* 30 he vehemently condemns some consecrated virgins who "spurn the commandments"; he says, "We know many consecrated virgins who exemplify this, for they are garrulous, inquisitive, drunken, argumentative, greedy, and arrogant." I have edited these two texts in *Oxford Early Christian Texts* (2001).

9. See J. N. D. Kelly 1975, 180ff. For the impact of this treatise on writers of the Middle Ages, see P. Delhaye 1951, 65ff.

10. Theophrastus *De nuptiis*, cited at Jerome *Adv. Iov.* 1.47.

11. *Adv. Jov.* 1.47. Jerome appends other arguments against marriage from Theophrastus: expense of clothes, jewelry, and furniture; midnight nagging; adulterous behavior; the notion that friends are better than children as heirs; and so forth. John of Salisbury echoes all these accusations (see n. 15).

12. For a review of educated laity in the Middle Ages, see Thompson [1939] 1960.

13. See Gilson 1960, 9ff., on the clerics' status vis-à-vis marriage.

14. I cannot here enter into the age-old controversy about the authenticity of the *Historia calamitatum* and the correspondence between Abelard and Heloise; the topic is well treated by Peter Dronke (1976, 5ff.). For the *Historia calamitatum*, see the edition of J. Monfrin (1967). There is a translation by Betty Radice in *The Letters of Abelard and Heloise* (1974); for the citation, see p. 71 of this translation.

15. Despite his more moderate tone, John devotes an extended chapter of the *Policraticus* to a critique of marriage. The chapter (8.11) is headed: "The troubles and burdens of marriage according to Jerome and other philosophers; the destructive nature of lust; the kind of fidelity shown by the woman of Ephesus and the like." The lengthy citation from Jerome's *Adversus Iovinianum* quotes the observation of Theophrastus that "a wise man should therefore not marry" and Cicero's riposte to Hirtius noted earlier. Later, John cites Juvenal *Sat.* 6.165, on the chaste woman (*rara avis in terra, nigroque simillima cygno*) and follows with Petronius's story of the Widow of Ephesus. Elsewhere he brands the man who embraces the life of the court yet proposes to practice the role of the philosopher as "a hermaphrodite" (5.10). I cite these passages from the edition of C. C. J. Webb (1909). For John's knowledge of Petronius, see Martin 1979.

16. On Map, see chap. 10 in this volume.

17. I discuss the literary and historical aspects of the "courtly love" controversy in Walsh 1982, 5ff. See also Boase 1977.

18. I cite the various suggestions for the change of heart in Walsh 1982, 25.

19. The catalogue of the vices of women is at 3.65–112 (I provide the section numbers in my 1982 edition for easier reference). Earlier in book 3, Andreas's concern is to condemn love in extramarital relations. So far as marriage is concerned, he argues that "even in the case of married people, it [sexual intercourse] is rarely regarded as a pardonable fault not involving serious sin" (3.33), a doctrine congenial to Jerome but opposed to Augustine's view in *De bono coniugali.*

20. *De amore* 1.11.3. With characteristic hypocrisy—or perhaps irony—Andreas adds: "I say this not with the desire to persuade you to the love of peasant women but so that through brief instruction you may know the procedure to follow if through lack of foresight you are compelled to make love to them."

21. See Piguet 1927; W. P. Jones 1973; Bate 1983.

22. Strecker 1925, no. 32; the text is conveniently available in Raby 1957, 194.

23. *Carmina Burana* 158; see Walsh 1993, 177ff.

24. See my comments in Walsh 1993, 178.

25. Cf. Marbod's statement at the outset of his *Liber decem capitulorum: Quae iuvenis scripsi, senior dum plura retracto, paenitet, et quaedam vel scripta vel edita nollem* [As I review several of the things that I wrote as a young man, I regret them, and I wish that I had not written or uttered some of them].

26. For a general introduction, see Raby 1953, 265–87.

27. For *Missus sum in vineam,* see Strecker 1929, no. 6; conveniently published in Raby 1957, 156ff. In addition to lines from Horace, Ovid, Persius, and Juvenal, there are citations from the *Disticha Catonis* and from Lucan. On Bernard of Cluny's poem, see the discussion later in the present chapter.

28. For the text, see Scott 1969, nos. 50, 40–41.

29. Scott (1969) usefully cites parallels from other satirical poems, not only by Marbod, Petrus Pictor, and Bernard of Cluny (treated shortly), but also by anonymous authors in the collections published by C. Pascal (1907, 175) and Novati (1883, 21), as well as an extract from an unpublished poem cited from a Bodley MS.

30. For the text, see *PL* 171. 1693–1716. For discussion, see Raby 1957, 273; Manitius 1931, 719ff. Quotations in the following discussion are from *PL* 171. 1698B–C, 1698B–1699A.

31. For Lot's daughters, see Gen. 19:31ff.; for Delilah, Judges 16:4ff.; for Herodias and her daughter, Matt. 14:3ff.; for Bathsheba, 2 Sam. 11:3ff.; for Solomon's turning away from God after marrying foreign wives, 1 Kings 11:2ff.; for Jezebel, 1 Kings 21:8ff.; for Athaliah, 2 Kings 11:1ff.

32. The groups of women from mythology are all clustered together at the close of Juvenal's sixth satire (644, 655–56) without elaboration of their misdeeds, with which Marbod was familiar from Ovid, Horace, and other classical sources.

33. The point is well made in Blamires 1997, 20; see also Blamires, Pratt, and Marx 1992, in which (100, 228) there is discussion of both *De meretrice* and *De matrona*.

34. For a more flattering assessment of Serlo and a survey of his career, see Raby 1957, 111ff. The text of the poem is included in the poems ascribed to Serlo by Thomas Wright (1872, 2:232–58). The lines quoted in our text come from 234–35.

35. For the career of Petrus Pictor, see Manitius 1931, 877–83; for the text of the poem, *PL* 171.1193–96.

36. See D. S. Robertson's Budé edition of Apuleius's *Metamorphoses* (1956, 1:xxxvi-iiff.). All the manuscripts are descended from F, copied in France at this early date.

37. For Bernard of Cluny (earlier erroneously named Bernard of Morlais) and his background, see De Ghellinck 1954, 449–50. The poem has recently been published, with facing translation, by R. E. Pepin (1991).

38. *De contemptu mundi* 2:155–59, 516–18, 529.

39. Manitius 1931, 85ff. The poem is published in *PL* 158.687–706 and by Thomas Wright (1872). The passage quoted is from 186–87(*PL* 696 A-C).

40. It is clear that here, as elsewhere, the abuse of women forms part of the strategy for defense of the monastic life. Elsewhere in the poem, women are sternly counseled to steer clear of monks (e.g., . . . *a sacro sit procul ipsa viro* [let her stay far from the holy man] 188).

41. The passage thus begins with an Ovidian phrase, *dulce malum* (*Amores* 2.9.36), and ends with a reminiscence of Juvenal *Sat.* 6.165 (quoted in n. 15 earlier in this chapter).

42. *Speculum naturale* 32.115. There is no modern edition of this work; for details of early editions, see *The Oxford Dictionary of the Christian Church* (3d ed. 1997), s.v. "Vincent of Beauvais."

43. This is presumably Vincent's purpose. Macrobius (*Saturnalia* 1.6.19ff.) derives the story from Aulus Gellius 1.23.4ff., where the story is told to account for the cognomen *Praetextatus* acquired first by the youth and thereafter by the gens Papiria.

Twelve

The Wife of Bath and
Dorigen Debate Jerome

Warren S. Smith

*This is the only chapter in this book centering on an author writing in the vernac-
ular. Its inclusion, I believe, is justified by the close relationship between the* Wife
of Bath's *prologue and Dorigen's lament in the* Canterbury Tales *and some of the
literature discussed earlier in this book, most obviously Jerome's* Against Jovinian *but also the work of Walter Map and Ovid. There is considerable interest also
gained from the status of the Wife of Bath and Dorigen as female characters react-
ing to the writings of males.*

*I argue in this chapter that Alison, Chaucer's Wife of Bath, defends the plain
truth of Scripture against the polemics of St. Jerome and adopts what in essence is
an Augustinian position on marriage. This trend continues in the "Franklin's Tale,"
where Dorigen's lament (1355–1456) again extensively borrows from Jerome but
uses this material in such a way as to change its emphasis and meaning, so that the
lament prefigures the favorable resolution of Dorigen's dilemma.*

DRAWING BATTLE LINES

C ritical discussions of the prologue to Chaucer's "Wife of Bath's Tale"
have sometimes taken it for granted that the wife's arguments are distorted—or "agitated and incoherent"—in contrast with her main source, Jerome's

Against Jovinian (*Adversus Iovinianum*, hereafter referred to as *A.J.*), which is imagined to be "straightforward, hard hitting, and unambiguous."[1] In fact, *A.J.* is a sprawling treatise, neither consistent nor easy to follow. The awkward attempts at sarcasm and the scattershot approach of Jerome can make his positions even on crucial issues difficult to pin down, including his attitude toward marriage. He claims once to defend marriage as a gift from God (*A.J.* 1.9), whereas more often he satirizes and ridicules marriage and women with a barrage of quotations from biblical and classical sources and seems "only a hair's breadth from the Manichaean view that marriage itself is evil." On several occasions (*A.J.* 1.7, 9) Jerome even seems to turn against St. Paul himself, supposedly his ally, to chide him for the apparent inconsistency or absurdity of his argument. The variety of sources and methods in the work of this intemperate polemicist gives the two books of *A.J.* a curious kind of wide-ranging recklessness, the product of a rhetorician-satirist who will stop at nothing—even resorting to biblical distortion—to score points on behalf of Christian asceticism. When published, *A.J.* shocked some of Jerome's own friends, who felt that he was doing "incalculable damage" to his own cause, and Jerome responded to their objections in three separate letters (*Ep.* 48, 49, and 50); in these letters, he defends, not entirely convincingly, his belief in the goodness of marriage, which the rhetorical flourishes of *A.J.* often seem to call into question. The harshness of Jerome's work was an impetus for the publishing in 401 of Augustine's *De bono conjugali* (On the good of marriage), a moderate defense of Christian marriage.[2]

In the prologue to the "Wife of Bath's Tale," Chaucer (though without naming his Latin source until lines 674ff.) provides a response to Jerome's strident defense of celibacy. In the first part of the prologue (1–162, up to the Pardoner's interruption), Alison closely follows the reasoning of sections of book 1 of *A.J.*; she again returns to many of its themes in, especially, lines 235–36 (closely imitating Jerome's *A.J.* 1.47, the quotation from Theophrastus) and 669–70, the description of Jankyn's "book of wikked wyves." Critical judgments are very harsh on the Wife of Bath as biblical interpreter. It has been argued that "she mangles St. Jerome sadly, and the Bible with him," and that she "embodies all the vices which Jerome feared Jovinian's heresies would promote."[3] Such a view underrates the subtlety of Alison's debate with Jerome's intemperate treatise, the inconsistencies and absurdities of which she exposes at many points. What she offers is far from a "rebuttal of St. Paul," as is sometimes claimed; indeed, time and again, she defends the plain sense of the Bible—of the "literal text," in Carolyn Dinshaw's phrase—and of St. Paul in particular, against Jerome's sometimes biased and distorted interpretations of Scripture. A few critics have noted that her thought on marriage is actually quite orthodox; moreover, as Lawrence Besserman has argued, the

Wife of Bath's "carnal, i.e. literal, exegesis" of Scripture may be closer to Chaucer's own view than is generally acknowledged. As this chapter will argue, the Wife of Bath, while at times mocking Jerome's pro-celibacy biblical exegesis, is not quick to contradict Jerome's positions. She accepts, emphatically and repeatedly, his argument that celibacy is preferable to marriage (75–76, 105–6, 142–43); she gladly seizes on his grudging concession that marriage is allowed by God (51–52); she concedes Jerome's argument that marriage represents "servitude" of the husband; and she mocks his horror by saying that she "liketh every deel" such an idea (162). The Wife of Bath's method of defense is technically effective, following the rhetorical device of *concessio* (cf. Cicero *De inventione* 2.31.94ff.; *Rhetorica ad Herrenium* 2.26.23ff.), in which the defendant acknowledges guilt but minimizes the offense or pleads attenuating circumstances. It is my contention that ultimately the Wife of Bath arrives at a humorously presented but reasonable, balanced, and, in basic outline, even Augustinian view of celibacy and marriage that triumphantly defends a literalist interpretation of the Bible against the mischief of its male glossators.[4]

The monk Jovinian, according to accounts by Jerome, Augustine, and others, attracted followers in Rome by his teachings and his published pamphlet, which made a moral equation between marriage and virginity. This "proto-Protestant" stressed the efficacy of faith above works, said that one could not fall again after baptism, and put second marriage on a par with first.[5] The contemporary church reacted with anger and shock to Jovinian's teaching and his treatise. Jerome, at Pammachius's request, set to work to refute him, producing *A.J.*, his most ambitious satirical work, in two books, about A.D. 393. In this ambitious, if crude, attack, Jerome summons up all his rhetorical skills; all his knowledge of the Greek, Latin, and Hebrew classics; and biting wit. There is never the slightest question of Jerome finding any common ground with the "Epicurus of Christianity." Jerome's attack is the all-out war of the diatribe satirist, out to combat his archenemy.

Jerome's satiric mode is already suggested in *A.J.* 1.3, when the author launches a full-scale attack, then checks himself.

> In saying this I have followed my own impatient spirit rather than the course of the argument. For I had scarcely left harbor, and had barely hoisted sail, when a swelling tide of words suddenly swept me into the depths of the discussion. I must stay my course, and take in canvas for a while. . . .

The ship at full sail is the metaphorical dilemma of a satirist who is so outraged he does not know where to strike first (closely similar is Juvenal in *Sat.*

1.149–50).[6] Jerome's bombastic tone here is characteristic of the preface, in which Jovinian's words are compared to the "hissing of the old serpent," while virgins are urged to "close their ears" lest they be corrupted by such blasphemy (*A.J.* 1.4). (The sailing metaphor, after being temporarily abandoned for that of an army led by Paul in *A.J.* 1.6, is picked up again toward the end of the treatise, at *A.J.* 2.35, where Jerome finally catches sight of his harbor.)

ALISON'S COUNTERATTACK

Jerome's presence is quickly felt in the prologue to the "Wife of Bath's Tale." Alison, who sometimes seems to weave into her discourse the point of view of male speakers, begins as though she herself intended to follow the plan of an anti-marriage satiric tract, saying she can speak from experience of the "wo" that is in marriage (3). In the bulk of her argument, she by no means follows Jovinian's view that marriage is equal to celibacy. She accepts the primacy of celibacy and the validity of many of Jerome's arguments about the nature of purity and holiness, though she restricts such purity to those who would "lyve parfitly" (111), from which company she excludes herself. In her utter honesty and refusal to claim more for herself than is due, Alison accepts the down-to-earth practicality of, for example, Cicero in *De amicitia*, who proposes "to look at things as they are in the experience of everyday life and not as they are in fancy or in hope."[7]

In lines 9ff. of her prologue, with the phrase "me was toold," the Wife of Bath begins consideration of the first of a series of arguments that are taken, without acknowledgment, from *A.J.*

> But me was toold, certeyn, nat longe agoon is,
> 10   That sith that Crist ne wente nevere but onis
> To weddyng, in the Cane of Galilee,
> That by the same ensample taughte he me
> That I ne sholde wedded be but ones.

Alison alludes to Jerome *A.J.* 1.40 (Migne *PL* 23.282A): *Qui enim semel venit ad nuptias, semel docuit esse nubendum* [For he who came once to a wedding, taught that marriage should occur once]. Jerome has borrowed this idea from Tertullian, one of his favorite Christian antifeminist sources, who was nonetheless controversial for his embracing of the Montanist heresy. Tertullian, in *De monogamia* 8, stresses that Jesus went only once to a wedding, thereby indicating how often he thought men should be married. The Wife of Bath's cynical tone especially—"Me was toold, certyn"—indicates her skepticism at male biblical interpreters, a point made with increasing vehemence.

Herkne eek, lo, which a sharp word for the nones,
15 Biside a welle, Jhesus, God and man,
 Spak in repreeve of the Samaritan:
 "Thou hast yhad fyve housbondes" quod he,
 "And that ilke man that now hath thee
 Is noght thyn housbonde," thus seyde he certyn.
20 What that he mente therby, I kan nat seyn;
 But that I axe, why that the fifthe man
 Was noon housbonde to the Samaritan?

It may seem obvious to us today, as it also did to Augustine, that the Samaritan woman in John 4:17 has been married five times but is now living with a man to whom she is not married. Yet several of the early church fathers found other lessons in the passage. Tertullian, in *De Monogamia* 8, argues that, on the basis of his reproof of the Samaritan woman, Jesus had condemned multiple marriage as adulterous.[8] Seizing on Tertullian's interpretation and eager to find support for his own disapproval of remarriage, Jerome, in *A.J.* 1.14 (Migne *PL* 23.244B), writes that Jesus "reproved" the Samaritan woman for claiming to have a sixth husband—though in fact she makes no such claim (Jerome repeats the mistake in *Ep.* 48.18 [Migne *PL* 22.508]). The Wife of Bath's account of John 4 is written with an eye on Jerome's version, to which her phrase "spake in repreeve" makes allusion (Jerome's *castigavit*). Alison here parodies Jerome's mistake (cf. especially the sly mockery of "What that he mente therby, I kan nat seyn"), just as later, in her tale, she will provide a commentary on Ovid by twisting the details of the story of Midas and his ass's ears. Alison's comments mock those who, like Tertullian and Jerome, falsely read into John 4:17 a condemnation of polygamy—a meaning that she doubts Jesus intended. All such speculation about the meaning of "numbers" is part of the wasted effort of men to "devyne and glosen" over small details in texts.[9]

 How manye myghte she have in mariage?
 Yet herde I nevere tellen in myn age
25 Upon this nombre diffinicioun.
 Men may devyne and glosen, up and doun,
 But wel I woot, expres, withoute lye,
 God bad for us to wexe and multiplye;
 That gentil text kan I wel understonde.

Alison's literalist interpretation of God's injunction to Adam and Eve corrects the reading by Jerome (*A.J.* 1.16 [Migne *PL* 23.246B–C]; cf. 1.24 fin.), who casts doubt on God's blessing of marriage in Genesis 2:22 by arguing that since God failed to find his creation "good" on the second day (Gen. 1:8), the number two, as seen in the coming together of husband and wife, destroys unity and is not good. Jerome's Old Testament exegesis, in particular, often seeks forced interpretations to explain away the approval by the patriarchs not only of marriage but of polygamy (cf. J. N. D. Kelly 1975, 183). The Wife of Bath's interpretation is strikingly close to the more moderate position of Augustine, who at times considers the possibility of spiritual and allegorical meanings of Genesis 1:28 (cf. *De Genesi contra Manich.* 1.13 [Migne *PL* 34.187]), but who insists on the plain truth of a literal interpretation in *De civitate Dei* 14.22 (Migne *PL* 41.1429).

> It is quite clear that they were created male and female, with bodies of different sexes, for the purpose of begetting offspring and so increasing, multiplying, and replenishing the earth; and it is great foolishness [*magnae absurditatis*] to fight against [this meaning].

Augustine, in casting doubt on allegorical readings of Genesis 1:28, compares it, as does Alison, with Christ's injunction in Matthew 19:4–5 for a man to leave his father and mother and cleave to his wife (cf. the Wife of Bath's prologue, lines 31–32, quoted shortly); in the same context, Augustine implies the sanctity of the marriage bond when he quotes the apostle's injunction to love their wives (Eph. 5:25; cf. the Wife of Bath's prologue, lines 160–61).

Alison quotes Matthew 19:5 to verify Jesus' approval of marriage, but she adds that polygamy is not at issue in that passage.

> 30 Eek wel I woot, he seyde myn housbonde
> Sholde lete fader and mooder and take to me.
> But of no nombre mencion made he,
> Of bigamye, or of octogamye;
> Why sholde men thanne speke of it vileynye?

Lines 33–34 allude to a mocking passage in Jerome (A.J. 1.15 [Migne *PL* 23.246C]).

> If more than one husband be allowed, it makes no difference whether he be a second or a third, because there is no longer a question of single marriage. "All things are lawful, but not all things are expedient" [1 Cor 6:12, 10:23]. I do not condemn second, third, nor, pardon the expression, eighth marriages; I will go still further and say that I welcome even a penitent whoremonger. Things that are equally lawful must be weighed in an even balance.

In her counterthrust to Jerome, Alison exposes the ineptness of his heavy-handed attempts at humor, by taking literally a concession that he may have meant only ironically—that eight marriages are no worse than two. Jerome makes this concession only on the basis of the neo-Stoic position that "all sins are equal"; he follows Tertullian (e.g., *Ad uxorem* [Migne *PL* 1.1385—418]) in arguing or implying the sinfulness of multiple marriages. The Wife of Bath, despite her comic emphasis, is certainly within the bounds of centralist church teaching on multiple marriage. In addition to the seemingly unambiguous permission by Paul in 1 Corinthians 7:39, Augustine, in *De bono viduitatis liber* (Migne *PL* 40.433), while favoring celibacy, insists that the remarriage of a widow is blessed and "altogether legitimate" [*omnino licitas*]; Augustine condemns those who, like Tertullian, foster heresy by teaching otherwise.

In lines 35–43 of her prologue, the Wife of Bath gleefully cites "the wise kyng, daun Salomon," as a precedent for multiple marriages, and she is sure that "the firste nyght [he] had many a myrie fit / With ech of hem." Jerome tries to explain away the many wives of Solomon by saying that he built his temple before his wives could turn away his heart from the Lord. But such justifications pale before the sheer number of Solomon's seven hundred wives and three hundred concubines (1 Kings 11:3), and there is leaden humor in Jerome's argument that if Jovinian approves the example of Solomon, he will no longer confine himself to second and third marriages but adopt seven hundred wives and three hundred concubines. Alison goes on to defend multiple successive marriages.

> 46 For sothe, I wol nat kepe me chaast in al.
> Whan myn housbonde is fro the world ygon,
> Som Cristen man shal wedde me anon,
> For thanne, th'apostle seith that I am free
> 50 To wedde, a Goddes half, where it liketh me.
> He seith that to be wedded is no synne;
> Bet is to be wedded than to brynne.

Jerome, writing on 1 Corinthians 7:9 (*A.J.* 1.9 [Migne *PL* 23.232Cff.]), claims to be preoccupied with degrees of moral worth. Finding no absolute goodness in the claim "it is better to marry," he develops the point to a farcical extreme and uses it to discredit the worth of marriage, by adding, "It is as though he said, it is better to have one eye than neither, it is better to stand on one foot and support the rest of the body with a stick, than to crawl with broken legs" (here, Jerome is influenced again by similar rhetoric in Tertullian). Similarly, in *A.J.* 1.13 Jerome is forced to admit that, in view of the

explicit statement in 1 Corinthians 7:36, to be married is "no sin." But he seems
to condemn marriage and retract this admission soon afterward, when he says
(*A.J.* 1.15 [Migne *PL* 23.244B]) that it is better to marry only once; "that is,
it is more tolerable for a woman to prostitute herself to one man than to many."
Such Parthian shots by Jerome, which seem to retract his original concession,
are countered by the Wife of Bath, who, in her prologue, repeatedly insists on
getting back to the actual text of Scripture and pits the plain meaning of St.
Paul against Jerome's twists and turns ("th'apostle seith," 49; "He seith," 51;
"Th'apostel . . . He seyde," 64–65; "Poul dorste nat comanden," 73).

Alison repeats the concession, made by Jerome, that Christ nowhere commands virginity (similarly, lines 73–78 of her prologue echo *A.J.* 1.12 [Migne
PL 23.238C]).

> Wher can ye seye, in any manere age,
> 60 That hye God defended mariage
> By expres word? I pray yow, telleth me.
> Or where comanded he virginitee?
> I woot as wel as ye, it is no drede,
> Th'apostel, when he speketh of maydenhede,
> 65 He seyde that precept therof hadde he noon.
> Men may conseille a womman to been oon,
> But conseillyng is no comandement.

Jerome had already admitted that God never commanded virginity, which
would have implied a condemnation of marriage (*A.J.* 1.12 [Migne *PL*
23.237B–C]: *si praecidisset radicem, quomodo fruges quaereret?* [if he had cut
off the root, how could he have sought any fruit?]; cf. *Ep.* 22.20). He further
explains the lack of a command by pointing to the need for marriages to give
birth to virgins. It must be admitted that Jerome seems to call his own admission into doubt when he claims soon afterward (*A.J.* 1.12 [Migne *PL* 23.239C],
based on Matt. 24:15) that Christ condemns "swollen wombs, wailing infants,
and the fruits and works of marriage" (cf. Tertullian *De monogamia* 1.16). Yet
Alison, in not acknowledging the afterthought but holding Jerome to the
original point ("And certes, if ther were no seed ysowe, / Virginitee,
thanne wherof sholde it growe?" 71–72), again repeats Jerome's argument
and admits the superiority of virginity over marriage—yet, curiously, she has
sometimes been accused of adopting the position of Jerome's opponents on
this issue.[10]

In lines 79–82 of her prologue, Alison interprets Jerome's permission to
marry as advice, not a command, to remain a virgin.

> I woot wel that th' apostel was a mayde;
> 80   But nathelees, thogh that he wroot and sayde
> He wolde that every wight were swich as he,
> Al nys but conseil to virginitee.

This echoes Jerome's argument on 1 Corinthians 7:7 at *A.J.* 1.8 (Migne *PL* 23.232A): *Volo autem omnes homines esse sicut meipsum* [But I wish all men were like myself]. Jerome implies that Paul's "permission" to marry is an indulgence of which we are wrong to take advantage (*in venia abutimur* [we abuse as an indulgence]), and he interprets the granting of "permission" as if it alluded to the pardoning of a crime; the church, he says, opens its doors to repentant sinners such as fornicators and the incestuous (*quasi non et fornicatoribus per poenitentiam fores aperiantur Ecclesiae*).

    Alison offers her commentary on 1 Corinthians 7:7.

> Al were it good no womman for to touche—
> He mente as in his bed or in his couche;
> for peril is bothe fyr and tow t'assemble:
> 90   Ye knowe what this ensample may resemble.

She picks up the warning made by Jerome in *A.J.* 1.7 (Migne *PL* 23.228), which exaggerates the urgency of the passage by forcing *bonum* into an extreme position, arguing that "good" can only be seen as the opposite of "bad"; if it is good not to touch a woman, it is bad to touch one (cf. Tertullian *De monogamia* 3 [Migne *PL* 2.932B]). Jerome also insists on taking "touch" in the most literal sense (*quasi et in tactu periculum sit: quasi qui illam tetigerit, non evadat* [as if there is danger even in one touch; as if he who has touched her cannot escape]). (He repeats this interpretation in *Ep.* 48.4.) Alison's pointed explanation is a correction of Jerome's: she interprets "touch" as a euphemism for sexual union (perhaps a Hebraism, compared by Thayer's *Greek-English Lexicon of the New Testament* [1889] with Gen. 20:6 and Prov. 6:29). This interpretation is careful and conservative. Desiderius Erasmus, for example, in his 1516 New Testament commentary on 1 Corinthians 7, like Alison, connects "touch" with sexuality and explicitly refutes Jerome's interpretation of the word for "touch" as a distortion (Le Clerc [1703] 1961–62, 6: col. 685).

    In lines 99ff. of her prologue, Alison turns to 2 Timothy 2:20, a passage that Jerome had already interpreted in terms of marriage.

> For wel ye knowe, a lord in his houshold,
> 100   He nath nat every vessel al of gold;

Somme been of tree, and doon hir lord servyse.
God clepeth folk to hym in sondry wyse,
And everich hath of God a propre yifte—
Som this, som that, as hym liketh shifte.

Alison connects the gold vessels of the household in 2 Timothy 2:20 with virginity, the wooden vessels with marriage. Critics sometimes claim that Alison misreads the biblical passage (Cooper) or that by associating herself with
wooden vessels rather than gold or silver, she puts herself "firmly among the
evil who are in the Church but not of it" (Robertson, basing his reading on a
passage from the *Glossa ordinaria*).[11] In fact, Alison is here not far from the
position of Jerome himself as presented in *A.J.* 1.40 (Migne *PL* 23.282B) and
more clearly spelled out in *Epistle* 48.2, written in justification of *A.J.* In the
letter, Jerome himself quotes 2 Timothy 2:20 in defense of the validity of marriage: "We know that in a large house there are vessels not only of silver and
of gold but of wood also and of earth. . . . We are not ignorant that 'marriage is honorable . . . and the bed undefiled' (Heb. 13:4). We have read the
first decree of God: 'Be fruitful and multiply and replenish the earth.' But
while we allow marriage, we prefer the virginity that springs from it"
(Migne *PL* 22.494–95). Jerome explains the passage similarly in *Epistle* 123.9
(Migne *PL* 22.1052). Others among the early patristic writers anticipated the
Wife of Bath in interpreting 2 Timothy 2:20 as encouraging a spirit of tolerance of diversity—the acceptance of many kinds of "vessels" in the household
of God, in a sense wider than the issue of marriage. Compare Augustine in
Sermo 32 (Morin 1930, 571) and Ambrose (in *Corpus Christianorum* 14.312),
who compares the passage with the lesson learned by Peter in Acts 10:9–16
(but for a harsher interpretation of 2 Tim 2:20, cf., e.g., Augustine *Operis
imperfecti contra Julianum* [Migne *PL* 45.1124]).

In lines 101–3 of her prologue, Alison's allusion to 1 Corinthians 7:7 derives
from *A.J.* 1.8 (Migne *PL* 23.232B), where Jerome acknowledges both marriage
and celibacy as legitimate, though diverse, gifts from God. Alison's humility
in calling virginity a superior gift strengthens her argument. She emerges as a
moderate on this position, in contrast with Jerome's enemy the heretic Jovinian, who had argued for the equality of baptized virgins, widows, and wives (cf.
A.J. 1.4 [Migne *PL* 23.224B]: *Dicit virgines, viduas, et maritatas, quae semel in
Christo lotae sunt, si non discrepent caeteris operibus, ejusdem esse meriti* [he [Jovin-
ian] says that virgins, widows, and married women, once they have been washed
in Christ, if they do not differ in other works, are of the same merit].

Alison continues to press the issue of more than one legitimate response
to a biblical injunction.

105   Virginitee is greet perfeccion,
       And continence eek with devocion,
       But Crist, that of perfeccion is welle,
       Bad nat every wight he sholde go selle
       Al that he hadde, and gyve it to the poore,
110   And in swich wise folwe hym and his foore.
       He spak to hem that wolde lyve parfitly:
       And lordynges, by youre leve, that am nat I.

The injunction "if you wish to be perfect" is emphasized by Jerome in *A.J.* 2.6 (Migne *PL* 23.307C). By advocating the possession of property, the Wife of Bath may echo the materialistic spirit of the church of Chaucer's day; moreover, by disclaiming any effort to attain moral perfection, she follows one of the methods of *concessio* outlined in Cicero: the defendant should emphasize his good intentions, say it was impossible to do more than he did, and say that if he is to be condemned, the weakness of all mankind is at fault (*De inventione* 2.101).[12]

Jerome, in *A.J.* 1.7, in a typically forced attempt at irony, compares Paul's permission to marry (1 Cor. 7ff.) with the giving of permission to eat barley bread (*hordeum*) as an extreme measure to avoid resorting to cow dung (*stercus bubulcum*). Alison counters with an allusion to John 6:9 (wrongly cited as "Mark") on Jesus feeding the crowd with barley bread, as a perfectly acceptable food for the masses.

       Let hem be breed of pured whete-seed,
       And lat us wyves hoten barly-breed:
145   And yet with barly-breed, Mark telle kan,
       Oure Lord Jhesu refresshed many a man.

The connection between the everyday "barley bread" of John 6:9 and the commonness of marriage, however, is not original with the Wife of Bath—as Robertson (1983, 329) seems to imply—but is already made by Jerome in *Epistle* 48 (Migne *PL* 22.503–4).

I call virginity fine corn, wedlock barley, and fornication cow dung.
Surely both corn and barley are creatures of God. But of the two
multitudes miraculously supplied in the Gospel, the larger was fed on
barley loaves and the smaller on corn bread. . . .

Nor is the analogy new even with Jerome, who in the same passage cites Ambrose's *De viduis* 13.79 (Migne *PL* 16.272), where the validity of marriage is affirmed though its difficulties are acknowledged: "The Lord Jesus gave to some barley bread, lest they should faint by the way, but offered to others his own body. . . . The nuptial tie, then, is not to be avoided as a crime but to be refused as a hard burden."

It has been argued that Alison's next paragraph, in particular, represents a perversion of Paul's arguments on marriage.

> An housbonde I wol have—I wol nat lette—
> 155 Which shal be bothe my dettour and my thral,
> And have his tribulacion withal
> Upon his flessh, whil that I am his wyf.
> I have the power durynge al my lyf
> Upon his propre body, and noght he.
> 160 Right this the Apostel tolde it unto me;
> And bad oure housbondes for to love us weel.

It is quite true that the Wife of Bath "quotes Paul's injunction to husbands while failing to mention his injunction to wives to submit to their husbands [Eph. 5:25]" and that she "lays claim to the power over her husband's body without bothering to point out the other half of the Pauline equation [1 Cor 7:4]."[13] But her insistence on the husband's need to pay a sexual "debt" to his wife is consistent with the provisions of medieval canon and civil law, which put a wife on an equal footing with her husband in regard to the conjugal duty;[14] and Alison's stress on the husband's need to pay his debt reflects or parodies a preoccupation of Jerome.

> And at the same time the meaning of the words must be taken into account. He who has a wife is regarded as a debtor, and is said to be uncircumcised, to be the servant of his wife, and like bad servants to be bound [*alligatus*]. But he who has no wife, in the first place owes no man anything. . . . (A.J. 1.12 [Migne *PL* 23.239D])

It is a key ingredient in antifeminist satire, to which Jerome here conforms, that women are seen as all-powerful and that men cringe and submit helplessly to the commands of their cruel and greedy wives. That men must submit to many indignities from women is one of the main arguments Jerome uses elsewhere against marriage and is key to the argument of Theophrastus that Jerome quotes (A.J. 1.47). The Wife of Bath, in this instance, deliciously turns Jerome's argument against him by following up his reasoning; she quotes the phrases from Paul only in the sense that Jerome interprets them, and she welcomes the submission of men as part of the fruits of marriage. These fruits include the "tribulations in the flesh" of 1 Corinthians 7:8, which Alison happily interprets—in a sense easily derived from Jerome (A.J. 1.13 [Migne PL 23.240B])—as the sexual struggles of a man who seeks to satisfy his wife.

Much of lines 235–307 of the Wife of Bath's prologue follows a purported book by Theophrastus, De nuptiis, as quoted in Latin translation (the work is unknown from other sources) by Jerome in A.J. 1.47 (Migne PL 23.288–91). At this point in Jerome's argument, he has temporarily left biblical criticism behind and is pursuing Greek and Roman examples. The stock charges in Theophrastus's arsenal, which is less of an argument against marriage and more of an ad mulierem attack, have to do with wives' jealousy, luxury, and nagging. In accordance with the shift in Jerome's method of attack, the Wife of Bath no longer responds directly to individual points but goes on the defensive, claiming it is impossible for any clerk to speak well of wives. She sets her own sense of decency against the macabre taste of Jerome and questions the purity of his motives in complaining that "folke seye vileynye" of Lameth (53–54). Moreover, Jerome's obsessive emphasis on Jovinian's book itself as an evil thing, as the hissing of the old serpent, having a power in itself to seduce, is strongly paralleled by Chaucer in the Wife of Bath's focus on the "book of wikked wyves" as exuding a kind of evil all by itself ("this cursed book," 789), arousing her disgust ("fy! spek namoore," 735) apart from her relation with her fifth husband, Jankyn, who delights in quoting from the book. To improve her relationship with Jankyn, she attacks the book first. She pulls three leaves out and punches him, then she finally persuades him to burn it, a fate appropriate to a heretical book.[15] Jerome's fight against the heresy of Jovinian has truly come full circle; Alison has made a strong case that Jerome himself and other misogynists like him have distorted Scripture and become the heretics. In addition, Alison wins a concession from Jankyn.

> And whan that I hadde geten unto me,
> By maistrie, al the soverayyntee,
> And that he seyde, "Myn owene trewe wyf,
> 820 Do as thee lust the terme of al thy lyf;
> Keep thyn honour, and keep eek myn estaat":
> After that day we hadden never debaat

A CENTRIST POSITION

Overall, Alison, in her shadow debate with St. Jerome, is actually much closer than is Jerome to a centrist position on marriage, at least in the Western tradition of biblical interpretation of St. Paul. The controversy over the extremism of Jerome's position led to an important corrective even in his own day. Jerome's younger contemporary Augustine, strongly disapproving of Jerome's denunciation of women, spoke out in defense of marriage in such treatises as *De bono viduitatis* and *De bono conjugali* (Migne 40.348ff., 430ff.). Augustine convincingly argued that it does not detract from the "good" of marriage to say that celibacy is better, and he varies from Jerome's emphasis at a number of points. For example, Jerome had satirized the "wailing of infants" as one of the evils of marriage (A.J. 1.12), following Tertullian (*Ex castitate* 9) in twisting Jesus' words in Matthew 24:19 into a condemnation of childbearing. Augustine responds by making the procreation of children the first good fruit of marriage.[16]

Alison, for her part, shows her cleverness—and conciliatory approach—most vividly by deriving much of her position from out of the heart of the very misogynist treatise that she bitterly denounces later on. She brilliantly plays the role of an ironical defendant, mocking Jerome's heavy-handed satiric prosecutor. Her response to Jerome is devastating: she plays Scripture off against him, eagerly accepts his concessions about marriage, and shows the consequences of his most extreme claims by taking them all seriously. Her willingness to compromise is in contrast with Jerome's extreme arguments and his ill-timed playing the fool, which cloud the logic of his treatise.

The misogynistic diatribes of Theophrastus, Lucretius, Juvenal, and Jerome present a nightmarish picture of women winning over helpless men, who are unable to fight back against the seductive qualities and power of women. In the Wife of Bath's prologue, it is the wife who ultimately prevails over the husband. Thus far the pattern is that of the misogynistic diatribes, but in Chaucer the result is far softer, a satisfactory resolution of the conflict between the sexes: Alison wins out over her husband, and they live in bliss forever, just as her embracing of the text of Scripture, her literalist reading, prevails over the "gloses" favored by Jankyn. This is perhaps a "fairy-tale ending" and the fantasy of the male author (as Dinshaw says),[17] but in its optimism, it is a liberating fairy tale that, with the burning of a "wicked book," seeks to break the cynical spell of the misogynistic treatises that regularly close in defeat and despair.

DORIGEN'S LAMENT

In the "Franklin's Tale," we have another instance of a passage of considerable length in which Chaucer reacts to an argument from Jerome's A.J., this time relating to the virginity and marital relationships of pagan (non-Christian) wives.

In arguments that repeat some of the epithets from the scholarly debate about the Wife of Bath's prologue, Dorigen's lament has been accused of reflecting disorganized and hasty writing (Dempster 1937, 22) and has been called a "tragicomic role call" marked by "irrelevance" (Sledd 1947, 43) and an argument that "degenerat[es] into confusion" (Baker 1961, 61) and even "incoherence" (Murtaugh 1971, 489). Even Dorigen's most eloquent defenders, those who see her as the most sympathetic character in the tale, tend to be numbed by the rhetoric of her lament, so that Anne Thompson Lee (1984), for example, says, "The biggest problem with her speech . . . is its utter dreariness" (174).[18] A few defend the relevance of the speech; for example, Morgan (1977), closely studying the analogies with Jerome, claims to find the lament divided into clear patterns.[19] In this part of this chapter, I will argue that, as in the Wife of Bath's prologue, Chaucer's clear and careful distinctions from Jerome's A.J. point to a differentiation from Jerome's position on marriage, again with a favorable glance toward the position of Augustine in contrast with that of Jerome. I also argue that the manner in which Dorigen presents her lament clearly points toward a favorable resolution of her dilemma.

Dorigen's lament in the "Franklin's Tale," just over one hundred lines long (1355–456), comes after Aurelius has succeeded, at least in appearance, in removing all the rocks from the coast of Brittany. Dorigen has promised to give her love to him—thus violating her marriage vow to Averagnus—if he can remove the rocks. Her lament contains a series of approximately twenty-two exempla—some consisting of a single proper name, others several lines long—which she examines as possible precedents for her to decide whether suicide is justifiable as an alternative, either to breaking her word with Aurelius (now that he has fulfilled the condition she set down in return for giving her love to him, of removing the rocks from the coast of Brittany) or to shaming herself by committing adultery with him. She sets forth the seeming hopelessness of her plight in her opening words (1355–58).

> "Allas" quod she "on thee, Fortune, I pleyne,
> That unwar wrapped hast me in thy cheyne,
> Fro which t'escape woot I no socour,
> Save only deeth or elles dishonour."

As so stated, she indeed has no hope, but the exaggeration has a humorous side, since she seems to have already reached her conclusion at the start of her lament rather than using it as an aid to judgment; we, as readers, are thereby invited to study the examples she lists, looking between the lines for a possible way out.

The twenty-two exempla of the lament are all taken from St. Jerome's *Against Jovinian* 1.41–46, the second half of book 1, where Jerome has finished his look at biblical examples and announces,

> I will quickly run through Greek and Roman and Foreign History, and will show that virginity ever took the lead of chastity. (1.41)

The Wife of Bath's prologue draws its Jerome material largely from the first forty chapters of book 1 of *A.J.*, where the issue is biblical exegesis. In the "Franklin's Tale," Chaucer focuses on the pagan exempla of the later chapters, to be consistent with the pre-Christian setting of his tale. As a highly rhetorical passage, the lament gives the lie to the disavowal of rhetorical color made by the Franklin in his prologue (716–27); this inconsistency certainly has an ironic effect, but those who dismiss the lament as a long-winded rhetorical exercise miss its more serious point, which only becomes evident in close comparison with its source. The rhetoric of Dorigen can be said to "correct" the highly artificial rhetoric of Jerome's treatise along with its stern moral system, which is seemingly rigid but also riddled with inconsistency and inappropriate humor. By subtle and unmistakable touches, Dorigen sends Jerome's rhetoric in a different and more humane direction, one that strongly insists on the moral difference between right and wrong in human behavior.

Moreover, whereas Dorigen's lament continues the sharp analysis that Chaucer already gives to the "Jovinian" treatise in the Wife of Bath's prologue, the approach of the analysis here is entirely different. The Wife of Bath mocks and refutes the views of Jerome, though not mentioning him by name until later; she exposes the fanaticism of his extremist, neo-Stoic ascetic views and uses the very Scripture quoted by Jerome to arrive at a commonsense moral compromise that elevates and sees goodness in marriage. In the "Franklin's Tale," the situation is changed, and the examples are now pagan instead of Christian. Dorigen follows Jerome's treatise faithfully in one sense; but by additions and omissions and, above all, by the emotional and moral asides she makes, she softens and transforms the "acid and polemical" chapters in Jerome that are her source—perhaps one might say she "Christianizes" them, by additions of sympathy for the victimized women and disapproval for the actions of their oppressors.[20]

Let us briefly consider how the chapters in question fit into the structure of Jerome's first book. Having considered the biblical evidence at length, though selectively (and frequently resorting to allegory to move beyond the literal meaning), Jerome, at *A.J.* 1.41, turns to Greek, Roman, and other examples as his "ace in the hole," proving that chastity has always been honored even among pagans, as though such a surprising and more difficult argument will clinch his biblical examples. The breadth of the pagan examples, however, creates a new kind of challenge for Jerome. In fact, Jerome's argument in this part of the treatise never entirely escapes confusion and uncertainty, because he is combining several kinds of examples whose lessons cannot easily be reconciled with each other. Thus some women are praised for maintaining their virginity (A.J. 1.41–42), because they resisted all offers by suitors (e.g., Atalanta), because they resisted rape (the daughters of Phidon, borrowed by Dorigen as her first example), or because, while still remaining virgin, they had given their heart to a fiancé who subsequently died (the daughter of Demotion, Dorigen's eighth example, at "Franklin's Tale" 1426–27). It will be obvious that Jerome is including both stories that extol virginity and those that extol fidelity to a single partner. Adding to the complexity is the fact that some of Jerome's virgins killed themselves to avoid violation, while others (the Theban virgin who is Dorigen's example in lines 1432–34) killed themselves as a result of being dishonored by rape.

The section on virginity concludes at the end of A.J. 1.42; the examples are complex, but the general point is clear, that many women who have chosen virginity have resorted to suicide, either when they had been raped or to avoid rape or forced marriage. In chapter 43, Jerome shifts the issue to marital fidelity rather than virginity, when he moves on to list widows whose love for their husbands leads them to take desperate measures when they are pressured to take on a second husband. The bliss and faithfulness of married love, which motivates this group of women to remain faithful to their former spouses, seems to come to Jerome almost as an afterthought, and his use of such examples risks contradicting him at several points: it blunts his attempt to prove the universal desire for virginity over married life, and it is also inconsistent with his barbs, borrowed from the satiric tradition, against female lechery and the natural tendency of wives to be unfaithful (a tone he adopts most prominently in the last three chapters of the book, A.J. 1.47–49, starting with the "Theophrastus" passage). In chapter 43 he considers two North African women, Dido and the wife of Hasdrubal. In chapters 44 and 45 he considers Greek wives, and in chapter 46, Roman wives. Sometimes he lists women who died rather than submit to marriage with a second husband. Dido is supposedly an example of this; in the version of the story followed by Jerome, she does not die for the love of Aeneas, as Virgil and Ovid relate, but kills herself because of the insistence of her suitor Iarbas; Jerome is following Servius or Tertullian here (see Hanna and Lawler 1997, 238–39). Others died after their husband's death rather than face life alone (this category includes Artemesia but also even includes a concubine—namely, the lover of Alcibiades, included by

Chaucer at "Franklin's Tale" 1439–41); and virgins continue to be listed in Jerome's account, mingled in with stories of married women (e.g., Lucretia; see *A.J.* 1.46). (On problems and inconsistencies in Jerome's list, see, further, Morgan 1977, 78.)

Jerome's penchant for anticlimax is evident when, writing on Roman wives, he passes quickly over the suicide of the noble Lucretia (46 init.), only to dwell at greater length on Bilia, the wife of the naval hero Duilus. Bilia was counted virtuous for never remarking on her husband's bad breath "because she thought all men had bad breath." Similarly, the reference to Dido thinking it "better to burn than to marry" illustrates how a cynical sneer can replace serious argument. It is also noteworthy, in remembering the variety and flexibility of the genre into which Jerome's work falls, that immediately after his presentation of the examples so plentifully to be mined by Chaucer's Dorigen, Jerome, at the start of *A.J.* 1.47, makes a semi-serious apology for the length of his list, then, abandoning all pretense of a serious theological argument, lists a satirical passage against women supposedly written by the Greek philosopher Theophrastus (on this passage, see the detailed discussion in Hanna and Lawler 1997, 14–17).

Dorigen's "allas" in the introduction to her lament (quoted earlier) sets the tone for the greater part of the lament (until about line 1437, where the mood changes), but it would be out of place in Jerome's account, which wants to show that virginity (or fidelity to a single partner) always held precedent among women of virtue. In the "Franklin's Tale," the outbursts that intersperse Dorigen's list of married women may seem to us today a natural and spontaneous human reaction, one that bursts from the heart of a good and simple person such as she; but it is important to remember that such sympathy is an innovation by Chaucer that would be out of place in Jerome's account. The moral tone of *A.J.* is extremely narrowly focused. The resolve of the women who would die rather than submit to rape is to be applauded, not deplored. The men who would do the outrage are rarely explicitly condemned by Jerome; indeed, any moral disapproval of their violence and their lust is tempered by a realization that their cruelty had a good result after all, by providing the opportunity to test the honor of these women and demonstrate their bravery. He has no time to feel grief for his female victims amid his applause for their preservation of their "honor." I have argued that the Wife of Bath, in her prologue, chooses to mock and expose the absurdities of Jerome's biblical arguments about marriage. In the case of Dorigen, Chaucer causes her to turn to the examples of the virtuous pagan women, in this instance not so much mocking the examples as transforming them, giving them a lesson and a moral tone sympathetic to the women and disapproving of the violence of the men, human reactions for which one looks in vain in Jerome.

Before Dorigen ever made her rash promise about the removal of rocks from the coast, she had already brooded over those rocks in her prayer ("Franklin's Tale" 865–94), in which she cannot imagine why God would create black rocks on the seacoast to "destroy . . . mankynde" (876). Noteworthy in this prayer is her seemingly reluctant admission that the will of God will make all turn out right (885–87).

> I woot wel clerkes wol seyn as hem leste,
>> By argumentz, that al is for the beste,
> Though I ne kan the causes nat yknowe.

Though she seems to regard the argument that "al is for the beste" as a kind of cliché devised by scholars, without much meaning for her, this aside by Dorigen, like her later comments in the lament, ultimately points to a happy resolution of the dilemmas of the tale, in ways she cannot anticipate. She prays that all the rocks might sink into hell, not for the sake of her own pleasure, but for her absent lord. Her prayer, so guileless and unselfish in its origin and intent, really prefigures and, in fact, contains already within itself, even while the complications of the plot unfold, a happy ending. Aurelius will hire a magician to cause the rocks to disappear. This fulfills Dorigen's heartfelt wish, but ironically it puts Dorigen in the position of finding that she has inadvertently forfeited either her honor or her chastity. By using the inexorable logic she finds in Jerome, Dorigen finds herself on the horns of a dilemma, forced to accept Jerome's choice between loss of chastity and loss of life. No matter which of these she chooses, it will be "agayns the proces of nature," as Dorigen remarks in line 1345 in reference to the removal of the rocks. She will be so torn until Aurelius, a second time performing the impossible, reveals to her a third alternative. But her earlier prayer had already suggested the same, by establishing her as a person of pity and compassion who cannot abide the senseless destruction of other human beings.

Dorigen's first example taken from Jerome (1368–78, A.J. 1.41) is the story in which the Thirty Tyrants of Athens murdered Phidon and made his daughters strip and dance lewdly in their father's blood. Jerome makes the women sound like Stoic or Christian martyrs; they do not even show any emotion but, when faced with this outrage, "hide their grief" [dissimulato dolore] and jump into a well in order to preserve their virginity (for a Stoic parallel, see Seneca *Troades* 1151–52, of Polyxena; for a Christian one, see Bede *Ecclesiastical History* 1.7, of St. Alban). In Chaucer's version, the whole emphasis is on the wickedness of the tyrants. Dorigen says that they are "ful of cursednesse" ("Franklin's Tale" 1368), damns their sadistic demand by calling it a "foul delit" (1372), and even includes an imprecation against them ("God yeve hem meschaunce!" 1374) Finally, instead of implying praise, as Jerome does, for the maidens' refusal to show any emotion (a detail that Jerome stresses again in the case of the deflowered Theban maiden at the end of A.J. 1.41; cf. Chaucer "Franklin's Tale" 1434–36), Dorigen calls them "woful maydens, ful of drede," not only ascribing human feelings to them but firmly establishing the emotional tone of the story—grief for the suffering maidens, contempt for their barbarous torturers (see Morgan 1977, 85).

Even in the shorter examples, Dorigen so tilts the emotional emphasis. In the next story, on the men of Messene who attempt to rape fifty Lacedaemonian maidens, Chaucer stretches Jerome's bare verb *violare* (A.J. 1.41; Migne *PL* 23.284A) into an entire line dripping with contempt, "On whiche they wolden doo hir lecherye" ("Franklin's Tale" 1381). And in the case of Dorigen's fourth example (1399–1404), she turns to Jerome's list of married women (A.J. 1.43) to consider the wife of Hasdrubal. Jerome's slant on the story is that "Carthage was built by a woman of virtue" (Dido!) and that "its end was a tribute to the excellence of the virtue." Jerome reports that Hasdrubal's wife leapt, with her children, into the burning ruins of her house at Carthage, after she saw that she could not escape capture by the Romans. Chaucer takes away the praise of the "virtue" of Hasdrubal's wife and adds a reference ("Franklin's Tale" 1403–4) to the wickedness of the Romans who wanted to outrage her (Jerome merely states that she was afraid of "capture" by the Romans).

> . . . and chees rather to dye
> Than any Romayn dide hire vileynye.

The fifth example on Dorigen's list is Lucretia, whose story is told at much greater length in Chaucer's *Legend of Good Women* (where the sources are Livy and Ovid's *Fasti*). In the "Franklin's Tale" reference, however, Chaucer continues to play off Jerome, jumping ahead to A.J. 1.46 to take the reference from Jerome's list of Roman women.

> I may pass on to Roman women; and the first that I shall mention is Lucretia, who would not survive her violated chastity but blotted out the stain on her person with her own blood.

Typical of Jerome's tone, this statement makes Lucretia's suicide sound justifiable and wise: by killing herself, she atoned for her shame. There is no mention of the guilt of her rapist. But Chaucer alters this by reminding the reader that a crime had been committed against her "whan that she oppressed was / Of Tarquyn" ("Franklin's Tale" 1406–7), and he qualifies the suicide by transferring the rationale for it to Lucretia's own mind (1407–8).

> Did not Lucretia slay herself
> For hire thoughte it was a shame
> To lyven when she hadde lost hir name?

The reminder "hire thoughte" makes all the difference, casting doubt on the validity of her suicide.

The justification of Lucretia was already a point of controversy between Jerome and Augustine. Her suicide becomes a central point in Augustine's discussion of the episode in book 1 of *City of God*, where Augustine strongly argues against Christian suicide in the case of a victim such as Lucretia, whose body, he argues, cannot be said to have truly been violated in a sense that involves any sin on her part, since she did not give her consent. Even if Lucretia had sinned willingly with Tarquinius, Augustine argues, "she ought still to have held her hand from suicide, if she could with her false gods have accomplished a fruitful repentance" (*City of God* 1.25). Augustine in fact uses the suicide of Lucretia as a cornerstone in his argument of the sinfulness of suicide and the need for Christians to seek a higher morality, though he is willing to turn to pagan, preChristian material if it will support his point, as when he quotes Virgil *Aeneid* 6.434 for its apparent implication that those who, though guiltless, have killed themselves will spend an eternity lamenting the rashness of their deed (*City of God* 1.24).

In lines 1395ff. of the "Franklin's Tale," Dorigen turns from the examples of virgins to those of wives who would rather kill themselves than submit to men's lust.

> Now sith that maydens hadden swich despit
> To been defouled with mannes foul delit,
> Wel oghte a wyf rather hirselven slee
> Than be defouled, as it thynketh me.

"Defouled . . . foul delit . . . defouled"—this emphasis on the nature of the outrage that men wished to do to the wives totally changes the emphasis from Jerome's, at the start of *A.J.* 1.43.

> I will proceed to married women who were reluctant to survive the decease or violent death of their husbands for fear they might be forced

into a second marriage, and who entertained a marvelous affection for the only husbands they had. This may teach us that second marriage was repudiated among the heathen.

It is "defoulment," not loss of virginity or second marriage, that occupies the mind of Dorigen, and thus, in the first part of her lament, covering at least the first ten examples ("Franklin's Tale" 1367–434), she changes not only the emotional response but, in the case of some of Jerome's examples, even the nature of the evidence. Although she professed in lines 1395ff. (quoted earlier) to move on from virgins to start considering married women, in lines 1426–37, where she gives her eighth through eleventh examples, she actually returns to Jerome's list of virgins from his chapter 41. The category that Dorigen is trying to maintain in this part of the lament is not centered on whether her women were virgins or married: rather, the central ingredient is whether they committed suicide either to avoid or in consequence of rape ("defoulment").

In lines 1419–27 Dorigen uses the already overworked word *defouled* three times to describe the alternative to committing suicide, including the following instance, her eighth (1426–27).

> As dide Demociones doghter deere
> By cause that she wolde nat defouled be.

But it would appear that Dorigen has added the attempted rape to try to make her examples consistent, since in Jerome's version (A.J. 1.41), there is no question of Demotion's daughter being "defouled"; rather, the point is that her betrothed Leostenes has been killed in war, and she can think of no other man as husband after him.

Dorigen's next example, her ninth ("Franklin's Tale" 1428–30), relates to the daughters of Cedasus ("Scedasus" in Jerome), of whom Jerome asks, "How shall we sufficiently praise the daughters of Scedasus at Leutra in Boetia?" (A.J. 1.41). These maidens, raped by two young men whom they had entertained, killed one another because they did not wish to survive the loss of their virginity. Jerome applauds their murder-suicide; Dorigen, little interested in the details of the crime and far from applauding their deed, deplores the young women's deaths.

> O Cedasus, it is ful greet pitee
> To reden how thy doghtren deyde, allas,
> That slowe hemself for swich manere cas.

Dorigen's tenth example is the Theban maiden who killed herself when she was desired by Nicanor after the capture of the town: Jerome, in this instance, highlights the grief that Nicanor felt at her death, but he still leaves the impression of his own admiration that the Theban woman prized chastity so highly. Dorigen extends this emotion to universalize the pathos of the maiden's death: "As greet a pitee was it, or wel moore . . ." ("Franklin's Tale" 1431). So begins Dorigen's eleventh example, the case of "another Theban mayden" who committed suicide after being defloured by a Macedonian. In Jerome, this woman "hides her grief" and kills her oppressor as well (A.J. 1.41); Dorigen omits the latter fact, thereby stressing the woman's status as victim.

Almost all of Dorigen's eleven examples so far have followed a clear pattern: each of them describes maidens, concubines, or wives who died rather than be "defouled" by men, and she repeats various versions of the sentiment "Why sholde I thanne to dye been in drede?" ("Franklin's Tale" 1386). Eleven examples have been gleaned from Jerome in sixty-nine lines, in most cases with a change from Jerome's emphasis. He praises the women's example; Dorigen grieves for them. He leaves neutral the rape or violent action of their captors; Dorigen speaks of the men with a mixture of anger and contempt, in one instance (her eighth example, on Demotion's daughter) even exaggerating the facts by deploring a "defoulment" that is not to be found in Jerome. By deploring the suicides and stressing the sinfulness on the part of the men who drove them to it, Dorigen has completely shifted the moral impact that had been implied in A.J., transforming it by her compassion and *gentilesse*.

Dorigen's final eleven examples occupy a total of only twenty lines (1437–56), less than a third of the space given to the first eleven. None of these eleven examples are taken from Jerome's chapter 41, where virgins are under consideration; rather, they come from chapters 43–45, where the majority of the examples are married women. In such a condensed space of twenty lines, there will be a much restricted opportunity to develop any story or make any moral point. Moreover, clearly these last eleven stories have been chosen by Chaucer for a different purpose. These are no longer women who died to avoid rape or in consequence of rape; instead, Chaucer has searched through Jerome's examples in chapters 43–45 to find instances of wives outstanding for their love of their husbands. As a result, there is no further "allas" or deploring of the "foul" deeds of men who drove women to suicide; instead of the note of lamentation, we find praise for women whose love for their partners was outstanding. Chaucer transforms the tone of Jerome to make Dorigen consistently sympathetic with the suffering women of the examples and contemptuous of the violent men.

The wife of Nicerates marks the transition passage ("Franklin's Tale" 1389–90).

> What shal I seye of Nicerates wyf,
> That for swich cas birafte hirself hir lyf?

Although Nicerates' wife was a suicide and, as such, strictly speaking, belongs with the preceding examples, to Dorigen's mind the Greek woman's love for her husband suggests a change of topic, which introduces the entire concluding section of her lament (1439–44).

> How trewe eek was to Alcebiades
> His love, that rather for to dyen chees
> Than for to suffre his body unburyed be.
> Lo, which a wyf was Alceste," quod she,
> What seith Omer of goode Penalopee?
> Al Grece knoweth of hire chastitee.

At last, here is the praise of women for which we may have looked in vain during the bulk of Dorigen's lament: she would not praise women who chose suicide but reserves praise for wives who were faithful to their husbands; there is emphasis only on their devotion (of which Penelope is the most famous example), not their sacrifice. Some of the women in this final list, such as Laodamia and Portia, killed themselves rather than live without their husbands, but this only serves to verify the depth of their love; Alcestis, indeed, is the supreme example of a wife's obedience, since she obeyed his request to die for her and was rewarded, as a result, with a return to life. The inclusion on the list of Bilia—the wife whose nobility consisted in never telling her husband he had bad breath—may include an implied sneer (a kind of aside for the cognoscenti) at the absurdity of some of the examples on Jerome's list; but mockery of Jerome is not a central focus for Chaucer in the "Franklin's Tale," which prefers to correct the emphasis of A.J. while drawing from it freely as a source and to tilt the emotional impact away from the approval of suicide that is implicit in the original.

Thus the lament of Dorigen divides roughly into two sets of examples: women whose tragic suicide is to be deplored, because it resulted from the cruelty of their male oppressors; and women whose love for their husbands, even to the point of death, is to be admired. In dividing the material this way, with categories quite different from Jerome's, she has picked and chosen her examples from various parts of the chapters in A.J. that deal with pagan women. Even as Dorigen repeatedly asks variations on the question "Why sholde I thanne to dye been in drede?" her own account of the deaths of nearly a dozen pagan women leaves a clear indication of her horror at their suicides, which were a consequence not of their own heroism but of the shame forced on them by the barbarous cruelty of their male oppressors. It could be said that Dorigen's head gives her one answer but her heart another. While it may technically be true that "the Church's ban on suicide cannot be relevant to Dorigen"[21] in any overt sense, Dorigen follows the lead of the Wife of Bath, who, in her prologue, tilts her moral frame of reference toward the moderation of Augustine. The latter is highly sympathetic to Lucretia, who "killed herself for being subjected to an outrage in which she had no guilty part" (City of God 1.19), yet he also argues with great emphasis (perhaps in response to Jerome; see Hanna and Lawler 1997, 242) that suicide, even in the case of loss of chastity, merely compounds one crime with another and is "a detestable and damnable wickedness" (City of God 1.25). This opinion of Augustine's was certainly known by Chaucer, who actually mentions Augustine's "gret compassioun" for Lucretia in The Legend of Good Women (5.1690–91). In that version of the story, Lucretia's friends, after she has confessed to them that Tarquin raped her, follow Augustine in urging her not to take any action to atone for the rape, which was not her fault (LGW 5.1848–949).

That they forgave yt hir, for yt was ryght,
It was no gilt, it lay not in hir myght.

In short, Dorigen's examples affirm marriage and the true heroism and nobility of women who remained true to their husbands. No such emphasis is to be found in Jerome, where virginity emphatically takes the preferred position and where the moral goodness of marriage is by no means a given.

Chaucer's use of A.J. in the "Franklin's Tale" is an improbable, but ultimately inspired, choice. There is some unmatched leg-pulling in including extensive citations from Jerome's anti-marriage treatise in a tale that many, following Kittredge, regard as Chaucer's "resolution of the marriage debate" (Benson 1987, 895). Dorigen's natural and human reaction to Jerome's "chamber of horrors" gives a foretaste of the gentle denouement of Chaucer's tale. That reaction also implies Dorigen's righteous horror at the prospect of being forced, similar to the women in her lament, to give in to the sexual request of Aurelius. In short, Dorigen's lament reveals her struggling toward a resolution to her dilemma that will keep her from suicide and preserve both her "trothe" and fidelity to her husband.

Notes

Versions of this chapter appeared in the *Chaucer Review* 36 (2002): 374–90 and 32 (1997): 129–45. Copyright 2002 © University of Pennsylvania Press.

I wish to thank Professors Diana Robin, Patrick Gallacher, and Susanna Morton Braund and my wife, Anne Marie Werner, whose comments greatly assisted me in writing this chapter.

1. "Agitated and incoherent": Wurtele 1983; "Straightforward, hard-hitting": Pratt 1962, 8.

2. The text of *Adversus Iovinianum* follows Migne *PL* 23.222–351; the translations are quoted from Freemantle [1892] 1980. The text of Chaucer follows Benson 1987. On *Adversus Iovinianum*, see Wiesen 1964, 159–60; Brooke, 1989, 61–63 (the quotation "only a hair's breadth . . ." is from p. 62). On contemporary reaction to the work, see J. N. D. Kelly 1975, 188; see now also the text and study in Hanna and Lawler 1997. On Augustine's reply, see Chadwick 1986, 114.

3. The first quote is from Helen Cooper (1989, 144); the second is from Graham D. Caie (1976, 351), who adds, "She is 'deaf' to the spiritual significance of the Pauline teaching on marriage which Jerome elucidates, prefers to follow the Old Law literally, and attempts to discredit the writing of Paul and Jerome as antifeminist and anti-marital, in order to justify her lechery." D. W. Robertson Jr. (1983, 324) says the Wife of Bath distorts Paul or quotes him out of context; cf. Bishop 1987, 123. More balanced are Donaldson 1977, 1–16; Aers 1980, 83–88 (also see n. 4 in the present chapter).

4. "Literal text": Dinshaw 1989, 120; Besserman 1984, 65–73; cf. Root 1994, esp. 256–59. Donaldson (1977) while defending the Wife of Bath's good sense, still speaks misleadingly of her "rebuttal of St. Paul." The orthodoxy of the Wife of Bath's thought on marriage is defended by Howard (1976, 248–55); see, further, Carruthers 1979, 209–22; H. Kelly 1975, esp. chap. 10, "The Too Ardent Lover of His Wife Classified."

5. On Jovinian, see, further, *De haer.* 1.82 (Migne *PL* 42.45–46); *Contra Iul. Pel.* 1–2 (Migne *PL* 44.643); Delhaye 1951, 66 and n. 1; J. N. D. Kelly 1975, 181–82. The Stoic idea that "all sins are equal" is presented by Cicero in *Paradoxa Stoicorum*, proposition 3.

6. On the sailing metaphor in Juvenal see Kenney 1962, 29–40.

7. Cicero *De amicitia* 5, trans. Falconer in *LCL*. For the argument that the Wife of Bath sporadically adopts the point of view of an omniscient male speaker, see Breuer 1992, 418–27; for a parallel in Juvenal, see S. H. Braund 1995, 207–19.

8. *Cum Samaritanae maritum negat, ut adulterum ostendat numerosum maritum . . .* [When he denies the Samaritan woman a husband to show that a numbered husband is an adulterer . . .] (Tertullian in Migne *PL* 2.940B). On Tertullian and Montanism and on Jerome's use of him, see J. N. D. Kelly 1975, 95–97; Wiesen 1964, 14.

9. In contrast with the struggles of Tertullian and Jerome to understand the passage, Augustine (*Tractatus in Joannis Evangelium* 15.20 [Migne *PL* 35.1517–18]) instantly gets the point: "you must understand that the woman at that time had no husband, but lived with [reading *utebatur*] some sort of illegitimate husband—an adulterer, not a husband." One of the few Chaucerians who calls attention to Jerome's mistake is Donaldson (1977,

6), who adds, in reference to Jerome's frequent distortions, "What interests me is that modern scholars have let him get away with it." However, Donaldson thinks the Wife of Bath's knowledge of the Bible was too "spotty" for her to catch Jerome's mistake. On the Wife of Bath's story from Ovid, see Patterson 1983, 656–57.

10. See J. N. D. Kelly 1975, 183.

11. "The Wife reduces the contrast to a question of domestic economy" (H. Cooper 1989, 145). D. W. Robertson Jr. (1953, 327) is ready to align the Wife of Bath among the "evil," according to his reading of the *Glossa* in Migne *PL* 114.635. Robertson claims that Jerome "does not actually identify the married with wooden vessels." Yet it is clear that Jerome does so identify the symbol of the "vessels," implicitly in *Adversus Iovinianum*, then explicitly in *Ep.* 48.2 and 123.9, where he explicates that work.

12. See, further, Bishop 1987, esp. 33 (on Chaucer and Cicero), 120–24 (on the Wife of Bath's prologue). On lines 107–12 of the prologue, see Aers 1980, 86–88. Aers points out that the Wife of Bath's position on property ownership is consistent with position of Pope John XXII, who advocated the possession of earthly rights and lordship over their renunciation.

13. Donaldson 1977, 5. Wood (1984, 37–38) says the Wife of Bath, like the devil, quotes Scripture for her own purpose. See, further, Makowski 1990, 129–43.

14. See Makowski 1990, 137.

15. See Pratt 1963, 319.

16. See, further, Murstein 1974, 88–91; Brooke 1989, 54–56.

17. Dinshaw 1989, 120. See also Patterson 1983, 660.

18. Similarly, Spearing (1985, 184–85) notes, "the longer she goes on, the more remote the exemplary cases become from her own. . . ."

19. Jerome is quoted from Freemantle [1892], 1980. The text, translation, and interpretative notes of selections from *Adversus Iovinianum* can now be found in Hanna and Lawler 1997, 158–93, 231–58. On the Breton lay, see Donovan 1969, 186–87.

20. "Acid, polemical": Wiesen 1964, 51. On the pagan setting for the "Franklin's Tale," see, further, Larson 1996, 144–45. For Dorigen as "inquiring Christian," see Wright 1998 (quote from p. 181); Hume 1972, esp. 371.

21. H. Cooper 1989, 239.

Bibliography

Adamietz, J. 1987. Zum literarischen Charakter von Petrons *Satyrica*. *RhM* 120:329–46.

———. 1995. Circe in den *Satyrica* Petrons und das Wesen dieses Werkes. *Hermes* 123:320–34.

Adkin, N. 1992. "Istae sunt, quae solent dicere": Three Roman Vignettes in Jerome's "Libellus de Virginitate Servanda" (*Epist.* 22). *Museum Helveticum* 49:131–40.

———. 1994. Juvenal and Jerome. *Classical Philology* 89: 69–72.

Aers, David. 1980. *Chaucer, Langland, and the Creative Imagination*. London.

Albrecht, M. 1994. *Geschichte der röm. Literatur*. Munich.

Allen, P. 1985. *The Concept of Woman: The Aristotelian Revolution, 750 B.C.–A.D. 1250*. Montreal.

Anderson, W. S. 1982. *Essays on Roman Satire*. Princeton.

Archer, L., S. Fischler, and M. Wyke, M. 1994. *Women in Ancient Societies: An Illusion of the Night*. London and New York.

Arthur, M. B. 1984. Early Greece: The Origins of the Western Attitude toward Women. In *Women in the Ancient World: The Arethusa Papers*, ed. J. Peradotto and J. P. Sullivan, 7–58. New York.

Baker, Donald C. 1961. A Crux in Chaucer's "Franklin's Tale": Dorigen's Lament. *Journal of English and German Philology* 60:57–64.

Bakhtin, M. M. 1981. *The Dialogic Imagination: Four Essays*. Ed. M. Holquist, trans. C. Emerson and M. Holquist. Austin.

Barchiesi, Alessandro. [1988] 1997. Ovid the Censor. *AJAH* 13:96–105.

Barnes, T. D. 1971. *Tertullian: A Historical and Literary Study*. Oxford.

Barrett, W. S. [1964] 1992. *Euripides' "Hippolytus."* Oxford.

Barsby, John. 1999. Love in Terence. In *Amor: Roma; Love and Latin Literature*, ed. S. M. Braund and R. Mayer, 5–29. Cambridge.

Barwick, K. 1959. *Martial und die zeitgenossische Rhetorik*. Berlin.

Bastiaensen, M., ed. 1997. *La femme lettrée à la Renaissance*. Brussels.

Bate, K. 1983. Ovid, Medieval Latin, and the Pastourelle. *Reading Medieval Studies* 9:26–33.

Bauman, Richard A. 1992. *Women and Politics in Ancient Rome*. London.

Beard, M. 1980. The Sexual Status of Vestal Virgins. *JRS* 70:12–27.

Beare, W. 1950. *The Roman Stage*. London.

Bechtle, G. 1995. The Adultery-Tales in the Ninth Book of Apuleius' *Metamorphoses*. *Hermes* 123:106–16.

Beck, R. 1979. Eumolpus *Poeta*, Eumolpus *Fabulator*: A Study of Characterization in the *Satyricon*. *Phoenix* 33:239–53.

Benoit, A. 1961. *L'actualité des Pères de l'Église*. Neuchâtel.

Benson, Larry D., ed. 1987. *The Riverside Chaucer*. 3d ed. Boston.

Besserman, Lawrence. 1984. Glosynge Is a Glorious Thyng: Chaucer's Biblical Exegesis. In *Chaucer and the Scriptural Tradition*, ed. David Jeffrey, 65–73, Ottawa.

Bettini, Maurizio. 1991. Verso un'antropologia dell'intreccio: Le strutture semplici della trama nelle commedie di Plauto. In *Verso un'antropologia dell'intreccio e altri studi su Plauto*, 11–76. Urbino. First published in *MD* 7 (1982): 39–101.

Bickel, E. 1915. *Diatribe in Senecae philosophi fragmenta*. Vol. 1, *De Matrimonio*. Leipzig.

Bieber, Margarete. 1961. *The History of the Greek and Roman Theater*. 2d ed. Princeton.

Bigelmair, A. 1902. *Die Beteiligung der Christen am öffenlichen Leben in vorkonstantinischer Zeit*. Munich.

Bishop, Ian. 1987. *The Narrative Art of the "Canterbury Tales."* London.

Blamires, Alcuin. 1997. *The Case for Women in Medieval Culture*. Oxford.

Blamires, Alcuin, ed., with K. Pratt and C. W. Marx. 1992. *Women Defamed and Woman Defended: An Anthology of Medieval Texts*. Oxford.

Bloch, R. Howard. 1991. *Medieval Misogyny and the Invention of Western Romantic Love*. Chicago.

Blumstein, Andree Kahn. 1977. *Misogyny and Idealization in the Courtly Romance*. Bonn.

Boase, R. 1977. *The Origin and Meaning of Courtly Love*. Manchester.

Boberg, B. 1999. Schoenheitsideale. Ovids Frauen- und Männerbild in der Ars Amatoria; Eine handlungsorientierte UE für die Oberstufe. *AU* 42:18–23.

Bock, F. 1898. *Aristoteles Theophrastus Seneca de Matrimonio*. PhD. diss. University of Leipzig.

Bonner, S. F. 1949. *Roman Declamation in the Late Republic and Early Empire*. Liverpool.

———. 1977. *Education in Ancient Rome*. London.

Bourdieu, P. [1979] 1984. *Distinction: A Social Critique of the Judgement of Taste*. Trans. R. Nice. Cambridge.

Bowie, E. L. 1977. The Novels and the Real World. In *Erotica Antica: Acta of the International Conference on the Ancient Novel*, ed. B. P. Reardon, 91–96. Bangor, Wales.

Bowie, E. L., and S. J. Harrison. 1993. The Romance of the Novel. *JRS* 83:59–178.

Brandt, P. [1902] 1991. *P. Ovidi Nasonis De Arte Amatoria*. Leipzig. Reprint, Hildesheim.

Braun, R. 1966. Le problème des deux livres du De Cultu Faminarum de Tertullien. *Studia Patristica* 7:128–37. (= *Texte und Untersuchungen* 92).

Braund, S. H. 1995. A Woman's Voice—Laronia's Role in Juvenal *Satire* 2. In Hawley and Levick 1995, 207–19.

———, ed. 1989. *Satire and Society in Ancient Rome*. Exeter.

Braund, Susanna Morton. 1988. *Beyond Anger: A Study of Juvenal's Third Book of Satires*. Cambridge.

————. 1992. Juvenal: Misogynist or Misogamist? *JRS* 82:71–86.

————. 1996. *The Roman Satirists and Their Masks*. London.

Breuer, Horst. 1992. Narrative Voices in Chaucer's Wife of Bath's Prologue. In *Anglistentag 1991 Düsseldorf*, 418–27. Tübingen.

Brewer, J. S. [1861] 1964–66. *Giraldi Cambiensis Opera*. Vol. 1. London.

Bright, D. 1971. The Plague and the Structure of the De Rum Natura. *Latomus* 30: 607–32.

Brochet, J. 1905. *Saint Jérôme et ses ennemis*. Paris.

Brooke, Christopher. 1989. *The Medieval Idea of Marriage*. Oxford.

Brown, Peter. 1967. *Augustine of Hippo*. Berkeley.

————. 1988. *The Body and Society: Men, Women, and Sexual Renunciation in Early Christianity*. New York.

————, ed. 1993. *Horace: "Satires" I, with an Introduction, Text, Translation, and Commentary*. Warminster, Eng.

Brown, Robert D. 1987. *Lucretius on Love and Sex: A Commentary on "De Rerum Natura" IV, 1030–1287 with Prolegomena, Text, and Translation*. Leiden.

Buddenhagen, F. 1919. Peri Gamou: Antiquorum Poetarum Philosophorumque Graecorum de Matrimonio Sententiae. . . . Ph.D. diss., University of Basel.

Buecheler, F., ed. 1895. *Petronii Saturae et Liber Priapeorum*. Berlin.

————. [1895] 1962. *D. Junii Juvenalis Saturarum Libri V*. Leipzig. Reprint, Amsterdam.

Bugge, J. 1975. *Virginitas*. The Hague.

Bultmann, R. 1955. *The Theology of the New Testament*. Trans. K. Grobel. New York.

Burchill, Julie. 1999. *Married Alive*. London.

Caie, Graham D. 1976. The Significance of the Early Chaucer Manuscript Glosses (with Special Reference to the *Wife of Bath's Prologue*). *Chaucer Review* 10:350–60.

Cameron, A. D. E. 1964. Literary Allusions in the *Historia Augusta*. *Hermes* 92:363–77.

Capelle, E., and H. I. Marrou. 1957. Diatribe. *RAC* 3:990–1009.

Carr, J. E. 1982. The View of Women in Juvenal and Apuleius. *Classical Bulletin* 58:61–64.

Carruthers, Mary. 1979. The Wife of Bath and the Painting of Lions. *PMLA* 94:209–22.

Cartlidge, Neil. 1997. *Medieval Marriage: Literary Approaches 1100–1300*. Cambridge and Rochester.

Carver, R. H. F. 2000. "Old-Wives' Tales" and "Eloquent Narrations": Humanist Encounters with the Ancient Novels and Romances. In *ICAN 2000: The Ancient Novel in Context: Abstracts of the Papers to Be Read at the Third International Conference on the Ancient Novel to Be Held at the University of Groningen, the Netherlands*, ed. M. Zimmerman, S. Panayotakis, and W. Keulen, 14–15. Groningen.

Cassell, Anthony, trans. and ed. 1975. *The Corbaccio/Giovanni Boccaccio*. Urbana, Ill.

Centrone, B., ed. 1990. *Pseudopythagorica Ethica: I trattati morali de Archita, Metopo, Teage, Eurifamo*. Naples.

Chadwick, Henry. 1986. *Augustine*. Oxford.

Charlton, H. B. 1938. *Shakespearian Comedy*. London.

Clark, Elizabeth A. 1979a. Friendship between the Sexes: Classical Theory and Christian Practice. In Clark 1979b, 35–106.

————. 1979b. *Jerome, Chrysostom, and Friends: Essays and Translations*. New York.

————. 1991. Adam's Only Companion: Augustine and the Early Christian Debate on Marriage. In Edwards and Spector 1991, 15–31.

————. 1999. *Reading Renunciation: Asceticism and Scripture in Early Christianity*. Princeton.

Coccia, M. 1989. *Multa in muliebrem levitatem coepit iactare* . . . : Le figure femminili del Satyricon di Petronio. In Uglione 1989, 121–40.

Coffey, Michael. [1976] 1989. *Roman Satire*. 2d ed. Bristol.

Cohen, Jeremy. 1989. *Be Fertile and Increase; Fill the Earth and Master It: The Ancient and Medieval Career of a Biblical Text*. Ithaca.

Commager, H. S. 1957. Lucretius' Interpretation of the Plague. *HSCP* 62:105–18.

Conte, G. B. 1996. *The Hidden Author: An Interpretation of Petronius' "Satyricon."* Berkeley.

Cooper, Helen. 1989. *Oxford Guides to Chaucer: "Canterbury Tales."* Oxford.

Cooper, K. 1996. *The Virgin and the Bride: Idealized Womanhood in Late Antiquity*. Cambridge, Mass., and London.

Corbier, Mireille. Divorce and Adoption as Roman Familial Strategies (Le divorce et l'adopton "en plus"). In Rawson 1991, 47–78.

Cornish, C. L., trans. 1994. Augustine's *De Bono Conjugali*. In Schaff 1994.

Costa, C. D. N. 1965. The Amphitryo Theme. In *Roman Drama*, ed. T. A. Dorey and D. R. Dudley, 87–122. New York.

Courcelle, P. 1948. *Les lettres grecques en occident de Marcobe à Cassiodore*. Paris.

Courtney, E. 1962. Parody and Literary Allusion in Menippean Satire. *Philologus* 106:86–100.

———. 1980. *A Commentary on the Satires of Juvenal*. London.

Crow, J., ed. 1969. *Les quinze joyes de mariage*. Oxford.

Csillag, P. 1976. *The Augustan Laws on Family Relations*. Budapest.

Curtius, E. 1965. *Europaeische Literatur und Lateinisches Mittelalter*. 5th ed. Bern and Munich.

Dalzell, A. 1996. *The Criticism of Didactic Poetry: Essays on Lucretius, Virgil, and Ovid*. Toronto.

Dawson, Christopher. 1967. *The Formation of Christianity*. New York.

De Decker, Josue. 1913. *Juvenalis Declamans: Étude sur la Rhétorique Declamatoire dans les Satires de Juvenal*. Ghent.

Del Corno, D. 1989. Anzia e le Compagne, Ossia le Eroine del Romanzo Greco. In Uglione 1989, 73–84.

Delhaye, P. 1951. Le Dossier Anti-Matrimonial de l'Adversus Jovinianum et Son Influence sur Quelques Écrits Latins du XIIe Siècle. *Medieval Studies* 13:65–86.

Dempster, Germaine. 1937. Chaucer at Work on the Complaint in the "Franklin's Tale." *Modern Language Notes* 52:16–23.

Diehl, E. 1922–25. *Anthologia Lyrica Graeca*. Leipzig.

Dillon, J. 1994. A Platonist Ars Amatoria. *CQ* 44:387–92.

Dinshaw, Carolyn. 1989. *Chaucer's Sexual Politics*. Madison, Wisc.

Dixon, S. 1991. The Sentimental Ideal of the Roman Family. In Rawson 1991, 99–113.

Donaldson, E. T. 1977. Designing a Camel; or, Generalizing the Middle Ages. *Tennessee Studies in Literature* 22:1–16.

Donovan, Mortimer J. 1969. *The Breton Lay: A Guide to Varieties*. Notre Dame.

Döpp, S. 1992. *Werke Ovids: Eine Einführung*. Munich.

Douglas, Mary. 1966. *Purity and Danger: An Analysis of the Concepts of Pollution and Taboo*. London.

Downing, E. 1999. Anti-Pygmalion: The Preceptor in Ars Amatoria 3. In *Constructions of the Classical Body*, ed. J. Porter, 235–51. Ann Arbor.

Dronke, Peter. 1968. *Medieval Latin and the Rise of the European Love-Lyric*. Vol. 2, *Medieval Latin Love-Poetry*. Oxford.

————. 1976. *Abelard and Heloise in Medieval Testimonies*. Glasgow.

Duckworth, George E. 1952. *The Nature of Roman Comedy*. Princeton.

Dudley, D. R., ed. 1965. *Lucretius*. London.

Duff, J. W. 1936. *Roman Satire: Its Outlook on Social Life*. Berkeley.

Duval, Y. M. 1980. Pélage est-il le censeur inconnu de l'Adversus Iovinianum à Rome en 393? Ou: Du "Portrait-robot" de l'hérétique chez S. Jérôme. *Revue d'Histoire Ecclésiastique* 75:525–57.

————, ed. 1988. *Jérôme entre l'Occident et l'Orient*. Paris.

Eck, w.1971. Das Eindringen des Christentums in den Senatorenstand bis zu Konstantin dem Großen. *Chiron* 1:388–95.

Edwards, Catharine. 1993. *The Politics of Immorality in Ancient Rome*. London.

Edwards, R., and S. Spector, eds. 1991. *"The Olde Daunce": Love, Friendship, Sex, and Marriage in the Medieval World*. Albany.

Egger, B. 1988. Zu den Frauenrollen im griechischen Roman: Die Frau als Heldin und Leserin. *GCN* 1:33–66.

————. 1994. Women and Marriage in the Greek Novels: The Boundaries of Romance. In *The Search for the Ancient Novel*, ed. J. H. Tatum, 260–80. Baltimore.

Ehrman, Bart. 1998. *The New Testament and Other Early Christian Writings: A Reader*. Oxford.

Eijk, T. H. C. van. 1972. Marriage and Virginity, Death and Immortality. In Fontaine and Kannengiesser 1972, 209–35.

Fantham, E. 1975. Sex, Status, and Survival in Hellenistic Athens: A Study of Women in New Comedy. *Phoenix* 29:44–74.

————, et al. 1994. *Women in the Classical World: Image and Text*. New York.

Farrell, Joseph. 2001. *Latin Language and Latin Culture from Ancient to Modern Times*. Cambridge.

Favez, C. 1946. La Satire dans les Lettres de Saint Jérôme. *Revue des Études Latines* 24:209–26.

Feichtinger, Barbara. 1995. *Apostolae Apostolorum. Frauenaskese als Befreiung und Zwang bei Hieronymus*. Frankfurt and New York.

————. 1997a. Zäsüren, Brüche, Kontinuitäten: Zur aristokratischen Metamorphose des christlichten askeseideals am Beispiel des Hieronymus. *Wiener Studien* 110:187–220.

————. 1997b. Verehrte Schwestern. Antike Frauengestalten als Identifikationsmodelle für gebildete Frauen in der Renaissance. In Bastiaensen 1997, 27–29.

Ferguson, E., D. Scholer, and P. Finney, eds. 1993. *Studies in Early Christianity: A Collection of Scholarly Essays*. New York.

Ferrante, Joan. [1975] 1985. *Woman as Image in Medieval Literature*. New York.

Foerster, Richardus, ed. 1903–27. *Libanii opera*. 12 vols. Leipzig.

Fontaine, J. 1988a. L'esthétique littéraire de la prose de Jérôme jusqua' à son second départ en Orient. In Duval 1988, 323–42.

————. 1988b. Un sobriquet perfide de Damasus: "Matronarum auriscalpius." In *Mélanges Le Bonniec*, 177–92. Brussels.

Fontaine, J., and Ch. Kannengiesser, eds. 1972. *Epektasis*. Paris.

Foucault, Michel. 1986. *The Care of the Self*. Vol. 3 of *The History of Sexuality*. Trans. Robert Hurley. New York.

Fraenkel, E. 1960. *Elementi Plautini in Plauto*. Florence.

Frassinetti, P. 1955. Gli scritti matrimoniali di Seneca e Tertulliano. *Rendiconti: Classe di Lettere e Scienze Morali e Storiche* 88:151–88.

Fredericks, S. C. 1971. Rhetoric and Morality in Juvenal's Eighth Satire. *TAPA* 102:114–32.

Fredershausen, O. 1912. Weitere Studien über das Recht bei Plautus und Terenz. *Hermes* 47:199–249.

Fredouille, J.-C. 1967. *Adversus Marcionem* 1, 29. Deux états de la rédaction du traité. *R.E.* 1–13.

———. 1972. *Tertullien et la conversion de la culture antique*. Paris.

Freemantle, W. H., trans. [1892] 1980. Jerome, *Letters and Select Works*. Vol. 6 of *Nicene and Post-Nicene Fathers*. Edinburgh.

Freudenburg, Kirk. 1993. *The Walking Muse: Horace on the Theory of Satire*. Princeton.

Friedmann, Herbert. 1980. *A Bestiary for St. Jerome: Animal Symbolism in European Religious Art*. Washington, D.C.

Frye, Northrop. 1957. *Anatomy of Criticism: Four Essays*. Princeton.

Funke, H. 1965–66. Univira. Ein beispiel heidnischer Geschichtsapologetik. *Jahrbuch für Antike und Christentum* 8–9:183–88.

Gaiser, Konrad. 1974. Für und Wider die Ehe: Antike Stimmen zu einer Offenen Frage. Munich.

Galinsky, K. 1981. Augustus' Legislation on Morals and Marriage. *Philologus* 125:126–44.

Gardner, Jane F. 1986. *Women in Roman Law and Society*. London.

Ghellinck, H. de. 1954. *L'essor de la littérature latine au XII siècle*. 2d ed. Brussels.

Giebel, M. 1999. Wer denkt an die Wolle? Adressatenvielfalt in Ovids Ars Amatoria. In *Festschrift M. von Albrecht*, ed. W. Schubert, 245–54. Frankfurt am Main.

Gilchrist, J. 1967. *The Church and Economic Activity in the Middle Ages*. New York.

Gilson, E. 1960. *Heloise and Abelard*. Ann Arbor.

Giordani, Igino. 1944. *The Social Message of the Early Church Fathers*. Trans. Alba Zizzamia. Paterson, N.J.

Godwin, John, ed. 1986. *Lucretius: "De Rerum Natura" IV*. Warminster.

Goldhill, S. 1994. *Foucault's Virginity: Ancient Erotic Fiction and the History of Sexuality*. Cambridge.

Goody, J. 1989. *Die Entwicklung von Ehe und der Familie in Europa*. Frankfurt am Main.

Grant, Robert M. [1970] 1990. *Augustus to Constantine: The Thrust of the Christian Movement into the Roman World*. New York.

Gratwick, A. S., ed. 1993. *Plautus: "Menaechmi."* Cambridge.

Griffin, Dustin. 1994. *Satire: A Critical Reintroduction*. Lexington, Ky.

Griffin, J. 1977. Propertius and Anthony. *JRS* 67:17–26. Reprinted in *Latin Poets and Roman Life* (London, 1986), 32–47.

Grilli, A. 1953. *Il problema della vita contemplativa nel mondo greco-romano*. Milan.

Grisebach, E. 1889. *Die Wanderung der Novelle von der treulosen Wittwe durch die Weltliteratur*. 2d ed. Berlin.

Grossgerge, F. 1911. *De Senecae et Theophrasti libris de matrimonio*. Regimonti.

Guthrie, K. S., ed. 1987. *The Pythagorean Sourcebook and Library: An Anthology of Ancient Writings Which Relate to Pythagoras and Pythagorean Philosophy*. Grand Rapids, Mich.

Haase, F. [1898] 1902. *L. Annaei Senecae, opera quae supersunt*. Leipzig.

Hagendahl, H. 1958. *Latin Fathers and the Classics: A Study of the Apologists, Jerome, and Other Christian Writers*. Göteborg.

Haines, C. R., trans. 1969. *Marcus Aurelius*. Cambridge.

Haller, W. 1897. *Iovinianus: Die Fragmente seiner Schriften, die Quellen zu seiner Geschichte, sein Leben und seine Legre*. Leipzig.

Handley, W. E. 1965. *The "Dyskolos" of Menander*. London.

Hanna, Ralph, III, and Traugott Lawler, eds. 1997. *Jankyn's Book of Wikked Wyves*. Vol. 1, *The Primary Texts*. Athens, Ga.

Hansen, G. C. 1963. Molestiae Nuptiarum. *WZ Rostock* 12:215–19.

Hanson, J. Arthur, ed. and trans. 1989. *Metamorphoses/Apuleius*. Cambridge.

Harnack, A. von. 1904. *Die Chronologie der altchristlichen Literatur bis Eusebius*. Leipzig.

———. 1980. Tertullian in der Litteratur der alten Kirche, *Kleine Schriften zur Alten Kirche*. Vol. 1, *Berliner Akademieschriften 1890–1907*. Leipzig.

Harris, Barbara J., and JoAnn McNamara, eds. 1984. *Women and the Structure of Society: Selected Research from the Fifth Berkshire Conference on the History of Women*. Durham, N.H.

Harrison, S. J. 1997. From Epic to Novel: Apuleius' *Metamorphoses* and Vergil's *Aeneid*. *Materiali e Discussioni* 39:54–73.

———. 1998. The Milesian Tales and the Roman Novel. GCN 9:61–73.

———. 2000. *Apuleius: A Latin Sophist*. Oxford.

———, ed. 1999. *Oxford Readings in the Roman Novel*. Oxford.

Hawley, Richard. 1994. The Problem of Women Philosophers in Ancient Greece. In Archer, Fischler, and Wyke 1994, 70–87.

———. 1995. Female Characterization in Greek Declamation. In *Ethics and Rhetoric: Classical Essays for Donald Russell on His Seventy-fifth Birthday*, ed. D. Innes, H. Hine, and C. Pelling, 255–68. Oxford.

———. 1999. Practicing What You Preach: Plutarch's Sources and Treatment. In Pomeroy 1999, 116–27.

Hawley, Richard, and Barbara Levick, eds. 1995. *Women in Antiquity: New Assessments*. London and New York.

Haye, Th. 1997. *Das Lateinische Lehrgedicht im Mittelalter: Analyse eine Gattung*. Leiden.

Heinze, Richard. 1899. Petron und der griechische Roman. *Hermes* 34:494–519.

———. 1962. Tertullians Apologeticum. In *Berichte über die Verhandlungen der Königlich Sächsischen Gesellschaft der Wissenschaften zu Leipzig*. Philolog.-hist. Klasse 62. Leipzig.

Henderson, A. A. R., ed. 1979. *P. Ovidi Nasonis Remedia Amoris*. Edinburgh.

Henderson, J. G. W. 1989. Not "Women in Roman Satire" but "When Satire Writes 'Woman.' " In S. H. Braund 1989, 89–125.

———. 1999. Satire Writes Women: Gendersong. In *Writing Down Rome: Satire, Comedy, and Other Offences in Latin Poetry*, 173–201. Oxford.

Henderson, John. 1997. *Figuring Out Roman Nobility: Juvenal's Eighth Satire*. Exeter.

Herrmann, E. 1980. *Ecclesia in Re Publica: Die Entwicklung der Kirche von pseudostaatlicher zu staatlich inkorporierter Existenz*. Frankfurt.

Hilhorst, T. 1998. Erotic Elements in *The Shepherd of Hermas*. GCN 9:193–204.

Hollis, A. S. 1977. *Ovid: "Ars Amatoria," Book 1*. Oxford.

Holloway, J., et al. 1990. *Equally in God's Image: Women in the Middle Ages*. New York.

Holzberg, N. 1990. Ovids Version der Ehebruchnovelle von Ares und Aphrodite in der Ars Amatoria. *Würzburger Jahrbuecher* 16:137–52.

———. 1997. *Ovid*. Munich.

Horney, K. 1967. *Feminine Psychology*, ed. H. Kelman. London.

Howard, Donald R. 1976. *The Idea of the "Canterbury Tales."* Berkeley.

Huber, G. 1990. *Das Motiv der Witwe von Ephesus in lateinischen Texten der Antike und des Mittelalters*. Tübingen.

Hübner, H. G., ed. [1828–33] 1981. *Diogenes Laertius de vitis, dogmatis, et apophthegmatis clarorum philosophorum libri decem.* 4 vols. New York. Reprint, Leipzig.

Humbert, M. 1972. *Le remariage à Rome: Étude d'histoire juridique et sociale.* Milan.

Hume, Kathryn. 1972. Why Chaucer Calls the "Franklin's Tale" a Breton Lay. *Philological Quarterly* 51:365–79.

Hunter, D. S. 1987. Resistance to the Virginal Ideal in Late Fourth-Century Rome: The Case of Jovinian. *Theological Studies* 48:45–64.

Ireland, S. 1990. *Terence: "Hecyra."* Warminster.

James, M. R., ed. and trans. [1983] 1994. *De Nugis Curialium = Courtiers' Trifles/Walter Map.* Revised by C. Brooke and R. Mynors. Oxford/New York.

Janka, M. 1997. *Ovid, Ars Amatoria Buch 2: Kommentar.* Heidelberg.

Jaspert, B., and R. Mohr, eds. *Traditio, Krisis, Renovatio aus Theologischer Sicht.* Marburg.

Jeffrey, David, ed. 1984. *Chaucer and Scriptural Tradition.* Ottawa.

Johnson, W. R. 2000. *Lucretius and the Modern World.* London.

Jones, A. H. M., J. R. Martindale, and J. Morris. [1971] 1980. *The Prosopography of the Later Roman Empire.* Vol. 1, A.D. 260–395. Cambridge.

Jones, D. 1997. *Enjoinder and Argument in Ovid's "Remedia Amoris."* Stuttgart.

Jones, W. P. 1973. *The Pastourelle.* 2d ed. New York.

Kaibel, George. 1899. *Comicorum Graecorum Fragmenta.* Berlin.

Kaimio, M. 1995. How to Manage in the Male World: The Strategies of the Heroine in Chariton's Novel. *A. Ant. Hung.* 36:119–32.

Kakridis, J. Th. 1962. Zum Weiberjambos des Semonides. *Wiener Humanistische Blätter* 5:3–10.

Kannicht, R. 1969. *Euripides: "Helena," Band 1.* Heidelberg.

Kelly, Henry. 1975. *Love and Marriage in the Age of Chaucer.* Ithaca.

Kelly, J. N. D. 1975. *Jerome: His Life, Writings, and Controversies.* London.

Kenney, E. J. [1961] 1994. *Ovid: "Amores." "Medicamina faciei femineae." "Ars amatoria." "Remedia amoris."* Oxford.

———. 1962. The First Satire of Juvenal. *PCPS* 8:29–40.

———. [1971] 1994. *Lucretius: "De Rerum Natura," Book III.* Cambridge.

———. 1990. Introduction and notes to *Ovid: The Love Poems,* trans. A. D. Melville. Oxford.

Kenney, E. J., and W. V. Clausen. 1982. *The Cambridge History of Classical Literature.* Vol. 2, *Latin Literature.* Cambridge.

Kerényi, K. [1927] 1964. *Die griechisch-orientalische Romanliteratur in religionsgeschichtlicher Beleuchtung.* Tübingen. Reprint, Darmstadt.

Kittredge, George. 1911–12. Chaucer's Discussion of Marriage. *Modern Philology* 9: 435–67.

Klein, J. 1940. *Tertullian, Christliches Bewußtsein und sittliche Forderungen.* Abhandlungen aus Ethik und Moral. Düsseldorf.

Knoche, U. [1971] 1975. *Roman Satire.* Bloomington. Reprint, London.

Köhne, J. 1931. *Die Ehen zwischen Christen und Heiden in der ersten Christlichen Jahrhunderten.* Paderborn.

Konstan, David. 1983. *Roman Comedy.* Ithaca and London.

———. 1994. *Sexual Symmetry: Love in the Ancient Novel and Related Genres.* Princeton.

Körte, A., and A. Thierfelder, eds. 1953. *Menander "Reliquiae" Pars II.* Leipzig.

Kötting, B. 1957. Digamus. *RAC* 3:1018–19.

———. 1964. Zu den Strafen und Bußen für die Wiederverheiratung in der Frühen Kirche. *Oriens Christianus* 48:143–49.

———. 1988. *Die Bewertung der Wiederverheiratung (der zweiten Ehe) in der Antike und in der Frühen Kirke.* Opladen.

Küppers, E. 1981. Ovids "Ars Amatoria" und "Remedia Amoris" als Lehrdichtungen. *ANRW* II.31.4:2507–51.

Labriolle, P. de. 1913. *La crise montaniste.* Paris.

Lachmann, R. 1974. *Der Dienst der Kirche. Gesammelte Aufsätze.* Kassel.

Laistner, M. L. W. 1952. The Study of St. Jerome in the Early Middle Ages. In F. X. Murphy 1952, 235–56.

Larson, L. J. 1996. Love, Troth, and Magnanimity: The Weltanschauung of the Breton Lay from Marie de France to Chaucer. Ph.D. diss., University of Southwestern Louisiana.

Lateiner, D. 2000. Marriage and the Return of Spouses in Apuleius' *Metamorphoses. CJ* 95:313—32.

Lattimore, R. 1942. *Themes in Greek and Latin Epitaphs.* Urbana, Ill.

Lea, H. C. 1966. *History of Sacerdotal Celibacy in the Christian Church.* 4th ed. New York.

Leach, Eleanor W. 1969. *Meam quom formam noscito:* Language and Characterization in the *Menaechmi. Arethusa* 2:30–45.

Le Clerc, Jean, ed. [1703] 1961–62. *Desiderius Erasmus Omnia Opera.* 11 vols. Leiden. Reprint, Hildesheim.

Lee, Anne Thompson. 1984. "A Woman True and Fair": Chaucer's Portrayal of Dorigen in the "Franklin's Tale." *CR* 19:169–78.

Le Saint, William P. 1951. *Tertullian: Treatises on Marriage and Remarriage; "To His Wife"; "An Exhortation to Chastity"; "Monogamy."* New York.

Levine, R. 1988. How to Read Walter Map. *Mitlateinisches Jahrbuch* 23:91–105.

Lightman, M., and W. Zeisel. 1977. Univira: An Example of Continuity and Change in Roman Society. *Church History* 46:19–32.

Lloyd-Jones, Hugh. 1975. *Females of the Species: Semonides on Women.* London.

Lucas, A. 1983. *Women in the Middle Ages.* New York.

Lucke, Ch. 1982. *P. Ovidius Naso: "Remedia Amoris"; Kommentar zu Vers 397–814.* Bonn.

Lutz, C. 1947. Musonius Rufus: The Roman Socrates. *YCS* 10:3–147.

MacCary, W. T., and M. M. Willcock, eds. 1976. *Plautus: "Casina."* Cambridge.

MacDonald, M. Y. 1966. *Early Christian Women and Pagan Opinion: The Power of the Hysterical Woman.* Cambridge.

Mack, Maynard. 1951. The Muse of Satire. *Yale Review* 41:80–92.

Makowski, E. M. 1990. The Conjugal Debt and Medieval Canon Law. In Holloway 1990, 129–43.

Manitius, M. 1931. *Geschichte der lateinischen Literatur des Mittelalters.* 3 vols. Munich.

Manning, C. E. 1973. Seneca and the Stoics on the Equality of the Sexes. *Mnemosyne* 26:172–76.

Marquardt, J. [1886] 1980. *Das Privatleben der Römer.* 2d ed. Leipzig. Reprint, Darmstadt.

Martin, Janet. 1979. Uses of Tradition: Gellius, Petronius, and John of Salisbury. *Viator* 10:57–76.

Marx, F., ed. [1904–5] 1963. *C. Lucilii Carminum Reliquiae.* Leipzig. Reprint, Amsterdam.

Mason, Hugh. 1968. Is Juvenal a Classic? In *Satire: Critical Essays on Roman Literature,* ed. J. P. Sullivan, 93–176. Bloomington. First published in *Arion* 1 (1962): 8–44; 2 (1962): 39–79.

Matsen, P., P. Rollinson, and M. Sousa, eds. 1990. *Readings from Classical Rhetoric*. Carbondale and Edwardsville.

Mattiacci, Silvia. 1996. *Le novelle dell'adulterio (Metamorfosi IX) Apuleio*. Florence.

McDonough, C. J. 1984. *The Oxford Poems of Hugh Primas and the Arundel Lyrics*. Toronto.

McGrath, Alister E. 1985. *Luther's Theology of the Cross: Martin Luther's Theological Breakthrough*. Oxford.

McKay, K. L. 1964. Animals in War and *Isonomia*. *American Journal of Philology* 85:124–35.

McKeown, J. C. 1979. Augustan Elegy and Mime. *PCPS* 25:71–84.

McLeod, Glenda. 1991. *Virtue and Venom: Catalogues of Women from Antiquity to the Renaissance*. Ann Arbor.

Micaeli, C. 1979. L'influsso di Tertulliano su Girolamo: Le opere sul matrimonio e le seconde nozze. *Augustinianum* 19:415–29.

———. 1985. Richerche sulla fortuna de Tertulliano. *Orpheus*, n.s., 6:118–35.

Miller, J. F. 1983. Callimachus and the *Ars Amatoria*. *CP* 78:26–34.

Minadeo, Richard. 1969. *The Lyre of Science: Form and Meaning in Lucretius' "De Rerum Natura."* Detroit.

Momigliano, A. 1966. Review of *St. Jerome as a Satirist*, by D. S. Wiesen. *Journal of Theological Studies*, n.s., 17:476–77.

Monfrin, J., ed. 1967. *Historia Calamitatum*. 3d ed. Paris.

Moore, A. 1943. Studies in a Medieval Prejudice: Anti-Feminism. Ph.D. diss., Vanderbilt University.

Morgan, Gerald. 1977. A Defence of Dorigen's Complaint. *Medium Aevum* 46:78–97.

Morgan, J. 1928. *The Importance of Tertullian in the Development of Christian Dogma*. London.

Morgan, J. R. 1978. A Commentary on the Ninth and Tenth Books of the *Aithiopica* of Heliodoros. Ph.D. diss., Oxford University.

Morin, G., ed. 1930. *Sancti Augustini Sermones*. Rome.

Mücke, Frances. 1987. *Plautus: "Menaechmi"; A Companion*. Bristol.

Muckle, J. T. 1964. *The Story of Abelard's Adversities*. Toronto.

Muller, C. W. 1980. Die Witwe von Ephesus: Petrons Novelle und die *Milesiaka* des Aristeides. *Antike und Abendland* 26:103–21.

Muller, K., ed. 1995. *Petronius: "Satyricon Reliquiae."* Stuttgart.

Mulvagh, Jane. 1998. *Vivienne Westwood: An Unfashionable Life*. London.

Murley, C. 1939. Lucretius and the History of Satire. *TAPA* 70:380–95.

Murphy, F. X., ed. 1952. *A Monument to Saint Jerome: Essays on Some Aspects of His Life, Works, and Influence*. New York.

Murphy, G. M. H. 1966. Review of *St. Jerome as a Satirist*, by D. S. Wiesen. *Downside Review* 276:322–24.

Murstein, B. 1974. *Love, Sex and Marriage throughout the Ages*. New York.

Murtaugh, Daniel M. 1971. Women and Geoffrey Chaucer. *ELH* 38:473–92.

Myerowitz, Molly. 1985. *Ovid's Games of Love*. Detroit.

———. 1992. The Documentation of Desire: Ovid's *Parva Tabella* and the Theater of Love. In Richlin 1992, 131–57.

Nauck, A., and B. Snell, eds. 1964. *Tragicorum Graecorum Fragmenta*. Hildesheim.

Neff, Théodore Lee. 1900. *La satire des femmes dans la poésie lyrique française du moyen âge*. Paris.

Newman, J. K. 1990. *Roman Catullus and the Modification of the Alexandrian Sensibility.* Hildesheim.

Niebergall, A. 1974. Zur Entstehungsgeschichte der Christlichen Eheschliessung: Bemerkungen zu Ignatius an Polykarp 5.2. In Lachmann 1974, 185–87.

———. 1976. Tertullians Auffassung von Ehe und Eheschliessung. In Jaspert and Mohr 1976, 56–72.

Niederwimmer, K. 1975. *Askese und Mysterium: Über Ehe, Ehescheidung und Eheverzicht in den Anfängen des christlichen Glaubens.* Göttingen.

Norwood, G. 1931. *Greek Comedy.* London.

Novati, Francesco. 1883. *Carmina Medii Aevi.* Florence.

Oepke, A. 1959. Ehe I. *RAC* 4:650–66.

Oldfather, W. A., ed. and trans. [1928] 1985. *Epictetus.* Cambridge.

Oltramare, A. 1916. *Les origens de la diatribe romaine.* Geneva.

Opelt, I. 1973. *Hieronymus' Streitschriften.* Heidelberg.

———. 1993. Saint Jerome and the History of Sex. *Viator* 24:1–22.

Oswald, Hilton. 1955. *Luther's Works.* St. Louis.

Panayotakis, Costas. 1995. *Theatrum Arbitri: Theatrical Elements in the "Satyrica" of Petronius.* Leiden, New York, and Cologne.

Papaioannou, S. 1998. Charite's Rape, Psyche on the Rock, and the Parallel Function of Marriage in Apuleius' *Metamorphoses*. *Mnemosyne* 51:302–24.

Parker, H. 1992. Love's Body Anatomized: The Ancient Erotic Handbooks and the Rhetoric of Sexuality. In Richlin 1992, 90–111.

———. 1996. Plautus vs. Terence: Audience and Popularity Re-examined. *AJP* 617:585–617.

Parry, John Jay, ed. [1941] 1969. *The Art of Courtly Love: Andreas Capellanus Translated With Introduction and Notes* (New York).

Pascal, C. 1907. *Poesia latina medievale.* Catania.

Patterson, Lee. 1983. For the Wyves Love of Bathe. *Speculum* 57:656–57.

Paulsen, T. 1992. *Inszenierung des Schicksals: Tragodie und Komodie im Roman des Heliodor.* Trier.

Pecere, O. 1975. *Petronio: La novella della matrona de Efeso.* Padua.

Pelling, C. B. R., ed. 1988. *Plutarch: "Life of Antony."* Cambridge.

Pepin, R. E. 1988. *Literature of Satire in the Twelfth Century: A Neglected Mediaeval Genre.* Lampeter, Wales.

———, ed. and trans. 1991. *Scorn for the World: Bernard of Cluny's "De Contemptu Mundi."* East Lansing, Mich.

Petitmengin, P. 1988. Saint Jerome et Tertullein. In Duval 1988, 43–59.

Pétré, H. 1940. *L'exemplum chez Tertullian.* Dijon.

Phillips, Adam. 1996. *Monogamy.* London and Boston.

Phillips, Jane E. 1985. Alcumena in the *Amphitruo*: A Pregnant Lady Joke. *CJ* 80:121–26.

Piguet, E. 1927. *L'evolution de la pastourelle du XIIe siècle a nos jours.* Basel.

Pike, J. B. 1938. *Frivolities of Courtiers and Footprints of Philosophers.* Minneapolis.

Plepelits, K., ed. and trans. 1976. *Kallirhoel Chariton von Aphrodisias, Callirho.* Stuttgart.

Pomeroy, Sarah. 1985. *Frauenleben im klassischen alterum.* Stuttgart. Translation of *Goddesses, Wives, Whores and Slaves: Women in Classical Antiquity* (New York, 1975).

———, ed. 1994. *Xenophon: "Oeconomicus"; A Social and Historical Commentary.* Oxford.

———. 1999. Plutarch's *"Advice to Bride and Groom" and "A Consolation to His Wife":* *English Translations, Commentary, Interpretive Essays, and Bibliography.* New York.

Porter, Stanley. 1997. *Handbook of Classical Rhetoric in the Hellenistic Period,* 330 B.C.–A.D. 400. Leiden.

Pratt, R. A. 1962. Jankyn's Book of Wikked Wyves: Medieval Antimatrimonial Propaganda in the Universities. *Annuale Mediaevale* 3:5–27.

———. 1963. Saint Jerome in Jankyn's Book of Wikked Wyves. *Criticism* 5:319.

Raby, F. J. E. 1953. *A History of Christian-Latin Poetry.* 2d ed. Oxford.

———. 1957. *A History of Secular Latin Poetry in the Middle Ages.* 2d ed. Oxford.

Radice, Betty. 1974. *The Letters of Abelard and Heloise.* Harmondsworth.

Raditsa, L. F. 1980. Augustus' Legislation concerning Marriage, Procreation, Love Affairs and Adultery. *ANRW* II.13:278–339.

Rajna, P. 1891. Tre studi per la storia del libro di Andrea Capellano. *Studi di Filologia Romanza* 5:266–72.

Ramage, E. S., D. L. Sigsbee, and S. C. Fredericks. 1974. *Roman Satirists and Their Satire: The Fine Art of Criticism in Ancient Rome.* Park Ridge, N.J.

Ramirez de Verger, A. 1999. Figurae Veneris (Ovid *Ars* 3.769–88). In *Festschrift M. von Albrecht,* ed. W. Schubert, 237–43. Frankfurt am Main.

Rawson, Beryl, ed. 1991. *Marriage, Divorce, and Children in Ancient Rome.* Canberra and Oxford.

Relihan, J. C. 1993. *Ancient Menippean Satire.* Baltimore and London.

Reynolds, R. W. 1946. The Adultery Mime. *CQ* 40:77–84.

Rice, Eugene F., Jr. 1985. *St. Jerome in the Renaissance.* Baltimore.

Richlin, Amy. 1983. *The Garden of Priapus: Sexuality and Aggression in Roman Humor.* New Haven.

———, ed. 1992. *Pornography and Representation in Greece and Rome.* New York and Oxford.

Rigg, A. G. 1983. *Gawain on Marriage: The Textual Tradition of the "De Conjuge non Ducenda," with Critical Edition and Translation.* Toronto.

Robertson, D. S., ed. and trans. 1956. *Apuleius: Les Métamorphoses.* 3 vols. 2d ed. Paris.

Robertson, D. W., Jr. 1970. *The Literature of Medieval England.* New York.

———. 1983. *Preface to Chaucer.* Oxford.

Rogers, Katharine M. 1966. *The Troublesome Helpmate: A History of Misogyny in Literature.* Seattle.

Root, Jerry. 1994. Space to Speke: The Wife of Bath and the Discourse of Confession. *Chaucer Review* 28:252–74.

Rose, F. F. C. 1971. *The Date and Author of the "Satyricon."* Leiden.

Rosenmeyer, Patricia A. 1995. Enacting the Law: Plautus' Use of the Divorce Formula on Stage. *Phoenix* 49:201–17.

Ross, W. D., trans. 1947. Aristotle's *Nicomachean Ethics.* In *Introduction to Aristotle,* ed. Richard McKeon, 309–543. New York.

Rouse, W. H. D., and M. F. Smith, trans. and eds. 1982. *Lucretius De Rerum Natura.* Cambridge.

Rudd, Niall. 1986. *Themes in Roman Satire.* London.

———. 1990. Dido's *Culpa.* In *Oxford Readings in Vergil's "Aeneid,"* ed. S. J. Harrison, 145–66. Oxford. First published in *Lines of Enquiry* (Cambridge, 1976), 32–53.

Ruiz-Montero, C. 1991. Aspects of the Vocabulary of Chariton of Aphrodisias. *CQ* 41:484–89.

Russell, D. A. 1979. Rhetors at the Wedding. *PCPS* 205:104–71.

———. 1983. *Greek Declamation*. Cambridge.

Rynaud, G., ed. 1894. *Eustaches Deschamps, "Le miroir de mariage." Oeuvres complètes.* Paris.

Saller, R. P. 1993. The Social Dynamics of Consent to Marriage and Sexual Relations: The Evidence of Roman Comedy. In *Consent and Coercion to Sex and Marriage in Ancient and Medieval Societies*, ed. A. E. Laiou, 83–104. Washington, D.C.

Sandy, G. 1969. Satire in the *Satyricon*. *AJP* 90:293–303.

Scafuro, Adele. 1997. *The Forensic Stage: Settling Disputes in Graeco-Roman New Comedy*. Cambridge.

Schaff, Philip, ed. 1994. *Nicene and Post-Nicene Fathers*. First series, vol. 3, *Augustine*. Peabody, Mass.

Schanz, M., and C. Hosius. 1959. *Geschichte der römischen Literatur*. 5 vols. Munich.

Schlam, C. C. 1978. Sex and Sanctity: The Relationship of Male and Female in the *Metamorphoses*. In *Aspects of Apuleius' "Golden Ass,"* ed. B. Hijmans and R. Van der Paardt, 95–105. Groningen.

Scholer, David M., ed. 1993. *Gnosticism in the Early Church*. New York.

Schuhmann, Elisabeth. 1977. Der Typ der uxor dotata in den Komodien des Plautus. *Philologus* 121:45–65.

Schultzen, F. 1894. Die Benutzung der Schriften Tertullians de monogamia und de ieiunio bei Hieronymus adv. Iovinianum. *Neue Jahrbucher fur Deutsche Theologie* 3:487–502.

Scott, A. B. 1969. *Hildeberti Cenomannensis, Carmina Minora*. Leipzig.

Sedley, D. N. 1998. *Lucretius and the Transformation of Greek Wisdom*. Cambridge.

Segal, Charles. 1990. *Lucretius on Death and Anxiety: Poetry and Philosophy in "De Rerum Natura."* Princeton.

Segal, Erich. 1987. *Roman Laughter*. 2d ed. New York and Oxford.

Sharrock, A. 1994. *Seduction and Repetition in Ovid's "Ars Amatoria" 2*. Oxford.

Shelton, Jo-Ann. 1998. *As the Romans Did*. 2d ed. New York and Oxford.

Sider, R. D. 1971. *Ancient Rhetoric and the Art of Tertullian*. Oxford.

Sledd, James. 1947. Dorigen's Complaint. *Modern Philology* 45:36–45.

Smith, Lesley, and Jane H. M. Taylor. 1997. *Women and the Book: Assessing the Visual Evidence*. London.

Smith, M. L., ed. 1975. *Cena Trimalchionis: Petronii Arbitri*. Oxford.

Smith, Susan. 1995. *The Power of Women: A Topos in Medieval Art and Literature*. Philadelphia.

Smith, Warren S. 1969. Speakers in the Third Satire of Persius. *CJ* 64:305–8.

———. 1972. The Narrative Voice in Apuleius' *Metamorphoses*. *TAPA* 103:513–34. Reprinted in Harrison 1999, 195–216.

———. 1980. Husband vs. Wife in Juvenal's Sixth Satire. *Classical World* 73:323–32.

———. 1989. Heroic Models for the Sordid Present: Juvenal's View of Tragedy. *ANRW* II.33.1:811–23.

———. 1997. The Wife of Bath Debates Jerome. *Chaucer Review* 32:129–45.

———. 1998. Cupid and Psyche Tale: Mirror of the Novel. In *Aspects of Apuleius' "Golden Ass,"* vol. 2, *Cupid and Psyche*, ed. M. Zimmerman, S. Panayotakis, et al., 69–82. Groningen.

———. 2002. Dorigen's Lament and the Resolution of the "Franklin's Tale." *Chaucer Review* 36:374–90.

Smith-Werner, Warren. 1996. The Satiric Voice in the Roman Novelistic Tradition. In *Unity and Diversity: Proceedings of the Fourth International Conference on Narrative*, ed. Joachim Knuf, 308–17. Lexington, Ky.

Spearing, A. C. 1985. *Medieval to Renaissance in English Poetry*. Cambridge.

Stadele, A. 1980. *Die Briefe des Pythagoras und der Pythagoreer*. Beitrage zur klassischen Philologie 115. Meisenheim am Glan.

Stählin, Otto, and Ludwig Früchtel, eds. 1985. *Clemens Alexandrinus: Works*. 2 vols. Berlin.

Stapleton, M. L., ed. 2000. *Thomas Heywood's "Art of Love": The First Complete English Translation of Ovid's "Ars Amatoria."* Ann Arbor.

Stephens, S., and J. Winkler, eds. 1995. *Ancient Greek Novels: The Fragments; Introduction, Text, Translation, and Commentary*. Princeton.

Steudel, M. 1992. *Die Literaturparodie in Ovid's Ars Amatoria*. Hildesheim.

Stone, L. 1977. *The Family, Sex, and Marriage in England, 1500–1800*. London.

Strecker, K. 1925. *Die Lieder Walters von Chatillon in der Handschrift 351 von St Omer*, no. 32. Berlin.

———. 1929. *Moralisch-satirische Gedichte Walters von Chattillon*. Heidelberg.

Stroh, W. 1979. Ovids Liebeskunst und die Ehegesetze des Augustus. *Gymnasium* 86:323–52.

Stücklin, C., ed. 1974. *Tertullian, "De virginibus velandis": Übersetzung, Einleitung, Kommentar: Ein Beitrag zur altkirchlichen Frauenfrage*. Frankfurt.

Sullivan, J. P. 1968. *The "Satyricon" of Petronius: A Literary Study*. London.

———. 1979. Martial's Sexual Attitudes. *Philologus* 123:288–302.

———. 1991. *Martial: The Unexpected Classic*. Cambridge.

Suss, W. 1938. Der heilige Hieronymus und die Formen seiner Polemik. *Giessener Beitrage zur Deutschen Philologie* 60:212–38.

Svarlien, Diane, trans. 1995. "Women," by Semonides of Amargos (Poem 7). *Diotima*. www.stoa.org/diotima/anthology/sem_7.shtml.

Tanner, T. 1979. *Adultery in the Novel: Contract and Transgression*. Baltimore.

Tatum, J. H. 1969. The Tales in Apuleius' *Metamorphoses*. *TAPA* 100:487–527.

Taylor, Mark. 1997. Servant and Lord/Lady and Wife: The "Franklin's Tale" and Traditions of Courtly and Conjugal Love. *Chaucer Review* 32:64–81.

Thayer, J. H. 1889. *Thayer's Greek-English Lexicon of the New Testament*. Grand Rapids, Mich.

Thesleff, H. 1965. *The Pythagorean Texts of the Hellenistic Period*. Abo.

Thibault, J. C. 1964. *The Mystery of Ovid's Exile*. Berkeley and Los Angeles.

Thomas, K. V. 1959. The Double Standard. *Journal of the History of Ideas* 20:195–216.

Thompson, J. W. [1939] 1960. *The Literacy of the Laity in the Middle Ages*. New York.

Tibiletti, C. 1960–61. Un opuscolo perduto di Tertulliano: *Ad amicum philosophum*. *AAT* 95: 122–66.

———. 1969. Verginita e matrimonio in antichi cristiani. *Annali della Facolta de Lettere e Filosofia della Universita de Macerata* 2:9–217.

Toohey, P. 1996. *Epic Lessons: An Introduction to Ancient Didactic Poetry*. London and New York.

Townend, G. B. 1973. The Literary Substrata to Juvenal's *Satires*. *JRS* 63:148–60.

Treggiari, Susan. 1991. *Roman Marriage: Iusti Coniuges from the Time of Cicero to the Time of Ulpian*. Oxford.

Tupper, F., and M. B. Ogle. 1924. *Master Walter Map's Book "De Nugis Curialium" (Courtiers' Trifles)*. London.

Uglione, R., ed. 1989. *La donna nel mondo antico: Atti del convegno nazionale de studi*. Turin.

Utley, F. L. 1944. *The Crooked Rib: An Analytical Index to the Argument about Women in English and Scots Literature to the End of the Year 1568*. Columbus, Ohio.

Van Geytenbeek, A. C. 1962. *Musonius Rufus and Greek Diatribe*. Bangorcum.

Van Leeuwen, Arend. 1964. *Christianity in World History: The Meeting of the Faiths of East and West*. Trans. H. H. Hoiskins. New York.

Verdennius, J. 1968–69. Semonides über die Frauen. *Mnemosyne* 21:132–58; 22:299–302.

Wachsmith, Curtius, and Otto Hense, eds. [1884–1912] 1958. *Ioannes Stovaius Anthologium*. 5 vols. Berlin.

Walsh, P. G. 1970. *The Roman Novel*. Cambridge.

———. 1978. Petronius and Apuleius. In *Aspects of Apuleius' "Golden Ass,"* ed. B. Hijmans and R. Van der Paart, 1:12–24. Groningen.

———. 1982. *Andreas Capellanus on Love*. London.

———, ed. and trans. 1993. *Love Lyrics from the "Carmina Burana."* Chapel Hill.

———, ed. and trans. 1996. *The Satyricon/Petronius: Translated with Introduction and Explanatory Notes*. Oxford.

———, ed. 2001. *Oxford Early Christian Texts*. Oxford.

Warmington, E. H. 1935–40. *Remains of Old Latin, Newly Edited and Translated*. 4 vols. Cambridge.

Watson, A. 1967. *The Law of Persons in the Later Roman Republic*. Oxford.

———. 1971. *Roman Private Law around 200 B.C.* Edinburgh.

Webb, C., ed. 1909. *Joannis Saresberiensis episcopi Carnotensis "Policrati sive De nugis curialium et vestigiis philosophorum" libri VIII*. Vol. 2. Oxford.

West, David. 1969. *The Imagery and Poetry of Lucretius*. Edinburgh.

Weston, A. H. 1915. *Latin Satirical Writing Subsequent to Juvenal*. Lancaster, Pa.

Wiesen, David S. 1964. *St. Jerome as a Satirist: A Study in Christian Latin Thought and Letters*. Ithaca.

———. 1973. Juvenal and the Intellectuals. *Hermes* 101:464–83.

Wildberger, J. 1998. *Ovids Schule der "elegaischen" Liebe: Erotodidaxe und Psychagogie in der Ars Amatoria*. Frankfurt am Main.

Wiles, David. 1989. Marriage and Prostitution in Classical New Comedy. In *Themes in Drama*, vol. 11, *Women in Theatre*, ed. J. Redmond, 31–48. Cambridge.

———. 1991. *The Masks of Menander*. Cambridge.

Williams, Gordon. 1958. Some Aspects of Roman Marriage Ceremonies and Ideals. *JRS* 48:16–29.

———. 1968. *Tradition and Originality in Roman Poetry*. Oxford.

Williams, R. D. 1973. *The "Aeneid" of Virgil*. 2 vols. London.

Wilson, K., and E. Makowski. 1990. *Wikked Wyves and the Woes of Marriage: Misogamous Literature from Juvenal to Chaucer*. Albany.

Winkler, J. J. 1985. *Auctor and Actor: A Narratological Reading of Apuleius' "The Golden Ass."* Berkeley.

Winkler, M. M. 1983. *The Persona in Three Satires of Juvenal*. Altertumswissenschaftliche Texte und Studien 10. Hildesheim.

Witke, Charles. 1970. *Latin Satire: The Structure of Persuasion*. Leiden.

Wood, C. 1984. Artistic Invention and Chaucer's Use of Scriptural Allusion. In Jeffrey 1984, 37–38.

Wright, F. A., ed. and trans. 1963. *Select Letters of St. Jerome*. Cambridge.

Wright, Michael. 1998. Isolation and Individuality in the "Franklin's Tale." SP 70:181–86.

Wright, T., ed. [1841] 1968. *The Latin Poems Commonly Attributed to Walter Map*. Hildesheim.

———. 1850. *Gualteri Mapes "De nugis curialium" distinctiones quinque*. London.

———. 1872. *The Anglo-Saxon Satirical Poets and Epigrammatists of the Twelfth Century*. 2 vols. London.

Wulff, A. 1914. *Die frauenfeindlichen Dichtungen in den romanischen Literaturen des Mittelalters bis zum Ende des XIII. Jahrhunderts*. Halle am Saale.

Wurtele, Douglas. 1983. The Predicament of Chaucer's Wife of Bath: St. Jerome on Virginity. *Florilegium* 5:214.

Wyke, M. 1997. Women in the Mirror: The Rhetoric of Adornment in the Roman World. In Archer, Fischler, and Wyke 1994, 134–51.

Zeitlin, F. 1995. Signifying Difference: The Myth of Pandora. In Hawley and Levick 1995, 58–74.

Zimmerman-de Graaf, M. 2000. *Apuleius Madaurensis: "Metamorphoses," Book X; Text, Introduction, and Commentary*. Groningen.

List of Contributors

SUSANNA MORTON BRAUND is professor of classics at Stanford University. She is the author of books and articles on Roman satire, Roman epic, and other aspects of Roman literature. Her books include *Beyond Anger: A Study of Juvenal's Third Book of Satires* (Cambridge, 1988), *Juvenal: "Satires" Book 1* (Cambridge, 1996), and *The Roman Satirists and Their Masks* (Bristol, 1996). Her new Loeb Classical Library volume of Juvenal and Persius has just been published (Cambridge, 2004).

ELIZABETH A. CLARK is John Carlisle Kilgo professor of religion at Duke University. A specialist in late ancient Christianity, she has written on women, asceticism, heresy, and biblical interpretation. Among her books are *Jerome, Chrysostom, and Friends: Essays and Translations* (New York, 1979) and *History, Theory, Text* (Cambridge, 2004). A fellow of the American Academy of Arts and Sciences, she has been president of the American Academy of Religion, the American Society of Church History, and the North American Patristics Society.

BARBARA FEICHTINGER is Ordinaria für Latinistik at the University of Konstanz, Germany. Her research areas, on which she has published numerous articles, include literary theory, early Christian literature, and gender studies. Among her publications are *Apostolae Apostolorum: Frauenaskese als Befreiung und Zwang bei Hieronymus* (Vienna, Frankfurt, and New York, 1995) and *Iphis: Beiträge zur alterumswissenschaftlichen Gender-Forschung*, with Georg Wöhrle (Trier, 2001).

RALPH HANNA III is professor of paleography at the University of Oxford and tutorial fellow of Keble College. His research interests include *Piers Plowman* and alliterative poetry, and he does extensive work with English manuscript books. His publications include *Pursuing History: Middle English Manuscripts and Their Texts* (Stanford, 1996) and, edited with Traugott Lawler, *Jankyn's Book of Wikked Wyves* (Athens, Ga., 1997).

RICHARD HAWLEY is lecturer in classics at Royal Holloway, University of London. He has published numerous articles on ancient concepts of gender in Greek drama, Greek women philosophers, Plutarch, Dio Chrysostom, and Greek declamation. He co-organized for ten years the innovative Oxford "Women in Antiquity" seminar series and coedited *Women in Antiquity: New Assessments* (London and New York, 1995). He is currently working on a commentary on Plutarch's *Banquet of the Seven Sages*.

REGINE MAY is fellow in classical languages and literature at Merton College, Oxford University. Her academic interests include Greek and Latin literature (especially drama and the novel), papyrology, and paleography. She has published articles on Apuleius and the novel; contributed to editions of literary papyri for the Oxyrhynchus Papyri, Oxford; and prepared a forthcoming lemmatized concordance on Cornelius Nepos.

KARLA POLLMANN, currently professor of classics at the University of St. Andrews, Scotland, is a former Humboldt scholar and member of the Institute for Advanced Studies at Princeton. Her books include a major study (Freiburg, 1996) and German edition (Stuttgart, 2002) of Augustine's hermeneutical treatise *De doctrina Christiana* and the edited volumes *History, Apocalypse, and the Secular Imagination* (Bowling Green, Ohio, 1999) and *Double Standards in the Ancient and Medieval World* (Göttingen, 2000).

WARREN S. SMITH is professor of classics and chairman of the Foreign Languages and Literatures Department at the University of New Mexico, Albuquerque. He has published extensively on Apuleius and the Roman novel, Juvenal and Roman satire, and the Latin sources of English literature, and he was coeditor and translator, with Robert Sider and others, of two volumes of Erasmus's New Testament scholarship published by University of Toronto Press: *Paraphases on Romans and Galatians* (1984) and *Annotations on Romans* (1995).

P. G. WALSH is emeritus professor and professorial research fellow at the University of Glasgow, Scotland. His many books on classical and medieval literature include *The Roman Novel: The "Satyricon" of Petronius and the "Metamorphoses" of Apuleius* (2d ed., Bristol, 1995); *Andreas Capellanus on Love*, edited with an English translation (London, 1982); and *Augustine, "De Bono Coniugali" and "De Sancta Virginitate,"* edited with introduction, translation, and notes (Oxford, 2001).

Index